standardized tests
in education

WILLIAM A. MEHRENS
Michigan State University

IRVIN J. LEHMANN
Michigan State University

HOLT, RINEHART AND WINSTON, INC.

NEW YORK   CHICAGO   SAN FRANCISCO   ATLANTA
DALLAS   MONTREAL   TORONTO   LONDON   SYDNEY

Dedicated to
our wives: Beth and Ruth
our children: Lori, Machell, Ilene, and Allan

preface

Educators have always been concerned with measuring and evaluating the progress of their students. As the goals of education have become more complex and as the number of students has increased enormously, this task has become much more difficult. The area of educational measurement can be considered as twofold: the construction, evaluation, and use (1) of teacher-made classroom tests and (2) of standardized tests. This text is intended to serve the latter purpose.

Educators have found that the use of standardized tests, constructed by various educational specialists in conjunction with psychometric experts, can be very helpful in the pervasive problem of evaluation. Thus, standardized tests have permeated educational establishments. Particularly within the past few years, with the impetus provided by the 1958 National Defense Education Act and the 1965 Elementary and Secondary School Act, the use of standardized tests in the public schools has expanded rapidly. The education of our teachers in measurement has not kept abreast of this change. Far too many teachers are untrained in the selection, administration, and interpretation of standardized tests. This fact has been recognized by many teacher training institutions across the nation, and they are providing courses to alleviate this problem.

Although many books are designed for use in basic measurement courses, most attempt to cover the whole domain of topics possible in measurement. This book has a more limited goal. *Standardized Tests in Education* is an outgrowth of the authors' convictions that there are certain things classroom teachers, counselors, and school administrators must know to select, administer, and use standardized tests correctly. The basic aim of this text is to provide that information. No formal course work in testing or statistics is necessary to understand the text.

This book can serve as the main text in the first course in standardized testing at either the undergraduate or graduate level. If so, the material should be supplemented by detailed examinations of various test specimen sets and selected outside readings. This book also is appropriate as a supplemental text in introductory educational psychology courses, methods courses, special education courses, and guidance and counseling courses.

We do not claim to have considered every possible approach to the assessment of cognitive and noncognitive traits. In fact, we have knowingly omitted teacher-made tests and such assessment techniques as observations, ratings, anecdotal records, and sociometric techniques. We felt that there are many textbooks available today that try to cover too much in a single text. The selection of topics in this book and the coverage given them have benefited from the advice of many colleagues. At all times the needs of educators have been kept foremost in mind.

When we felt that the topic being considered could not be treated without some theoretical background, we attempted to present a simple but clear treatment of the theory. When we felt that the topic being discussed did not require a full theoretical treatment, we chose to omit the erudition.

A preliminary draft of this text was used in courses taught at Michigan State University. Students helped considerably in the determination of educators' needs regarding knowledge in this area. The text has benefited from student reactions to the preliminary manuscript. When necessary, we have rewritten material so that it will be easier to comprehend. We have tried to obtain simplicity but not at the expense of accuracy.

Chapter I introduces the student to the basic nature and functions of standardized tests. The section on statistical concepts emphasizes the understanding, meaning, and potential use of a statistic rather than its computation or theoretical derivation. This chapter also includes some of the basic principles in test selection, technical and practical aspects of testing, and interpretation of test scores.

Because educators make more use of aptitude and achievement tests than they do of interest and personality measures, we have devoted more attention to the cognitive tests. Aptitude tests are discussed in Chapter II. Achievement tests are treated in Chapter III. With respect to these cognitive measures, we have discussed a larger number of achievement tests than aptitude tests because they are used more frequently in the public schools.

Because school personnel must also know about the noncognitive characteristics of their students, we have discussed interest, personality, and attitude measures in Chapter IV. Because educators, in general, are more qualified to use interest rather than personality inventories and since interest inventory results are of greater educational value, we have stressed them accordingly. "Types of Standardized Interest Inventories" in Chapter IV may present a bit more detailed information than the classroom teacher needs to know. It would not be unreasonable for the elementary school teacher to skip this section. Junior high and high school teachers may wish to skim over the material. Counselors or prospective counselors should read this section as thoroughly as they read the other portions of the book.

We have emphasized the important principles to be considered by the user in selecting, administering, and interpreting a particular type of test for his specific needs. We have done this by looking at some of the more common standardized tests used in our schools in a brief fashion and by evaluating one (or more) tests in each of Chapters II, III, and IV in a somewhat comprehensive fashion. Our goal in many of these evaluations has been to do more than present a brief synopsis or abstract of the test. We have tried to evaluate critically the various tests—pointing out their strengths and weaknesses—so that the user will have some general notion as to what questions should be asked when he selects a test; how to interpret the information presented in the test manual regarding the test's psychometric problems; and what this test has to offer, if anything, over other available tests.

The last chapter includes some of the factors that must be considered in setting up a school testing program, gives some public views of testing, and includes a brief look towards the future of testing.

We feel indeed fortunate for the assistance received throughout all the stages of writing this book. Fred Brown, Phil Jackson, Jack Merwin, and Jim Molineux have all reviewed the manuscript in detail and have made many fine suggestions. Robert Ebel, Don Freeman, Walker Hill, Arvo Juola, Allan Lange, Lee Olson, Nick Rayder, Bruce Rogers, John Schweitzer, and Bill Warrington have all read, corrected, and made valuable suggestions on various portions of the manuscript. Students in several sections of a course on standardized tests in education have presented written critiques of a previous draft of the entire manuscript. All these sources were extremely valuable, and we are grateful. The authors owe a great deal to the patience and conscientious attention of their typists, Patricia J. Martens and Mary Ann Powell. We are also very appreciative of the thorough training given us by our advisers, Jack C. Merwin and Chester W. Harris. Any errors of fact or awkward phrasings that remain are, however, the responsibility of the authors.

East Lansing, Mich.   *W.A.M.*
November 1968   *I.J.L.*

contents

CHAPTER I

Measurement in Education

CHAPTER II

Aptitude Tests

CHAPTER III

Standardized Achievement Tests

CHAPTER IV

Interest, Personality, and Attitude Inventories

CHAPTER V

Educational Testing: A Broader Viewpoint

chapter

I

measurement in education

NATURE OF STANDARDIZED TESTS

Testing, measurement, and evaluation have been with us for a long, long time. The original evaluation was when God, after forming the earth, the sun, the moon, and the stars, looked at everything he made and saw that it was *very good.*[1] An oft quoted, though probably not the first, standardized test was one used by the Gileadites.

> And the Gileadites took the passages of Jordan before the Ephraimites: and it was so, that when those Ephraimites which were escaped said, Let me go over; that the men of Gilead said unto him, Art thou an Ephraimite? If he said Nay; then said they unto him, Say now Shibboleth; and he said Sibboleth; for he could not frame to pronounce it right. Then they took him, and slew him at the passages of Jordan; And there fell at that time of the Ephraimites forty and two thousand.[2]

As Stanley points out, "Here indeed is an old final examination."[3]

[1]Gen. 1:1–31, Holy Bible, King James Version.
[2]Judg. 12:5–6, Holy Bible, King James Version.
[3]Julian C. Stanley, *Measurement in today's schools.* (4th ed.) Englewood Cliffs, N.J.: Prentice-Hall, 1964, p. 8.

The use of these Biblical examples is not to suggest measurement and evaluation were procedures ordained by God—although some psychometrists might wish or act as if this were the case. Rather, these examples are used to illustrate the point that man has always been concerned with measurement and evaluation. Educators particularly have been concerned with measuring and evaluating the progress of their students. As the goals of education have become more complex, and as the numbers of students have increased enormously, this task has become much more difficult. Standardized tests constructed by various educational and psychological specialists in conjunction with psychometric experts have been found to be quite useful in the task of measurement and evaluation. As a result, the use of standardized tests has permeated the educational establishments.

INCREASED USE OF STANDARDIZED TESTS

One of the major reasons for the rapid increase of testing in the public schools has been the guidance movement. The National Defense Education Act[4] of 1958 provided funds for public school testing, and school administrators were quick to make use of these funds.

The increase in the number of state-wide testing programs has also contributed toward the increased use of tests in the public schools. Most of these programs are voluntary, but some states, such as New York and California, have enacted laws requiring the use of aptitude and achievement tests in the elementary and secondary schools.

The Elementary and Secondary School Act of 1965 has also had an impact on the use of standardized tests. Part of this act deals directly with evaluation. Section 205 in Title II reads:

> ... effective procedures including provision for appropriate objective measures of educational achievement will be adapted for evaluating at least annually the effectiveness of the program in meeting the special educational needs of educationally deprived children.[5]

These "appropriate . . . measures of educational achievement" have been, no doubt, for the most part, standardized tests.

Table 1–1 shows the number of test booklets and answer sheets sold in the United States from 1955 through 1967. Of interest is the big jump in sales from 1958 to 1959 (following the National Defense Education Act) and from 1964 to 1965 and 1965 to 1966 (Elementary and Secondary School

---

[4]Public Law 85–864. *United States statutes at large*. Washington, D.C.: United States Government Printing Office, 1959, Vol. 72, Part 1, pp. 1580–1605.

[5]Public Law 89–10, *United States statutes at large*. Washington, D.C.: United States Government Printing Office, 1966, Vol. 79, p. 31.

Act of 1965). The decrease from 1966 to 1967 may be due, in part, to any or all of the following reasons: (1) reuse of test booklets purchased earlier; (2) oversale of booklets and answer sheets in 1964 and 1965; (3) a decrease in external funds to purchase test supplies; and (4) the possibility that some schools may be illegally reproducing answer sheets with their own equipment.

Test publishers are well aware of the financial aid that federal legislation provides. The California Test Bureau,[6] for example, devotes two pages in its catalog to informing its readers of the federal programs that are relevant to the testing industry. With such a pervasive use of standardized tests in the public schools, it is certainly important that educators have an understanding of these instruments. This book is designed to develop that understanding.

Table 1–1

Net Sales of Standardized Tests and Answer Sheets[a]

Year	K–12	Total
1955		83,800,000
1956		91,070,000
1957		97,810,000
1958		109,710,000
1959		133,620,000
1960	122,650,000	140,750,000
1961	123,820,000	141,290,000
1962	125,520,000	146,630,000
1963	122,680,000	146,710,000
1964	122,300,000	149,100,000
1965	132,020,000	163,930,000
1966	169,990,000	205,070,000
1967	153,830,000	188,710,000

[a]Figures obtained from the 1967 *Annual Survey of Standardized Test Publishing*, prepared by Stanley B. Hunt and associates, New York. The sales for 1955–1959 were not subdivided for K–12 and others. The statistics reported do not include tests such as those of the College Entrance Examination Board, American College Testing, or Merit Scholarship, where test materials are not really sold but merely furnished as part of a total service. Thus, the survey figures are low as indicators of volume of standardized test activity. Figures are reprinted by permission of the American Educational Publishers Institute, New York.

[6]Catalog. Monterey, Calif.: California Test Bureau, 1967.

DEFINITION OF STANDARDIZED TESTS

In order to facilitate understanding of standardized tests in education, it would probably be wise to define *standardized tests*. Cronbach has defined a test as "a systematic procedure for comparing the behavior of two or more persons."[7] The key words in this definition are *systematic, comparing*, and *behavior*. If one had a systematic procedure for comparing the behavior of one individual with his later development, this also could be considered a test. Noll presents the following definition of a standardized test:

> A standardized test is one that has been carefully constructed by experts in the light of acceptable objectives or purposes; procedures for administering, scoring, and interpreting scores are specified in detail so that no matter who gives the test or where it may be given, the results should be comparable; and norms or averages for different age or grade levels have been pre-determined.[8]

This definition is very good but perhaps too restrictive. Most standardized tests do have norm data that serve as a useful interpretive tool. However, inventories such as the Mooney Problem Check List do not have norms, yet they are ordinarily considered standardized.

CLASSIFICATION OF TYPES OF STANDARDIZED TESTS

There are many ways in which standardized tests can be classified. For example, they can be classified according to administrative procedures, such as individual administration versus group administration or as oral instructions versus written instructions. However, the most popular broad classification is according to what is measured. We will employ the following classification of tests:

1. Aptitude tests (general, multiple, and special)
2. Achievement tests
3. Interest, personality, and attitude inventories

Often the first two categories are considered to contain tests of maximum performance and the third tests of typical performance. Some classify aptitude and achievement tests as cognitive measures, and interest, personality, and attitude inventories as noncognitive measures. Because the noncognitive measures have no factually right or wrong answers, some people prefer to

---

[7]Lee J. Cronbach, *Essentials of psychological testing.* (2nd ed.) New York: Harper & Row, 1960, p. 21.

[8]Victor H. Noll, *Introduction to educational measurement.* (2nd ed.) Boston: Houghton Mifflin, 1965, p. 5.

refer to them as inventories. This change in terminology may lessen the anxiety of the test taker. Whether or not these measures are referred to as tests or inventories, they do fit the definition of standardized tests presented in the previous section. The word *test* will be used in this text to simplify the language. However, it should not be used in the title of noncognitive measures.

FUNCTIONS OF STANDARDIZED TESTS IN SCHOOLS

The functions of standardized tests are many and varied; however, one can in essence sum up their function by saying that they should help in decision making. Throughout his school career, a student makes many decisions, and many decisions are made about him. It is a truism that the more and more accurate the information on which a decision is based, the better the decision is likely to be.

The kinds of decisions made are often classified as institutional and individual decisions. *Institutional decisions are ones in which a large number of comparable decisions are made. Individual decisions are ones where the choice confronting the decision maker will rarely or never recur.* In education, institutional decisions are typically the ones the school personnel make concerning the students (for example, homogeneous grouping and college admission). Individual decisions are typically the ones the individual makes about himself (for example, vocational choice). Test information is helpful for both kinds of decision making. Tests per se, however, do not make decisions, and they are not the only information that should be considered in making decisions. This point can best be explained by considering decision-theory models.

One can conceptualize every decision as a choice among various alternatives. Each alternative has many possible outcomes. Each outcome has a certain probability attached to it and has a certain utility value (desirability). In general, tests do provide us with information concerning the probability of the outcomes, but they provide little information on the desirability of the outcomes.

Let us take an oversimplified example. Suppose a high school senior is faced with the decision of whether to go to college. We can dichotomize the alternatives as follows:

1. Go to college.
2. Don't go to college.

Following the path of Alternative 1 we can dichotomize the possible outcomes of this alternative.

a. The person will maintain a high enough average to eventually be graduated from college.

b. The person will fail.

Now, in decision making, both the probability of each outcome and the utility value (or desirability) of each outcome must be considered. Test information can certainly help us in determining probabilities. But they help little, if any, in determining utilities. Two senior boys, Bill and John, may both have the same estimated probability (say 75 chances out of a hundred) of being graduated from college. This does not mean that both boys should make the same decision about college attendance. Perhaps Bill thinks that it is very desirable to be graduated from college but thinks that the other possible outcome — failing — although undesirable, is not really a catastrophe. John may not care much whether he ever obtains a college degree but may think that failing, once he is enrolled, would be a fate worse than death. These two boys, having the same probability estimates, would not make the same decision. Thus, test information does not make decisions for us; it only provides us with additional information that, when incorporated with data we already have, helps us arrive at better decisions.

At times institutional decision making will restrict individual decision making. This occurs, for example, if college admission is dependent upon a minimum estimated probability for success. Where this minimum probability should be set depends upon the cost (utility value) one places upon two different kinds of errors: admitting a student who does not succeed (referred to as a miss) or excluding a student who would have succeeded (a false positive). Suppose, for example, we have the relationship between Y (success in college defined as a grade-point average equal to or greater than 2.0), and X (some numerical value derived from a combination of variables such as test score information or past grades) represented by the scattergram shown in Figure 1–1(a). Here each tally above the horizontal line (defining success in college) and to the left of $X = 4$ (the minimum admission score) would represent a false positive. Every score below the horizontal line and to the right of the X cutoff score would be a miss. The other tallies would represent correct decisions.

If the decision maker equated the costs (utility values) of the two kinds of errors, then the proper approach would be to minimize the total errors and to therefore set the cutting score at 4, as is shown in Figure 1–1(a). This would give six false positives and five misses (or 11 total errors). If, however, it was decided that false positives are three times as costly as misses (in terms of loss to society or whatever) then the proper cutting score should be changed. If the cutting score were kept at 4 one would have

6 false positives at a cost of 3 units each = 18 cost units
5 misses at a cost of 1 unit each   = 5 cost units
                                               ─────────────
                                               23 cost units

A cutting score of 3, as in Figure 1–1(b), would produce 15 total errors but only 21 cost units as follows:

$$3 \text{ false positives at a cost of 3 units each} = 9 \text{ cost units}$$
$$12 \text{ misses at a cost of 1 unit each} \quad\quad = \underline{12 \text{ cost units}}$$
$$21 \text{ cost units}$$

This simple example illustrates again that test information does not make decisions. It is used (often in conjunction with other information) to help us set probability values. Once we have set some utility values on the various outcomes of the alternatives, we can combine probabilities and utilities to arrive at better decisions.

What are some of the specific kinds of decisions in which test information can assist? Are there some specific functions for which tests are best qualified? Yes, of course. Although different authors use different systems of classifying these functions, this book will extend the system used by Thorndike and Hagen.[9] They classify the functions into three categories:

1. Tests for teaching (instructional purposes)
2. Tests for guidance
3. Tests for administration

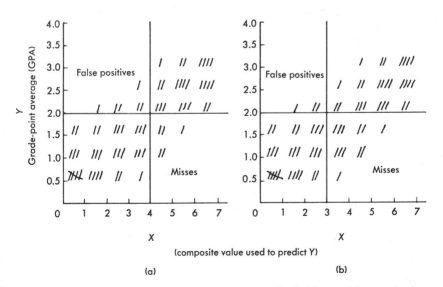

Figure 1-1 Scattergrams depicting (for the same data) false positives and misses for cutting scores of 4 and 3, respectively, when a GPA of 2.0 is required for success.

[9]Robert L. Thorndike and Elizabeth Hagen, *Measurement and evaluation in psychology and education.* (2nd ed.) New York: Wiley, 1961, p. 446.

One shortcoming of this classification system is that different kinds of tests serve different functions within each of the three categories listed above. A second, less important deficiency is that the system does not contain a research category. A two-way classification such as is shown in Table 1–2 is much more meaningful.

Table 1–2

Purposes of Standardized Tests[a,b]

Purposes	Aptitude	Achievement	Interest	Personality	Attitude
		Kinds of Tests			
Instructional					
Evaluation of learning outcomes	X	X	?	?	
Evaluation of teaching	X	X			
Evaluation of curriculum	X	X	?		?
Learning diagnosis	X	X			
Differential assignments within class	X	X	?	?	?
Grading	?	?			
Motivation		?			X
Guidance					
Vocational	X	X	X	X	X
Educational	X	X	?	?	X
Personal	?	?	X	X	X
Administrative					
Selection	X	X	?	?	
Classification	X	X	X	X	
Placement	X	X	?		
Public relations (information)	X	X	?		
Curriculum planning and evaluation	X	X	?		
Evaluating teachers	?	?	?	?	
Providing information for outside agencies	X	X			
Research	X	X	X	X	X

[a]An X indicates that a test can and should be used for that purpose.
[b]A ? indicates that there is some debate concerning whether or not a test can serve that purpose.

The functions, as shown in the table, will be explained in more detail within each of the chapters devoted to the four kinds of tests. Note that interest and personality tests serve fewer instructional purposes; although, these tests can be very useful in the guidance functions of the school.

For all the specific functions mentioned, it should be remembered that the ultimate purpose of a standardized test is to help in making decisions. Some examples of the kinds of decisions that can be aided by using standardized test results are as follows:

    1. Do the pupils in Miss Perriwinkle's third grade need a different balance of curricular emphasis?

    2. Is it advisable for Erskine to take a remedial reading course?

    3. Should Billy take a college-preparatory program in high school?

    4. Is the phonics method of teaching reading more effective than the sight method?

If knowledge of a test result does not enable one to make a better decision than the best decision that could be made without the use of the test, then the test serves no useful purpose and might just as well not be given. However, if one used and interpreted test information correctly, it would be impossible to make poorer decisions using the additional information.

SOME BASIC PRINCIPLES IN TESTING AND TEST SELECTION

Because a test, once selected by a school, is ordinarily used for many years, it certainly behooves the purchaser to delve into the problem of test selection to a considerable extent. Some of the many questions that always arise in public schools are "What kind of information is needed?" "How should this information be obtained?" If it is agreed that test information would be helpful, "Who should select the tests?" One way to stimulate test use is to have all the professional staff who will ever use the tests help in the test selection process. If teachers are expected to use test information, then they should assist in selecting the tests; if guidance personnel will be using test results, then they should be involved; and if the principal also plans to use the test results to help him in certain decisions, then he should assist in the test selection. Test selection should be a cooperative venture by all the professional staff who intend to use the test information.

There are many different factors to consider when selecting a test, such as purpose, administration, scoring, cost, format, interpretation, reliability, and validity. In the rest of this section, we will discuss the purposes of testing and the sources of information about tests.

PURPOSES OF TESTING

When deciding which test(s) to select, the first consideration should be a detailed examination of the purposes for which the testing is to be done. If general uses of the test results are not known in advance, the best decision would be not to test. If one is only going to administer the tests, obtain the results, and file them away in a vault, it makes little difference which test is administered. To be sure, there may be more status among your fellow professionals in giving one test over another, but that is hardly sufficient reason for selecting a test!

If, however, specific uses are anticipated, then test selection can occur in a more sensible and systematic fashion. Quite often one can easily decide what general kind of test is most desirable. Aptitude, achievement, interest, and personality tests are not used for exactly the same specific purposes. Although Table 1–2, for example, shows that all kinds of tests *can* be used for vocational guidance, they obviously don't all serve the same *specific* purpose. *Many* purposes could fall under the heading of vocational guidance, and adequate test selection demands more specific preplanning. Knowing that a test is to be used for the purpose of comparing Johnny's interests to the interests of people in various professional occupations would make the selection much easier.

Even knowing precisely the purposes for which one is testing, though, does not necessarily make selection automatic. Suppose you are a seventh grade mathematics teacher and you wish to measure the achievement of your students in mathematics so you can evaluate (1) whether or not they have learned enough material to undertake the eighth grade math curriculum and (2) whether you have been an effective teacher. Furthermore, suppose you wish to use a standardized test in addition to your own classroom test to help make the evaluations. How do you decide which of the many standardized seventh grade mathematics tests to administer? To make this decision you must be precise in considering your purposes. One difference in all the tests you might choose from is that they do not all cover the same mathematics content. Some of the tests will cover "modern math." Others will cover the content taught in traditional courses. To make a decision among these tests you have to decide what your specific objectives are and exactly what area of mathematics you wish to test. Although this is a problem of content validity and will be mentioned later in this chapter, it is also a problem of determining just exactly why you wish to use the test. It cannot be emphasized too strongly that the first and most important step in test selection is to determine exactly *why* you are giving the test, *what* type of information you expect from it, and *how* you intend to use that information once you have it.

SOURCES OF INFORMATION

Although "sources of information" is not one of the principles of test selection per se, knowledge of these sources is so important that they will be considered here. Once you have determined specifically what sort of information you want to obtain from a test, how can you find out what tests will give this information, and how should you choose between them? There are many sources of information that can assist in this decision. Some of these are Buros' *Mental Measurements Yearbook* and his *Tests in Print*, publishers' catalogs, specimen tests, professional journals, measurement texts, and bulletins published by testing corporations.

A good place to start is the latest edition of the *Mental Measurements Yearbook*.[10] The sixth edition lists most of the published standardized tests that were in print at the time the yearbook went to press. Those tests not reviewed in earlier editions (and those previously reviewed that have been revised) are described and criticized by educational and psychological authorities. All reviewers of this 1714 page volume praise it highly. Each school district should own a copy of this book and use it extensively in the test selection process.

Tests in Print[11] is a comprehensive test bibliography and index to the first five books in the *Mental Measurements Yearbook* series. Each test mentioned in *Tests in Print* includes information concerning:

1. Test title
2. Appropriate grade levels
3. Publication date
4. Special short comments about the test
5. Number and type of scores provided
6. Authors
7. Publisher
8. Reference to test reviews in *Mental Measurements Yearbooks*

Test publishers' catalogs are a particularly good source for locating new and recently revised tests. These catalogs provide basic information about the purpose and content of the test, appropriate level, working time, cost, and scoring services available. An important piece of information that is not provided in all publishers' catalogs is the copyright date (or norm date).

After locating some promising tests by searching the *Mental Measurements Yearbooks* and the publishers' catalogs, it is essential that the tests be examined before you make a final selection and order large quantities. Most

[10]Oscar K. Buros (Ed.), *The sixth mental measurements yearbook*. Highland Park, N.J.: Gryphon Press, 1965.
[11]Oscar K. Buros, *Tests in print*. Highland Park, N.J.: Gryphon Press, 1961.

publishers will send, for a very nominal price, specimen sets of tests. These sets usually include the test booklet, answer sheet, administrator's manual, and technical manual, as well as complete information on cost and scoring services. Careful study of the set is essential in determining whether or not that test will meet the specific purposes you have in mind. For example, a seventh grade modern math teacher may receive a brochure describing a modern math achievement test. From published reviews as well as from the descriptive literature provided, this test appears to be appropriate. But is it? Even though the professional reviewers laud the test from a technical standpoint and praise its modern content, it is still quite conceivable that this test may be inappropriate. This seventh grade teacher may stress fundamental operations in set theory, but the test may only have two items devoted to testing this concept. The teacher may skim over binary operations, but over 25 percent of the test may be devoted to this. The teacher may stress commutative, associative, and distributive properties without resorting to technical jargon. The test, however, although measuring these same properties, may assume the pupils' understanding of this mathematical language. This disparity between what the test is designed to measure and what the teacher actually teaches will not be evident except by detailed examination of the test and the test manual.

Other sources of information are the test reviews found in the professional periodicals. Journals such as *Educational and Psychological Measurement*, the *Journal of Educational Measurement*, the *Journal of Counseling Psychology*, and the *Personnel and Guidance Journal* typically carry reviews of some of the more recently published or revised tests. *Educational and Psychological Measurement* also publishes a validity studies section twice a year. The bulk of the articles in this section are reports of studies using various standardized instruments for predictive purposes. Textbooks on measurement also typically include information on various tests.

It should be obvious by now that there is an abundance of sources of information about tests. These sources should be used to a considerable extent. It makes test selection both easier and better.

PRACTICAL ASPECTS
OF TESTING AND TEST SELECTION

The range of tasks begins with test selection but also includes administration, scoring, and interpretation. These are aspects that, although separate tasks, should be taken into consideration at the time of test selection. These factors will therefore be considered both in terms of their importance in test selection as well as their unique aspects in the whole process of test use.

Let us assume that we have three tests. Which one of these should we choose? Our choice should be guided in part by such factors as ease of administration and scoring, availability of norms, availability of equivalent or parallel forms, and the test's ultimate utility (utility depends upon the test's reliability and validity, which will be discussed later). Other things being equal, we will want to select the test that is easiest to administer and score, and the one that is accompanied by the most detailed manual that outlines the procedure to be followed. Factors to be considered in this section are administration, scoring, cost, and format.

ADMINISTRATION

A characteristic of the standardized test that distinguishes it from the teacher-made test is that the standardized test has a uniform procedure with respect to administration. This procedure refers to the physical arrangements made for the actual testing as well as to the directions to be employed in administering the test. Conditions prior to the actual testing also are relevant.

Who, When, and How

Questions such as *who* should administer the test, *when* should the test be given, and *how* should the test be administered are very pertinent.

For most group tests, the ordinary classroom teacher is capable of administering the test without any formal or specialized training provided he follows the directions exactly as they are stated in the test manual.

There are many views on the question of the time at which the tests should be administered. Some feel that all tests should be administered in the morning, when individuals are physically and mentally at their peak. Some feel that tests should never be given on Mondays or Fridays. Some feel that tests should be administered at the same time of the year that the tests were given to the standardization sample while others feel that interpolations or extrapolations of the norm data can be validly made to correct for differing time conditions.

In general, time of day, and day of the week, are not too important. It would probably be best not to give the test right after lunch or right before a pep rally for the homecoming game, but there is no valid evidence suggesting that some days or times of day are particularly bad. It is, however, important in achievement testing to try to administer the test at the same time of year as when the norming was done. Assume a test's normative data were gathered in October. The norm group's seventh graders might have a mean raw score of 85; the eighth graders a mean raw score of 125. Can one predict from these data what a mean raw score for the norm group's seventh graders would have been had they been tested in June (nine months after the norm group was actually tested)? Some test companies would answer affirmatively and provide interpolated norms depicting this mean to be 115 (three-fourths the distance between 85 and 125). However, in some subjects it might well be that at the end of the year seventh graders perform better than beginning eighth graders due to the latter's forgetting during the summer months. This illustrates one of the dangers of attempting to use test companies' interpolated norms — norms that are arrived at mathematically rather than empirically. For this reason, it is best to administer achievement tests at the same time of year as the actual norm data were gathered. Another possibility is to choose a test that has norms gathered during the time of year you wish to test.

Suppose one must make a choice between two equally valid achievement tests. They differ only insofar as the time the normative data were gathered — fall and spring. Which test should be used? This is indeed an important point to consider. If the data are to be used to assist the teacher during the regular school year, it might be advisable to test in the fall. On the other hand, if the data are to be used to help determine which students are in need of summer instruction, it would be advisable to test in the spring. All in all, the time of testing will depend, in large part, upon the uses to which the data will be put.

The question of *how* the test should be administered is one over which the test administrator has little control because it is essential that he rigidly follow the directions outlined in the test manual.[12] For example, if Test A has three subparts and the manual states that Part 1 is to be given first, then the administrator must administer Part 1 first even though he feels that it would be better to administer the test in a different order. Should the test administrator deviate from the directions given, the norms provided will be misleading.

Occasionally the instructions for a test are purposely vague. For example, because it is not always made clear, test administrators frequently are asked whether there is a penalty imposed for guessing. Although at one time test publishers attempted to provide specific instructions with respect to guessing,[13] they have now abandoned this approach and, in their general instructions, urge individuals to attempt only those items about which they have some knowledge and to avoid random guessing.

If the test administrator knows how the test is to be scored (that is, whether or not a guessing formula will be applied) but the directions read to

[12]See Karou Yamamoto and Henry F. Dizney, Effects of three sets of test instructions on scores on an intelligence scale. *Educ. psychol. Measmt.*, 25, 1965, 87–94.

[13]Sheer random guessing is seldom used by individuals in their selection of the correct answer. One of the major criticisms about guessing formulas is that they are based upon the assumption that all wrong answers are due to chance guessing, and we know that this is not so.

the students are vague, it is necessary that any questions students raise related to the use of guessing formulas be answered without giving additional information. This could be done, for example, by the administrator's saying something like "The directions suggest that . . ." and then rereading the directions. Any direct answer providing more information than the original directions would destroy the test makers' attempt to establish a certain mental set without providing specific instructions.[14]

Physical Conditions

Test administrators often neglect to ensure that pupils take the test under similar physical testing conditions. In other words, they sometimes neglect to consider the seating arrangements, the ventilation, the heat, the lighting, and the other physical conditions.

There is no doubt that an individual's test score can be somewhat influenced by the physical conditions under which the test is taken. Let us assume that two boys are equally motivated and of comparable ability. Both are tested in their regular classrooms. The thermostat in one room breaks down, and the room becomes extremely hot. Would we not expect to obtain different scores because of the variance in testing conditions? Although this illustration might be far fetched, it is used to show the importance that physical conditions could play in determining an individual's score. All individuals should take the test under conditions that duplicate as closely as possible the conditions that existed when the test was standardized. (One usually assumes these conditions were optimal.) Even though reliability formulas are typically not used to estimate the error variance due to differing physical conditions, this does not imply that the errors are nonexistent, nor does it detract from the fact that we are obligated to provide testees with optimal testing conditions.

Psychological Aspects

Individuals usually perform better at any endeavor, including test taking, if they approach that experience with a positive attitude. And yet, test administrators frequently fail to establish a positive mental attitude in the individuals being tested. At present, the research on the general mental attitude and motivation of individuals and the correlation of these traits with test performance is inconclusive. We do know, however, that test anxiety affects optimum performance. It is the task of the administrator to

---

[14]For further references on guessing formulas see Frances Swineford and Peter M. Miller, Effects of directions regarding guessing on item statistics of a multiple-choice vocabulary test. *J. educ. Psychol.*, *44*, 1953, 129–139. The study illustrated that some students will guess regardless of the penalties imposed. Also see L. K. Waters, Effect of perceived scoring formula on some aspects of test performance. *Educ. psychol. Measmt*, *27*, 1967, 1005–1010.

prepare the student emotionally for the test. Students should be motivated to do their best but should not be made unduly anxious. If students are made aware of the benefits they will derive from accurate test results, this should do much toward setting the proper emotional climate.

Besides the motivating factor, there are other characteristics of students that may affect their test performance but that are not related to what the test is attempting to measure. All individuals have certain personality characteristics that govern their test-taking behavior. For example, some individuals, when in doubt, will tend to say "yes" in a true-false question. Some individuals will tend to select either the first, middle, or last response in a multiple-choice test item. Some individuals will tend to guess even though they have been warned and instructed not to guess. This tendency to respond to test items on the basis of personality habits (rather than on direct or peripheral knowledge) is referred to as response set, and research has demonstrated that these traits can affect the obtained score.

Students also vary in their degree of test wiseness or in their ability to pick up cues from the format of the test item or from the format of the test. Nearly every student taking objective examinations learns quickly that, in true-false questions, items that contain specific distractors such as *never* or *always* should be answered in a certain way, and they learn that the various alternatives appear with approximately equal frequency in any test. Hence, a "test-wise" individual can obtain a good score because he is cognizant of the "tricks of the trade." To equate for this variable, it would be best to attempt to have all students at approximately the same level of test-taking sophistication.[15]

Ease of Administration

In selecting tests, one must consider ease of administration as well as the adequacy of the directions presented. The nature of the test with respect to time limits will also influence the selection of one test over another. If one test takes 75 minutes to administer but consists of three parts, the longest of which takes 30 minutes, while another test takes 55 minutes but must be given at one time, class schedules may dictate which test should be used because most schools operate with periods of from 30 to 50 minutes. Any test that necessitates a change in the school's operating procedure should be considered carefully before being selected. Naturally, if the so-called inconvenient test is a much better test, it should be selected regardless of the slight inconvenience that might be caused.

Test users must critically examine the test manual and render judgments concerning the adequacy of directions for administration. The test publisher has an obligation to furnish a manual that provides a description of standard

[15]Arvo E. Juola, *Examinations (skills and techniques)*. Lincoln, Neb.: Cliff's Notes, 1968.

testing conditions, as well as norms and directions that are clear and concise. On the other hand, test administrators have an obligation to provide for standard testing conditions and qualified test administrators. Only when these conditions are realized will the student be able to perform maximally according to clear and concise instructions that both he and the examiner fully comprehend.

Summary of Test Administration

Because there are conditions (other than the individual differences on the trait being measured) prior to and during the test taking that can influence the obtained score, it is essential the test administrator be aware of the conditions and try to minimize the influence of some of them through proper student preparation and by following the directions contained in the test manual.

Because it is of vital importance that the test be administered under uniform conditions and that these conditions duplicate as closely as possible the conditions existing when the validity and reliability data were obtained, it is suggested that the test administrator thoroughly familiarize himself with the instructions for administration at least two or three weeks before the test is given. In this way any ambiguities or errors can be clarified by communicating directly with the test publisher so that clarification and/ or further instructions may be received. We must remember that all subjects should operate under optimal physical and psychological conditions.

SCORING

In this section, we will consider the variety of scoring devices that are currently available. Briefly, there are three types of scoring processes: (1) hand scoring either in the booklets themselves or on separate answer sheets, (2) machine scoring, and (3) self-scoring answer sheets.[16] The manner in which the tests are to be scored will be governed, at least in part, by the availability of special scoring equipment or the monetary resources available to have the answer sheets scored by the test publisher or by an independent scoring service.

Hand Scoring

This method is primarily used in the preschool or primary grades because it is relatively easy for the children to understand. Here the subject is asked to perform a task such as "Cross out the thing that doesn't belong in this

---

[16]For a discussion on the effect of the type of answer sheet used on test performance see Priscilla Hayward, A comparison of test performance on three answer sheet formats. *Educ. psychol. Measmt.*, 27, 1967, 997–1004.

group" or "Draw a line from the wagon to the horse," and he proceeds to record his answer directly in the test booklet. The test booklets are then hand scored. Pupils can also record their answers to multiple-choice test items on a separate answer sheet, and a punched key can then be placed over the answer sheet to obtain the score. This key is nothing more than the regular answer sheet with the correct responses punched out. The teacher then places the key over the pupils' answer sheets and counts the number of blackened spaces to determine the number of items answered correctly. One advantage of separate answer sheets is that the test booklet can be used repeatedly, which reduces the cost of test administration. The carbon booklet is another technique that may be used to record and score responses. The pupil records his answer on the top sheet, and these marks are transferred to a scoring sheet below. Should the student wish to alter a response, he completely fills in the square of the original answer. After the test has been completed, the teacher need only separate the two answer sheets and count the number of responses in the squares to obtain the number of items answered correctly.

A recent adaptation of the carbon booklet is the silver overlay answer sheet. Here the correct answers are previously placed in the appropriate squares, and the total answer sheet is covered by a silver overlay that conceals the correct answers. The student erases the square he feels corresponds to the correct answer. This procedure has not found its way into commercially prepared tests as yet but is used quite effectively in classroom testing because it provides immediate feedback. The pin-prick method is similar to both the carbon booklet and the silver overlay. Instead of checking the answer by placing an "X" in the appropriate space or by erasing the appropriate square, the subject sticks a pin in the square (or circle) near the answer he feels is correct. Squares (or circles) corresponding to the correct answer are printed on the back of the page so that when the booklet is torn open the number of pinholes falling within the designated squares indicates the score. It should be readily evident that the hand-scoring method does not restrict the process to written answers in the test booklet. The carbon booklet, the pin-prick method, the silver overlay, or the separate answer sheet can all be used.

Machine Scoring

Most answer sheets can be either hand or machine scored. With machine scoring one can employ any correction formula desired to obtain the total score, which is then recorded on the answer sheet. The kind of answer sheet to be used, the type of pencil used, and the speed of scoring is dependent upon the type of scoring equipment available. Some scoring equipment presently being used at the Measurement Research Center (Iowa City) and the National Computer Systems (Minneapolis) is capable of scoring test responses recorded directly in the test booklet. Such systems obviate the need for separate answer sheets.

A major advantage of electronic scoring is that many papers can be scored accurately in a relatively short time. For example, with the IBM 1230 scoring machine, about 900 answer sheets can be scored in one hour. A disadvantage of machine scoring is that, unless directions are explicitly followed by the student, scoring errors will occur. The errors can be minimized by a preliminary screening; however, the time required for correcting sloppy and/or smudgy papers can prove to be costly. This need for remarking or correcting can be almost entirely eliminated by careful administrative directions prior to taking the test.

Although schools with small testing programs would not be in a position to purchase or lease test-scoring equipment, the major test publishers provide this service for a nominal charge. When the test publisher's equipment is to be used, the answer sheets are mailed directly to the publisher. In addition to scoring the papers, these scoring centers will provide print-outs of the pupils' raw and converted scores, percentiles, grade and age equivalents, distributions of test scores, and the like. It is also possible to have answer sheets scored by some state universities or large school districts for a small charge. Those persons using tests should compare the costs and services offered by the various agencies so that they will be able to process their answer sheets most economically.

Although such factors as validity, reliability, availability of norms and equivalent forms (to be discussed later), and ease of administration and scoring are all to be considered heavily in test selection, one should also consider two other minor points in selecting a test: cost and format.

COST

The cost of testing should only be an ancillary factor to be considered when deciding which test is to be employed. Other things being equal of course, the teacher or counselor should select the test that will have the lowest per pupil cost in terms of administration and scoring. However, the factor of cost should not be a primary factor in selecting Test A over Test B. Validity, reliability, norms, an adequate manual, and the like are all more important than cost. Just as in any purchase, one test at ten cents may be a good buy while another at six cents may be too expensive. We should consider *what* we are getting for our money rather than *how* much will it cost us to provide an adequate and meaningful testing program in our school.[17]

[17]As Dr. Harold Seashore pointed out, the most costly aspect of testing *should* be the salaries paid to professional staff to make proper use of the tests. He states: "For every $500 a school spends on the tests themselves, it should spend $15,000 on salaries for personnel to supervise and interpret the tests" (*Newsweek*, July 20, 1959, p. 93).

FORMAT

Just as we should not judge a book by its cover, we should not judge a test by its initial appearance. Nevertheless, other things being equal, we should select the test that is most attractive in appearance and that is printed in clear type of a size appropriate for the grade level. In addition, if pictures or illustrations are used in the test, they should be of high quality. Too often we find tests used at the preschool or primary level containing illustrations that are fuzzy, hazy, and ambiguous. When the quality of reproduction is such that pupils might answer incorrectly because of the illustrations used rather than because they do not know the correct answer, it behooves us to find a better test.

SOME BASIC STATISTICAL CONCEPTS
RELATED TO TESTING AND TEST SELECTION

Often, teachers are given a set of scores for their pupils and flounder in an attempt to determine the meaning of the scores. The understanding of some basic statistical concepts will enable the user to obtain a better understanding of two of the most essential qualities of any test—reliability and validity—as well as to derive more meaning from the scores themselves.

Given an ordered set of scores, often called a distribution, it is of value to use statistics to summarize certain characteristics of this distribution. Two characteristics that are of particular interest are a measure of central tendency that gives some idea of the average or typical score in the distribution and a measure of variability that gives an indication of how much the scores vary (or the spread of scores). When given two distributions for the same set of people, a statistic describing the relationship between the distributions is valuable. Measures of *central tendency, variability,* and *relationship* will be briefly discussed at this time.[18]

MEASURES OF CENTRAL TENDENCY

There are two commonly used measures of central tendency encountered in testing: the mean and the median. A third measure, the mode, is used occasionally. All are points on the score scale. *The arithmetic mean ($\bar{X}$) is the average of a set of scores.* It is found by adding all the scores in the distribu-

---

[18]For a fuller discussion of these measures, one should turn to a basic statistics text such as Jimmy R. Amos, Foster L. Brown, and Oscar G. Mink, *Statistical concepts.* New York: Harper & Row, 1965.

tion and dividing by the total number of scores (N). The formula is as follows:

$$\bar{X} = \frac{\Sigma X}{N} \qquad (1)$$

where
$\bar{X}$ = the mean
X = the raw score for a person
N = the number of scores

and
Σ = a summation sign indicating that all X's in the distribution are added

The median (Mdn) is the point below which 50 percent of the scores lie. It is obtained by simply arranging the scores from high to low (or low to high) and finding the score in the middle of the distribution. This middle score is the median. With an odd number of scores, such as 25, the median would be the score above and below which 12 scores lie. That is, the median is considered to be the 13th score. With an even number of scores, such as 24, the median would be the score halfway between the 12th and 13th scores in the distribution.[19]

Table 1–3

Hypothetical Distribution of IQ Scores for a Class of 20 Students

IQ Scores	
185	
185	
83	
83	
82	$N = 20$
81	
81	$\Sigma X = 1780$
80	
80	$\bar{X} = \dfrac{\Sigma X}{N} = \dfrac{1780}{20} = 89$
80	
78	Mdn = 79
78	
78	Mode = 74
77	
77	
76	
74	
74	
74	
74	

[19]For grouped data a slightly different approach is used. See William L. Hays, *Statistics for psychologists.* New York: Holt, Rinehart and Winston, 1963, pp. 159–161.

The mode is the most frequently occurring score in the distribution. It, however, is seldom used as a measurement of central tendency in educational measurement.

The mean is generally the preferred measure of central tendency. The mean takes into account the actual numerical value of every score in the distribution. The median is preferred if one wants a measure not affected by the values of the extreme scores in a distribution.

The distribution of IQ scores for a class of 20 students shown in Table 1–3 is an example where the median would be a better indicator of central tendency than the mean. The mean of 89 is a somewhat misleading figure, influenced greatly by two students with very high IQ's. Note that in this case the mean is actually six points above the third highest score! The median of 79 is a much more representative figure. (Note that the mode of 74 is actually the lowest score in this distribution.)

For fairly normal distributions with large N's (which is the case in most distributions obtained from standardized test results) the mean, median, and mode are ordinarily close in value.

MEASURES OF VARIABILITY

The two measures of variability most often used in testing are the standard deviation (S) and the variance (S^2).[20] These have a very precise mathematical relationship to each other: The standard deviation is the square root of the variance. This relationship is indicated in the symbols by use of the exponent *2* when indicating variance. The variance can be computed with the following formula:

$$S_x^2 = \frac{\Sigma(X - \bar{X})^2}{N} \tag{2}$$

where all symbols on the right-hand side have been previously defined and the subscript x on the S_x^2 identifies the distribution whose variance is being computed. The standard deviation is

$$S_x = \sqrt{\frac{\Sigma(X - \bar{X})^2}{N}} \tag{3}$$

Two examples of computing the variance and standard deviation are illustrated in Table 1–4. Figure 1–2 is a graph of these two distributions. If a new student with an IQ score of 120 (Assume all IQ scores were obtained from the same test.) were to join a class of pupils with IQ scores as shown in Table 1–4(a), he would be 20 points above the mean and 11 points above the second pupil in his class in measured academic ability. If he were to join

---

[20]Occasionally the range (High − Low + 1) is used, but this measure, like the mode, is very unstable.

a class with scores as shown in Table 1–4(b) he would still be 20 points above the mean, but there would be three pupils who would have higher measured academic ability. The class depicted in Table 1–4(b) would be much harder to teach due to the extreme variability in academic ability of the students.

To know only a person's raw score is of little value. To know that a person's score is so much above or below the mean is of some value. If one has an indication of the variability of a distribution of scores as well, much more information is obtained.

Table 1–4

Two Distributions of IQ Scores with Equal Means but Unequal Variances

Table 1–4(a)			Table 1–4(b)		
X	$(X - \bar{X})$	$(X - \bar{X})^2$	X	$(X - \bar{X})$	$(X - \bar{X})^2$
109	9	81	185	85	7225
108	8	64	147	47	2209
107	7	49	121	21	441
105	5	25	108	8	64
105	5	25	106	6	36
103	3	9	104	4	16
102	2	4	103	3	9
101	1	1	103	3	9
101	1	1	102	2	4
101	1	1	101	1	1
99	−1	1	99	−1	1
99	−1	1	96	−4	16
97	−3	9	91	−9	81
97	−3	9	83	−17	289
96	−4	16	82	−18	324
95	−5	25	80	−20	400
95	−5	25	74	−26	676
94	−6	36	74	−26	676
93	−7	49	71	−29	841
93	−7	49	70	−30	900

$\Sigma X = 2000 \qquad 480 = \Sigma(X - \bar{X})^2$

$N = 20 \qquad \bar{X} = \dfrac{\Sigma X}{N} = \dfrac{2000}{20} = 100$

$S_x^2 = \dfrac{480}{20} = 24$

$S_x = \sqrt{24} \doteq 4.9$

$\Sigma X = 2000 \quad \Sigma(X - \bar{X})^2 = 14{,}218$

$N = 20 \qquad \bar{X} = \dfrac{\Sigma X}{N} = \dfrac{2000}{20} = 100$

$S_x^2 = \dfrac{14{,}218}{20} = 710.9$

$S_x = \sqrt{710.9} \doteq 26.66$

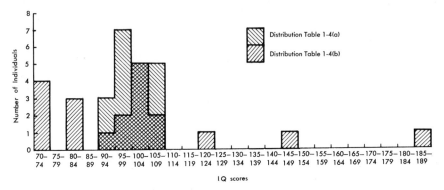

Figure 1-2 Two distributions of IQ scores with equal means but unequal variances.

A MEASURE OF RELATIONSHIP

If we have two sets of scores from the same group of people, it is often desirable to know the degree to which the scores are related. This is true when we wish to study the reliability or validity of a test. For example, we might like to know the linear relationship between the scores on two different administrations of the same test. Or we may be interested in the relationship between reading ability and grade-point average (GPA). The Pearson product moment correlation coefficient (r) is the statistic most often used to give us an indication of this relationship. It can be calculated from the formula:

$$r = \frac{\Sigma(X - \bar{X})(Y - \bar{Y})}{NS_xS_y} \tag{4}$$

If a desk calculator is available, or when the N is large, the following formula is often employed.

$$r = \frac{N\Sigma XY - \Sigma X\Sigma Y}{\sqrt{[N\Sigma X^2 - (\Sigma X)^2][N\Sigma Y^2 - (\Sigma Y)^2]}} \tag{5}$$

where　　X = the score of a person on one variable

Y = the score of the same person on the other variable

$\bar{X}$ = the mean of the X distribution

$\bar{Y}$ = the mean of the Y distribution

S_x = the standard deviation of the X scores

S_y = the standard deviation of the Y scores

N = the number of scores within each distribution

The value of r can range from $+1.00$ to -1.00. When an increase in one variable tends to be accompanied by an increase in the other variable (such as aptitude and achievement), the correlation is positive. When an increase in one tends to be accompanied by a decrease in the other (such as speed and accuracy), then the correlation is negative. A perfect positive correlation (1.00) or a perfect negative correlation (-1.00) occurs when a change in the one variable is always accompanied by a commensurate change in the other variable. A zero (.00) correlation occurs when there is no relationship between the two variables.

The example shown in Table 1–5 illustrates the computation of r. This r of .75 indicates that there is considerable relationship between scores on X

Table 1–5

The Calculation of r

X[a]	Y[b]	X	Y
3.6	95	2.7	45
3.5	83	2.7	34
3.4	93	2.6	77
3.4	72	2.6	61
3.3	83	2.6	42
3.3	64	2.6	29
3.2	93	2.5	71
3.2	76	2.5	59
3.2	55	2.5	50
3.1	86	2.5	36
3.1	68	2.4	53
3.0	92	2.4	42
3.0	80	2.4	31
3.0	54	2.4	24
3.0	45	2.3	64
2.9	88	2.3	47
2.9	70	2.3	35
2.9	63	2.2	55
2.8	82	2.2	21
2.8	75	2.1	49
2.8	58	2.1	34
2.8	49	2.0	40
2.8	39	2.0	19
2.7	66	1.9	31
2.7	53	1.8	17

$N = 50$

$\Sigma X = 135$

$\Sigma X^2 = 373.9$

$\Sigma Y = 2848$

$\Sigma Y^2 = 185{,}048$

$\Sigma XY = 8037.9$

$$r = \frac{N\Sigma XY - \Sigma X \Sigma Y}{\sqrt{[N\Sigma X^2 - (\Sigma X)^2][N\Sigma Y^2 - (\Sigma Y)^2]}}$$

$$= \frac{50(8037.9) - (135)(2848)}{\sqrt{[50(373.9) - (135)^2][50(185048) - (2848)^2]}}$$

$$= \frac{17415}{\sqrt{(472)(1141296)}} \doteq .75$$

[a] X = Grade point average
[b] Y = A scholastic aptitude test score

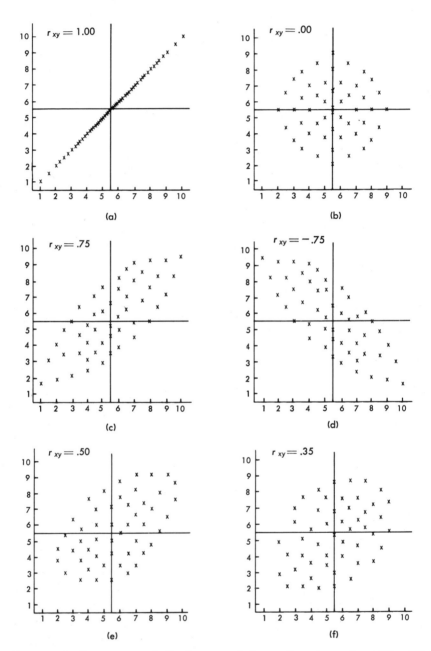

Figure 1-3 Scattergrams indicating correlations of various sizes ($N = 50$).

(grade-point average) and Y (a scholastic aptitude test). How high (positively or negatively) an r must be in order to indicate that a significant relationship exists is difficult to specify. It is dependent upon how one defines *significance*. Significance can be considered in either a statistical or practical sense. For example, a correlation coefficient of .08 (say between teaching method and grades) will be statistically significant if the number of cases used to compute the correlation is sufficiently large. But, this correlation is so low that it has no practical significance in educational decision making. There will be instances when the decision to be made is vital to life (for example, decisions based on pharmacological research) when a correlation of .08 is both of statistical and practical significance. The scattergrams in Figure 1–3 depict the amount of relationship for various correlation coefficients.

Two cautions should be mentioned concerning the interpretation of a Pearson product moment correlation coefficient:

1. It is not an indication of cause and effect. One can find all sorts of variables that are related but have no causal relationship. For example, for children, the size of the big toe is slightly correlated with mental age — yet one does not cause the other. They are correlated simply because they are both related to a third variable: chronological age.

2. It is a measure of linear relationship. In Figure 1–4 there is a high relationship between variables X and Y. The Pearson product r, however,

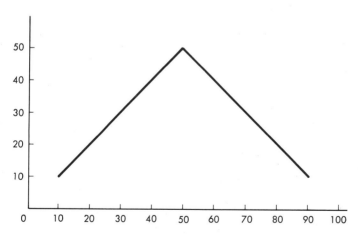

Figure 1-4 A scattergram showing two variables that are perfectly related but with a zero Pearson product moment r.

is zero. If one suspects that two variables have a relationship other than linear, a different index of correlation should be computed.[21]

THE NORMAL CURVE

The normal curve is a bell-shaped curve as shown in Figure 1–5. It has two characterisics that are of particular importance in measurement theory: (1) a symmetry about the mean and (2) a specified percent of scores falling within each standard deviation from the mean. As can be seen from Figure 1–5, about 68 percent of the scores fall between $\pm 1S_x$, 95 percent between $\pm 2S_x$, and 99 percent between $\pm 3S_x$.

There has been considerable discussion in the past about whether human characteristics are normally distributed. Evidence on physical characteristics such as height and weight lend some support to those who take the position such characteristics are normally distributed. Whether one can infer anything about the distribution of psychological characteristics from this observation is debatable. The distributions obtained on psychological characteristics cannot be used as evidence because the test score distributions can be influenced greatly by the characteristics of a test. The position a test publisher takes on this will affect the kind of transformation he makes on the data. If one assumes that the underlying characteristic is normally distributed, then a normal transformation of the data is warranted; otherwise it is not. Most test publishers do transform scores so they will fall into a normal distribution.

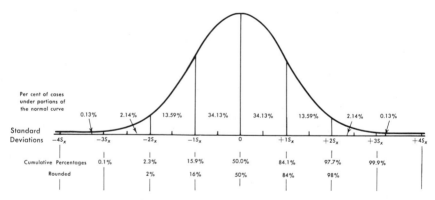

Figure 1-5   Chart showing the normal curve and the percent of cases under various portions of the normal curve. (Adapted and reproduced with the permission of The Psychological Corporation.)

[21]An explanation of curvilinear relationships can be found in William A. Hays, *Statistics for psychologists.*

TECHNICAL CONSIDERATIONS OF TESTING AND TEST SELECTION

Up to this point our major consideration has been on some of the *extrinsic* factors (factors independent of test construction per se) that can influence the obtained score and that therefore should be considered in test selection. We shall now consider some of the *intrinsic* factors (reliability and validity) involved in testing that should be taken into account in test selection. In conjunction with this discussion, the reader may wish to consult the American Psychological Association's *Standards for Educational and Psychological Tests and Manuals*.[22] This guide, which recommends uniform professional standards for commercially published tests, treats six specific topics, namely:

- a. Dissemination of information
- b. Interpretation
- c. Validity
- d. Reliability
- e. Administration and scoring
- f. Scales and norms

The standards are intended to apply to "most published devices for diagnosis, prognosis and evaluation."[23] They do not apply to devices used only for research but rather to those that will be used as an aid in practical decision making. The importance of the individual recommendations made in the manual is indicated by three levels: essential, very desirable, and desirable. An example of an essential recommendation in the interpretation section is as follows:

> B2. The test manual should state implicitly the purposes and applications for which the test is recommended. ESSENTIAL[24]

Following each recommendation is a paragraph or two explaining its importance. On the technical considerations of test selection, this booklet can be extremely valuable reading for the personnel within a school system who serve as consultants for the rest of the staff.

However, all the staff should know something about the technical considerations of tests. It is necessary not only for test selection but also for test interpretation. The technical characteristics of a test that will be discussed

---

[22]John W. French and William B. Michael, *Standards for educational and psychological tests and manuals*. Washington, D.C.: American Psychological Association, 1966.
[23]French and Michael, p. 3.
[24]French and Michael, p. 10.

under this heading are reliability and validity. Interpretation, although not considered a technical aspect, is also an important factor to be considered in test selection. It will be discussed in a separate section.

RELIABILITY

Reliability can be defined as the degree of consistency between two measures of the same thing. This is neither a theoretical nor an operational definition but is more of a conceptual (or layman's) definition. In physical measurement we ordinarily obtain reliable measures. This is true primarily for three basic reasons:

1. Physical characteristics can usually be measured directly rather than indirectly.
2. The instruments used to obtain the measures are quite precise.
3. The traits or characteristics being measured are relatively stable.

However, even in physical measurement there is some unreliability or inconsistency. If we are interested in determining the reliability with which we can measure a person's weight, we may proceed in a variety of ways. We may, for example, have a person get on and off a scale several times, and we may record his weight each time. These recorded weights may differ. The person may stand somewhat differently on the scale from one time to the next, which would influence the reading, or the person doing the measuring may not read or record the numbers correctly.

Another method of checking the consistency with which we can measure weight would be to record the weight of a person as obtained on ten different scales and to compare these values. These values may vary for the reasons just given. In addition, they may vary due to whatever differences exist in the scales. Thus, one would expect to obtain a more variable (less consistent) set of values.

Still different methods of checking the consistency of weight measures would be to weigh a person on ten successive Saturday mornings on (1) the same scale each time or (2) ten different scales. With these two procedures one would have an additional source of variance from those already mentioned: the stability of the person's weight from one week to the next. Thus, there are many different procedures for estimating the consistency or reliability of measurement. Each procedure considers a slightly different source of variance for the values obtained.

Psychological measurement is typically much less reliable than physical measurement. Psychological measurement is indirect and is conducted with less precise instruments on traits that are not always stable or well defined. As with the physical example mentioned, there are many reasons a pupil's test score may vary. A partial listing of sources of variance (error variance) in psychological measurement follows:

1. Trait instability
2. Sampling error
3. Administrator error
4. Scoring error
5. Health, motivation, degree of fatigue of the person
6. Good or bad luck in guessing

The variance in a person's scores is typically called *error variance* and the sources of the variance are known as *sources of error*. The fewer and smaller the errors, the more consistent (reliable) the measurement. With this general background, let us turn to a brief discussion of the theory of reliability.

Theory of Reliability

The theory of reliability can best be explained by starting with observed scores (X's). These observed scores can be conceptualized as containing various component parts. In the simplest case we think of each observed score as being made up of a "true score" and an "error score" such that

$$X = T + E \tag{6}$$

where
$$X = \text{observed score}$$
$$T = \text{true score}$$
$$E = \text{error score}$$

People, of course, differ from each other with regard to both their true scores and their observed scores. If the errors are assumed to be random, the positive and negative errors will cancel each other, and the mean error will be zero. Also, if the errors are random, they will not correlate with the true scores or with each other. Making these assumptions we can write the variance of a *test* as

$$S_x{}^2 = S_t{}^2 + S_e{}^2 \tag{7}$$

where $S_x{}^2$ = the variance of a group of individuals' observed scores

$S_t{}^2$ = the variance of a group of individuals' true scores

and $S_e{}^2$ = the error variance

Theoretically, reliability is defined as the ratio of two variances:

$$r_{xx} = \frac{S_t{}^2}{S_x{}^2} \tag{8}$$

Reliability, then, tells us to what extent the observed variance is due to true score variance. The symbol r_{xx} is used for reliability because so many of the reliability estimates are via the correlation coefficient (r) procedure. The double x subscript is used to indicate measurement of the same trait(s). Formulas (7) and (8) are basic formulas from which most of the commonly written expressions concerning reliability and the standard error of measurement (see next section) are derived. Rewriting (7) as $S_t^2 = S_x^2 - S_e^2$ and substituting into (8), we get

$$r_{xx} = 1 - \frac{S_e^2}{S_x^2} \qquad (9)$$

The definition of reliability is also often written in this fashion.

Standard Error of Measurement

From either (8) or (9) it can be seen that reliability increases as error variance decreases if S_x^2 remains constant.

Solving (9) for S_e we get

$$S_e = S_x\sqrt{1 - r_{xx}} \qquad (10)$$

which is called the standard error of measurement. Although this statistic is typically estimated from group data via (10), it is frequently conceptualized as the standard deviation of a person's observed scores (from many administrations of the same test) about his true score on that test. Theoretically, the true score of an individual does not vary. If we retested the same person many times, there would be some inconsistency (error), and the observed scores (X's) of this single person would vary, sometimes being greater than T, sometimes less. Making the assumption that the errors within a person, across testing sessions, is random, the positive and negative errors will cancel each other, and the mean error will be zero. Thus, the mean of the observed scores over repeated testings is the individual's true score ($\bar{X} = T$).

It is assumed that these observed scores (being random) will fall in a normal distribution about the true score. The standard deviation of the observed scores across repeated testings of the same individual is the standard error of measurement.

Why (10), which is computed from group data, is considered to be a good estimate of the standard error of measurement of a person's observed scores across repeated testings should become clear if we look at (7).

$$S_x^2 = S_t^2 + S_e^2$$

If we think of these values as being obtained from the data for a single individual over many testings (so that the true score does not change and hence $S_t^2 = 0$), then from (7) we get

$$S_x^2 = 0 + S_e^2$$

and $$S_x = S_e$$

Note that this holds only for the case where S_x represents the standard deviation of a person's observed scores over repeated testing. If a test has any reliability at all, S_e will be much smaller than S_x for a group of individuals each tested once, because their true scores will vary.

To reiterate, the standard error of measurement is conceptualized as providing information about the variability of a person's scores on repeated testings. Ordinarily we do not give a person the same test many times because it is uneconomical and because these tests would result in changes in the individual (fatigue, learning effects). Thus, the standard error of measurement is estimated from group data. Under this procedure it is assumed that every individual in the group has the same standard error. This is never precisely true in actual practice, particularly if the group is fairly heterogeneous. Better tests report different standard errors of measurement for different homogeneous subgroups along the continuum of the trait being measured.

The standard error of measurement is often used for what is called band interpretation. Band interpretation helps convey the idea of imprecision of measurement. Because it is assumed that the errors are normally distributed about an individual's true score, one can say that a person's observed score will lie between $\pm 1S_e$ of his true score approximately 68 percent of the time, or $\pm 2S_e$ of his true score about 95 percent of the time. Although it is not precise mathematically, one usually interprets with about 68 percent (or 95 percent) certainty a person's true score to be within $\pm 1S_e$ (or $\pm 2S_e$) of his observed score. The interval $X \pm 1S_e$ is ordinarily the band used when interpreting scores to others.[25]

Suppose, for example, that an individual obtains an IQ score of 112 on a test that has 6 as a standard error of measurement. We could be about 68 percent confident that his true IQ would lie between 112 ± 6 (or 106 to 118). We could be about 95 percent confident that this true IQ would lie between $112 \pm 2(6)$ (or 100 to 124).

Estimates of Reliability

Now that reliability has been defined and discussed conceptually and theoretically, let us consider the operational definitions of reliability. How do we obtain estimates of the theoretically-defined reliability? Given one set of observed scores for a group of people, we can obtain $S_x{}^2$. From equation (9) we can see that one must get an estimate of either r_{xx} or $S_e{}^2$ to solve the equation. Ordinarily, one estimates r_{xx} first and then uses equation (10) to estimate S_e.

---

[25]See Leonard A. Feldt, Reliability of differences between scores. *Amer. educ. res. J.*, March 1967, 4, 139–145. Feldt discusses the use of confidence bands in interpreting scores and score differences.

The methods used to estimate reliability differ in that they allow different sources of error to show up. There are many different approaches that can be used to estimate reliability, but the more common ones reported in test manuals are as follows:[26]

1. Measures of stability
2. Measures of equivalence
3. Measures of internal consistency
   a. Split-half
   b. Kuder-Richardson estimates
   c. Hoyt's analysis of variance procedure

MEASURES OF STABILITY   A measure of stability, often called a test-retest estimate of reliability, is obtained by administering a test to a group of individuals, readministering the same test to the same individuals at a later date, and correlating the two sets of scores. There are various possible time intervals. The estimate of reliability will vary with the length of interval and thus this interval length must be considered in interpreting reliability coefficients. Any change in score from one setting to the other is treated as error (it is assumed the trait is stable). This is analogous to weighing a person at two different times and ascribing the difference in the two recorded measures to error. The difference may be due to standing on the scale somewhat differently, it may be due to the scale's breaking (becoming inaccurate) between measures, it may be due to a mistake in reading or recording the numbers, or it may be due to an actual weight change (trait instability) over time. We cannot in this type of estimate isolate which of the scources of error contribute to the difference in performance (weight). What is really being measured is the consistency over time of the examinees' performances on the test.

MEASURES OF EQUIVALENCE   In contrast to the test-retest procedure, the equivalent forms estimate of reliability is obtained by giving two forms (with equal content, means, and variances) of a test to the same group of individuals on the same day and correlating these results. Here, also, any change in performance is considered error, but instead of measuring changes from one *time* to another, we measure changes due to the specificity of knowledge. That is, a person may know the answer to a question on Form A and not know the answer to the equivalent question on Form B. The difference in the scores would be treated as error. This procedure is somewhat

[26]Methods 1, 2, and 3-a all use the Pearson product moment correlation coefficient. It is not obvious why this should be a reasonable estimate of reliability as defined in fomula (8). Space does not allow us to present all algebraic derivations. However, given the assumption that the error is random error and that the variances of the two distributions are equal, it can be shown that formula (8) is equal to formula (4) for the Pearson product moment coefficient. Thus, a correlation coefficient is a good estimate of reliability to the extent that the assumptions are met.

analogous to weighing a person on two different scales on the same day. Here we are unlikely to have much of a difference score (if any) due to weight change, but a difference could exist because two different scales are being used.

The two methods of estimating reliability discussed above are quite different and may give different results. Which, then, should be used? It depends on the purposes for which the test is administered. If one wishes to use the test results for long-range predictions, then he would want to use a coefficient of stability. For example, in order for a scholastic aptitude test in grade 9 to predict college grade-point average, the scores must be fairly stable. If not, we would fail in long-term predictions. Thus, we would want a reliability estimate to reflect any trait change as error so that our confidence in any prediction would be appropriately tempered by a lower reliability coefficient.

If the purpose of giving a test is not for long-range prediction but rather, say, for the purpose of making inferences about the knowledge one has in a subject matter area, then one would be primarily interested in a coefficient of equivalence. In this case we are less interested in how stable the knowledge is over time but are more interested in whether we can infer to a domain of knowledge from a sample. If there were a considerable change in score from one equivalent form to another, then the score on either or both forms is due, in large part, to specificity of knowledge. Inferences to the domain of knowledge from a score so influenced by the properties of a specific sample are hazardous. This fact would be reflected by a low equivalent forms reliability estimate.

At times people are concerned with both long-range prediction and inferences to a domain of knowledge. In that case, a coefficient of equivalence and stability could be obtained by giving one form of the test and, after a period of time, administering the other form and correlating the results. This procedure allows for both changes in scores due to trait instability and changes in scores due to item specificity. This estimate of reliability is thus usually lower than either of the other two procedures.

MEASURES OF INTERNAL CONSISTENCY   The above two estimates of reliability both require data from two testing sessions. At times it is not feasible to obtain these kinds of data. Using the methods to be described, it is possible to obtain reliability estimates from only one set of test data. These estimates are really indices of the homogeneity of the items in the test, or the degree to which the item responses correlate with the total test score.

Split-Half   The split-half method of estimating reliability is theoretically the same as the equivalent forms method. Nevertheless, the split-half method is ordinarily considered as a measure of internal consistency because the two equivalent forms are contained within a single test. That is, instead of administering an alternate form of the test, one splits the single test into two parts, and these two subscores are correlated. This correlation coefficient ($r_{\frac{1}{2}\frac{1}{2}}$) is an estimate of the reliability of a test only half as long as the original. To estimate what the reliability of the whole test would be, a correction factor needs to be applied. The appropriate formula is a special case of the Spearman-Brown prophecy formula and is as follows:

$$r_{xx} = \frac{2r_{\frac{1}{2}\frac{1}{2}}}{1 + r_{\frac{1}{2}\frac{1}{2}}} \tag{11}$$

where $\quad r_{xx} = $ the estimated reliability of the whole test

$\qquad r_{\frac{1}{2}\frac{1}{2}} = $ the reliability of the half test

Thus, if two half tests correlated .60 ($r_{\frac{1}{2}\frac{1}{2}} = .60$), the estimated reliability of the whole rest would be:

$$r_{xx} = \frac{2(.60)}{1 + .60} = \frac{1.20}{1.60} = .75$$

The advantage of the split-half method is that there need be only one form of the test and one administration to estimate reliability.

The Spearman-Brown prophecy formula assumes that the variances of the two halves are equal. If they are not, the estimated reliability of the whole test will be greater than that obtained by other methods of internal consistency. Thus, one of the problems that exist in the split half method is how to make the split. This problem can be approached in a variety of ways. But if one really attempts to make the two halves equivalent, it requires all of the same efforts necessary to construct two equivalent forms (except only half as many items are needed). Ordinarily the test is just split into two parts by a preconceived plan (for example, odd items versus even items) without statistically attempting to make the two parts equivalent.

Kuder-Richardson Estimates One way to avoid the problems of how to split the test is to use one of the Kuder-Richardson formulas. The formulas represent the average correlation obtained from all possible split-half reliability estimates. K-R 20 and K-R 21 are two formulas that are used extensively. They are as follows:

$$\text{K-R 20} \quad r_{xx} = \frac{N}{N-1}\left[1 - \frac{\Sigma pq}{S_x^2}\right] \tag{12}$$

$$\text{K-R 21} \quad r_{xx} = \frac{N}{N-1}\left[1 - \frac{\bar{X}(1 - \bar{X}/N)}{S_x^2}\right] \tag{13}$$

where $\quad N = $ the number of items in the test

$\qquad p = $ the percent of people who answered the item correctly. (If, for example, on Item 1, six of 30 people answered the item correctly, p for this item would be $6/30 = .20$)

$\qquad q = $ the percent of people who answered the item incorrectly. ($q = 1 - p$)

Σ = a summation sign indicating that pq is summed over all items

S_x^2 = the variance of the total test

$\bar{X}$ = the mean of the total test

The distinction between K-R 20 and K-R 21 is that the latter assumes all the items are of equal difficulty; that is, p is constant for all items. Given this assumption, K-R 21 is simply an algebraic derivation of K-R 20. If the assumption is not met, K-R 21 will give a lower estimate of reliability. Both formulas are frequently used by the authors of standardized tests.

Hoyt's Analysis of Variance Procedure Hoyt's[27] method has certain theoretical and conceptual advantages, but they will not be discussed because understanding analysis of variance is prerequisite to understanding Hoyt's procedure. This method has been mentioned here only because you will probably find results using it being reported occasionally in the literature. The important point to remember is that this method yields exactly the same results as K-R 20.

Factors Influencing Reliability

As has been pointed out, the specific procedure (equivalent forms, test-retest) used will affect the estimate of reliability obtained. There are other factors as well that affect the reliability estimates. Three of these will now be discussed.

TEST LENGTH When discussing the split-half method of estimating reliability, a specific case of the Spearman-Brown prophecy formula (11) was illustrated. The more general expression of this formula is:

$$r_{xx} = \frac{Kr}{1 + (K - 1)r} \tag{14}$$

where r_{xx} = the predicted reliability of a test K times as long as the original test

r = the reliability of the original test

K = the ratio of the number of items in the new test to the number of items in the original one

Thus, if a test has an original reliability of .60 and if the test were made three times as long ($K = 3$), we would predict the reliability of the lengthened test to be

$$r_{xx} = \frac{3(.60)}{1 + 2(.60)} = .818$$

As previously stated, when $K = 2$, as in the case of split-half reliability, the Spearman-Brown prophecy formula makes the assumption that the two subtests are equivalent. A more general way of stating this assumption is

[27]Cyril J. Hoyt, Test reliability estimated by analysis of variance. *Psychometrika*, 1941, 6, 153–160.

that the items added to a test must be equivalent to the items already in the test. We would not increase the reliability of a test by adding items that are markedly different.

Just as adding equivalent items makes a test more reliable, so deleting equivalent items makes a test less reliable. A person may have a test with very high reliability but simply too long to be usable. One can also use formula (14) to estimate the reliability of a test shorter than the original. For example, if one wanted to know what the estimated reliability of a test half as long as the original would be, one would use $K = \frac{1}{2}$ in the formula.

SPEED   A test is considered a pure speed test if everyone who reaches an item gets it right but if no one has time to finish all the items. Thus, score differences depend upon the number of items attempted. A pure power test is one in which everyone has time to try all the items but because of the difficulty level, ordinarily no one obtains a perfect score. Few tests are either pure speed or pure power tests. However, to the extent that a test is speeded, it is inappropriate to estimate reliability through the methods of internal consistency, and the measures of stability or equivalence should be used.

GROUP HOMOGENEITY   A third factor influencing the estimated reliability of a test is group homogeneity. Other things being equal, the more heterogeneous the group the higher the reliability. The reason for this can best be explained by looking at one of the definitional formulas (9) for reliability.

$$r_{xx} = 1 - \frac{S_e^2}{S_x^2}$$

Because S_e^2 is the variance of a person's observed score about his true score, there is no reason to expect the observed score to vary as a result of group characteristics. S_x^2 increases with group heterogeneity. If S_e^2 remains constant and S_x^2 increases, r_{xx} increases. Thus, when evaluating tests for selection purposes, it is important to note the heterogeneity of the group from which the reliability was estimated. If the reported reliability were estimated on a group of sixth through ninth graders and if the test were then administered to only seventh graders, it would be safe to conclude that because the students in the seventh grade are more homogeneous, the reliability of the test for those seventh graders would be considerably lower than the reported reliability.

Reliability and Test Selection

A question often asked in measurement courses is as follows: How reliable should a test be in order for it to be useful? This question cannot be answered in a simple manner. It depends upon the purposes for which the test is to be used. If it is to be used to help make decisions about individuals, then it should be more reliable than if it is to be used to make decisions about groups of people. Although there is no universal agreement, it is generally accepted that tests used to assist in making decisions about individuals should have reliability coefficients of at least .85. For group decisions, a reliability coefficient of about .65 may suffice. These are only guidelines. There are no absolutes; one should use the best test available. A more relevant factor is the consideration of how good a decision can be made without the help of the test data. If there is very little other information on which to base a decision, and a decision must be made, it may be helpful to use a test with low reliability rather than none at all. (A test with low reliability can still have some validity and can therefore be useful.) On the other hand, if a good decision (or accurate prediction) can be made without any test data, it may not be worthwhile to give a test even though it is reliable.

In test selection the crucial matter for the reader of a test manual is to be able to understand the reliability information reported. This of course implies that reliability data must be reported in the test manual. A knowledge of the theory of reliability, different estimates of reliability, and effects upon these estimates should help lead to such an understanding.

The kinds of reliability data that one should expect to find in a test manual depends on the type of test and on how one expects to use it. For general aptitude tests the most important kind of reliability estimate would be a stability estimate. Because aptitude test results are used to help make long-range predictions, it is important to know how stable the aptitude results are. (If the test scores are not stable they can't predict themselves, much less a criterion.) For multiple aptitude tests it is also essential to have data on the reliabilities of the subtests and the difference scores. Equivalence and internal consistency estimates are also of value for interpreting any aptitude test.

For achievement tests, equivalence reliability estimates seem almost essential. One wants to infer from the responses to a specific set of items the degree to which a person has mastered the essential skills and/or knowledge in a much larger universe. In addition, it would be valuable to have some indication about the homogeneity of the content. Thus, internal consistency estimates should also be provided. As with multiple aptitude tests, achievement test batteries should provide data on subtest reliabilities and on the reliabilities of difference scores. Inasmuch as most achievement tests are intentionally designed to fit the curriculum, one would not expect these scores to remain constant. Hence, long-range stability coefficients would be rather meaningless.

For noncognitive measures, the types of reliability information needed varies. For example, if one wishes to use an interest test to predict long-term job satisfaction, then one must assume that interests are stable, and information relevant to this assumption is needed. On the other hand, if one wishes to obtain a measure of a transient personality characteristic (such as temporary depression), high stability coefficients would not be expected.

In addition to indicating the type(s) of reliability estimates obtained, the manual must also provide other information. It is essential to know the characteristics of the sample on which the reliability estimates were computed. One should know the sample size, its representativeness, and the mean and standard deviation of sample scores.

Standard errors of measurement (and how they were obtained) should be provided. Separate age and/or grade estimates should be reported. Even within an age or grade level, different S_e's should be reported (for example, an aptitude or achievement test should report separate S_e's for students performing at the high, middle, and low levels).

VALIDITY

The degree of validity is the single most important aspect of a test. Validity can best be defined as the degree to which a test is capable of achieving certain aims. It is sometimes defined as truthfulness—does the test measure what it purports to measure. The truthfulness aspect refers only to content and construct validities, not to criterion-related validity (See following.). In order for a test to be valid, or truthful, it must first of all be reliable. (Neither validity nor reliability is an either/or dichotomy. There are degrees of each.) If we cannot get even a bathroom scale to give us a consistent weight measure, we certainly cannot expect it to be accurate. Note, however, that a measure might be very consistent (reliable) and not accurate (valid). A scale may record weights as two pounds too heavy each time. In other words, reliability is a necessary but not sufficient condition for validity.

Since a single test may be used for many different purposes, there is no single validity index for a test. A test that has some validity for one purpose may not be at all valid for another.

Kinds of Validity

While many different authors have used many different terms for validity,[28] the latest *Standards for Educational and Psychological Tests and Manuals*[29] delimits only three kinds of validity coefficients:

[28]See Robert L. Ebel, *Measuring educational achievement*. Englewood Cliffs, N.J.: Prentice-Hall, 1965, p. 380. Two terms he mentions that are occasionally used but not included in this section for discussion are *face validity* (what the test appears to measure), and *factorial validity* (the correlation between a test and a factor — arrived at through factor analysis).
[29]French and Michael.

1. Content validity
2. Criterion-related validity
3. Construct validity

Content validity is related to how adequately the content of the test samples the domain of subject matter about which inferences are to be made. It is particularly important for achievement tests. There is no numerical expression for content validity: It is determined by a thorough inspection of the items. An achievement test that may have good content validity for one teacher may prove to have low content validity for another teacher. Not all teachers (even those teaching the same course titles in the same grade) are teaching the same domain of subject matter. One of the main reasons teachers should help in the selection of achievement tests is that they are best able to judge the content validity of a test for their particular course.

Criterion-related validity pertains to the technique of studying the relationship between the test scores and independent external measures. Some writers make a distinction between two kinds of criterion-related validity: concurrent validity and predictive validity. The only distinction between these pertains to the time the criterion data are gathered. When they are collected at approximately the same time as the test data, we speak of concurrent validity. When they are gathered at a later date, we have a measure of predictive validity. Predictive validity will generally be less than concurrent validity. This is to be expected if the trait measured by the test is not stable over time. Whether criterion-related validity should be expressed as concurrent or predictive depends on whether we are primarily interested in prediction or in assessment of current status.

Construct validity is the degree to which the test scores can be accounted for by certain explanatory constructs[30] in a psychological theory. If an instrument has construct validity, people's scores will vary as the theory underlying the construct would predict. A simplified example may help. If one is interested in studying a construct like creativity, it must be because he hypothesizes that people who are creative will perform differently from those who are not creative. It is possible to build a theory (or theories) specifying how creative people (people who possess the construct creativity) behave differently from others. Once this is done, creative people can be identified by observing the behavior of individuals and classifying them according to the theory. (They could be rated rather than classified.) Now, suppose one wished to build a paper-and-pencil test to measure creativity. Once built, the creativity test would be considered to have construct validity to the degree that the test scores are related to the judgments made from

[30]Constructs are normally considered as unobservable phenomena (such as intelligence, motivation, and interest) that help to explain an individual's behavior.

observing behavior identified by the psychological theory as creative. If the anticipated relationships are not found, then the construct validity of the test is not indicated. This could result from several reasons. For example, the test may really not measure the construct of creativity, or the psychological theory concerning how creative people behave may be faulty. Theoretical psychologists are probably more apt to believe that the test is faulty rather than the theory. While this is the most probable reason, it is suggested that psychologists should be a little more willing to re-examine their theories if empirical evidence does not support them.

Methods of Expressing Validity

As mentioned, there is no numerical expression for content validity. The methods to be discussed below are used in expressing both criterion-related and construct validities. However, it should be kept in mind that one must obtain many more indices before feeling justified in suggesting that any degree of construct validity has been demonstrated.

CORRELATION COEFFICIENTS AND RELATED EXPRESSIONS The Pearson product moment correlation coefficient is probably the most often used procedure for reporting validity. A fairly standard notation is to use the symbol r_{xy} for correlations representing validity coefficients. (Recall that r_{xx} was used for reliability.) The x subscript stands for the test score, the y subscript for the criterion measure. For example, a correlation coefficient of .80 ($r_{xy} = .80$) between Scholastic Aptitude Test scores (X) obtained in 11th grade and college freshmen GPA's (Y) may be reported. This correlation would indicate a substantial relationship. From this relationship we could say that the Scholastic Aptitude Test has considerable predictive validity with regard to college freshmen grades. The correlation coefficient can also be used in a regression equation to derive predicted criterion measures.[31]

The relationship between the test and the criterion is often expressed using algebraic modifications of the correlation coefficient. One such expression is $(r_{xy})^2$, that is, the squared correlation between the test and the criterion. An often heard expression is that $(r_{xy})^2$ indicates the proportion of criterion variance accounted for by the test. Thus, in the example above, where $r_{xy} = .80$, $(r_{xy})^2 = .64$. This would mean that 64 percent of the variation in grades can be accounted for (predicted) from knowledge of the aptitude test scores. A correlation of .60 (perhaps a more realistic expectation judging from research evidence) would mean that only 36 percent of the GPA variance could be accounted for by differences in the students' Scholastic Aptitude Test scores.

[31]See, for example, Hays, pp. 490–538.

Another statistic often reported is the standard error of estimate $(S_{y.x})$. This is read "the standard deviation of y for a given value of x." It can be computed by

$$S_{y.x} = S_y\sqrt{1 - (r_{xy})^2} \qquad (15)$$

where S_y = criterion standard deviation. $S_{y.x}$ can be used to set confidence limits about an estimated criterion score just as the standard error of measurement (S_e) was used in setting confidence limits on a true score. If Melinda has an aptitude test score of 80, and if r_{xy} = .60, from a regression equation one could predict a GPA for Melinda. Assuming a predicted GPA of 2.5, it would be desirable to know how much confidence can be placed in this predicted GPA. If the standard deviation of the GPA distribution (S_y) is .8, using the formula, one could obtain $S_{y.x}$ = $.8\sqrt{1 - (.60)^2}$ = .64. This means that the chances are about 68 in 100 (about 2 to 1) that Melinda's actual GPA will be between 2.5 ± .64. We can be about 95 percent confident (odds of 20 to 1) that her actual GPA will be between 2.5 ± 2 (.64).

We can see from the formula for $S_{y.x}$ that its numerical value is influenced by the standard deviation of the criterion measure (S_y). S_y can be manipulated by changing the units of measurement on the criterion variable (for example, by changing the grading system from a five-point scale (A to F) to a nine-point [stanine] scale). For this reason some people prefer to use a statistic called the coefficient of alienation,

$$S_{y.x}/S_y = \sqrt{1 - (r_{xy})^2} \qquad (16)$$

which is not influenced by the unit of measurement.

We know that validity depends upon the reliability of the test and criterion scores. We also know that in many instances the reliabilities of the test and criterion scores are low. In an attempt to compensate for these low reliabilities, test publishers occasionally employ a statistical manipulation called the correction for attenuation. This correction tells us what the relationship would be had there been perfectly reliable measures. The correction can be applied to either correct for unreliability of the test score, unreliability of the criterion measure, or unreliability in both the test and criterion scores. Corrections for attenuation are certainly subject to misinterpretation. Naive users may easily be led into believing that the test is a better predictor than is warranted. In general, we are opposed to such statistical manipulations being reported in a test manual. If they are reported, however, the uncorrected validity coefficient must also be reported, and the manual should caution the user regarding the interpretation of the statistic.

EXPECTANCY TABLES Ordinarily students and teachers find expectancy tables easier than correlation coefficients to understand and interpret. A hypothetical expectancy table is given in Table 1–6.

Table 1–6

Sample Expectancy Table

Expectancy Table for First Year Grade Point Average
Based on Scholastic Aptitude Test Scores of Freshmen
Entering Central College in the Fall of 1967

Predictions Based on Scholastic Aptitude Test

(1) Percentile Rank on the Scholastic Aptitude Test (National Norms)	Chances in 100 of a Freshman Obtaining an Average Grade of			
	(2) D or Higher	(3) C or Higher	(4) B or Higher	(5) Size of Group (n)
80–99	99	81	32	100
60–79	95	52	12	100
40–59	80	15	—	60
20–39	50	—	—	30
0–19	30	—	—	10

Column 1 gives the Scholastic Aptitude Test score in percentile rank form. The numbers in columns 2, 3 and 4 of the table represent the percent of people within each of the five categories of the test who achieved college freshman GPA's of D or higher, C or higher, and B or higher. While such a table is usually easily understood by high school students, two limitations (or possible misinterpretations) should be noted. First, the column giving the size of the group is important. From column 5 we can see that the percentages for the last row were based on only ten people. Percentages based on such a small number of people are subject to extreme fluctuation. Second, the table should not be interpreted as if a person in the bottom fifth (0–19) on the Scholastic Aptitude Test has no chance of receiving a GPA of C or greater, or that a person in the middle fifth (40–59) has no chance of receiving a GPA of B. The table only shows that of the group sampled, no students fell in these cells of the table. It would not be impossible to do so; in fact, using a different sample, we would expect to find slight deviations in our predictions.

Counselors would be well advised to build expectancy tables such as the one shown for their own school system. The tables can be very useful in helping students make decisions about colledge attendance. However, one must remember that just as there would be errors in prediction with regression equations, so would there be with expectancy tables.

DISCRIMINANT STATISTICS   Other methods of expressing validity employ various statistics describing the degree of difference between groups (*t* tests, *F* tests, the discriminant function, and the percent of overlap are examples of this type of statistic). To learn to compute these statistical values requires a complete course in statistics. However, the test user need only understand that these procedures allow for a numerical expression of the degree to which various groups perform differently on the test. If we wish to use a test to differentiate people with various psychiatric disorders (as in the Minnesota Multiphasic Personality Inventory) or to differentiate between various occupational interest groups (as in the Strong Vocational Interest Blank), it is important to know how successful the test is in that endeavor.

The percent overlap is the most common method test publishers use to express the difference between groups. If two groups have a 30 percent overlap on a test, 30 percent of the total number of people in the two groups have scores higher than the lowest score in the better group and lower than the highest score in the poorer group. As illustrated in Figure 1–6, there are 50 people in group A and 50 people in group B. Of these 100 people, 30 (30 percent) have scores in the shaded area; so there is a 30 percent overlap.

Factors Affecting Validity

There are many factors that can affect any of the validity measures discussed: validity coefficients, expectancy tables, and those measures reporting group differences. As has already been pointed out, the reliabilities of both the test (predictor) and the criterion measures are important. Another factor is the heterogeneity of the group(s) with respect to both the test data and the criterion measures. For validity coefficients, as with reliability coefficients, other things being equal, the more heterogeneous the group the higher the validity coefficient. Thus it may not be reasonable, for example, to expect the Millers Analogy Test and grades in a doctoral program to be highly related since the doctoral candidates are fairly homogeneous with respect to both variables. This is particularly true when the group on which the correlation has been obtained has already been screened (selected) on the basis of the test score. For example, if everyone

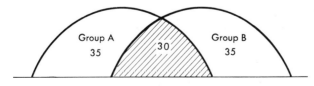

Figure 1-6   Diagram showing 30 percent overlap between two groups.

who took an algebra aptitude test took algebra regardless of their test score, we would anticipate obtaining a higher correlation between test score and grade than if only those who scored in the upper half of the test could take algebra. For group-difference statistics, such as percent overlap, significant differences are more apt to be found if each group is homogeneous but different from the other group(s).

A third factor that can affect criterion-related validity is criterion contamination. Suppose, for example, in correlating an aptitude test score with teacher grades, the teachers who assign the grades know the children's aptitude test scores. The teachers' grades may be influenced by the knowledge of the aptitude test results. This would, then, unduly affect the correlation coefficient.

Thus, one can see that just as the size of the reliability coefficient can be affected by so many variables, so too, can the validity measures. To correctly interpret validity data, it is necessary to be aware of these various factors.

Validity and Decision Making

Let us assume that a test manual reports a correlation coefficient of .50 between scores obtained on a mathematical aptitude test administered in the eighth grade and scores in a ninth-grade algebra course. Will this information have any effect on the kind(s) of educational decisions made? What if the school's policy is to have all students take ninth-grade algebra in heterogeneous classes? In this case, the benefits derived from the test score information could only be used for instructional purposes. If the school's policy is to have all students take ninth-grade algebra and if students are also grouped homogeneously, then the test score information can be used for both instructional and administrative purposes. If the school's policy is to permit students to select either ninth-grade algebra or general math, then the test score information could be used for instructional, administrative, and counseling purposes. For any of these decisions — instructional, guidance, or administrative — the important question is whether or not better decisions could be made using test score results in addition to other data already available (for example, teacher recommendations and previous school grades). This is an empirical question, one we would not necessarily expect the ordinary classroom teacher or counselor to answer. However, they should be cognizant of the factors that are apt to make test score information useful. We will now consider some of these factors.

1. *Availability of Other Data.* Tests should be used only if better decisions can be made with the data than without it. How much better the decision would be using the test data than decisions based on chance alone is not

the relevant consideration.[32] One never, or almost never, is forced to make an educational decision on the basis of no information. If fairly valid decisions can be made without test data, then the probability that the test data will improve the accuracy of the decision decreases. If the probability of making a correct decision without the test data is very low, then it may well be beneficial to give the test even though it has only a modest correlation with the criterion.

2. *Selection Ratio.* In the example dealing with ninth-grade algebra, it was pointed out that, if all students were required to take ninth-grade algebra, the test data would be of no value for selection purposes. If conditions are such that either almost everyone or very few are to be selected, then the test data will not be as valuable in selection decisions as in cases where the selection ratio is closer to 50 percent.

3. *Cost of Faulty Decisions.* Decisions are subject to two kinds of errors: (1) a false positive, predicting failure when success would have occurred, and (2) a miss, predicting success when failure is the result. The value of a test is dependent upon the difference between the cost of testing (such factors as the cost of purchasing the test, student and examiner time, and scoring) and the savings in the cost of errors. In the "algebra" example, a student could take algebra and fail or not take algebra even though he could have passed it. To decide whether the test information is worth gathering is dependent upon the cost of these errors. As discussed earlier, where to set the cutting score is dependent upon the relative cost of these two errors. If a false positive is expensive as compared to a miss, then the cutting score should be lower (that is, the selection ratio should be higher), than if the reverse is true.

4. *Success Ratio.* Another factor affecting whether test data are likely to improve decision making is the success ratio (the proportion of people selected who succeed). The success ratio depends in part upon the selection ratio. Other things being equal, the smaller the selection ratio the larger the success ratio. The success ratio, however, is also highly dependent upon base rates.[33] *Base rates* refers to the proportion of people in the general population who fall in a certain category. If 99 percent of the general ninth-grade population can succeed in ninth-grade algebra, one can predict success with 99 percent accuracy simply by predicting success for everyone. It would take a very valid test to enable one to predict more accurately than that. If only 1 percent can succeed, an analogous situation exists. Base rates in clinical psychology are often so high or low (for example, the proportion of people who commit suicide) that tests cannot improve prediction. In

[32]Lee J. Cronbach and Goldine C. Gleser, *Psychological tests and personnel decisions.* (2nd ed.) Urbana, Ill.: University of Illinois Press, 1965.
[33]Paul E. Meehl and Albert Rosen, Antecedent probability and the efficiency of psychometric signs, patterns, or cutting scores. *Psychol. Bull.*, 1955, *52*, 194–216.

educational decisions the base rates are usually much closer to 50 percent, the value that best enables a test score to improve the predictive accuracy.

Validity and Test Selection

Just as people want to know how reliable a test should be, they also want to know how valid a test should be. The same answer must be given: it depends upon the purposes for which the test is to be used. Naturally, one should select the best test possible. Suppose, however, that no test is very valid for our purpose. Does that mean we should not test? To decide, we must answer the question raised in the previous section: How much better decision can we make using the test information in addition to all other information than we could make just from the other data alone? Once that question is answered, we must inquire whether this increase in accuracy of prediction is sufficiently greater to justify the use of the test. This could theoretically be answered by cost analysis procedures if we could specify the cost of faulty decisions.

Validity is a matter of degree, and a test has many validities, each dependent upon the specific purposes for which one uses the test. Thus, just as for reliability, the kinds and extent of validity data that one should expect to find in a test manual depend upon the type of test and upon how one wishes to use it. For achievement tests, content validity is by far the most important type of validity. Aptitude, interest, and personality measures probably, depending upon their use, should have evidence of criterion-related validity. If one wishes to use test data as evidence to support or refute a psychological theory, then construct validity is necessary.

In addition to reporting the type(s) of validity evidence, the manual must also provide other relevant information. The characteristics of the group(s) from which the evidence was obtained must be reported in detail. Tables of specifications and their rationale should be given in support of content validity claims; standard errors of estimates should be reported for validity coefficients; and a large number of studies should be reported if one wishes to make a claim for construct validity.

INTERPRETATION

Once one has administered and scored a test, the next task is interpretation. As mentioned earlier, the purpose of testing can be summarized by saying that tests are an aid in decision making. Interpretation involves making statements about the wisdom of future decisions (or about the courses of action) from a knowledge of present characteristics or sets of characteristics. In interpreting a test score, we are seeking to find some meaning outside the test. That is, we must make inferences. The value of a test and, therefore, the wisdom of any decision based partly on the test score depends upon the degree to which we can make accurate inferences.

The basic responsibility for making correct interpretations from the data lies with the test user. However, in drawing such inferences the user is dependent upon whatever information he can obtain about the test. Thus, the test publisher has a responsibility to provide the information necessary for accurate interpretation. Such factors as the degree of and method of estimating reliability as well as the extent and type of validity are certainly relevant information and should be clearly specified in the test manual. These factors have already been discussed. The publisher also has the responsibility of clearly defining the norm population (and the method of sampling) and using scores, the meanings of which have been carefully described. It is the consumer's responsibility to know whether the norms are appropriate and adequate for his purpose and how to interpret the type(s) of scores used in the manual.

NORMS

Norms are important in that they tell us how others have performed on the test. We have no clear idea of the meaning of a person's score in and of itself. It must be compared to other scores. The importance of comparison can be illustrated by the story of the psychometrist who, when asked "How's your wife?" responded with "Compared to whom?" She may appear pretty good compared with some women but not appear as good compared with others.

The appropriateness of the norm group depends on the degree to which the population sampled is comparable with the group with which users of the test wish to compare their students. If, for example, we wish to compare a student's ability to that of students who intend to go to college, then the norm group should be a sample of students who wish to go to college, not a sample from a general population.

Another important factor is the kind of sampling. A large sample (even if sampled from the appropriate population) alone is not sufficient. The sampling procedure must be correct. Space does not permit us to delve into sampling problems extensively. In general, however, stratified random sampling is the best procedure where the stratification is done on all relevant independent variables. The relevant independent variables would vary from one kind of test to another, but examples might be such thing as age, sex, socioeconomic status, race, size of community, and geographic location of the subject.

The user of test information must be very cautious in his interpretation of the norms provided by the test publisher. Questions like the following must be considered: How representative are the norms? Were the norms derived from a random sample of pupils? What were the characteristics of the standardization and norming sample? How old are the norms? Are the norms useful for the kinds of comparisons to be made? These questions must be satisfactorily answered before one can correctly and meaningfully use the norm data.

Test manuals at times do not seem to provide the data necessary to answer all the above questions. If not, it is possible that the information may be available in a technical supplement. At any rate, one should not accept the norms on faith. A manual may state that it has a "national" sample without providing the data necessary for the user to judge for himself the adequacy of the norms. The norm group must necessarily consist of those who are willing to be tested, and the test manual should state the refusal rate. The user must then decide how this will affect his interpretations. Many older tests were often locally normed so that the norm data really represented, say, only the Midwest, or only the East Coast, or only the Far West. Generally, the newer tests, particularly those published by the larger reputable companies, have adequate norm data. Highly sophisticated sampling procedures have been worked out so that a truly national sample can be obtained if the publishers are able and willing to go to the effort to achieve such an end.

There are instances where local norms are more useful than national norms. If one wishes to make some interschool comparisons, or intercity comparisons, local norms are better. Not that one couldn't make such comparisons using national norms, but the users may find it more difficult to make the comparison with the data in that form. If test scoring is done by machine — whether by a test company or locally — local norms can be easily constructed. In general, it is worth the slight extra charge to have these local norms prepared. It facilitates interpretation to the teacher, the parent, the student, and the community.

It should be stressed that norms are not standards. Norm information tells us how people *actually* perform, not how they *should* perform. Comparing a person's score with a norm group does not automatically tell us whether that person's score was above or below where it should be. It only tells us how he performed in comparison with others. A description in relative terms is not an evaluation.

Several types of scores (related to the norm data) that help us in interpretation of the data will now be discussed.

TYPES OF SCORES

Simply knowing a person's raw score and the distribution of all the raw scores in the norm group is of little help in test interpretation. However, if a person's raw score is changed into a score that by itself gives normative or relative information, we have a single value that is interpretable. Such expressions as *types of scores, kinds of scales, kinds of norms,* or *derived scores* all refer to those various procedures that involve using the normative information to transform the raw scores to scores that have normative or relative meaning. Examples of these derived scores found most frequently in test manuals are percentiles, linear z and T scores, normalized z and T scores, stanines, grade equivalents, and ratio and derived IQ's. These will be explained, and the advantages and disadvantages of each will be discussed.[34]

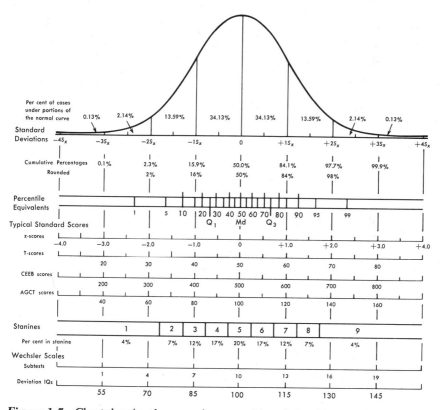

Figure 1-7 Chart showing the normal curve and its relationship to various derived scores. (Adapted and reproduced with the permission of The Psychological Corporation.)

[34]The literature on transformed scores is not consistent with regard to terminology. In general, normalized z scores are not used as such but are only found as an intermediate step to normalized T's. Some refer to a normalized T score with just the symbol T and use Z to refer to what we have called a linear T.

Percentiles

A percentile is defined as a point on the distribution below which a certain percent of the scores fall. For example, the 98th percentile is the point below which 98 percent of the scores in the distribution fall. This does not mean that the student who scores at the 98th percentile answered 98 percent of the items correctly. He may have a raw score of 76 on an English test composed of 100 items. If this score is equivalent to the 98th percentile, it means that 98 percent of the students who took the test received a score below 76.

Percentiles have the advantage of being fairly easily interpreted. Parents and students can understand the basic idea of percentiles easily. (Occasionally people will confuse *percentiles* with *percentage correct*, but the distinction can easily be made with only a little explanation.) However, percentile scores have a disadvantage in that the size of the percentile units is not constant in terms of raw score units. For example, if the raw score distribution is normal, the raw score difference between the 80th and 90th percentiles is much greater than the raw score difference between the 40th and 50th percentiles (See Figure 1–7.). This can lead to faulty interpretation of either intra- or interindividual difference scores.

Linear z and T Scores

Linear scores are transformed scores where the resulting set of values has a distribution shape identical to the original raw score distribution. In other words, if the original raw scores are plotted on one axis and the transformed scores on another, a straight line will connect the plotted points. Linear *z* and *T* scores express raw scores as a function of the mean and standard deviation of the original distribution.

The formulas are

$$z = \frac{X - \bar{X}}{S_x} \tag{17}$$

$$T = 10z + 50 = 10\left(\frac{X - \bar{X}}{S_x}\right) + 50 \tag{18}$$

where all symbols except *z* and *T* have been previously defined.

The relationship between *z* and *T* is shown in equation (18). Figure 1–7 also depicts this relationship. As can be seen from equations (17) and (18), the mean of the *z* scores is 0 and the standard deviation is 1; the mean of the *T* scores is 50 and the standard deviation is 10. Thus, a person with a $z = 1$ or a $T = 60$ is one standard deviation above the mean of the norm group. Using raw scores, it would take three different values (the raw score, mean, and standard deviation of the raw scores) to provide the same amount of information.

Although there is no theoretical advantage for the z score over the T score, or vice versa, practitioners often prefer T scores because negative numbers can generally be avoided. Also, T scores usually obviate the need for decimals.

Normalized z and T Scores

When raw scores are normalized the shape of the distribution of the transformed (normalized) scores is normal regardless of the shape of the original distribution. Test publishers often provide normalized scores, and the wise test user should be able to discern the difference between these and linear-transformed scores. If normalized z and T values are given, then the relationship between these values and percentiles as shown in Figure 1–7 is accurate regardless of the shape of the raw score distribution. Thus, knowing that a person had a normalized z of 1, we would know that he was at about the 84th percentile. This interpretation could not be made with a linear z of 1 unless the original raw score distribution was normal. (It should be emphasized that the relationships shown in Figure 1–7 hold for a *normal* distribution of raw scores, not for *all* raw score distributions.)

Stanines

Stanines are often simply defined (actually misdefined) as standard scores with a mean of 5 and a standard deviation of 2. If this were their only characteristic, they would be linear-derived scores. However, only the whole numbers of 1 to 9 can occur, and they are typically computed so that a certain percent of the scores are transformed to each stanine. The percentages are determined so that a plot (histogram) of the stanines would approach a normal distribution. Thus, stanines are really normalized scores with the possible values curtailed at each end of the distribution. For an originally normal distribution, the relationship between stanines and the other derived scores mentioned is shown in Figure 1–7. That is, each stanine is 1/2 a z score unit (1/2 S_x of the original distribution) in width, and the percentage of scores at each stanine is 4, 7, 12, 20, 17, 12, 7, and 4.

Grade Equivalents

Grade equivalents can best be explained by an example. If a student obtains a score on a test that is equal to the median score for all the beginning sixth graders in the norm group, then that student is given a grade equivalent of 6.0. If a student obtains a score equal to the median beginning fifth grader, then he is given a grade equivalent of 5.0. If a student would score between these two points, interpolation would be used to determine his grade equivalent.

Grade equivalents suffer from at least three major limitations. One of these limitations is the problem of extrapolation. When a test author standardizes his test, he normally does not use students of all grade levels in his normative sample. Suppose a particular test is designed to be used in grades 4, 5 and 6. Ordinarily the norming would be done on only these three grades. Now, if the median sixth grader receives a grade equivalent of 6.0, then half the sixth graders must have a grade equivalent higher than this. How much higher? 7.0, 7.8, 9.0, 12.0? We don't know. Because the test was not given to any students beyond the sixth grade, there is no way to know how they would have done. However, we can guess, and that is just what is done. A curve can be constructed showing the relationship between raw scores and grade equivalents as shown in Figure 1–8. The actual data (that is, the median raw scores for each grade) are only available for grades 4, 5, and 6. However, the curve can be extrapolated so that one can guess what the median raw scores would be for other grade levels. The extrapolation procedure is based in the assumption that there would be no points of inflection (that is, no change in the direction) in the curve if real data were available. This is a very unrealistic assumption.

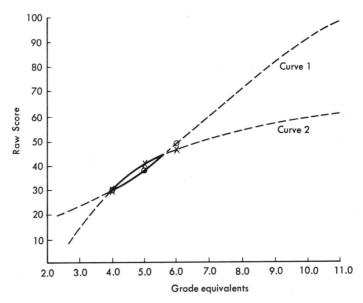

Figure 1-8   Curves for determining grade equivalents from raw scores. O's = population median raw scores for grades 4-6; X's = sample median raw scores for grades 4-6.

Another major problem in extrapolation relates to sampling error. Look at the two curves in Figure 1–8. Let us assume that Curve 1 is accurate for grades 4 through 6. That is, given the whole population of students in these grades, the median raw scores would fall as indicated by the circles on Curve 1. However, because of sampling error within grades 5 and 6, we may obtain the medians shown by the X's on Curve 2. The differences between the medians of the two curves are well within the range of sampling error we might expect. Now when these two curves are extrapolated we get completely different estimated grade equivalents. For example, a raw score of 60 is given a grade equivalent of 7.0 using Curve 1 (the one we assumed to be accurate) while it would get a grade equivalent of about 10.3 using Curve 2. Thus, small measurement errors can make extrapolated grade equivalents very misleading.

A second limitation of grade equivalents is that they give us little information concerning the percentile standing of a person within his class. A fifth-grade student may, for example, because of the differences in the grade equivalent distributions for various subject matter, have a grade equivalent of 6.2 in English and 5.8 in mathematics and yet have a higher fifth-grade percentile rank in mathematics.

The third limitation of grade equivalents is that (contrary to what the numbers indicate) a fourth grader with a grade equivalent of 7.0 does not know the same amount or the same kinds of things as a ninth grader with a grade equivalent of 7.0. For example, a bright fourth grader who can do very well on an arithmetic test involving speed and accuracy may perform equally as well as the average seventh grader. A weak ninth grader may be poor in speed and accuracy and perform at the seventh-grade level on a test demanding those skills. Yet those two respective students, receiving equal scores on an arithmetic test, do not know the same things about mathematics in a more general sense.

Grade equivalents remain popular in spite of their serious inadequacies. Teachers are under the impression that such scores are easily and correctly understood by both children and parents. This is unfortunate. It is probably not too dogmatic to suggest that grade equivalents, although useful if used in conjunction with other kinds of scores such as percentiles, should never be used alone.

Modal Age Norms

Modal age norms are grade equivalents when the norm group is composed only of students who are in the appropriate grade for their chronological age. Thus, people who have been retained or accelerated and are older or younger than the majority of the students will not be included in the original norm group. In the past, when retention was more prevalent, modal age norms were a more rigorous set of norms than regular grade equivalents. That is, a higher raw score would be necessary to obtain the same grade equivalent under modal age norms. This was true because older children who had been retained were not able to score as well as the average child in the test. Thus, they would depress the mean or median. Exclusion of these students makes the norm group more select. As promotion policies change in our schools—as there is less retention and more automatic promotion from year to year—it will be less certain that modal age norms will remain more rigorous.

Ratio and Derived IQ's

The intelligence quotient (IQ) is one of the most misunderstood concepts in measurement. Much of this confusion exists because of a lack of understanding of intelligence tests. (In Chapter II we will consider what an aptitude or intelligence test really measures, and how the scores can be usefully interpreted.) Part of the confusion, however, exists because people do not understand the type of score typically used to report the results of intelligence tests, that is, the IQ. Originally the IQ was actually a quotient (a ratio). It was found by dividing a person's mental age by his chronological age and then multiplying by 100 ($IQ = MA/CA \times 100$). The problem was in determining a person's mental age. This was accomplished differently on various tests, but essentially the process was similar to obtaining grade equivalents. Thus, if a student obtained a raw score equal to the median raw score of all nine-year-olds, he would be given a mental age of nine years.

The ratio IQ had many inadequacies. One weakness was that the standard deviations of the IQ's were not constant for different ages. A second problem was that opinions varied concerning what the maximum value of the denominator should be. When does a person stop growing intellectually — at 12 years, 16 years, 18 years? Because of these various inadequacies of the ratio IQ, test constructors now report derived IQ's. These are not literally intelligence quotients. They are transformations much like the z or T values (usually normalized) discussed earlier. Typically these derived IQ's have a mean of 100 and a standard deviation of 15 or 16, although some tests have standard deviations as low as 12, others as high as 20. Derived IQ's are computed separately for each age group within the norm sample.

INTERPRETING TEST SCORES TO OTHERS

It is essential that a professional educator understand the meaning of scores and understand the kinds of inferences that can be drawn from them. It is also important that teachers be able to interpret test score information to others in order to assist them in their decision making. Parents and students are the most likely recipients of this test score interpretation. The methods of interpreting scores to others will be covered in Chapter V.

CHAPTER SUMMARY

There has been an increased use of standardized tests in education. Educators are becoming increasingly aware of the role of standardized tests in instructional, guidance, administrative, and research functions. For their tests to be most helpful in decision making, it is necessary that they be chosen properly, administered correctly, and interpreted accurately.

The first task in test selection is to determine the purposes of testing. Once it is determined what decisions the tests should help make, and what general types of tests can do this task, the next step is to choose the specific tests. Sources of information about tests such as Buros' *Mental Measurements Yearbooks* and his *Tests in Print*, publishers' catalogs, specimen tests, professional journals, and measurement texts should all be consulted prior to final selection.

Some basic statistical concepts were presented to assist the test user to understand the technical and interpretative aspects of testing. The computation, meaning, and usefulness of measures of central tendency (mean and median), measures of variability (variance and its square root, the standard deviation), and a measure of relationship (the Pearson r) were discussed.

Two technical considerations that are very important in test selection are reliability and validity. Reliability is the degree of consistency or precision of measurement. The standard error of measurement, conceptualized as the standard deviation of a person's observed scores on repeated testings, is another way of expressing this precision. Some ways to estimate reliability are measures of stability, equivalence, and internal consistency. Each estimate allows for somewhat different sources of error to affect the score variability. It is important that the test constructor report which method was used in obtaining reliability estimates.

Validity is defined as the degree to which a test measures what it purports to measure. A test may measure reliably and not validly, but a test cannot be valid unless it is reliable. Three kinds of validity (content, criterion-related, and construct) were discussed.

Some practical aspects of testing to be considered in test selection are administration, scoring, cost, format, and interpretation of the test. Administration, scoring, and interpretation are unique aspects of testing that need to be considered beyond the role they play in test selection. In administering tests the most important point to remember is that the instructions given in the manual should be followed exactly if one wishes to compare the results of his students to the norm group.

Interpretation is perhaps the hardest aspect of testing. Three major points must be considered when interpreting test data: (1) what information the test scores give us (in terms of what construct is being measured), (2) the type of score (percentile, stanine, z score, etc.) used, and (3) the precision of the information.

POINTS TO PONDER

1. All measurement is subject to error. List at least eight types of errors of measurement.

2. Why should the split-halves method of reliability not be used with speeded tests?

3. Is a reliable test valid? Why?

4. Assume that you were the teachers' representative at a salary negotiating session with your school board. If you wished to show the low salary of teachers in the system, would you use the *mean* or *median* salary? Why?

5. You are responsible for selecting a standardized achievement survey battery for your elementary school. You have finally narrowed your selection to Test A. At the staff meeting, you announce your choice. One of your colleagues challenges your selection and says that Test B is equally as good. What types of evidence or support should you present in defense of your choice of Test A?

6. If you were only permitted evidence on one type of validity, which would you select for each one of the following tests: an intelligence test, an art test, an achievement test, an interest test, an attitude test? Why do you think that knowledge of this type of validity is most germaine?

7. Given a normal distribution of raw scores, which of the following standard scores is furthest from the mean?

$$T = 65$$
$$z = -2.0$$
$$\text{percentile rank} = 90$$
$$\text{stanine} = 7$$

8. You wish to use an algebra aptitude test to help decide who should take ninth-grade algebra. Two tests (A and B) are equal in every respect (cost, format, ease of scoring) except for their reliabilities and predictive validities, shown in the chart below:

	Test A	Test B
Reliability	.84	.95
Validity	.85	.80

Which test should you choose?

9. Which of the scattergrams shown in Figure 1–2 would you expect to obtain if you were studying the relationship between
    a. chronological age and intelligence
    b. car age and car value
    c. height and weight
    d. raw scores and linear z's
    e. aptitude test scores and college grade point average

10. Test administration involves many aspects. What factors must the examiner be alert to during the test administration? (Hint: cheating would be one such factor.)

chapter

II

aptitude tests

INTRODUCTION

That the school should assist each pupil to achieve the maximum of which he is capable is a motto often heard in educational circles. But behind that well-meaning phrase lurk impelling problems. How do we know what a person's capabilities are? Can we define *capacity?* Can we measure capacity? Does a person have a general capacity to acquire knowledge, or are there many different capacities, each specific to a given type of knowledge? Is capacity constant over time? If not, what conditions affect capacity? These are all relevant questions. Unfortunately, psychologists do not agree on all the answers. Nevertheless, for the past 75 years psychologists have been using various labels such as *capacity, intelligence, potential, aptitude,* and *ability* to identify a construct that appears to be useful in helping to predict various kinds of behavior. The tests that have been designed to measure this construct (or set of constructs) vary considerably because test authors may not define a construct the same way or indeed may be talking about different constructs.

The definitions of *intelligence* generally fall into one or more of three categories: the capacity to (1) think abstractly, (2) learn, or (3) integrate new experiences and adapt to new situations. Some of the more common definitions of *intelligence* are as follows:

Binet:

> ... the capacity to judge well, to reason well, and to comprehend well.[1]

Goddard:

> ... the degree of availability of one's experiences for the solution of immediate problems and the anticipation of future ones.[2]

Stoddard:

> ... the ability to undertake activities that are characterized by difficulty, complexity, abstractness, economy, adaptiveness to a goal, social value, emergence of originals, and to maintain such activities under conditions that demand a concentration of energy and a resistance to emotional forces.[3]

Terman:

> ... the ability to think in terms of abstract ideas.[4]

Wechsler:

> ... the aggregate or global capacity of the individual to act purposefully, to think rationally, and to deal effectively with his environment.[5]

In order to more fully understand the uses and misuses of the various instruments typically identified as intelligence or aptitude tests, it is first necessary to study briefly the various theories of the structure and development of intelligence.

THEORIES OF INTELLIGENCE STRUCTURE

The formal movement in testing intelligence began in the latter part of the nineteenth century. Sir Francis Galton, an English biologist, began to apply the principles of variation and selection set forth by his cousin Darwin to the measurement of physical and mental traits, and Galton then devised many instruments for this purpose. He believed that tests of sensory discrimination and reaction time were estimates of intellectual functioning,

---

[1] Alfred Binet and Th. Simon. *The development of intelligence in children*. Vineland, N.J.: Training School Publication #11, 1916, p. 192.

[2] Henry H. Goddard, What is intelligence? *J. soc. Psychol.*, 1946, *24*, p. 68.

[3] George D. Stoddard, *The meaning of intelligence*. New York: Macmillan, 1943, p. 4.

[4] Lewis M. Terman, *The measurement of intelligence*. Boston: Houghton Mifflin, 1916.

[5] David Wechsler, *The measurement of adult intelligence*. Baltimore: Williams & Wilkins, 1944, p. 3.

and his tests were largely of this type. James McKeen Cattell, an American psychologist, also theorized that differences in sensory keenness, reaction speed, and the like would reflect differences in intellectual functioning. Cattell[6] first introduced the term *mental test* in 1890. His tests measured such things as muscular strength, speed of movement, sensitivity to pain, weight discrimination, and reaction time. One of the major reasons that Cattell preferred these measures to what might be termed higher mental functions was that he was convinced these characteristics could be measured with more precision.

While other psychologists such as Jastrow[7] followed the leads of Galton and Cattell in measuring similar functions, Binet and Henri[8] began their research by measuring such characteristics as memory, attention, and comprehension. In other words, they measured complex functions rather than unitary characteristics such as reaction time previously employed. Although they employed many different kinds of tasks, they conceptualized intelligence as a very general trait, defining it as the ability to effectively adjust to one's environment. In 1905, Binet and Simon[9] developed the first individual intelligence test (the Binet Scale), designed to be a global measure of intellectual level.

Although many others have also conceptualized intelligence as a general characteristic, several opposing theories have developed. Wissler, in one of the first studies on the correlation between mental and physical tests, found, contrary to what Cattell would have expected, that there was little correlation between the two kinds of tasks. Physical tests showed a tendency to correlate among themselves but to correlate only very slightly with the mental tests. The tests of various mental abilities showed little intercorrelation with each other. As Wissler stated:

> Thus it becomes evident that the outcome of this research raises questions which throw us back into one of the great problems of psychology, viz., What constitutes mental ability? The significance of this question becomes apparent when we consider its relation to educational practice alone. It is plain that if we accept the conclusions of this research as final, an individual must be regarded as the algebraic sum of a vast array of small abilities of almost equal probability, the resulting combination conforming to the laws of chance.[10]

[6]James McK. Cattell, Mental tests and measurements. *Mind*, 1890, *15*, 373–381.

[7]Joseph Jastrow, Some currents and undercurrents in psychology. *Psychol. Rev.*, 1901, *8*, 1–26.

[8]Alfred Binet and Victor Henri, La psychologie individuelle. *L'Anne Psychologique*, 1896, *2*, 411–465.

[9]*The development of intelligence in children.*

[10]Clark Wissler, The correlation of mental and psysical tests. In James J. Jenkins and Donald G. Paterson (Eds.), *Studies in individual differences*. New York: Appleton, 1961, p. 43.

The controversy of whether mental ability can meaningfully be measured via a single score still continues. A variety of positions have been taken in the past 60 years.[11]

In 1927, Spearman[12] developed a two-factor theory suggesting that intelligence is composed of a general factor (g) and many specific factors (s_1, s_2, . . . s_n). Using factor analytic methods, Thurstone[13] developed a theory of multiple factors ($f_1, f_2, . . . f_n$), which led to his test of Primary Mental Abilities. Vernon,[14] has suggested a hierarchical structure of abilities starting with a general factor that is divided into two major group factors: verbal-educational and kinesthetic-mechanical. These major group factors are a little less general than Spearman's g but more general than Thurstone's group factors. Under each major group factor there are minor group factors; and under each of these are specific factors.

Guilford,[15] in a structure-of-intellect model, postulates many factors of intelligence. He categorizes these factors under three broad dimensions according to (1) the process or operation performed, (2) the kind of product involved, and (3) the kind of material or content involved. He then subclassifies under each of these dimensions five operations, six types of proproducts, and four types of content. Looking at the three main headings as faces of a cube, he ends up with 120 (4 x 6 x 5) cells within the cube, each representing a different aspect of intelligence. (See Figure 2–1.)

Thus a person could conceivably be capable of divergent thinking on symbolic content when the product is an implication and not be so capable when the product is a transformation. Guilford claims to have demonstrated empirically that 82 of the 120 different structure-of-intellect factors exist.[16] He argues that each factor should be tested separately and that tests giving a single score are somewhat misleading.

From the preceding discussion it should be readily evident that there are many different theories concerning the structure of intelligence.[17] Some theorists feel that intelligence is a general attribute; others feel that there are many different aspects to intelligence. However disconcerting it

---

[11]See Quinn McNemar, Lost: Our intelligence? Why? *Amer. Psychologist*, 1964, *19*, 871–882.

[12]C. Spearman, *The abilities of man.* London: Macmillan, 1927.

[13]Louis Leon Thurstone, *The theory of multiple factors.* Author, 1933.

[14]Philip E. Vernon, *The structure of human abilities.* (2nd ed.) London: Methuen, 1961.

[15]J. P. Guilford, Three faces of intellect. *Amer. Psychologist*, 1959, *14*, 469–479.

[16]J. P. Guilford, *The nature of human intelligence.* New York: McGraw-Hill, 1967, p. 65.

[17]We have curtailed this discussion drastically. Whole books are written on the issue. One of the most recent is J. P. Guilford, *The nature of human intelligence.* New York: McGraw-Hill, 1967. Cattell has also done research and written extensively in this area. See, for example, Raymond B. Cattell, Theory of fluid and crystallized intelligence: A critical experiment. *J. educ. Psychol.*, 1963, *54*, 1–22. This position has been criticized by Lloyd G. Humphreys, Critique of Cattell, Theory of fluid and crystallized intelligence, a critical experiment. *J. of educ. Psychol.*, 1967, *58*, 129–136.

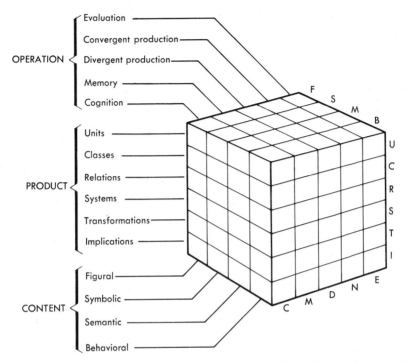

Figure 2-1 Guilford's "three faces of intellect." (Reproduced by permission of the author and McGraw-Hill Book Company from J. P. Guilford's *The Nature of Human Intelligence.* New York: McGraw-Hill Book Company, 1967.)

may be, one must realize that psychologists cannot agree as to the real nature of intelligence. While theoretical psychologists generally adopt the view that there are specific factors of intellect, most believe there is also a general factor. Practical psychologists are still very inclined to use tests of general intelligence because these tend to be well developed and predictive.

Due to this lack of agreement, there are a wide variety of tests that are often subsumed under the phrase *intelligence tests.* They do not all measure the same thing. They are not even designed to do so. A rather important implication is that, when selecting and interpreting an intelligence test, one must be completely aware of how the author defines the construct he is trying to measure.

DEVELOPMENT OF INTELLIGENCE

Because psychologists cannot agree as to what intelligence is or how many intellectual factors there are, they obviously cannot agree as to the etiology of intellectual differences. The score on any test of ability is a result of how well a person performs on that instrument at a particular time. Ignoring, for purposes of this discussion, chance errors we may ask the question: Why was that person able to perform as he did? Is the behavior on an aptitude test due to an individual's heredity or environment? Or does it really matter? For some purposes of testing, the preconditions affecting the test performance may not be relevant. If the purpose of a test is to use the results simply to predict some future behavior, then the question as to the usefulness of the test is an empirical one. However, one seldom wants solely to predict. In fact, educators are, or should be, in the business of attempting to upset negative or unfavorable predictions by changing the school environment. (This is not always easy, if indeed possible.) If we are to effectively change our educational process as a result of the predictive evidence, then it may well be helpful to understand why a person performs as he does. For this reason some understanding of the heredity-environment controversy is necessary. Without going into detail it may be said that, by far, the most popular current opinion is that there is an interaction between heredity and environment. The original question "which one of these factors affects an intelligence test score" was replaced by "which one contributes the *most*." This question, in turn, has been replaced by "how do heredity and environment interact to affect test scores." While psychologists do not as yet have the complete answer to this, progress has been made in terms of the sophistication of the question asked. Intelligence test scores are not solely dependent upon either environment or heredity: both are relevant.

STABILITY OF INTELLIGENCE

Because intelligence is now generally considered to be influenced by both heredity and environment, it logically follows that, as a person's environment changes, so might his intelligence or so at least might his score on an intelligence test, which is an operational definition of intelligence.

The extent to which intelligence is a stable or variable construct is very important. If there were no stability to intelligence test scores, then the test would be a useless instrument. On the other hand, if intelligence test scores were completely stable, then we might adopt fatalistic attitudes concerning a student's prognosis.

The research findings[18] suggest that intelligence test scores are very unstable during the early years of a person's life. Bayley,[19] for example, found no relationship between intelligence measured at age one and age

---

[18]See, for example, Benjamin S. Bloom, *Stability and change in human characteristics.* New York: Wiley, 1964, pp. 52–94 for an excellent review of the longitudinal research.
[19]Nancy Bayley, Consistency and variability in the growth of intelligence from birth to eighteen years. *J. genet. Psychol.*, 1949, 75, 165–196.

seventeen. Certainly the tested intelligence of children under five years old is unstable.[20] Although it is hard to know whether this instability is primarily caused by imprecise measuring instruments or trait instability, it nevertheless implies that important, irreversible decisions should not be based on early intelligence test performance.

With increased age, the stability of intelligence test performance increases rapidly. In general, longitudinal studies have suggested that intelligence is a fairly stable characteristic after age five. Bayley[21] found the correlations between intelligence test scores at age eleven and seventeen to be $+.92$. There is some evidence to suggest that a considerable change in environmental conditions is needed to affect a test score greatly after the first five formative years are past. This is one reason why there has been so much emphasis on such programs as Project Headstart.

There has also been some controversy concerning the stability of adult intelligence. Wechsler,[22] testing a cross-sectional sample of adults, found that the verbal aspects of intelligence increase until age thirty and then begin to gradually diminish. However, his method of sampling was somewhat faulty because the educational levels of the various age groups were not comparable. The younger groups had a higher educational level than the older groups, and this could have accounted for the differences he found. Bayley,[23] using longitudinal evidence, concluded that there is continued intellectual growth until age fifty. A safe conclusion would be that general intellectual functioning does not automatically decrease with age. The environment of the adult may serve to increase or decrease his intellectual performance, but barring health problems, the fifty-year-old may well have as much intellectual ability as he had at twenty-five.

INTELLIGENCE VERSUS APTITUDE

We have not yet attempted to distinguish between the terms *intelligence* and *aptitude*. These two terms are used interchangeably by some, while others suggest that subtle shades of meaning distinguish them. The distinctions have been made on two separate bases.

One distinction that has been made is whether the measure we obtain is considered a *general* measure. If so, the test is called an intelligence test. If the test measures *multiple* or *specific* factors, then it is termed an aptitude

[20]Data such as this has led one colleague to suggest that the best estimate we can obtain of a young child's intelligence is to take the average of his parents' intelligence. One would not have to lean heavily toward the hereditarian position to make this statement. Familial characteristics may be just as much due to environment as heredity.

[21]Consistency and variability in the growth of intelligence from birth to eighteen years.

[22]David Wechsler, *Wechsler Adult Intelligence Scale, Manual.* New York: The Psychological Corporation, 1955.

[23]Nancy Bayley, On the growth of intelligence. *Amer. Psychologist,* 1955, *10,* 805–818.

Figure 2-2   A global-to-specific continuum of intelligence (aptitude) test measures. Key: S-B (Stanford-Binet), WISC (Wechsler Intelligence Scale for Children), CQT (College Qualifications Test), CTMM (California Test of Mental Maturity), DAT (Differential Aptitude Test), FACT (Flanagan Aptitude Classification Test), MAT (Musical Aptitude Test).

test. Thus, we might conceptualize different measures of intelligence (aptitude) as lying on a continuum with global measures falling at one end and specific measures at the other. (See Figure 2–2.) At some point along the continuum we could arbitrarily change the label of the construct we are measuring from intelligence to aptitude. Although this schema has been suggested by some, it certainly is not universally followed. It does present some difficulties because there are some tests, such as the Wechsler Adult Intelligence Test, that are considered measures of a general factor, yet that report part scores.

Another distinction between the meaning of the two terms has a historical basis. During the time intelligence tests were first being developed, psychologists thought of intelligence as being an innate characteristic not subject to change. This assumption is invalid. However, the term *intelligence*, unfortunately still carries to some the connotation of complete innateness. To avoid the implications of innateness, many test makers prefer to use the term *aptitude*. Because these aptitude tests are most useful in predicting future school success, some persons have suggested that the phrase *scholastic aptitude tests* is the most honest and descriptive. Other people prefer to refer to all such tests as measures of learning ability.

Authors do differ in their attempts to construct intelligence (aptitude) tests that are free from cultural and educational influences and, therefore, that supposedly more closely measure innate ability. Thus, some authors prefer the term *intelligence* to *aptitude*. However, these terms as used by authors certainly do not reflect the degree of success test constructors have enjoyed in this endeavor. All test scores are influenced by both environmental and hereditary variables regardless of whether the test is termed an intelligence or aptitude test.

In this book both the terms *intelligence* and *aptitude* will be used. We will follow the general nomenclature used by the authors of the various tests. An author's use of a term does not necessarily reflect the position of the test on either the global-specific or innate-environmental continua.

APTITUDE VERSUS ACHIEVEMENT TESTS

The terms *aptitude* and *achievement* have been used interchangeably, coterminously, and separately. There really is no hard-and-fast rule to distinguish an achievement test from an aptitude test by cursory examination of the test format. Some people distinguish between an achievement and an aptitude test in terms of the amount or degree of the specific influence of past learning; that is, an achievement test measures specialized or formal instruction, whereas an aptitude test measures the cumulative impact of all kinds of learning. Although one is hard pressed to present a definition of achievement and aptitude that is acceptable to all people, the writers in general subscribe to the following definition: *An achievement test is used to measure an individual's present level of knowledge or skills or performance; an aptitude test is used to predict how well an individual may learn.* However, it has often been said that the best way to predict future performance is to look at past performance. If this is true, and if aptitude tests are best able to predict future scholastic success, how do they differ from achievement tests? The common distinction that achievement tests measure what a pupil has learned (or past learning activities) and aptitude tests measure ability to learn new tasks (or future performance), breaks down if past learning is the best predictor of future learning.

Thus, some people suggest that the difference is not in what the tests do but in the author's purpose and method of constructing the test. A certain achievement test may be a better predictor than a particular aptitude test for some specified purpose. If, however, the author originally constructed his test for the purpose of predicting future performance, then the test is called an aptitude test. If the purpose of the author is to measure past learning, then the test is considered an achievement test, even though it may well be a very successful predictive instrument. This distinction also has some limitations because one would never administer a test solely to measure past learning. We always want to use tests to help us in making decisions. Decision making involves prediction. Thus, either explicitly or implicitly, achievement tests as well as aptitude tests are used to make predictions.

Aptitude and achievement tests are sometimes classified according to the degree to which the tasks within a test are dependent upon formal school learning. This distinction is a matter of degree. Some aptitude tests are more like achievement tests than others. As the test tasks become more and more dependent upon specific educational instruction, the test becomes more and more an achievement test. Thus, we have a continuation of the distinction between the terms *achievement* and *aptitude* on the innate-environmental continuum. Being more dependent on specific school instruction, achievement tests are more environmentally influenced than aptitude tests.

Cronbach[24] has suggested that aptitude tests can be arranged along a spectrum. Tests at one extreme are strictly measures of the outcomes of education — these resemble achievement tests in content and usefulness. The School and College Ability Tests[25] would be examples that fall toward this end of the continuum. Tests at the other extreme are those whose scores are fairly independent of specific instruction (intelligence tests). The Raven Progressive Matrices would be an example at this extreme. The so-called culture-free tests are examples of tests that are supposedly restricted to tasks where success is independent of differences in educational instruction. More will be said about these tests later.

In summary, several possible distinctions have been suggested between aptitude and achievement tests. If the author's purpose is to develop a predictive instrument, he will no doubt call it an aptitude test. If his purpose is to develop an instrument to measure past performance he will call it an achievement test. For the latter goal, the test items will be based on past school instruction; for the former goal, that may or may not be the case. However, regardless of what an author calls his test, its uses may vary. Many achievement tests like aptitude tests are used to predict. This is ordinarily quite appropriate.

CLASSIFICATION OF APTITUDE TESTS

There are a variety of ways in which aptitude tests can be classified. One type of classification is verbal versus performance (language versus nonlanguage)[26] tests. Although the terms *verbal* and *language* scales have similar connotations, performance and nonlanguage scales can be quite different. A performance scale usually requires the subject to manipulate objects to complete a specified task. (An example might be to fit together a puzzle.) Nonlanguage tests are those where the subject is not required to use or understand the language. However, the subject need not be required to manipulate objects in a nonlanguage test. In spite of their differences, performance and nonlanguage scales are alike in that both are relatively independent of specific educational instruction. Test authors, however, do not always use these terms as appropriately as they should. In order to determine what a test demands, one should look at both the items them-

---

[24]Lee J. Cronbach, *Essentials of psychological testing.* (2nd ed.) New York: Harper & Row, 1960, pp. 234–236.

[25]Only tests discussed in this text will be referenced fully. For tests used solely as examples, the reader is referred to Oscar K. Buros (Ed.), *The sixth mental measurements yearbook* (Highland Park, N.J.: Gryphon Press, 1965) or *Tests in print* by the same author (Highland Park, N.J.: Gryphon Press, 1961) for information on publishers and copyright dates.

[26]Many consider *nonlanguage* to be a misnomer because mediation supposedly requires the covert use of verbal symbols. The use of nonverbal mediation, of course, is not what is meant by *nonlanguage tests*.

selves and the test manual, not only at the name of the tests or subtests.

For purposes of discussion, aptitude tests will be subdivided into four categories: (1) individually administered tests that give a general measure of intelligence[27] (or aptitude), (2) group administered tests that give a general measure of intelligence, (3) tests that give measures of multiple aptitudes, and (4) tests that are measures of some specific kind of aptitude.

Often a person is looking for a single measure of ability that will enable him to make a general prediction about future vocational or educational success. Tests of general intelligence best suit this purpose. If one wants to make differential predictions, then a multiple aptitude test would be best. If one wants to predict success in a specific vocation or course, a specific aptitude test may be most appropriate. The next four sections will be devoted to a consideration of the four categories just mentioned.

INDIVIDUALLY ADMINISTERED TESTS OF GENERAL INTELLIGENCE

For the most part, educational institutions make use of group tests of intelligence. However, occasionally it is more appropriate to administer an individual test to a person. Individual administration allows the psychologist to more closely observe and control the behavior of the individual. This generally leads to more reliable measurement and a better understanding of the factors underlying one's behavior. Perhaps we should examine these statements more closely. *Control*, as used here, has a positive connotation. One should control process variables such as the motivational level of the client. The outcome variables (responses) may also be controlled somewhat. However, this can be overdone. The amount of freedom a test administrator has in clarifying the questions so as to elicit the proper response is, appropriately, somewhat limited. When we suggest that individual administration leads to more reliable behavior, we are of course assuming that the test is correctly administered. Test scores could vary as a result of administrators' variability. However, the administrators' reliability is high if the administrators are correctly trained.

The most popular individual intelligence tests are the Stanford-Binet and the various Wechsler tests. These instruments, as well as examples of some infant and preschool scales and some performance scales, will be discussed in this section. However, because this book is designed to serve only as an introduction to standardized tests, these individual tests will not be covered

---

[27]The use of the term *intelligence* in no way implies that the authors of this book believe that intelligence test scores are solely measures of an innate characteristic. We know that is not true.

in great detail.[28] Proper administration of individual tests requires considerable training. To be adequately trained, one needs a basic knowledge of psychology plus at least one course in individual testing with considerable practice under supervision.

STANFORD-BINET

The present Stanford-Binet test is an outgrowth of the original Binet-Simon Scales. As previously mentioned, Binet was convinced that measures of simple sensory and motor processes were of little value as measures of intelligence. When Binet was charged with the task of identifying the mentally deficient children in the Paris schools, he collaborated with Simon to publish the 1905 Scale, which consisted of 30 tasks of higher mental processes arranged in order of difficulty. This scale was revised in 1908 and the tasks were grouped into age levels. Thus, the score of a child could be expressed as a mental age. The test was again revised in 1911.

Although there were several American revisions of these scales, the one that gained the most popularity was the Stanford revision, published in 1916.[29] A second Stanford revision appeared in 1937 and a third revision in 1960.[30] All three of these revisions have followed essentially the same format. A series of tasks are designed at each of several age levels. For this reason, the Binet is referred to as an age scale. For an average individual the administrator starts at a level just below the chronological age of the subject. He then works downward, if necessary, to lower age levels until the subject passes all the tasks within that age level. This is called the basal age. The examiner then proceeds upward from his original starting place to a level at which the subject misses all the tasks. This is called the ceiling age. An individual's total score (mental age) is computed by adding to the basal age appropriate weights for the items answered correctly up to the ceiling age.

The 1960 edition of the Stanford-Binet is not really a revision but a combination of the best items of the two forms of the 1937 edition. It groups the tasks into age levels ranging from age two to superior adult. Between the ages of two and five the tasks are spaced at half-year intervals. From ages five to fourteen the tasks are spaced at year intervals. There are four adult levels: one average adult and three superior adult.

[28]Books such as Anne Anastasi, *Psychological testing.* (3rd ed.) New York: Macmillan, 1968, and Frank S. Freeman, *Theory and practice of psychological testing.* (3rd ed.) New York: Holt, Rinehart and Winston, 1962, give much fuller coverage to individual intelligence tests.
[29]Lewis M. Terman, *The measurement of intelligence.* Boston: Houghton Mifflin, 1916.
[30]Lewis M. Terman and Maud A. Merrill, *Measuring intelligence.* Boston: Houghton Mifflin, 1937. Also, L. M. Terman and Maud A. Merrill, *Stanford-Binet intelligence scale: Manual for the third revision,* Form L-M. Boston: Houghton Mifflin, 1960.

Examples of tasks presented in the Stanford-Binet follow. It will be readily obvious that emphasis is placed upon the knowledge of words and comprehension of written material throughout the test — especially at the higher age levels. The few instances of performance-type items are to be found at the lower age levels. In addition, scattered at the various age levels are tests designed to measure memory and ability to follow directions.

Year II

1. Three-hole form board: A five-inch by eight-inch form board containing a cut-out square, circle, and triangle are shown to the child. The pieces are removed and the child is then asked to put them back.

2. Delayed response: Three small pasteboard boxes and a toy cat are used. While the child is watching, the cat is placed under the middle box. A screen is then placed in front of the boxes for about 10 seconds. After removal of the screen the child is asked to identify which box contains the cat. The procedure is repeated for each of the other two boxes.

3. Identifying parts of the body: The child is asked to identify various parts of the body on a large paper doll.

4. Block building: Using a set of one-inch cubes the examiner builds a four-block tower. He then asks the child to do the same.

5. Picture vocabulary: Eighteen cards with pictures of common objects are shown to the child. He is asked to name the objects.

6. Word combinations: The examiner is to note the child's spontaneous word combinations during the test. Two-word combinations such as *see man* are sufficient.

Year VIII

1. Vocabulary: The child is asked to define words read from a list.

2. Memory for stories: A story is read aloud to the child while he follows along on a separate copy. The child's copy is removed and six questions are asked concerning factual aspects of the story.

3. Verbal absurdities I: A set of four absurd statements such as "Bill now has to kick with his left foot since he lost both feet in an accident last year" are read to the child. After each statement he is asked, "What is foolish about that?"

4. Similarities and differences: The examiner names two things and asks the child in what way they are alike and different. This is repeated for four sets of two objects.

5. Comprehension IV: Six questions are asked such as the following hypothetical example: "What would you do if you found a billfold on the street?"

6. Naming the days of the week: The child is asked to name the days of the week.

Year XIV

1. Vocabulary: This is the same as the vocabulary list for Year VIII. More correct definitions are required for passing at this level.

2. Induction: Six sheets of tissue paper are needed. The first one is folded once and cut on the fold, and the child is asked how many holes there will be when the paper is unfolded. This procedure is repeated for the next five sheets, each being folded once more than the preceding one. On the sixth sheet, the child is asked to give the rule that tells how many holes there will be for the cut made on this sheet.

3. Reasoning: A reasoning problem (not mathematical) is presented on a card, which the examiner reads aloud while the child reads it to himself. A question is then asked to determine whether the child can reason through the problem.

4. Ingenuity I: Three "water jar problems" (where a child has two jars of different sizes and is to get an amount of water not equal to either size) are presented. The child is not allowed to use paper or pencil. Three minutes are allowed for each problem.

5. Orientation, Direction I: A child is given five sets of questions such as the following simplified hypothetical example: "You are facing north. If you turn left, what directions will you be facing?"

6. Reconciliation of opposites: The child is given five sets of paired words such as *big* and *small* or *fat* and *thin*. He is asked in each set to explain in what way the two words are alike.

Intelligence scores are computed as deviation scores with a mean of 100 and a standard deviation of 16. In other words, transformed scores (Dev. IQ = $16z + 100$). It should be pointed out, however, that the revision did not involve a new norm group. The deviation IQ was arrived at algebraically from the 1937 norms. Although this deviation IQ is an improvement over the 1937 revision when the ratio IQ (MA/CA $\times$ 100) concept was still employed, it would have been much better to have obtained a new norm group.

By most technical standards, the Stanford-Binet is a soundly constructed instrument. Most of the reported reliability coefficients are over .90. They do, however, tend to be somewhat lower for the younger subjects. This test, like other intelligence tests, is most useful in predicting future scholastic success. The predictive and concurrent validity coefficients using such criteria as school grades and achievement test scores tend to fall between .40 and .75.

There has been some debate as to whether the Stanford-Binet has adequate norms. Some argue that because the standardization sample did not include minority groups the test is not applicable to these subgroups. However, others argue that if the test is to be used for predicting success within the dominant U.S. culture the norm group is meaningful. Perhaps a more limiting aspect of the test is that it is primarily a measure of verbal ability. The popularity of the test is indisputable. The amount of research done on the Stanford-Binet can be attested to by the fact that Buros lists 728 references to professional journals and books regarding the test.[31]

THE WECHSLER SCALES[32]

The major competitors of the Stanford-Binet are the Wechsler Scales. The first form of the Wechsler Scales, published in 1939, was known as the Wechsler-Bellevue Intelligence Scale. This scale was specifically designed as a measure of adult intelligence. In 1949 the Wechsler Intelligence Scale for Children (WISC) was published. It is designed for ages five through fifteen, and follows the same format as the Wechsler-Bellevue. In 1955 the Wechsler-Bellevue was revised and renamed the Wechsler Adult Intelligence Scale (WAIS). The latest of the Wechsler Scales is the Wechsler Pre-school and Primary Scale of Intelligence (WPPSI), published in 1967 and designed for children of ages four to six and a half. These three tests will be discussed briefly below.

WAIS The WAIS (for ages sixteen and over) is composed of eleven subtests grouped into two scales: verbal and performance. The six subtests comprising the verbal scale are as follows: information, comprehension, arithmetic, similarities, digit span, and vocabulary. The subtests of the performance scale are: digit symbol, picture completion, block design, picture arrangement, and object assembly.

The individual's score is based on the number of items answered correctly. For this reason, the WISC is referred to as a point scale. (The items are not classified by age level as in the Binet.) The raw scores for each subtest are transformed into standard scores with a mean of 10 and a standard deviation of 3. Thus, each subtest score is expressed in comparable units permitting intra- and interindividual comparisons. Also, deviation IQ scores with means of 100 and standard deviations of 15 can be obtained for the verbal and performance scales as well as the total. An interesting aspect of these deviation IQ scores is that they are obtained separately for different age groups. (This, of course, is always done for children's scales, but it is somewhat unique for adult scales.) The age twenty-five to twenty-nine norm group performs better than any other group. Hence, adults in this age bracket must score higher (in raw score) in the test than those of any other age in order to receive the same deviation IQ. Computing IQ's separately for different age groups was done intentionally so that, even if intelligence

---

[31]Oscar K. Buros (Ed.), *The sixth mental measurements yearbook*, pp. 828–830.
[32]All Wechsler scales are published by The Psychological Corporation.

does decline with age, the average intelligence scores for each age group are equated. As mentioned earlier, however, it could well be that faulty sampling rather than a decline in intelligence with age was the cause of Wechsler's findings. Actually, the norm data of the WAIS has always been somewhat questionable. The data are now somewhat out of date as well, although they are still as satisfactory as the Stanford-Binet norms.

The WAIS is considered to give a very reliable measure of intelligence. The verbal and performance IQ's have split-half reliabilities in excess of .93, and the total scale IQ's have split-half reliability coefficients of .97 for the groups for which they were computed. The separate subtests, being quite short, have lower reliabilities. These range from about .60 to .96. Because the intent of Wechsler was to get a total or global measure of intelligence, he suggested that a profile interpretation of the scales for normal subjects would not be meaningful. There is some debate about the use of the subtest scores as clinical data.[33] Validity data is essentially lacking in the manual, although there are many studies that support the usefulness of the test in predicting various criteria.

In general, the WAIS is considered to be a very good measure of adult intelligence, perhaps the best. It is, however, in need of revision. The item content as well as the normative information is somewhat outdated.

WISC and WPPSI   The WISC (for ages five to fifteen) was originally prepared as a downward extension of the Wechsler-Bellevue. A quote from Anastasi appears fitting:

> It will be recalled that a major reason for the development of the original Wechsler-Bellevue was the need for an adult intelligence test that would not be a mere upward extension of available children's scales. Having presumably achieved this objective, the author then proceeded to prepare a children's scale that was simply a downward extension of the adult scale. Is this a case of "Heads I win and tails you lose"?[34]

In spite of this seeming inconsistency of logic, the WISC is considered a good instrument. It follows the same format as the WAIS, giving subtest scores and verbal, performance, and total IQ's.

The WPPSI (for ages four to six and a half) follows the same format as the WISC. The major advantage of it is not as a downward extension to younger children but, rather, as a replacement at the five- and six-year-old level for the WISC, which is too difficult for testing disadvantaged or mentally

---

[33]See Anastasi or Freeman for a fuller discussion of the Wechsler as a clinical instrument. Also see David Rapaport, Merton Gill, and Roy Shafer, *Diagnostic psychological testing*. Vol. II. Chicago: Year Book Medical Publishers, 1946.

[34]Anastasi, (2nd ed.) p. 320.

retarded children of this age. Because the WPPSI is so new, little can be said concerning its adequacy. However, it seems to be constructed with the same care as the other Wechsler instruments.

COMPARISON OF THE STANFORD-BINET AND WECHSLER SCALES

In terms of psychometric qualities such as validity and reliability, there is very little difference between the Binet and Wechsler scales. There are, however, some major differences between these tests. One of the major differences between the Stanford-Binet and the Wechsler is that the former is an age scale whereas the latter is a point scale. Because the 1960 revision of the Stanford-Binet provides deviation IQ's, there is some question as to whether the work involved in building an age scale is really worthwhile.[35] An age scale is more expensive to norm. Most psychologists are in agreement that point scales are preferable for adults. There is less agreement concerning which type of scale is preferable for children and young adolescents. However, many do prefer the age scale for children.

Another difference is in the norming procedure for adults. The Stanford-Binet was not designed to test adults. The standardization sample only included individuals through age eighteen. The WAIS was specifically designed to measure adult intelligence.

A third difference is that the Wechsler scales provide both verbal and performance IQ's whereas the Stanford-Binet provides only an overall IQ. Having separate verbal and performance tasks in the Wechsler tests makes it possible to obtain IQ's for illiterates, individuals who have language difficulties, and individuals who come from impoverished environments (and therefore have a very limited verbal experiential background), by using the performance subtests. The Binet cannot be used for such individuals.

The Stanford-Binet is considered to be more appropriate for younger children and to give more reliable measures at the lower ranges of intelligence for all ages. The first advantage may no longer hold now that the WPPSI has been published. The Wechsler scales are easier to administer.

In spite of these and other differences, however, the results of the two tests correlate very well. For example, one correlational study shows the following relationships between the WAIS and the Stanford-Binet.[36]

Stanford-Binet with WAIS full scale = .85
Stanford-Binet with WAIS verbal scale = .80
Stanford-Binet with WAIS performance scale = .69

---

[35]See Julian C. Stanley, Review of the Stanford-Binet. *Personnel guidance J.*, 1960, *39*, 226–227.

[36]David Wechsler, *The measurement and appraisal of adult intelligence.* (4th ed.) Baltimore: Williams and Wilkins, 1958, p. 105.

Much more could be said about these individually administered tests of intelligence. However, for one to be properly qualified to use the instruments, further training is required than could possibly be provided in a beginning course on standardized tests. Thus, we will stop at this point in our discussion of the instruments. Probably the most important point that educators should know about these two specific tests of intelligence are as follows:

1. They are highly reliable.
2. They are valid for predicting scholastic success.
3. The scores on the latest forms are derived scores with means of 100 and standard deviations of 16 and 15 for the Stanford-Binet and Wechsler scales respectively.
4. One must be thoroughly trained to administer the tests and to interpret their results.

INDIVIDUAL PERFORMANCE SCALES

A test is called a performance test if the tasks involved demand a manipulation of objects (for example, making geometrical configurations with blocks) rather than an oral or written response. This type of test is most helpful in assessing the level of intellectual functioning for people who have language disabilities. Those who speak only a foreign language, who are deaf, illiterate, or blind, or who have any type of speech or reading disability are unable to perform adequately on the instruments discussed in the previous section. In some instances, then, performance scales must be used as replacements for other tests. It should be pointed out, however, that originally, performance scales were conceived of as supplements rather than substitutes for the more verbally weighted tests. Some examples of performance scales are the Pintner-Patterson Scale, the Cornell-Coxe Scale, the Arthur Point Scale, the Cattell Infant Intelligence Scale, the Merrill-Palmer Scales (for preschoolers aged two and up), and the Leiter Adult Intelligence Scale. Although a variety of approaches can be and are used, some of the more commonly used subtests involve (1) manipulating small objects to form designs, (2) tracing and copying, (3) solving mazes or puzzles, (4) following simple directions, and (5) completing formboards.

All of the individual performance scales are valuable as clinical instruments. An examiner can observe the examinee's approach to problem solving, his reaction to stress, and his general test-taking behavior patterns thereby having the opportunity to gain valuable information. (It should be noted that this is also true for any individual test — verbal or performance. However, as noted earlier, there are instances where a verbal-type test is inappropriate.) Performance scales are most useful with young children and/or the mentally retarded because verbal tests are not very accurate for these groups. Although scales of this kind can be very helpful in assessing the level of intellectual functioning, they are not very predictive of immediate scholastic success, and they are seldom used in the schools.[37] If they are used, they should be given only by qualified personnel.

INFANT AND PRESCHOOL MENTAL TESTS

As mentioned earlier, the measures of intelligence prior to age five do not correlate very well with the measures obtained at a later point in a person's life. This is not entirely due to the impreciseness of the measuring instruments. (Split-half and alternate form reliabilities of the tests used at early ages are reasonably high.) The low correlations between earlier and later testings of intelligence are also caused by the instability of the construct of intelligence from early childhood to adult and/or the nonidentity of the constructs being measured.[38] That is, the change in intelligence test scores may occur because the construct of intelligence is affected radically by environmental conditions; or the change may occur because the tasks on intelligence tests, being different at different age levels, actually measure different aspects of intelligence; or change may occur because of a combination of these and other factors that are continually interacting. Is, then, a change in score due to a qualitative or quantitative change in mental functioning? The question is a difficult one to answer; and the answer one gives depends, in part, upon which theory regarding the structure of intellect he accepts.[39]

Doing experimental research and armchair philosophizing on the reasons for the low correlations may be enjoyable and beneficial to the theoretical psychologist. Yet the practitioner has a legitimate point if he questions the value of early testing. Because early intelligence testing does not allow us to do an accurate job of predicting future development, the use must be justified on the basis of measuring present developmental status. That is, these tests are really similar to achievement tests, and their use must be justified, if possible, on that basis.

Because the nonspecialist will not be involved with preschool testing, these kinds of tests will not be reviewed here. In terms of popularity the Stanford-Binet and WISC are two of the most popular tests for children under six.[40] The WPPSI will probably gain in popularity as research

---

[37]Performance tests measure abilities that are different from those measured by verbal tests such as the Stanford-Binet. Correlations between verbal and performance tests range from .50 to .80.

[38]Because the constructs measured at two different ages may, indeed, be different, many people would speak of the low correlation over time as a lack of validity rather than a lack of stability reliability.

[39]See Leland H. Stott and Rachel S. Ball, Infant and preschool mental tests: Review and evaluation. *Monogr. Soc. Res. child Develpmt.*, 1965, *30* (3), 151 pp.

[40]Stott and Ball, p. 136.

evidence is accumulated on it. Other tests used are the Goodenough-Harris Drawing Test, the Gesell Schedules, the Cattell Infant Intelligence Scale, Ammons Picture-Vocabulary, and the Merrill-Palmer Scales. Students interested in more details on these preschool scales should check such sources as the Anastasi or Freeman texts mentioned earlier as well as the various editions of Buros.

SUMMARY OF INDIVIDUAL TESTS

The field of individual intelligence testing is presently dominated by three tests: the Stanford-Binet, the WAIS, and the WISC. These tests are technically sound and are useful both as predictors of future academic success and as clinical assessment devices. In comparing individual tests with the group tests to be discussed, the major disadvantages are that individual tests are expensive to give and require a highly trained administrator. The major advantages are: (1) individual tests are generally more reliable; (2) they are potentially more useful in clinical settings — the good clinical psychologist can learn more about a person from an individual test than a score indicates; (3) they can be used with individuals who may be unable for reasons of shyness, reticence, anxiety, or whatever to perform validly on a group test, and (4) although many individual tests are highly verbal in nature, they do require considerably less reading ability than most of the group tests to be discussed in the next section.

GROUP TESTS
OF GENERAL INTELLIGENCE

In educational institutions group intelligence tests are used far more extensively than individually administered intelligence tests. They are much less expensive and generally give comparable results to the more time-consuming individual tests. Although in many schools the actual test administration may be performed by a counselor or someone else with special advanced training, most group tests are designed so that any teacher, with a minimum of training (such as in-service training or a basic course in standardized testing), should be capable of the administrative task.

The first group intelligence test (the Army Alpha) was produced during World War I when it became necessary to obtain a measure of general ability for one and a half million recruits very quickly. Because the Army Alpha required a reading level at about the sixth grade, and because many of the drafted men could not read at that level, the Army Beta was constructed. It was also a group test, but it required no reading on the part of the examinees. The directions could be given in pantomime if the subject could not understand spoken English.

The great demand for group tests can be attested to by the fact that within five years after the close of World War I over 50 group tests of intelligence were in print. Although it is laudable that so many psychologists were willing to fill the need for group intelligence tests by providing their own, the hasty construction of some of these ill-conceived tests certainly did much in the long run to disenchant the public with psychological testing.

The distinction between verbal and nonverbal group tests that began with the Army Alpha and Beta has continued to this day. Many group tests, designed to give a measure of general intelligence, actually give scores on two subtests. These may be given such titles as verbal and nonverbal or language and performance scales. In considering the use of subscores, one must keep in mind the continuum from global-to-specific measures mentioned earlier. It is always hard to know just when to consider a test a measure of general intelligence and when to consider it a measure of multiple aptitudes. The classification is not solely dependent upon the number of subscores. (For example, the California Test of Mental Maturity has eight subscores and is classified in Buros as a general intelligence test. The Academic Promise Test has seven subscores derived from only four subtests and is classified as a multiaptitude battery.) The author's definition of intelligence and the method of constructing the test are primarily what determines the classification.

Most authors of tests that give two part scores such as verbal and non-verbal are really attempting to measure the same construct (general intelligence) with two separate procedures rather than attempting to obtain measures of two separate aspects of intelligence. Tests giving a whole series of part scores are typically attempting to measure different aspects of intelligence and are referred to as multifactor aptitude tests. These will be considered in the next section. We will discuss in this section the tests that are group administered and that are considered as measures of general intelligence even though they may report more than one score.

Besides differing on the general-specific and innate-environmental continua discussed previously, group tests are usually classified according to grade or age level. Some tests have different levels, each level being appropriate for certain grades. For school purposes there are advantages to using such tests. The same construct is being measured at all levels of the test, and norm groups are chosen to be comparable from one level to another. This then permits one to compare measures obtained over a period of time.

It is impossible to review all appropriate group tests for each grade level. Because most group intelligence tests measure essentially similar skills (verbal and nonverbal), although they may employ a slightly different approach, we will only review briefly two of the more commonly used tests. One other test, the Lorge-Thorndike Intelligence Tests, will be described in detail so that the reader can ascertain some of the important considerations in selecting, administering, and interpreting a group intelligence test. Finally, there will be a short subsection on "culture fair" tests. Prior to choosing any test for school use, it should be examined thoroughly.

PRIMARY LEVEL GRADES (K–3) GROUP TESTS

Although some individually administered tests attempt to measure the intelligence of very young children, group tests should ordinarily not be used for children under five (preschool children). Children of this age have difficulty following the detailed directions necessary for group-testing procedures and need individual supervision. For five- and six-year-olds, group testing is feasible but it is necessary to keep the number within a group as small as possible. It is suggested that one not attempt to administer tests at the primary level to groups of more than 12 to 15 children.

Actually, there is some difference of opinion on whether or not it is worthwhile to give group intelligence tests to children in the early grades. If only a few individuals are to be tested for specific reasons, individual intelligence tests are often used. As discussed earlier, the long-range reliability (stability) of these tests for young children leaves much to be desired. For this reason, it is debatable just how useful the scores can be. Some persons, for example, argue that such measures can be helpful to the teachers in grouping their

Figure 2-3 Sample items from the Lorge-Thorndike Intelligence Tests, Level 2, Form A, Primary Battery. (Reproduced by permission of Houghton Mifflin Company, Boston, Mass.)

students. Others feel that any grouping should be very flexible and that scores on an intelligence test only serve the ill-advised purpose of making educators' decisions too rigid at this early school level. Decisions about grouping should be flexible. Using test information need not contradict this principle.

At any rate, there are several group tests that are appropriate for these grade levels. These tests require little reading or writing on the part of the student. Responses are marked directly on the test booklets because it is difficult for young children to use separate answer sheets. Most of the items are of the type that require the student to mark the correct picture.

Some sample questions taken from the Level 2 (Grades 2-3), Form A of the Lorge-Thorndike Intelligence Tests are shown in Figure 2-3. The directions for this type of item are as follows. For each row the administrator says: "Now look at row _____. Draw a ring around the picture that shows _____."

Other Primary (K-3) Group Intelligence Tests[41]

Kuhlmann-Anderson Intelligence Tests   Seventh edition. Personnel Press, Inc., 1963. One form. Eight levels: grades K, 1, 2, 3-4, 4-5, 5-7, 7-9, and 9-12. Three scores: verbal, quantitative, and total. Over 30 separate parts or subtests, each separately timed. Percentile ranks are reported for each of the three scores in each of grades 7-12 (based on beginning-of-year testing). Total raw score can be converted to deviation IQ's.

SRA Tests of General Ability   Science Research Associates, Inc., 1960. One form. Five levels: grades K-2, 2-4, 4-6, 6-9, and 9-12. Three scores: information, noncultural reasoning, and total. All test items at all levels are in pictorial form. Provides a measure of general intelligence using items not dependent upon formal school learning.

Otis-Lennon Mental Ability Test   Harcourt, Brace & World, Inc., 1967. One form. Six levels: first half of kindergarten, first half of grade 1, grades 1.6-3.9, 4.0-6.9, 7.0-9.9, and 10.0-12.9. Revision of the familiar Otis Quick-Scoring Mental Ability Tests. Samples a broad range of cognitive abilities. Deviation IQ's, percentile ranks, and stanines by age; percentile ranks and stanines by grade; mental age norms for the first three levels.

Primary Mental Abilities Test   Revised edition. Science Research Associates, Inc., 1963. One form. Five levels: grades K-1, 2-4, 4-6, 6-9, and 9-12. Five scores: verbal meaning, spatial ability, perception, number facility, and reasoning.

[41]The tests described here also have appropriate levels through grade 12.

Pre-School Inventory   Educational Testing Service, 1967. One form. Ages three to six. Five scores (four subtests and total): personal-social responsiveness (does the child know who he is and can he carry out simple and complicated verbal instructions), associative vocabulary (knowledge of words by either carrying out a task or by describing a role such as a dentist), knowledge and application of numerical concepts, and knowledge and application of sensory concepts (for example, geometrical shapes, weight, and color). Percentile norms by subtest, age (at six-month intervals), and socioeconomic status (middle and lower social class).

ELEMENTARY LEVEL (GRADES 4–8) GROUP TESTS

Tests at this level give more stable results and are therefore more useful than primary level group tests. The tasks in these higher levels are generally more verbal in nature. Examples from Level A (grades 3 and 4) of the Lorge-Thorndike are shown in Figures 2–5 and 2–6. All the tests just mentioned contain levels suitable for the elementary grades. In addition, the following tests have received wide use at this level.

The Henmon-Nelson Tests of Mental Ability   Revised edition. Houghton Mifflin Company, 1961. Two forms (A and B). Four levels: grades 3–6, 6–9, 9–12, and 13–17. Single IQ score. Highly verbal in nature. Scores can be expressed as mental ages, percentiles, and deviation IQ's (equated to those on the Stanford-Binet).

SRA Tests of Educational Ability   Science Research Associates, Inc., 1962. One form. Three levels: grades 4–6, 6–9, and 9–12. Four to five scores: language, reasoning, quantitative, total (grades 4–6 only), and nonreading total. Total score(s) converted to IQ's and percentiles. Referent used in establishing norms was grade level rather than age level. High educational loading.

Quick-Word Test   Harcourt, Brace & World, Inc., 1964. Three levels: Elementary (grades 4–6), Level 1 (grades 7–12 and average adult), and Level 2 (college and professional groups, superior 11th and 12th graders). Two forms for each level. Fifty words for the elementary level; 100 words for each of the other two levels. Untimed but takes about 15 minutes. Yields a quick measure of verbal intelligence. Scores converted to percentile ranks and stanines.

HIGH SCHOOL, COLLEGE, AND ADULT LEVEL GROUP TESTS

All of the primary and elementary tests just listed have levels appropriate for students through grade 12. Most are designed for even higher levels. When choosing a test for a certain age level, one should be careful to assure that the ceiling on the test is adequate. If, for example, one were to administer a test to a group of above-average high school seniors, it would be best to use a test that is designed for college students as well as high school seniors so that the test has an adequate ceiling.

Some tests, not mentioned above, that are particularly useful in predicting college success at the undergraduate level are as follows:

American College Testing Program Exam (ACT)   Revised annually. American College Testing Program. High school seniors and college freshmen. Four tests: English usage, mathematics usage, social studies reading, and natural science reading. Separate score for each test as well as a composite score. Scores reported in a variety of ways. Scored by publisher. (Note: This is classified as an achievement test in Buros, but it is often used as a predictive instrument.) Publisher provides extensive score reporting and research services for a fee.

College Entrance Examination Board Scholastic Aptitude Test (SAT)   Revised continually. Educational Testing Service. Candidates for college entrance. Two scores: verbal and mathematical. Percentile ranks by sex and by high school seniors and secondary school seniors who later entered college. Voluminous normative data. Scored by publisher.

College Qualification Tests (CQT)   The Psychological Corporation, 1961. Candidates for college entrance. Three forms (A, B, and C, with the latter two restricted to colleges and universities). Six scores: verbal, numerical, science information, social studies information, total information, and total. Separate sex norms. A variety of special norms tables are provided (for example, freshmen in state universities, in private colleges, college freshmen in various majors, and high school students in grades 11 and 12).

Terman-McNemar Test of Mental Ability   Harcourt, Brace & World, Inc., 1941. Grades 7–13. Two forms (C and D). Seven subtests: information, synonyms, logical selection, classification, analogies, opposites, and best answer. Age norms for computing deviation IQ's and percentile ranks.

The two tests often used for predicting success in graduate school are the Graduate Record Examination Aptitude Test and the Miller Analogies Test. Because these are of little use to primary and secondary school personnel, they will not be discussed here.

TWO BRIEF REVIEWS

California Test of Mental Maturity (CTMM)   Revised edition. California Test Bureau, 1963. There are six levels: Level 0 (K to entering grade 1), Level 1 (grade high 1–3), Level 2 (grades 4–6), Level 3 (grades 7–9), Level 4 (grades 9–12), and Level 5 (grade 12 to college and adult). These tests provide for continuous measurement with a series of articulated tests. One form. Testing time varies from 48 minutes for Level 0 to 81 minutes for Level 5. Each level consists of both language and nonlanguage sections. The language section has four subtests: number problems, inferences, verbal comprehension, and delayed recall. The nonlanguage section has eight subtests: opposites, similarities, analogies, rights and lefts, manipulation of areas, number series, numerical values, and immediate recall.

Scores are reported as mental ages, derived IQ's, percentiles, normalized T scores, and stanines. In addition to the scores that are provided for the language, nonlanguage, and total, the test also provides five factor scores: logical reasoning, spatial relationships, numerical reasoning, verbal concepts, and memory. It is interesting to note the similarity between these factor names and what the Binet and Wechsler scales seem to measure. With respect to these factor scores, the CTMM deserves the most criticism. These factor scores, as well as being less reliable than the total score, have little evidence concerning their differential predictability. We would recommend that little, if any, emphasis be placed on the interpretation of these factor scores.

The language, nonlanguage, and total scores are all reliable, and these scores correlate well with other general aptitude tests. The norming appears adequate both as to number and stratification. A somewhat elaborate profile sheet is provided upon which the pupil's scores can be plotted. Suggestions are presented in the manual on how to interpret the test scores. An aid to the teacher is a table presenting the factor and section (language and nonlanguage) standard score differences needed for various levels of statistical significance (.33, .05, .01).

The CTMM is one of the most popular tests of general intelligence used in the public schools. For example, a survey of the testing programs in Michigan schools[42] showed that 73 percent of the Michigan schools with a testing program administered the CTMM. This proportion has probably declined somewhat in recent years because of the increased popularity of the Cooperative School and College Ability Tests.

Cooperative School and College Ability Tests, Series II (SCAT, Series II) Educational Testing Service, 1967. This series of tests is composed of four levels: Level 4 (grades 4–6), Level 3 (grades 7–9), Level 2 (grades 10–12), and Level 1 (grades 12–14). There are equivalent forms at each level: three forms for the 12–14 grade level and two forms for each of the other levels. The test provides three scores: verbal, mathematical, and total. The verbal subtest is composed of 50 verbal analogy items. The mathematical subtest consists of 50 quantitative comparison items. Each quantitative question is

---

[42]Frank B. Womer, *Testing programs in Michigan schools.* Ann Arbor, Mich.: University of Michigan Press, 1963.

composed of two parts, and the testee must decide if one part is greater than the other, if the parts are equal, or if not enough information is given to decide. (See Figure 2–4.) Total administration time is 45 to 50 minutes (each subtest is a 20-minute timed test). Scores are presented in percentile ranks and percentile bands. The SCAT Series II was placed on the same score scale as the original SCAT, so the scores on the two series are roughly comparable. Also, one can compare scores across forms and levels of the tests. The norming of the test appears very adequate. The validity reported compares favorably with other general intelligence tests. Average validity coefficients (averaged on studies within grades by Fisher's Z transformation) between total score and GPA ranged from .59 to .68.

Internal consistency estimates of reliability were all high, ranging from the upper .80's to middle .90's. Equivalent form and test-retest correlations were not available in the Handbook. We hope such correlations will soon be reported because the subtests (particularly mathematics) are somewhat speeded and the internal consistency estimates may be misleading.

This test appears to be very promising. The vigorous efforts to improve and update the original SCAT, which in itself was a very promising instrument, has resulted in a shorter version but one that appears to remain reliable and valid.

CRITICAL EVALUATION OF THE LORGE-THORNDIKE INTELLIGENCE TESTS, MULTILEVEL EDITION[43]

This thorough review should illustrate some of the important aspects to consider in test selection and use. The choice of the Lorge-Thorndike is not meant to imply that the authors of this book consider it the best test available. We have tried to point out previously in this book that a test must be evaluated in accordance with its intended use. No test is best for all possible uses. The Lorge-Thorndike is considered a technically well-constructed test, but so are many others. The Lorge-Thorndike has been chosen as a representative example of those well-constructed tests that cover a wide age range.

Grade Level and Content

The Lorge-Thorndike Intelligence Tests are designed for all grade levels from kindergarten through college freshmen. The multilevel edition provides in a single reusable booklet a continuous set of group tests from grade 3 through 13. There is also available a primary battery for kindergarten through grade 3. This primary battery is issued in a consumable booklet form. The college freshmen level (H) of the multilevel edition is also issued in a separate booklet for the convenience of those who are working only

---

[43]Irving Lorge and Robert L. Thorndike, Lorge-Thorndike intelligence tests. (multilevel ed.) Boston: Houghton Mifflin, 1964.

Part I Directions

Each question begins with two words. These two words go together in a certain way. Under them, there are four other pairs of words lettered **A, B, C,** and **D.**

Find the lettered pair of words that go together in the same way as the first pair of words.

Then, find the row of boxes on your answer sheet which has the same number as the question. In this row of boxes, mark the letter of the pair of words you have chosen.

See how these examples are marked:

EXAMPLE 1 **calf : cow ::**

A puppy : dog
B nest : bird
C horse : bull
D shell : turtle

Answer

E 1 ■ B C D

In the first pair of words (**calf : cow**), calf goes with cow in this way— a calf is a young cow.

The only lettered pair of words that go together in the same way is **puppy : dog.** A puppy is a young dog.

Box **A** is marked because the letter in front of **puppy : dog** is **A.**

Part II Directions

Each of the following questions has two parts. One part is in Column A. The other part is in Column B.

You must find out if one part is greater than the other, or if the parts are equal.

Then, find the row of boxes on your answer sheet which has the same number as the question. In this row of boxes, mark:

A if the part in Column A is greater,
B if the part in Column B is greater,
C if the two parts are equal.

	Column A	Column B	Answer
EXAMPLE 1	10	9	

The part in Column A (10) is greater than the part in Column B (9). Box **A** is marked because the part in Column A is greater.

1 ■ B C

	Column A	Column B
EXAMPLE 2	2	$1 + 2$

The part in Column B (1 + 2) is greater than the part in Column A (2). Box **B** is marked because the part in Column B is greater.

2 A ■ C

	Column A	Column B
EXAMPLE 3	The value of 5 cents	The value of 1 nickel

The part in Column A is 5 cents. The part in Column B (1 nickel) is also equal to 5 cents. Box **C** is marked because the parts are equal.

3 A B ■

Figure 2-4 Examples of the verbal and mathematical items on the Cooperative School and College Ability Tests, Series II, Form 4A. (Reproduced by permission of the Educational Testing Service, Princeton, N.J.)

with college students and who, therefore, have no need for the complete series of levels. Only the multilevel edition (1964) will be reviewed here. *Multilevel* means that there are 8 different but overlapping levels within the same booklet. For example, in the vocabulary section of the verbal battery there are 60 exercises. Level A starts at Item 1 and ends at Item 25. Level B starts at Item 6 and ends at Item 30; Level C starts at Item 11 and ends at Item 35; and so forth up to Level H, which begins at Item 36 and ends at Item 60. Thus, each level has 25 vocabulary exercises, 20 (80 percent) of which overlap with adjacent levels. The levels have been indicated by letter (A to H) rather than by grade so that students will not be aware of what level corresponds to what grade. This is important because the authors suggest that the level used at any particular grade should be dependent upon the kinds of students in class or school. (See Table 2–1.)

There is both a verbal (V) and nonverbal (NV) battery within each booklet. There are two forms (1 and 2) for each battery so that one can retest individuals whose scores seem questionable.

Table 2–1

Chart Suggesting the Most Appropriate Grades
for Using the Lorge-Thorndike[a]

	Average Communities: Average Classes and Schools[b]	High Socioeconomic Communities: Above-Average Classes and Schools	Low Socioeconomic Communities: Below-Average Classes and Schools
Primary battery			
Level 1	Kindergarten to Grade 1	Kindergarten	Kindergarten to Grade 2
Level 2	Grades 2–3	Grades 1–2	Grades 3–4
Multilevel battery			
Level A	Grade 3 or 4	Grade 3	Grade 5
Level B	Grade 4 or 5	Grade 4	Grade 6
Level C	Grade 5 or 6	Grade 5	Grade 7
Level D	Grade 6 or 7	Grade 6	Grade 8
Level E	Grade 7 or 8	Grade 7	Grade 9
Level F	Grades 9–10	Grades 8–9	Grade 10
Level G	Grades 11–12	Grades 10–11	Grades 11–12
Level H	Superior grade 12, College	Grades 12–13	

[a]Taken from the *Manual for administration*, Lorge-Thorndike Intelligence Tests. (multilevel ed.) Boston: Houghton Mifflin, 1964, p. 35.

[b]It is recommended that Level A be given in grade 3 during the second semester. Similarly, for Levels B to E, if testing is done during the first half of the school year, it is recommended that the levels be given in the higher of the pair of grades listed.

According to the authors, the tests are designed to be measures of abstract intelligence defined as "the ability to work with ideas and the relationships among ideas."[44] Supposedly, both the verbal and nonverbal batteries measure this same abstract intelligence but do so with a different set of tasks.

The verbal battery is made up of five subtests composed of only verbal items: (1) vocabulary, (2) sentence completion, (3) arithmetic reasoning, (4) verbal classification, and (5) verbal analogy.

The items in the vocabulary subtest require the examinee to choose from five words the one that has most nearly the same meaning as the given word (stem). The sentence completion subtest requires the examinee to choose the one word out of five that best completes a sentence. The arithmetic reasoning subtest presents short story problems. The examinee is to choose the correct answer from five alternative answers (one of which is always "none of these"). The verbal classification items present a series of three words, and the examinee is to choose the one of five additional words that belongs with the original series. The verbal analogy subtest is composed of items that present three words. The first two words are related to each other in some way, and the examinee is to choose which one of five answers is related to the third word in the same way. Examples of items from each of these five subtests of the verbal battery are presented in Figure 2–5 below.

I. VOCABULARY:

For each exercise in this test you are to read the word in dark type at the beginning of that exercise. Then, from the five words that follow you are to choose the word that has the same meaning or most nearly the same meaning as the word in dark type. Look at sample exercise O.

O. **loud**　　A　quick　　B　noisy　　C　hard　　D　heavy　　E　weak

The word which has most nearly the same meaning as loud is noisy. The letter in front of noisy is B, so on your answer sheet make a heavy black pencil mark in the B answer space for exercise O.

II. SENTENCE COMPLETION:

In each exercise in this test, a word has been left out of a sentence. Read the sentence carefully; then. from the five words that follow, choose the one word that will make the best, the truest, and the most sensible complete sentence. Look at sample exercise O.

O. Hot weather comes in the _____.

　　A　fall　　B　night　　C　summer　　D　winter　　E　snow

The best answer is summer. The word summer makes the best, truest, and most sensible complete sentence. The letter in front of summer is C,

---

[44]*Manual for administration*, Lorge-Thorndike Intelligence Tests. (multilevel Ed.) Boston: Houghton Mifflin, 1964, p. 4.

so on your answer sheet make a heavy black pencil mark in the C answer space for exercise O.

III. ARITHMETIC REASONING:

In this test you are to work some arithmetic problems. After each problem are four possible answers and a fifth choice, "none of these," meaning that the correct answer is not given.

Work each problem and compare your answer with the four possible answers. If the correct answer is given, fill in the space on the answer sheet that has the same letter as the right answer. If the correct answer is not given, fill in the space on the answer sheet that has the same letter as "none of these." Look at sample exercise O.

O. If candy costs a cent a piece, how much will nine pieces cost?
        A 1¢   B 7¢   C 8¢   D 9¢   E none of these

The correct answer is 9¢. The letter in front of 9¢ is D, so on your answer sheet make a heavy black pencil mark in the D answer space for exercise O.

IV. VERBAL CLASSIFICATION:

For each exercise in this test, a series of words is given in dark type. You are to figure out how the words in dark type are alike, then you are to choose the one word among the five on the line below that belongs with the words in dark type. Look at sample exercise O.

O. **rose   daisy   violet**
        A red   B garden   C sweet   D grow   E lily

All the words in dark type are the names of flowers. Of the five words on the line below, only lily is the name of a flower. The letter in front of lily is E, so on your answer sheet make a heavy black pencil mark in the E answer space for exercise O.

V. VERBAL ANALOGY:

For each exercise in this test, a pair of words is given that are related to each other in some way. Look at the first two words and figure out how they are related to each other. Then, from the five words on the line below, choose the word that is related to the third word in the same way. Look at sample exercise O.

O. Laugh → happy: cry →
        A wonder   B sad   C hide   D lost   E rough

The right answer is sad because you laugh when you are happy and you cry when you are sad. The letter before sad is B, so on your answer sheet make a heavy black pencil mark in the B answer space for exercise O.

Figure 2-5 Examples of the five types of items on the verbal battery of the Lorge-Thorndike Intelligence Tests, Multilevel Edition. (Reproduced by permission of Houghton Mifflin Company, Boston, Mass.)

The nonverbal battery is composed of three subtests: pictorial classification, numerical relationships, and pictorial analogy. The ability to perform well on these subtests is not dependent upon reading ability. The
pictorial classification subtest is composed of items that contain drawings
(usually three) that are alike in some way. The examinee is to choose which
one of five alternative drawings goes with the first set. The numerical
relationship subtest presents a series of numbers or letters in a certain order.
The examinee is to choose which one of five other numbers (or letters)
should come next in the series. The pictorial analogy subtest is of the same
format as the word analogy subtest of the verbal battery, only pictures are

I. Pictorial classification:

For each exercise in this test, a series of drawings is given which are alike in a certain way. You
are to figure out in what way the drawings are alike. Then you are to find the drawing at the right
that goes with the first group. Look at sample exercise 0. The first three drawings in the row are
alike in a certain way. Find the drawing at the right that goes with the first three.

The first three drawings are alike in that they are all circles and they are getting smaller. At the right
the only one that is a circle and is still smaller is at **H**. Make a heavy black pencil mark in the **H**
answer space for exercise 0.

II. Numerical relationships:

For each exercise in this test a series of numbers or letters is given in a certain order. You are
to figure out the order (or way) in which the series of numbers or letters is arranged, then find the
number or letter at the right that should come next. Look at sample exercise 0.

1.   1   3   5   7   9 →   A 10   B 11   C 12   D 13   E 14

In the series of numbers, 1 3 5 7 9, each number is 2 more than the number before it; therefore, the
next number in the series should be 11. The letter in front of 11 is **B** so make a heavy black pencil
mark in the **B** answer space for exercise 0.

III. Picture analogy:

In each exercise in this test, the first two drawings go together in a certain way. You are to
figure out how the first two go together, then find the drawing at the right that goes with the third
drawing in the same way that the second goes with the first. Look at sample exercise 0.

The right answer is **K**, because the little circle at **K** goes with the little square just as the big circle
goes with the big square. Make a heavy black pencil mark in the **K** answer space for exercise 0.

Figure 2-6 Examples of the three types of items on the nonverbal battery of the
Lorge-Thorndike Intelligence Tests, Multilevel Edition, Level A. (Reproduced by
permission of Houghton Mifflin Company, Boston, Mass.)

used instead of words. Examples of items from each of the three subtests of the nonverbal battery are presented in Figure 2–6.

Administration

DIRECTIONS The multilevel tests have a 95-page manual for administration accompanying the tests. Twenty-seven of these pages are devoted strictly to the directions for administration. Separate specific directions are given for use with various answer sheets. All directions are clear and concise; the only real problem is that in this multilevel booklet it is possible for the students to get confused and start (or stop) at the wrong place within the subtest. The test administrator must be alert to this possibility and guard against its occurrence. There is little doubt but that a typical teacher would be capable of administering the test correctly — providing that the instructions are read carefully prior to the actual administration.

TIME LIMITS The testing time for each of the five tests on the verbal battery is 7 minutes, and 9 minutes for each of the three subtests on the nonverbal battery.

Considering the time it typically takes to distribute and collect booklets and answer sheets, fill in personal data on answer sheets, and so forth, the authors recommend that a total of one hour be allotted for each battery. The two batteries should not be scheduled for the same testing session.

Although all subtests of both the verbal and nonverbal batteries are timed, the authors suggest that "the tests are primarily power tests since the time limits were chosen so that very few pupils would make a higher score if they had more time."[45] However, the empirical data from which that statement was determined were not presented in either the administrator's or the technical manual.

Scoring

All answers to the various levels and forms of this test are recorded on one of three kinds of answer sheets: MRC (Measurement Research Center) Answer Sheets, IBM 805 Answer Sheets, or IBM 1230 Answer Sheets. If either of the IBM-type answer sheets is used, the scoring may be either by hand (a punched out cardboard key is provided) or by machine. However, the Houghton Mifflin Scoring Service is not available for the IBM Answer Sheets. If MRC Answer Sheets are used, they may be either hand scored by means of a plastic overlay key or they may be sent to the Houghton Mifflin Scoring Service located in Iowa City. The instructions for hand

[45] *Manual for administration*, p. 36.

scoring are clear and can easily be followed by a competent secretary. The scoring service provides a list report of pupil scores by grade and school building, containing for each pupil his name, sex, grade, date of birth, age, raw scores on each battery (verbal and nonverbal), and nine derived scores. Class averages are also reported. A variety of optional services are provided for a slight additional cost.

Types of Scores

The following nine derived scores can be obtained:

1. Verbal IQ
2. Nonverbal IQ
3. Composite IQ (average of 1 and 2)
4. Verbal age equivalent
5. Nonverbal age equivalent
6. Verbal grade equivalent
7. Nonverbal grade equivalent
8. Verbal grade percentile
9. Nonverbal grade percentile

The IQ's are all deviation IQ's with a mean of 100 and a standard deviation of 16. Because the various levels in this test are composed of overlapping items, it was possible for the authors (using these common items) to derive equivalent scores for different levels. Thus, for example, if on the nonverbal battery (Form 1) a nine-year-old received a raw score of 30 on Level B, he would have a nonverbal IQ of 96. If, however, he took Level C rather than Level B, he would only need a raw score of 22 to obtain the same nonverbal IQ of 96. This comparability of levels, possible because of the common items, allows an administrator flexibility in picking the appropriate level of difficulty for a particular set of students. (See Table 2–1.)

Norming

The standardization of the test was excellent. The authors used a sample of communities in the United States stratified on size, median family income, and median education of adults in the community. The final norms were based on approximately 19,000 students per grade (approximately 0.6 percent of the total school population) for grades 3 through 12 from a total of 72 sampling units. Two of the major assets of the norming procedure are that (1) the norms are comparable from grade to grade and (2) the Iowa Tests of Basic Skills and the Tests of Academic Progress were normed on the same school systems, thus providing the opportunity to compare intelligence and achievement scores.

Reliability

The reliability of the Lorge-Thorndike compares favorably with other well-constructed intelligence tests. The technical manual reports the reliability studies in a lucid fashion with no apparent attempt to mislead the reader. Alternate form reliabilities (with the two forms given within a week of each other) are reported for each grade level. These reliabilities for the verbal battery range from .83 to .94 and from .80 to .92 for the nonverbal battery.

The reported odd-even reliabilities are all above .90. It must be remembered that the tests were timed (although supposedly not speeded) so the odd-even reliabilities may be overestimates. Separate standard errors of measurement (S_e's) were computed from the odd-even reliabilities for different score levels within each battery. These range from 2.4 to 6.1 deviation IQ points. In general, the S_e's were lower at the middle IQ level. Very low and very high scores are expected to shift more on retesting than those at the middle range.

There is some stability information available showing the correlation between the multilevel and the earlier separate level scores. For a one year interval from grade 7 to 8, these correlations range from .71 to .88 for the verbal battery and from .58 to .82 for the nonverbal battery. The correlations between the primary battery given in grade 3 and the V and NV batteries given in grade 6 range from .49 to .55.

Correlations between the verbal and nonverbal batteries range from about .65 to .75. These correlations "are enough lower than the reliabilities of the two tests so that the differences do have some stability and some significance. (The reliability of the difference between the two scores is around .70.) In about 20 percent of cases, the two tests will yield IQ's differing by 15 points."[46]

A correlation matrix of part scores as well as the results of a factor analysis is also reported in the technical manual.

Validity

The technical manual devotes 13 pages (including 16 tables) to a discussion of the validity evidence on the Lorge-Thorndike. Much of the evidence is necessarily based on the 1954 separate level edition rather than on the 1964 multilevel edition, but because there is a high similarity between the two forms (many of the items are identical), it is reasonable to assume that similar results would be found using the newer scales.

---

[46]*Technical manual*, Lorge-Thorndike Intelligence Tests. (multilevel ed.) Boston: Houghton Mifflin, 1966, p. 14.

The manual discusses three kinds of validity: validity as representing (content validity), validity as predicting, and validity as signifying (construct validity).

Under the section on validity as representing the authors point out that the test avowedly measures abstract intelligence defined as the ability to use and interpret symbols. Because the items require the interpretation and use of verbal, pictorial, diagrammatic, and numerical symbols, the tasks do seem to represent what the test authors define as intelligent behavior. Some might argue that this is really face validity rather than content validity. However, since intelligent behavior is actually defined as the ability to do these tasks, we would agree with the authors that content validity is demonstrated.

The manual presents data on two kinds of predictive validity: correlation with achievement tests and correlation with school grades. Not all the data will be summarized here, but some examples will be presented. The correlations with the verbal battery and the subtests of the Iowa Test of Basic Skills are in the general range of .72 to .84; the nonverbal battery correlations run somewhat lower (.57 to .68). Correlations with the subscores of the Tests of Academic Progress are at about the same level. Correlations between the Lorge-Thorndike and average grades two years later range from .39 (nonverbal) to .56 (verbal).

Under the "validity as signifying" section, the manual presents data showing the correlations of the Lorge-Thorndike with other well-known tests of intelligence. These correlations range from the low .60's to the middle .80's.

In summarizing the validity aspects of the Lorge-Thorndike, we feel that the technical manual presents considerable data in a clear fashion. The Lorge-Thorndike certainly has as much (or more) evidence for its validity as most other group tests of general intelligence.

Format

The format of the test is very good. The test booklet itself is well constructed and set up in a pleasing style. A possible drawback is one inherent in a multilevel booklet, that is, the possibility of students becoming confused about the starting and stopping points within the subtests.

The manual for administration (95 pages) is easy to follow and the technical manual (31 pages) is, in general, written at such a level that people with a "one-course background" in tests and measurement should be able to understand it.

Interpretation and Use

The final section of this chapter will deal with the interpretation and use of all the types of aptitude tests discussed in this chapter: general, multiple, and specific. In discussing the uses of the Lorge-Thorndike, we will only mention three unique characteristics of it and how these are useful, rather than discuss all possible uses. The characteristics to be mentioned are unique in the sense that they are not common to all group general-intelligence tests. We do not mean that no other group intelligence tests would have these characteristics.

First, the continuous multilevel approach (with norms showing the comparability of levels) has two advantages: (1) it allows one to use a test of appropriate difficulty and (2) it allows one to observe an individual's relative intellectual growth over time.

Second, the nonverbal battery, purporting to measure abstract intelligence, allows one to obtain an estimate relatively unaffected by reading ability. The authors do not make the claim that the nonverbal battery is a culture fair test (or a measure of innate ability). However, it is less susceptible to the influences of formal schooling than is the verbal battery.

Third, because both the Iowa Test of Basic Skills and the Tests of Academic Progress are standardized on the same norm group as the Lorge-Thorndike, a comparison between level of achievement and aptitude is possible.

This fairly thorough review of the Lorge-Thorndike was presented as an example of what you should look for in choosing a group general-aptitude test. The Lorge-Thorndike compares well with other tests of the same type. We would classify it as one of the better measures of its kind.

CULTURE FAIR TESTS OF INTELLIGENCE

Intelligence tests have often been severely criticized for their "cultural biases." People of different nations as well as people in different subcultures within the United States place different values upon verbal fluency, speed, and other aspects that influence the scores on intelligence tests. Suppose individuals in one subculture are less verbal than individuals in another subculture and that the test used requires verbal skills. Is the test fair to individuals of the first subculture?

As already discussed, there is no doubt that a person's environment (subculture) can affect his intelligence test score. For this reason, some people argue that intelligence testing is not fair to some groups. This argument is particularly set forth in the testing of the disadvantaged. Should typical intelligence tests be used with culturally disadvantaged? Or should we use tests that are culturally fair?

Psychologists have attempted in the past to develop tests that are free from cultural influences. Failing in this — for no test can be free from cultural influences — there has, more recently, been an attempt to develop tests that are equally fair to members of all cultures. Examples of tests of this type are the Culture Fair Intelligence Test and the Davis-Eells Test of General Intelligence or Problem-Solving Ability. In attempting to achieve this cultural fairness, these tests have included tasks that involve nonsense material, or tasks that should be equally familiar or unfamiliar to all cultures. Figure 2–7 presents examples of sample items taken from Scale 2 of the Cattell Culture Fair Intelligence Test. Complete verbal directions are given to the subject so that he understands the task. These items do not appear to be unfair to any culture. However, the research evidence suggest that these tests are not culturally fair if, by this phrase, we mean groups from one culture score as well on the tests as groups from another culture.[47] It is very hard, if not impossible, to devise a test that will show no differences between such groups. Even if we could, would it be a worthwhile attainment? Some argue yes. They say such a measure would be relatively independent of cultural influences and, therefore, as nearly correlated to innate ability as possible. Others argue that to mask existing group differences by eliminating all items measuring these differences is to delimit the usefulness of the test. Tannenbaum, for example, in reviewing the Culture Fair Intelligence Test, takes the following position.

> In essence, then, it must be admitted that the long-pursued goal of demonstrating equality among national and international sub-populations on some measure of general ability has not been reached by this test. Is it, indeed, a goal worth pursuing? Even if it were possible to devise a test so antiseptic as to clean out inequality not only among subcultures but also among other groups showing differences in test intelligence, such as those classified by sex, age, education, geographic origin, body type, physical health, personality structure, and family unity—what kind of instrument would we then have? Since such a test must perforce be so thoroughly doctored as to omit tasks that reveal these group differences, or substitute others that show "no difference," what could it possibly measure? What could it predict? Covering up group differences in this way does not erase test bias. Rather, it delimits drastically the kinds of information one can gather about problem-solving strengths and weaknesses associated with groups as well as individuals.[48]

The debate as to the usefulness of a culture fair test depends on how we wish to use the instrument. Some people wish to get a measure of innate ability (whatever that is) and argue as follows:

---

[47]See the reviews in the 5th and 6th *Mental measurements yearbooks* of the two tests mentioned.

[48]Abraham J. Tannenbaum, Review of the Culture Fair Intelligence Tests in O. K. Buros, *The sixth mental measurements yearbook*, pp. 722–723.

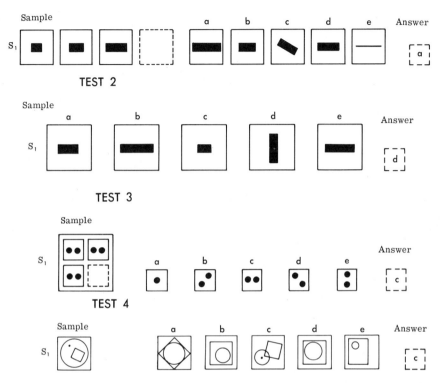

Figure 2-7 Sample items from Scale 2, Form A, of the Cattell Culture Fair Intelligence Test. (Copyright © 1949, 1957, by the Institute for Personality and Ability Testing, 1602 Coronado Drive, Champaign, Illinois, U.S.A. All rights reserved. Reprinted with permission.)

1. There are no genetic differences in intelligence among sub-cultures.[49]

2. Therefore, tests that are measures of innate ability will show no differences between subcultures.

3. Therefore, tests that show no differences between subcultures are tests that measure innate ability.

[49]This point has been debated by psychologists, but we will side-step the argument in this book. There is certainly no compelling scientific reason to reject this assumption, and there are some good humanitarian reasons for accepting it. See Arthur R. Jensen, Social class, race, and genetics: Implications for education. *Amer. educ. res. J.*, 1968, *5*, 1–42 for an interesting position concerning this.

The logic breaks down in going from step two to three. If A implies B, it does not follow that B implies A. We simply cannot (at the present time) obtain measures of innate ability.

Other people, realizing that we can never measure innate ability with a paper-pencil test, wish to use intelligence tests primarily as predictive instruments. If the environmental effects of one's culture are related to the criterion we are attempting to predict, then to eliminate these cultural differences would reduce substantially the validity of the test.

Paradoxically, there are a few psychologists and lay people who assert that tests are unfair to some subcultures and who also take the position that all differences in intellectual functioning are due to environmental factors. Now, if there really were no genetic differences between people and if we used a measuring instrument that ruled out (or equated) environmental effects, then everyone would get exactly the same score on the test! Such a test would be completely useless. The question of whether we wish to build culture fair tests is legitimately debatable, but only if we take the position that there are some nonenvironmental factors contributing to test per-performance.

The authors of this text take the position that if culture fair tests could be developed, they would be in general less useful measures than the presently existing measures that are influenced by environmental factors.[50]

MULTIFACTOR APTITUDE TESTS

As already mentioned, psychologists do not all agree as to the structure of intellect. Some contend that intellect is a general characteristic and that a single score can adequately represent the degree to which a person possesses intelligence. Others may subscribe to a multifactor theory of intelligence but argue that the measurement of these multifactors adds little, if any, to the predictive validity of single-factor tests. The advocates of multifactor testing generally support it on both theoretical and practical bases.

One of the early exponents of a multifactor theory of intelligence was Thurstone. Using a statistical technique called multiple-factor analysis,[51] he found many different factors of ability and, in 1941, published the first

[50]See Anne Anastasi, Psychology, psychologists, and psychological testing. *Amer. Psychologist*, 1967, *22*, 297–305, and J. E. Doppelt and George K. Bennett, Testing job applications from disadvantaged groups. *Test Service Bulletin*, no. 57, May 1967, for good commentaries on this issue.

[51]Factor analysis will not be covered in this book, other than noting that the intercorrelations between the tests determines the number of factors. If the tests are all highly correlated with each other, for example, then one would only have a single factor. If, at the other extreme, the tests do not correlate at all with each other, then we would have as many factors as tests. See, for example, Ben Fruchter, *Introduction to factor analysis*. Princeton, N.J.: Van Nostrand, 1954, for further discussions of this topic.

multifactor test — the Chicago Tests of Primary Mental Abilities. (The name SRA Primary Mental Abilities has been given to later editions of this same test.) In the years since this early multifactor test was developed, the popularity of both a multifactor theory of intellect and the use of multifactor tests has grown. At the present time, most school districts administer a multifactor aptitude test at some stage of a student's public school career. What are the reasons for this popularity of multifactor tests? Is this popularity justified? What are the characteristics of these tests? What are their advantages and limitations?

The development of factor-analytic techniques was certainly the major technical development affecting the popularity of the multifactor theory. Rather than simply arguing whether intelligence is general, multifactor, or composed of many specific abilities, one can perform a factor analysis on many different kinds of ability tests. If only one factor is obtained, then we have some support for the theory of general intelligence. If many factors are obtained, this lends support to the multifactor theory. If one obtained as many factors as kinds of tests, this would support the specific aptitude theory.

Some of the multifactor tests have not actually been constructed through a factor-analytic procedure but, rather, have been constructed by choosing items that have high correlations with other items in the *same* subtest but low correlations with the items (and subtest scores) in the *other* subtests. This results in a set of subtests that are internally consistent but that have low intercorrelations with each other. This should be a major characteristic of any multifactor test. Of course, the use of test construction techniques to develop a multifactor test does not enable us to argue that obtaining a set of factors proves the actual existence of the factors within a person.

Another aspect that led to the increased popularity of multifactor aptitude tests was the vocational and educational counseling movement. The discovery of differential abilities within a person should certainly facilitate vocational and educational counseling. But does it? Some argue that identification of differential abilities will only be helpful in counseling to the extent that this knowledge allows us to differentially predict how well an individual will be able to perform in various educational curricula or vocational tasks. The degree to which multifactor tests enable us to differentially predict is an important aspect in determining their usefulness.

In general, the data indicate that multifactor aptitude tests are not very good for differential prediction.[52] This is not solely because of the tests' inadequacies in subdividing intellect into its component subparts. The

[52]See *The use of multifactor tests in guidance*, a reprint series from *Personnel guidance J.*, Washington, D.C.: American Personnel and Guidance Association, 1957.

problem is that the criteria (for example, job success) are not solely dependent upon specific aspects of intelligence. Thus, although we may be able to obtain measures of numerical ability and verbal ability that are distinct, there simply are not any criteria that differentially demand one aptitude and not the other. Therefore, there is little evidence of differential predictive validity. [53] Whether this makes the test no more useful than the less expensive and less time-consuming test of general intelligence depends on the degree to which one believes that a more precise description is useful in counseling regardless of whether it increases predictability. As with any belief, there are differences of opinion on this. It is not a belief easily subjected to scientific verification.

EXAMPLES OF MULTIFACTOR APTITUDE TESTS

The sixth edition of Buros lists 16 multiple-aptitude batteries. Three of the most widely used of these will be mentioned here. A fourth, the Differential Aptitude Test, will be more thoroughly reviewed in the next section.

Academic Promise Tests (APT) The Psychological Corporation, 1961–1962. This test is designed for grades 6–9. There are seven scores: abstract reasoning, numerical, nonverbal total, language usage, verbal, verbal total, and total. Three of these (abstract reasoning, numerical, and verbal) are downward extensions of their counterparts in the Differential Aptitude Tests (DAT). It is a well-constructed test with good validity and reliability. However, differential validity is not particularly high. Because three of the seven scores are totals, there are actually only four different areas tested. The decision to classify the APT under multiaptitude batteries and the SCAT and the CTMM under tests of group intelligence is somewhat arbitrary.

Flanagan Aptitude Classification Tests (FACT) Science Research Associates, Inc., 1951–1960. Designed for grades 9–12 and adults, this test measures 19 areas of aptitude: inspection, mechanics, tables, reasoning, vocabulary, assembly, judgment and comprehension, components, planning, arithmetic, ingenuity, scales, expression, precision, alertness, coordination, patterns, coding, and memory.

Each subtest corresponds to a job element identified by (1) listing the critical behaviors in a group of occupations, (2) translating these critical behaviors into hypotheses about the nature of the aptitude involved and (3) determining whether variations in job performance are related to measures of aptitudes.

---

[53]Multifactor aptitude tests may increase in differential predictability as the more sophisticated analyses (such as multiple regression equations) are employed. However, to date, most of the validity evidence is reported using single correlations. Further discussion of this point is beyond the scope of this book.

Flanagan is conducting longitudinal follow-up research to gather further evidence on validity. This test could conceivably become the most popular multifactor aptitude test. It depends on the outcome of the continuing research. A disadvantage of the test is that it takes about 10.5 hours to administer.

General Aptitude Test Battery (GATB) United States Government Printing Office, 1946–1953. Designed for grades 9–12 and adults, GATB yields nine aptitude scores from 12 tests as follows: intelligence, verbal aptitude, numerical aptitude, spatial aptitude, form perception, clerical perception, motor coordination, finger dexterity, and manual dexterity. These aptitudes are not completely independent because some of the subtests are used in determining more than one aptitude score.

These tests have been widely used by the United States Employment Service (USES). Multiple cutoff scores (a series of minimum scores) are used in predicting job success in various occupations. The USES is continuing to do research on the GATB. It is considered by many to be a very well-constructed instrument. The total time required for testing is just a little over 2 hours.

CRITICAL EVALUATION OF THE DIFFERENTIAL APTITUDE TESTS (DAT)[54]

As with the choice of the Lorge-Thorndike for thorough review under the section on group tests of general intelligence, the choice of the DAT is not necessarily meant to imply that it is the best of the multifactor tests. It is a good test and is widely used in the public schools, but we must again emphasize that a test best for one use may be completely inadequate for other uses.

Grade Level and Content

The DAT has been designed for use in grades 8–12. There are two forms of the test (L and M), and each form is composed of eight subtests: verbal reasoning (VR), numerical ability (NA), abstract reasoning (AR), clerical speed and accuracy (CSA), mechanical reasoning (MR), space relations (SR), Language Usage I: Spelling (SPEL), and Language Usage II: Grammar (GRAM). The authors of the test also report a ninth score. It is simply VR + NA. This combined score is interpreted in the same way as a measure of general intelligence. Examples of the practice items contained in each subtest are shown in Figure 2–8. They are, of course, easier than the actual items in the subtest, but they are identical in form.

[54]George K. Bennett, Harold G. Seashore, and Alexander G. Wesman, Differential Aptitude Tests. New York: The Psychological Corporation, 1963.

Verbal Reasoning:

Example X.   ...... is to water as eat is to ....

    A.   continue —— drive
    B.   foot —— enemy
    C.   drink —— food
    D.   girl —— industry
    E.   drink —— enemy

Numerical Ability:

Example X.

Add	13	A	14
	12	B	25
		C	16
		D	59
		E	**none of these**

Abstract Reasoning:

    Each row consists of four figures called Problem Figures and five called Answer Figures. The four Problem Figures make a series. You are to find out which one of the Answer Figures would be the next, or the fifth one in the series.

Example Y.

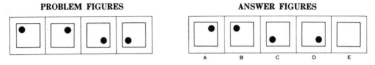

PROBLEM FIGURES   **ANSWER FIGURES**

Clerical Speed and Accuracy:

    This is a test to see how quickly and accurately you can compare letter and number combinations. On the following pages are groups of these combinations; each Test Item contains five. These same combinations appear after the number for each Test Item on the separate Answer Sheet, but they are in a different order. You will notice that in each Test Item one of the five is **underlined.** You are to look at the **one** combination which is underlined, find the **same** one after that item number on the separate Answer Sheet, and fill in the space under it.

    These examples are correctly done. Note that the combination on the Answer Sheet must be exactly the same as the one in the Test Item.

TEST ITEMS   SAMPLES OF ANSWER SHEETS

Mechanical Reasoning:

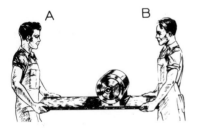

X

Which man has the heavier load?

(If equal, mark C.)

Space Relations:

Example X.

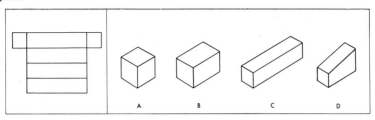

Language Usage I: Spelling:

EXAMPLES   SAMPLES OF ANSWER SHEETS

W.   man

X.   gurl

Y.   catt

Z.   dog

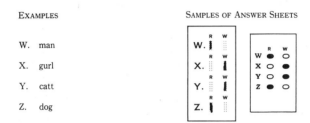

Language Usage II: Grammar:

This test consists of a series of sentences, each divided into four parts lettered A, B, C and D. You are to look at each sentence and decide which part has an error in grammar, punctuation or spelling. When you have decided which part is wrong, fill in the space under the letter for that part. Be sure the item number on the separate Answer Sheet is the same as that of the sentence on which you are working.

Some sentences have no error in any part. If there is no error in a sentence, fill in the space under the letter E.

SAMPLES OF ANSWER SHEETS

Example X.   Ain't we / going to / the office / next week?
            A   B   C   D

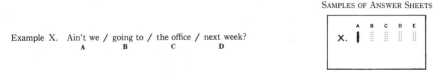

Figure 2-8   Examples of practice items from the subtests of the DAT. (Reproduced by permission. Copyright 1947, © 1961 for Verbal Reasoning, Numerical Ability, Abstract Reasoning, and Clerical Speed and Accuracy. Copyright 1947, © 1961, 1962 for Mechanical Reasoning, Space Relations, Language Usage–Spelling, and Language Usage–Grammar. The Psychological Corporation, New York, N.Y. All rights reserved.)

109

The verbal reasoning test is a measure of ability to understand verbal relationships and concepts. The analogy-type item used (see Figure 2–8) is considered to be very versatile. It requires more than simple vocabulary recognition and can become quite complex without being tricky.

The numerical ability items are of the computation rather than of the reasoning variety, and thus they are free from reading ability. The abstract reasoning test is a nonverbal measure of a student's reasoning ability. As can be seen from Figure 2–6, this kind of item is similar to the pictorial classification of the nonverbal L–T discussed in the previous section. The clerical speed and accuracy test is simply a measure of speed of response to a perceptual task. The test is heavily speeded. (Note the two kinds of answer sheets shown in Figure 2–8 for Language Usage I. Because of the speed factor, there are different norms for each type.) No intellectual ability is involved in the usual sense of the term. The mechanical reasoning test is composed of items consisting of pictorially presented mechanical situations and of a question. The terminology used in the questions was intentionally kept at a very simple level so as not to measure reading ability. The space relations test is composed of items that require "mental manipulation of objects in three-dimensional space."[55] Actually, much more could be said in describing the eight subtests. The brief descriptions given above are only meant to provide some idea of the abilities measured by the DAT.

Administration

The directions for the administration of the DAT are specified clearly in the manual. Specific directions are given for use with various answer sheets. The authors clearly specify the importance of planning for correct administration. They suggest that the staff go through a brief in-service training program prior to administering the test.

All the subtests are timed with limits as follows:

Booklet I	
Verbal reasoning	30 minutes
Numerical ability	30 minutes
Abstract reasoning	25 minutes
Clerical speed and accuracy	
Part I	3 minutes
Part II	3 minutes
	91 minutes
Booklet II	
Mechanical reasoning	30 minutes
Space relations	25 minutes
Language usage	
I Spelling	10 minutes
II Grammar	25 minutes
	90 minutes

[55]*DAT manual.* (4th ed.) New York: The Psychological Corporation, 1966, pp. 1-9.

Although all tests are timed, only the clerical speed and accuracy test is supposedly speeded. The manual suggests three alternative testing schedules (using two, four, or six sessions), so that the schools have some flexibility and can choose whichever schedule best fits their particular needs.

Scoring

Scoring may be done either by hand or machine using any of four types of answer sheets: IBM 805 and 1230 Answer Sheets, Digitek Answer Sheets, and MRC Answer Sheets.

Types of Scores

Percentile ranks and stanines can be obtained for the eight subtests and for the combined raw scores on the verbal reasoning and numerical ability tests. Only 23 designated percentile values (99, 97, 95, 90, 85, 80, 75, . . . 50, . . . 10, 5, 3, 1) are reported. "This method was chosen to avoid the appearance of exaggerated precision."[56] It is true that a more gross measure avoids the appearance of precision, and also fewer people are thus misclassified. The problem is that every misclassification is more serious. Under the method used on the DAT, there are people who, if they had scored only one raw score point higher, would have increased their reported percentile rank five points. There are certainly no psychometric reasons for regrouping people into 23 categories somewhat arbitrarily when they have already been more precisely differentiated.

Norming

The norm group includes more than 50,000 students from 195 schools (95 communities, 43 states). The term national norms is, indeed, appropriate. The norms are separate by sex and grade level (8–12). The testing of the normative sample was done in the fall. However, the authors also provide spring (second semester) norms for grades 8–11. These spring norms were obtained by interpolating between the fall norms of successive grades. The accuracy of these interpolated norms is debatable. It would be better to administer the test in the fall and to thus avoid having to use the spring norms.

Reliability

Split-half reliability coefficients computed separately for each sex and each grade are reported for both Forms L and M for all subtests except the clerical speed and accuracy subtest. Because this subtest is speeded (the others, remember, are timed but supposedly unspeeded), an alternate form reliability is reported. All coefficients for each grade were converted to Fisher's Z's prior to computing the means. These mean reliability coeffi-

[56]*DAT manual*, p. 3-1.

cients for the separate subtests range from .87 to .94 for boys and from .79 to .95 for girls. For both boys and girls, the mechanical reasoning subtest was the least reliable.

For each grade, standard errors of measurement (S_e's) were computed on each subtest separately for boys and girls. They ranged from about 2.3 to 5.5 raw score points. Separate S_e's were not computed for different ability levels within a grade.

The manual also reports a study on the long-term stability of the tests. The correlations between grade 9 and grade 12 scores range from .60 to .86. Mechanical reasoning and clerical speed and accuracy are the least stable subtests. Verbal reasoning is the most stable.

The reliability information on this instrument compares favorably with other multifactor aptitude batteries. Considering the length of the subtests, the obtained reliability estimates are, indeed, quite high. Because the subtests are supposedly measures of different aptitudes, their intercorrelations are more relevant to determining validity rather than reliability and will be discussed under that section.

Validity

Probably no test reports more validity information than the manual for the DAT. Three chapters within the manual are devoted to what could be classified as validity information: Chapter 5, "Validity"; Chapter 7, "Principles of Differential Measurement"; and Chapter 8, "Correlation with Other Tests." Although both Chapters 5 and 8 deal with what we have classified as criterion-related validity, the authors of the manual do differentiate between the studies showing validity evidence collected after the testing (predictive validity covered in Chapter 6) and validity evidence obtained concurrently (concurrent validity reported in Chapter 8).

Chapter 5, itself only a summary of research studies on the predictive validity of the DAT, is 59 pages long and contains 41 tables and 8 figures. The reported studies in this chapter are classified under three major headings: "Prediction of Course Grades," "Prediction of Achievement Test Results," and "Prediction of Vocational and Educational Success." The authors point out:

> The large amount of data presented in this manual may be confusing to test users who are accustomed to seeing a single validity coefficient for a test and accepting it as applicable to all situations. The more sophisticated test users, who understand that validity must differ as the course and the pupils differ, will recognize that data at least as plentiful as these are necessary for full understanding of the tests.[57]

[57]*DAT manual*, p. 5-28.

There is little doubt but that the voluminous amount of data coupled with the authors' position concerning the importance of studies within each school system should serve as an impetus for such tasks as building local expectancy tables and prediction equations. However, in spite of such urgings, many educators, unfortunately, are apt to feel that with all that validity information there is no reason for them to conduct their own investigations.

The research on the prediction of course grades is summarized according to subject areas. English grades are best predicted by VR + NA and by the GRAM and VR scores. Mathematics grades are best predicted by the VR + NA combination or by NA alone. VR, AR, and GRAM predict only slightly less well. Science grades can be best predicted by VR + NA, VR, NA, or GRAM subtests. Social studies grades can be predicted about equally well using VR + NA, VR, NA, or GRAM subtests. The four major subject-matter areas can all be predicted with a fair amount of success. Median correlations (across all studies) between the best subscores on the DAT and the criterion course grades range from the upper .40's to the low .60's. However, all four major subject-matter areas can be predicted successfully using the same score: VR + NA. Thus, the differential validity of the DAT in predicting course grades is not very well substantiated.

The prediction of achievement test results follows essentially the same pattern as the prediction of course grades. Again, the subscores on the DAT are fairly good predictors — they are not very adequate in differential predictions. The data showing the relationship between DAT scores and educational and occupational groups indicate the same thing.

The concurrent validity studies showing the correlation between the VR + NA score and tests of general intelligence reveal consistently high correlations. Their correlations, ranging mostly in the .70's and .80's, are as high as the correlations between most tests of general intelligence. Thus it certainly appears that the VR + NA score serves the same purpose as general intelligence test scores, and little would be gained by administering the DAT and a test of general intelligence in the same grade.

An interesting (and perhaps surprising to many) finding is the low correlations between the subscores on the DAT and the Kuder Preference Record scores. In general, interests and aptitudes are not highly correlated and, as the DAT manual points out, it is risky to base counseling on interest scores without having some information on a person's aptitude scores.

As mentioned in the introduction to this section on multifactor tests, one of the characteristics such tests should have if they are to be successful in differential prediction is low intercorrelations of the subtests. Table 2–2 shows the average (across grades) intercorrelations for Form L of the DAT. While the authors of the test feel that these data are favorable, most users would probably wish lower intercorrelations.

Table 2–2

Average (Mean) Intercorrelation Coefficients of the DAT by Sex for Form L[a]

Boys (N = 913)	VR	NA	AR	CSA	MR	SR	SPEL
Numerical Ability	.70						
Abstract Reasoning	.68	.66					
Clerical S and A	.19	.36	.33				
Mechanical Reasoning	.55	.50	.59	.16			
Space Relations	.58	.53	.63	.28	.62		
LU — I: Spelling	.59	.60	.41	.29	.27	.31	
LU — II: Grammar	.74	.66	.58	.21	.46	.46	.65
Girls (N = 930)	VR	NA	AR	CSA	MR	SR	SPEL
Numerical Ability	.72						
Abstract Reasoning	.68	.64					
Clerical S and A	.23	.29	.26				
Mechanical Reasoning	.59	.53	.59	.20			
Space Relations	.58	.58	.67	.20	.63		
LU — I: Spelling	.56	.52	.36	.27	.32	.28	
LU — II: Grammar	.75	.67	.57	.26	.52	.45	.64

[a]Reproduced by permission from *DAT manual*, p. 7-2. Copyright 1947, 1952, ©1959, 1963, 1966 for Fourth Edition Manual for the DAT. The Psychological Corporation, New York, N. Y. All rights reserved.

To summarize the validity of the DAT is almost an impossible task. The authors are certainly to be commended for their complete and accurate presentation of validity data. The subscores of the DAT predict, quite well, a variety of secondary-school course grades and standardized-achievement test results. They predict to a fair extent college course grades and job level within an occupational area. The evidence for differential validity is sketchy.

Format

The subtests are contained in two separate booklets: Booklet I contains the first four subtests and Booklet II contains the last four. The printing and pictures (figures) are all very clear and legible. The manual is complete and well written.

Interpretation and Use

The primary suggested use of multifactor aptitude tests has been for educational and vocational guidance. The DAT is no exception. The administration of the DAT in grade 8 or 9 can provide information that is relevant to the decisions a student must make concerning future educational plans. The general lack of differential predictive validity does not mean the test is useless. The subtests do predict a variety of criteria, and the descriptive value of the subtest scores is not to be underemphasized.

Many counselors are appreciative of the fact that students who would perform at a low level on a test of general intelligence may do well on some of the subtests of the DAT. Thus, the counselor can say something of a positive nature concerning the student's abilities, and the student leaves the counseling interview with a better self-concept than if one could only interpret the low score on a general intelligence test. The combined score (VR + NA) serves very well as a measure of general intelligence. A casebook prepared by The Psychological Corporation is of considerable value to counselors in interpreting the profile differences to students.[58]

The DAT is certainly a well-constructed and well-researched instrument. However, as other aptitude tests, it does lack the degree of differential predictive validity that multifactor aptitude tests should have.

SPECIAL APTITUDE TESTS

A special aptitude is usually defined as an individual's potential ability (or capacity to acquire proficiency) in a specified type of activity. Special aptitude tests were developed primarily for help in making vocational and educational selection decisions as well as for counseling. As compared with multifactor aptitude tests, they are probably more useful in selection (or placement) decisions by an institution, and generally less useful in personal counseling for individual decision making.

There are many kinds of aptitude tests that could be discussed in this section. Most textbooks relegate to this section tests that really are not aptitude tests but that are ability tests, such as for hearing and visual acuity. We will follow this same practice because these tests should be used in the public schools, and this is the most reasonable section under which to place them. Thus, this section will really contain a potpourri of special tests — the term aptitude will be used in a broad sense.

Because all readers will not be interested in the same areas, we will not spend a great deal of time on any particular test. The major purpose of this section will be to introduce the readers to the variety of special aptitude tests that exist. Those interested in a more thorough coverage of any test or area of testing should turn to the sources of information about tests discussed in Chapter I.

---

[58]George K. Bennett, Harold G. Seashore, and Alexander G. Wesman, *Counseling from profile — A casebook for the Differential Aptitude Tests*. New York: The Psychological Corporation, 1951.

TESTS OF VISION AND HEARING

Although seeing and hearing abilities are not aptitudes per se, both of these sensory functions are important in various educational and occupational endeavors. The ability to see or hear can be predictive in the sense that an uncorrected deficiency will adversely affect performance on many kinds of tasks. It is now routine to screen all school children for visual or auditory deficiencies. We will not discuss tests in these areas because ordinarily the testing is not performed by classroom teachers. However, all school personnel should be alert to the detection of such deficiencies even though screening may have occurred. The screening is often not done as thoroughly as it might be, and students often are not aware of their own sensory limitations. Examples of vision and hearing instruments are the Eames Eye Test, the Snellen Chart, the Auditory Discrimination Test, and the Maico Audiometers.

MECHANICAL APTITUDE TESTS

Various mechanical aptitude tests measure many different traits, and even the same test sometimes will measure more than one function. Such traits as spatial ability, perceptual speed, manual dexterity, and mechanical reasoning are all, at times, classified under the general rubric of mechanical aptitude. For this reason, mechanical aptitude tests have low intercorrelations and cannot be used interchangeably. Most schools do not routinely give to all students any tests of mechanical aptitude other than those related aspects measured by the DAT (space relations and mechanical reasoning). It would be advisable, however, to use other tests in counseling with students who are interested in vocations requiring one or more of these various aptitudes. The A.C.E.R. Mechanical Reasoning Test and the Revised Minnesota Paper Form Board Test are examples of other mechanical aptitude tests.

CLERICAL APTITUDE TESTS

Clerical aptitude, like mechanical aptitude, is not a unitary characteristic. There are many tasks that clerks must perform, and some of the more comprehensive clerical aptitude tests attempt to measure a variety of aptitudes. For example, aptitudes in verbal skills, alphabetical filing, grammar, and spelling are all important for success in clerical work. Again, as with mechanical aptitude, there are several subtests of the DAT related to clerical aptitude, and no other such tests are usually given to all the students in a public school. In the counseling of specific individuals other clerical aptitude tests such as the Beginner's Clerical Test or the Minnesota Clerical Test may well prove useful.

MUSICAL AND ARTISTIC APTITUDE TESTS

There are several musical and artistic aptitude tests available. These tests may be used by teachers in the specific areas or by counselors for certain individuals, but, in general, their use is not widespread. The Seashore Measures of Musical Talents, Revised Edition and the Wing Standardized Tests of Musical Intelligence are two of the most frequently used musical aptitude tests. The Meier Art Tests is one of the most frequently used art tests.

APTITUDE TESTS FOR SPECIFIC COURSES AND PROFESSIONS

Aptitude tests developed for particular school subjects such as algebra and foreign language have been used extensively in the past to help individual pupils with their curricular choice. However, in recent years this popularity has diminished. Research has shown that they do not significantly increase the predictive validity over what can be obtained by a general mental ability test, the relevant subscores on multifactor aptitude tests, or achievement test batteries. Because these tests are usually given in the schools, it may well be a waste of time and money to also administer special aptitude tests.

Many special aptitude tests have also been developed in recent years for use in various graduate and professional schools. These tests are designed to be of appropriate difficulty (harder than general aptitude tests for adults) and emphasize the abilities of importance to the particular profession. While these tests are usually slightly better predictors than general aptitude tests, their major advantage lies in their security. Many general aptitude tests could be obtained in advance by an enterprising person desirous of obtaining a high score and thereby admission into a professional school. The security of the professional tests rules out this sort of enterprising as a factor in admission decisions.

TESTS OF CREATIVITY

As already discussed, there is a wide diversity of opinions on the theory of intelligence. Some who subscribe to the general theory of intelligence suggest that creativity is an aspect of general intelligence and need not be measured separately. Others realize that, although tests of general ability are best able to predict future school success (that is, grades), this ability may be distinct from creativity. The majority of psychologists subscribe to the notion that creativity is something different from general intelligence; the problem is that it is hard to agree on constructual definitions of creativity, let alone operational definitions. Even if we could agree on an operational definition, it would be hard to indicate validity for the measure because of the lack of an adequate criterion measure. Does creativity imply a creative *process*, or a creative *product?* Or does the former lead to the latter? Is a creative person one who comes up with a variety of unique ideas, or is he one who has a variety of unique good ideas? That is, is there a quality criterion or simply a quantity criterion for judging creativity? If one is asked, as in the Torrance Tests of Creative Thinking, to name as many uses of a cardboard box as one can think of, how should the results be scored? To be sure, Torrance has created a scoring scheme, but it is doubtful if all would agree with it. As has been pointed out, the distinction between creative and asinine ideas is often hard to make. Most people feel that the production of a large number of unworkable ideas is of little use and to measure this type of creativity is a waste of time.

The authors of this book feel that more research on attempts to measure creativity and to investigate its correlates is warranted. There is now available enough evidence to suggest that creativity is something unique from the ability to perform well in an academic setting. There are many potential benefits available if one could effectively isolate and measure the construct of creativity. Creative people are important for an advancing society. If creativity can be further understood, if the identifying of creative people becomes possible, and if creativity can be taught in the schools, our society is sure to benefit.

At the present time there are some interesting creativity tests on the market such as the one by Torrance mentioned earlier. These, however, are only research instruments, and much more work is needed in the area before we can really feel comfortable with the results these tests give us. Fortunately, there is considerable investigation of this whole area, and, hopefully, psychologists will soon have available more adequate tests.[59]

USING APTITUDE TEST RESULTS

Considering all the types of aptitude tests discussed in this chapter (individual and group tests of general intelligence, multifactor aptitude tests, and special aptitude tests), it is surely a safe estimate to say that the average

---

[59]For further reading on this interesting topic the following books are highly recommended. (a) Jacob W. Getzels and Philip W. Jackson, *Creativity and intelligence.* New York: Wiley, 1962. (b) J. P. Guilford, *The nature of human intelligence.* New York: McGraw-Hill, 1967. (c) E. Paul Torrance, *Guiding creative talent.* Englewood Cliffs, N.J.: Prentice-Hall, 1962. (d) E. Paul Torrance, *Rewarding creative behavior.* Englewood Cliffs, N.J., Prentice-Hall, 1965. (e) Michael A. Wallach and Nathan Kogan, *Modes of thinking in young children.* New York: Holt, Rinehart and Winston, 1965. (f) Liam Hudson, *Contrary imaginations.* New York: Schorken Books, 1966.

child will be given the opportunity to take (or be subjected to) at least three aptitude tests before graduating from high school. A collegebound student may easily take five or more. How are these tests being used? Are they helpful or harmful?

Although aptitude testing is not as controversial a topic as personality testing, the public has been much concerned with the uses and possible misuses of these tests. This final section, devoted to the uses of aptitude tests, will also contain warnings against potential misuses.

Table 1-2 lists some various purposes of standardized tests under four headings: instructional, guidance, administrative, and research. The use of aptitude tests under each of these categories will be discussed in more detail here.

INSTRUCTIONAL USES

The level of aptitude test scores of students in a particular class should enable a teacher to evaluate the appropriateness of his class materials. One shouldn't teach the same kinds of material in the same fashion to two classes, one in which the students have a mean IQ of 85 and the other in which the students have a mean IQ of 120. Neither should two students within the same class who differ considerably in ability have similar assignments. Thus, knowledge of general aptitude test scores can enable a teacher to make better decisions about the kinds of class material presented to each student.

An argument that has occasionally been voiced against the use of aptitude tests for instructional purposes is that teachers will use low aptitude scores as an excuse for not attempting to teach the students ("The students can't learn anyway" attitude). Unfortunately, it is probably true that some teachers do this. Aptitude test scores should be used in helping teachers form realistic expectations of students; they should not be used to help teachers develop fatalistic expectations.

However, in agreeing that this potential danger of testing exists, we do not think it should be overemphasized. The teachers in slum schools who do not try their hardest because of preconceived ideas that their students can't learn have not obtained their ideas of student deficiency primarily from aptitude test scores. Such factors as the parents' educational level, socio-economic status, race, and occupation all help teachers form their opinions concerning a child's aptitude. Goslin,[60] a noted sociologist, in a comprehensive survey of teachers' opinions about tests, found that less than one-fourth of the teachers felt that abilities measured by intelligence tests are more important than other qualities for predicting school success. He also found

[60]David A. Goslin, *Teachers and testing*. New York: The Russell Sage Foundation, 1967.

that teachers tend to view intelligence test results as being more influenced by learning than by innate capacities. Whether or not test results actually are more influenced by learning, his findings would suggest that teachers are not likely to become fatalistic about a person's innate ability from intelligence test score information. Goslin summarizes the problems of teachers' opinions concerning the nature of intelligence as follows:

> Leaving for a moment the question of whether or not intelligence or aptitude tests actually measure innate capabilities to any substantial degree, we may conclude that there are likely to be certain advantages for the school system and for pupils in it if teachers are unwilling to accept the presupposition that a pupil's score reflects his inherent (and therefore, presumably, unchangeable) abilities. How one reconciles this proposition with the facts in the situation, namely, that intelligence tests do measure innate abilities to some degree, however, is less clear. It is probably unrealistic to consider seriously attempting systematically to dupe teachers into thinking that tests do not measure innate abilities or that there are no such things as genetically influenced individual differences in capacity for learning. . . . In attempting to hide the fact that individual differences in learning capacity do exist, such a policy may result in teachers and others using less appropriate measures . . . to make inferences about the intellectual capacities of children.[61]

Knowing that Denny has a measured IQ of 80, that his father is an unemployed alcoholic, and that his mother entertains men to pay for the groceries, the teacher may conclude (correctly or incorrectly) that Denny will have trouble in school learning. If the teacher accepts these factors in the spirit of a challenge and does his best — fine. If the teacher adopts a fatalistic attitude toward Denny — bad. However, there is no more compelling reason to blame the test for the improper attitude of the teacher than to blame his knowledge of all the other facts.

Let us make this point clear. Aptitude tests can help teachers develop realistic expectations for their students. While we, in no way, condone — in fact do condemn — teachers who develop fatalistic attitudes toward the learning abilities of their students, we do not think aptitude tests should be made the scapegoat. We admit this potential misuse of tests. There, however, is little evidence to suggest that teachers' attitudes toward the learning potential of their students are unduly influenced by test results. Teachers are probably more apt to be unduly influenced by other factors with much less predictive validity. One must remember, however, that if we use any kind of data (including aptitude tests) to label children, we need to take care

[61]Goslin, pp. 131–132.

not to misuse the labels. Labels must be treated as descriptions rather than as explanations. Too often a label is treated as an explanation.

Improvement in aptitude test scores should not be used in evaluating learning outcomes or teaching because these scores should be relatively unaffected by formal school learning. However, knowing something about the ability level of the students in a class or school can help the teachers determine whether the students are learning as much as is predicted from their ability level. While some people object to the term *underachiever* (for, really, it is just an overprediction) it is nonetheless helpful to know that a person is not performing as well as could be predicted on the basis of his ability scores. If a whole class or school is performing less well (say, for example, on a standardized achievement battery) than would be predicted from aptitude test scores, then this may be due to inadequate teaching.

GUIDANCE USES

Aptitude tests can be useful in vocational, educational, and personal counseling. Once the training necessary for entrance into the occupation has been completed, it is generally true that tests of general intelligence are not very predictive of vocational success. However, these test scores are still useful in counseling because the educational requirements of some vocations do require considerable general ability. Multifactor aptitude tests are often used in counseling to give students a better idea of their differential abilities. As discussed, the measurement of these differential abilities does not necessarily improve differential prediction, but it does lead to a fuller understanding of one's self.

With guidance, as with instructional purposes, there are some possible misuses of aptitude test scores. The problem of treating test scores as fatalistic predictors still exists. Counselors, teachers, in fact all school personnel should remember that their job, in part, is to attempt to upset negative predictions.

A related problem to educators becoming fatalistic is the development of a fatalistic attitude in the children. A popular topic of conversation these days is the importance of developing a good self-concept in the students. The Norman Vincent Peale approach is becoming the rage in some educational circles.[62] There is no doubt that students should be self-accepting and feel that others accept them also. If a counselor interprets a low test score so that the student feels unworthy, then that is, indeed, unfortunate. One of the advantages of a multifactor aptitude test is that a student usually performs at an acceptable level on some of the subtests, and these scores can and should serve as morale builders for the students.

[62]Norman V. Peale, *The power of positive thinking.* Englewood Cliffs, N.J.: Prentice-Hall, 1952.

As with other possible misuses of test results, we feel this problem of low aptitude scores resulting in poor self-concepts can be overemphasized. Just as test scores are not the major factors in forming teachers' opinions about the learning ability of children, so also low aptitude test scores are probably much less influential than other factors in contributing to an undesirable (inaccurately low) self-concept. Tests often seem to be blamed for educational problems that were not caused by the tests to begin with. To be sure, there is some relationship between what a person thinks he can achieve and what he will achieve. Nevertheless, it is a generally held position that counselors should help students obtain and accept an accurate self-concept, not an inaccurately high one. The interpretation of aptitude tests can be helpful in this endeavor.

ADMINISTRATIVE USES

There are many ways in which aptitude tests can be used by the administration. Some selection, classification, and placement decisions such as who should be admitted to kindergarten early, who should be placed in the enriched classes, who should be placed in the remedial classes, and who should be admitted to colleges are decisions that may be performed by counselors or school psychologists who may rightly not consider themselves as administrators. Nevertheless, these are administrative decisions.

As with almost any use of aptitude tests, there are accompanying potential misuses. Some persons charge that the major misuse of tests in administrative functions is that decisions made on the basis of test scores are often treated as if they were permanent, irreversible decisions. If a child is put into a remedial class in, say, grade 3 there is often too much a tendency on the part of the administration, having made a decision once, to forget about it. The child then gets lock-stepped into a curriculum.

Now, although we in no way support administrative inflexibility in the reconsideration of decisions, we should consider whether the use of test scores is really the causative factor of this inflexibility. We must admit that, in some cases, it is. Some people simply place far too much faith in test scores, and this unwarranted faith results in too much faith in the correctness of decisions — so they are made and then forgotten. However, not all, or not even most, inflexibility can be charged to test score misuse. Many of the decisions made would be incorrectly treated as permanent, even if there were no test score data on the students. It is worth noting that, if a decision must be made, it should be based on as much evidence as possible. Not to use test information in making decisions because of possible misuse is cowardly, foolish, and even unprofessional.

There are also some who argue against the use of aptitude tests for various decisions because they do not think the decision has to, or should, be made at all. For example, a sizeable group of educators are against ability grouping.[63] However, if a test is used to help implement a policy that is considered incorrect by some, there is no reason to blame the test. If there is a policy, right or wrong, to group on the basis of ability, it is not incorrect to use an aptitude test to help decide who should be placed in what group. If there is a policy, right or wrong, to limit college enrollment to those with some minimal level of scholastic aptitude, it is not incorrect to use aptitude test scores to help determine who should be admitted to college. Far too often the cry of test misuse is raised because the lamenter is against the policy that the correct use of test scores helps implement, rather than because the test is not being correctly used under the existing policy.

The uses of aptitude test results for public relations and for providing information for outside agencies do have some very real potential pitfalls. Occasionally press releases are made concerning how a school compares with others in the average ability of its students. While this sort of public relations may momentarily "feather the cap" of some school official, the chances of the public understanding the release are dim indeed, and one is hard put to verbalize any real advantages of this sort of public release of information.

The issue of whether or not schools should provide aptitude test score information to outside agencies is a cloudy one. All would agree that if aptitude test score information is provided to outside agencies, the provider has a moral obligation to make sure that the recipient of the information understands it and can interpret it correctly. There appears to be fairly general concensus that this means one should not ordinarily give out information in the form of a specific IQ score. Thus, there is some general agreement as to how test score information should be given out if it is released. There is much less agreement on whether test score information — in whatever form — should be released at all. The question is whether such information is to be treated as confidential. If so, then it should not be released without a student's permission. But does the consent have to be explicit, or can it be implied? For example, if a student applies for a job that requires security clearance, is the application to be interpreted as implied consent for the release of school records? These questions can not all be discussed in great detail in this book. The safest procedure (both morally and legally), however, is not to release test information to any outside agency without the explicit consent of the student and/or his parents.

Another possible use of aptitude tests is for relevant supplementary information in curriculum planning and evaluation. An idea of the general

---

[63]Because this book is not devoted to a discussion of the various methods of providing for individual differences in the schools, we will not enter that debate.

ability level of the school should help educators decide, for example, how much relative emphasis to place on college preparatory curricula.

Finally, some administrators feel that aptitude tests can be useful in deciding which teachers to hire or promote. While there is obviously a relationship between aptitude test scores and the obtaining of a teacher's certificate, there is little known evidence suggesting a relationship between aptitude test scores and on-the-job performance for certified teachers. Thus, hiring or promoting on this basis is of no merit.

RESEARCH USES

Aptitude test scores can be used in many, many ways in research. Ordinarily the scores are used as independent variables in a research design, although some research — such as that investigating the environmental effects on intelligence — treats the scores as dependent variables. Because this book is not designed for the researcher, we will preclude further discussion of this topic.

CHAPTER SUMMARY

Schools should assist each pupil to achieve the maximum of which he is capable. To evaluate the degree to which this is being accomplished requires both measures of achievement and measures of intellect or aptitude. In this chapter we have discussed the latter type of measure. Many problems exist in aptitude measurement. The definitions, structure, development, and stability of intellect are all unsettled issues in psychology. Theories regarding the structure of intelligence have ranged from the idea of a general factor of intelligence to the conceptualization of many specific factors. These various theories have resulted in many different kinds of tests, classified as tests of general intelligence, multifactor aptitude tests, and special aptitude tests.

The development of intelligence has received much research attention in the last 50 years. The nature-nurture issue is still being debated, but there seems to be little doubt but that both heredity and environment affect intelligence test scores. The manner in which these two interact is now considered to be a more relevant research question than attempting to decide what proportion of intelligence is due to each.

The stability of intelligence is related at least in part to the nature-nurture issue. If environment influences test scores, then, as a person's environment changes, so might his intelligence. Other factors such as the unreliability of tests and the changes in test content from one age level to the next also contribute to some instability. Research findings suggest in general that intelligence measures are not very stable in early childhood, but by the age of six or so they become quite stable. It takes considerable environmental change to drastically influence intelligence test scores of older youth and adults.

The majority of aptitude tests given in the public school fall under the classification of either general intelligence tests or multifactor aptitude tests. Tests of general intelligence can be administered either individually or in groups. The most popular individual intelligence tests are the Stanford Binet and the Wechsler instruments. Specialized training is required in order to correctly administer these tests. Individual tests are typically more reliable and can also be better used with individuals who, for motivational or other reasons, do not perform accurately on group tests. Also, more clinical information can be obtained from individual tests.

Group tests are much cheaper to administer than individual tests, and teachers are generally qualified to administer such instruments. Brief reviews were made of the California Test of Mental Maturity and the School and College Ability Tests: Series II. A thorough review of the Lorge-Thorndike Intelligence Tests was included in this chapter so that the reader could obtain a general idea of the composition of these tests as well as could learn, through example, how to thoroughly review such instruments. Some attempts have been made in the past to build culture fair intelligence tests. These results have largely failed if we define *culture fairness* as the equality of mean scores for various subcultures. Even if culture fair tests could be devised, the usefulness of such measures is open to question. Most psychometrists would suggest that the intentional masking of cultural differences would in general make tests less predictive.

Multifactor aptitude tests are used by the majority of school systems in either eighth or ninth grade. The original intent of multifactor tests was to give part scores that had low intercorrelations with each other and that could be used to predict differentially various criteria. Most multifactor tests do contain part scores with low intercorrelations. They have not been very successful in differential prediction. This has probably been due, in part, to the multidimensionality of the criteria measures. In spite of their lack of differential predictability, multifactor aptitude tests have remained a popular tool of the counselors to assist students in understanding themselves better. A thorough review of the Differential Aptitude Test was included to illustrate the general format and types of items of multiple aptitude tests.

Various kinds of special aptitude tests were mentioned, but no reviews of these tests were made because the tests that could be listed in this section would be of little interest to the majority of the readers.

There are many ways in which aptitude test results can be appropriately used by teachers, counselors, and administrators to help in selection, placement, and classification. Aptitude test results can also be misused. An example of a potential misuse would be to become fatalistic concerning a student's chances of success on the basis of an aptitude test score. In general we feel that the negative attitude the public correctly displays toward test misuse has been overgeneralized to the tests themselves. Tests have inadequu cies and limited use. Although the inadequacies should be alleviated as much as possible, limitations will always exist.

POINTS TO PONDER

1. Which theory of intelligence do you subscribe to? What are the advantages and limitations of accepting this theory?

2. Project Headstart implicitly makes an assumption that environment plays a significant role in intellectual development. If research shows that these headstart programs are ineffective, must we conclude the assumption is incorrect?

3. Can you write an item that you would defend as being a measure of aptitude and not a measure of achievement?

4. A married couple wishes to adopt an infant. They request assurance that the infant possess a normal intelligence. What should the social worker tell this couple?

5. List five specific situations where group intelligence tests would be more appropriate than individual intelligence tests. Do the same for the converse situation.

6. Assume two randomly chosen groups were given the Stanford-Binet at age four. One group (Group A) of students received nursery school instruction that included tasks similar to those asked on the Stanford-Binet. The other group (Group B) received no such instruction. Upon retesting at age five, Group A performs significantly better. Does this tell us anything about the stability of intelligence, the effects of environment on intelligence, or the validity of the test?

7. Why do you think there are no multifactor aptitude tests published for the early elementary grades?

8. What are the advantages and limitations of using a multifactor aptitude test rather than a set of special aptitude tests covering the same constructs?

9. What are the instructional advantages (if any) of being able to correctly identify highly creative children?

10. Given the question "What can books be used for?" a student responds, "To build fires." Is this a creative answer? Support your contention.

chapter

standardized
achievement tests

What is an achievement test? How do standardized achievement tests differ from teacher-made achievement tests? Are there achievement tests for all subject matter areas? Will the Stanford Achievement Test be valid for my purpose? What use can be made of achievement test results? What are some of the factors that must be considered in the selection of a standardized achievement test? These are some of the questions that the classroom teacher, counselor, and school administrator can be expected to ask. This chapter presents information that will assist the test user to answer these and other questions.

HISTORICAL DEVELOPMENT
OF ACHIEVEMENT TESTS

Pupils always have been and are being evaluated by their teachers, although the methods of evaluation — personal observations, oral quizzes, subjective evaluations or feelings, and written answers — differ widely from teacher to teacher and from course to course. Some teachers prefer the oral quiz, others the written test, and still others prefer a combination of the oral-written quiz. There are some teachers who prefer to use only objective evidence while there are other teachers who feel that both objective and subjective evaluation devices should be employed to assess the child's growth in, or status of, knowledge. For example, an assessment of a pupil's knowledge of arithmetic skills may be made by either asking the pupil orally "What is the sum of 2 + 2?" or by asking him the same question on a paper-and-pencil test. The teacher can use the oral approach in his daily instruction and the written item for the quiz or examination used at the end of the unit or term. Regardless of the method of examination employed, teachers are constantly concerned with evaluating their pupils' knowledge and progress. The basic fault of many of our evaluation devices lies in their lack of scientific rigor. The chance method of evaluating pupil progress was prevalent until 1845, the year of the Boston Survey. This survey, instigated by Horace Mann, was the first instance in which the same written examination was given to a sample of all pupils at the same school level, and where the papers were scored under uniform conditions.[1] Although the findings confirmed Mann's contention that the public schools were not as good as claimed, it would appear that the findings did not serve as a stimulus to more objective and refined evaluation techniques in American public schools.

In 1864, Reverend George Fisher,[2] an English schoolmaster, constructed the first objective educational test. We might, therefore, say that although Mann raised the issue of objective testing in 1845, it was not until 1864 that the first objective tests of achievement were constructed. Fisher devised a series of tests to measure accomplishment in spelling, grammar, handwriting, composition, mathematics, and other school subjects. He referred to his battery of tests as a Scale Book. In his Scale Book, various subscores and a total score could be obtained, and norms were provided so that inter- and intrapupil strengths and weaknesses could be plotted. Hence, not only did Fisher attempt to refine scoring procedures so that they would be more objective, but also he provided the beginning of what we now recognize as the pupil profile.

The first objective educational or achievement test in the United States was developed by Rice in 1895, almost 50 years after the Boston Survey. Rice's spelling test (consisting of 50 spelling words) was administered to over 16,000 pupils in grades 4 to 8. Because of the unexpectedly wide variation in results, Rice developed two more spelling tests so that he could be certain that the findings were the result of real differences in spelling ability rather than the result of the particular sample of words used. Although Rice is best known for his spelling test, he also developed tests in arithmetic and language. His major contribution to what is now called standardized

---

[1]Uniform scoring conditions as described by Mann are not analogous to what is now referred to as objective scoring.

[2]E. B. Chadwick, Statistics of educational results. *The Museum, A Quarterly Magazine of Education, Literature, and Science*, 1864, *3*, 480–484.

achievement tests lay in his objective and scientific approach to the assessment of pupil knowledge. In 1908, Stone published his arithmetic reasoning test. In 1909, Thorndike published a standardized achievement scale, the Scale for Handwriting of Children. In addition to producing numerous scales and tests, Thorndike taught many students who were later to make their contribution to the field of measurement and achievement testing.

Beginning in 1910, numerous studies indicated the unreliability of teachers' grading. In 1912 and 1913, Starch and Elliott had a group of teachers independently grade an English essay, a geometry paper, and a history paper. They found considerable variation in grades assigned (even with the geometry paper, which we would assume to be more amenable to objective evaluation).[3] In 1928, Falls had 100 English teachers grade an essay written by a high school senior (who, incidentally, wrote for a newspaper). The teachers were required to assign both a numerical grade to the essay as well as indicate the grade level of the student. Once again, as in Starch and Elliott's study, there was marked variation in both the numerical grades assigned and the estimated grade level of the writer. The grades varied from 60 to 98 percent and the grade level from 5 to 15.[4] (That this unreliability in teacher grading is still perceived as a problem is attested to by the fact that in some of our external, national testing programs, training sessions are conducted for the graders. In addition, papers are frequently recirculated among the graders to check on the reliability of their grading.) These kinds of studies led to the search for, and development of, more objective procedures for testing and grading students. Up to this time, with the exception of the Scale Book, all achievement tests were single tests.

In the early 1920s and 1930s an important development was the preparation of test batteries. In 1923, the first standardized survey battery, the Stanford Achievement Test, was published.[5] It was designed primarily for use at the elementary level. In 1925, the Iowa High School Content Examination, the first standardized survey battery for high school, was published. Since that time, hundreds of different standardized achievement tests (single subject-matter tests, test batteries, diagnostic and prognostic tests) have been developed. Since the 1940s, there has been a movement in test construction, from the specialized, single, subject-matter test to testing in broad content areas such as the humanities and natural sciences. In addition, more and more emphasis is now being placed upon the evaluation of work-study skills rather than focusing upon factual knowledge per se.

---

[3]Daniel Starch and Edward C. Elliott, Reliability of grading high school work in English. *Sch. Rev.*, 1912, *20*, 442–457. See also *Sch. Rev.* 1913, *21*, 254–259; and 676–681 for articles dealing with their mathematics and history studies, respectively.

[4]James D. Falls, Research in secondary education. *Kentucky sch. J.* 1928, *6*, 42–46.

[5]A survey test measures general achievement in a given subject or area. A survey battery consists of a group of survey tests (different content areas) standardized on the same population.

Much impetus was given to the testing movement in general and to standardized tests in particular by three noteworthy studies: (1) the Eight-Year Study of the Progressive Education Association[6] in 1942, (2) the College Entrance Examination Board[7] long-range study initiated in 1952, and (3) the Cooperative Study of Evaluation in General Education[8] completed in 1954. These three studies showed that the major development in standardized achievement testing in the 1940s and 1950s were (1) an increased use of standardized achievement tests in our public schools, (2) an emphasis on critical thinking, application of knowledge, synthesis, and evaluation because our tests must keep up with the changing public school curriculum, and (3) the refinement of techniques used to construct and standardize achievement tests.

Historically, there is much similarity in the development of standardized tests, whether they be individual intelligence tests, aptitude, or achievement tests, because they all received their major impetus from a source other than the concern of the individual pupil per se. When Binet developed his first scale, he was concerned with devising a means of removing dull pupils from the overcrowded schools in Paris rather than with constructing an instrument specifically designed to help the classroom teacher relate certain intellectal qualities to the learning process. Horace Mann really did not intend to devise an objective measure of pupil accomplishment. His criticisms of the public schools in Massachusetts infuriated a group of teachers and lay citizens in Boston. This group were intent in resisting and refuting Mann's opinions. In the end, as a solution to the problem, it was agreed to prepare written examination questions in history, geography, vocabulary, science, arithmetic, astronomy, and grammar. Hence, the impetus to objective measurement appears to have been mitigated by political and personal considerations rather than by a concern for the improvement of instruction or the subjectivity of evaluation practices in the Boston schools.

DIFFERENCES BETWEEN STANDARDIZED AND TEACHER-MADE ACHIEVEMENT TESTS

Any test that has a representative sampling of the course content (that is, possesses content validity) and that is designed to measure the extent of

[6]William M. Aikin, *The story of the eight-year study with conclusions and recommendations.* New York: Harper & Row, 1942.

[7]Henry S. Dyer and William E. Coffman, The tests of developed abilities. *Coll. bd. Rev.* 1957, No. 31, 5–10. These tests, which were designed to reflect the current emphasis on intellectual skills, are not commonly used in our school testing programs. Nevertheless, their rationale has guided the development of present-day tests so that our tests now measure the higher mental processes as well as factual knowledge.

[8]Paul L. Dressel and Lewis B. Mayhew, *General education: Explorations in evaluation.* Washington, D.C.: American Council on Education, 1954.

present knowledge is an achievement test, regardless of whether this test was constructed by the classroom teacher or by professional test makers. The major (but not the only) distinction between the standardized achievement test and the teacher-made test is that in a standardized achievement test, the systematic sampling of performance (that is, the pupil's score) has been obtained under prescribed directions of administration. They also differ markedly in terms of their sampling of content, construction, norms, and purpose and use.

SAMPLING OF CONTENT

Standardized achievement tests normally cover much more material (that is, they have a wider range of coverage, although they need not have more items) than teacher-made tests because they are designed to assess either one year's learning or more than one year's learning. Teacher-made tests usually cover a single unit of work, or that of a term. Standardized tests, in contrast to teacher-made tests, may not as readily reflect curricular changes, although test publishers attempt to "keep up with the times."[9]

The decision of whether to administer a commercially published standardized test or a teacher-made test is based, to a large degree, on the particular objectives to be measured. Standardized tests are constructed to measure generally accepted goals rather than specific or particular instructional objectives. Teacher-made tests will usually measure more adequately the degree to which the objectives of a particular course for a particular teacher have been met. For example, let us assume a teacher of 11th-grade history feels that his pupils should have an awareness of social conditions prior to the French Revolution. If this area is atypical to the conventional curriculum in this course, it should be readily evident that the teacher-made test would be more valid than the best standardized test that did not concern itself with this objective. In other words, the test user must ask himself, "How valid is this test for my objectives?"

CONSTRUCTION

Another difference between standardized achievement tests and teacher-made achievement tests is in the relative amount of time, money, effort, and resources that are available to commercial test publishers. The following example of how a standardized achievement test is constructed by test publishers may indicate why the teacher-made test is seldom as well prepared as the standardized test.

First, the test publisher arranges a meeting of curriculum specialists and subject matter specialists. After a thorough study and analysis of syllabi,

[9]This is less of a problem with single subject-matter tests than with survey batteries. It is easier (and often less expensive) to revise and renorm a single test than a survey battery.

Table 3–1

Distribution of Subject Matter as Related to Objectives in Grade 11 American History

Subject Matter / Objectives	Colonial Period	Revolutionary and Constitutional Period	The Westward Movement	Eve of the Civil War	The War between the States	Total
Knowledge[a]	4	6	2	4	4	20
Understanding	4	8	4	2	6	24
Application	2	6	6	4	8	26
Total	10	20	12	10	18	70

[a]If desired, the vertical axis could be more finely subdivided to represent the areas of knowledge, comprehension, application, analysis, synthesis, and evaluation as specified in Benjamin S. Bloom and others, *Taxonomy of educational objectives: The classification of educational goals, Handbook I: Cognitive domain.* New York: McKay, 1956. Often though, it is difficult to categorize an item in this specific classification scheme, and the more general one represented above is usually just as useful.

textbooks, and programs throughout the country, a list of objectives is prepared — what information the student should have, what principles he should understand, and what skills he should possess. These decisions concerning objectives to be sampled by the test are then reduced to a test outline that guides the test maker in constructing the test. One frequently used device is a two-dimensional grid as shown in Table 3–1. The horizontal entries represent divisions of subject matter, and the vertical entries represent classifications of objectives that are deemed important.

In Table 3–1, the cells of the chart indicate the planned number of test questions. These values represent the number of questions to be prepared under each of the headings (content sampling) and have been determined on the basis of the judgments of the various experts involved in the planning and construction of the test. Then, with the assistance of classroom teachers and subject matter experts, a professional team of test writers prepares the items according to the specification outlined in the grid.[10] After careful review and editing, the try-out or experimental items are ready to be arranged in a test booklet. Then, the general instructions (and specific instructions, if there are subparts) to both administrators and pupils and the try-out tests are given to a sample of students for whom the test is designed.

[10]The publisher's inclusion of such a grid in the test manual would aid the user immeasurably in ascertaining whether the test has content validity for him. Unfortunately, few publishers do so.

After the answer sheets have been scored, an item analysis[11] is made to remove the poor items. In addition, comments from test administrators are noted insofar as they pertain to timing and clarity of instructions for both administrator and pupils. Then, further editing is performed on the basis of the item analysis (or more items are written if too many need to be discarded and the content validity is rechecked) and the test is then ready to be standardized.[12] After a representative sample of pupils has been selected, the refined test is administered and scored. Reliability and criterion-related validity (if the test is to be predictive) evidence is obtained and norms are prepared for the standardization sample.

This brief description should demonstrate how much time, effort, and expense go into the preparation of a standardized achievement test. Without minimizing the enthusiasm, interest, and dedication of the classroom teacher in constructing his own tests, we may say the teacher-made test seldom compares in technical aspects with a commercially made standardized test. The teacher alone constructs his test; the standardized test is constructed by test specialists in cooperation with experts in the subject matter area, curriculum specialists, and statisticians. The teacher has a limited amount of time that can be devoted to test construction; standardized test makers can spend as much as two or three years on the preparation of their test. The teacher has little, if any, opportunity to examine his items in terms of difficulty and discrimination;[13] commercial test publishers have recourse to statistical tools in order to eliminate or to suggest ways to rewrite the poor items. The teacher, because he is unable to try out his test beforehand, does not have the opportunity to (1) clarify ambiguous directions before they occur, and/or (2) alter the speededness of the test by either increasing or decreasing the number of items; the commercial test publisher tries out his items in experimental or preliminary editions and is able to ascertain how well the test and the items function. On the whole then, it should be readily evident that commercial standardized achievement tests are superior in terms of technical features to teacher-made achievement tests. This does not imply that teacher-made achievement tests cannot be technically as sound as commercial tests. They can be, but,

---

[11] Item analysis is the procedure used to compute the difficulty and discriminating power of each of the items on a test. See *Short-cut statistics for teacher-made tests.* Princeton, N.J.: Educational Testing Service, Advisory Bulletin No. 5, 1964, for a simple treatment (this and other bulletins are available gratis from the publisher).

[12] It has commonly been assumed that reworking or rewriting test items on the basis of item analysis will improve the test. However, differential discarding of items could result in a biased test (such that the content validity is actually lowered). See Richard Cox, An empirical investigation of the effect of item selection techniques on achievement test construction. Unpublished doctoral dissertation, Michigan State University, 1964.

[13] An item that is either too easy or too difficult is generally a poor item. In addition, if the better pupils fail to answer an item correctly while the poorer or less able pupils obtain the correct answer, this item is also a weak or poor item.

because of the time, money, effort, and technical skill involved in preparing a good test, they normally are not.

The classroom teacher should not develop an inferiority complex because of the preceding remarks. He should recognize that he has been trained to be a teacher and not a test maker. Horst made the following comment regarding the teacher as a professional test maker:

> For some years considerable emphasis has been placed on the importance of teachers learning to develop objective measures of achievement based on subject matter. . . . The underpaid and overworked classroom teacher should not be expected to be a specialist in the development of measuring instruments.[14]

NORMS

Another feature distinguishing standardized from teacher-made achievement tests is that all standardized tests contain norms of one type or another: sex, rural-urban, grade, age, type of school (public, private, parochial). These types of norms are referred to as national norms. Their value is dependent upon the manner in which they have been constructed. With national norms, the classroom teacher, school psychologist, counselor, or others concerned with the pupil's education will be in a position to make numerous comparisons of the performance of individual pupils, classes, grades, schools, and school districts with the academic progress of pupils throughout the country. Naturally, the kinds of comparisons that can be made will depend upon the type of norms furnished by the test publisher. Although teacher-made tests can have norms, they usually do not.[15]

PURPOSES AND USE

Standardized achievement tests, especially survey batteries, by the nature of their construction have a broad sampling of content, and they may be too general in scope to meet the specific educational objectives of a particular school or teacher. Teacher-made achievement tests, on the other hand, will usually have narrow content sampling (although what is sampled is covered thoroughly)—especially those tests prepared for just a single unit of material or for material covered in a single semester. This does not imply that the standardized achievement test is superior to the teacher-made achievement

[14]Paul Horst. *Psychological measurement and prediction.* Belmont, Calif.: Wadsworth, 1966, p. 10.

[15]Local norms can be prepared for every test, teacher-made or standardized, used by the classroom teacher. However, with only 25 to 40 pupils, it is unlikely that separate age, sex, or geographical norms (even if they could be made) would be too meaningful. The variety of norms provided by the commercial test publisher permits many different kinds of comparisons to be made. Teacher-made norms have a somewhat restricted use.

test. Because of the emphasis placed upon the various course objectives, the standardized achievement test may be superior to the teacher-made test in one instance and not in another. Both standardized and teacher-made achievement tests serve a common function: the assessment of the pupil's knowledge and skills at a particular time. However, because standardized and teacher-made achievement tests often differ in scope and content (as well as the normative data provided), they also differ in their uses. It is usually agreed that the teacher-made achievement test will assess specific objectives more satisfactorily than does the standardized achievement test. It should be noted, however, that all educational decisions — assignment of course grades, vocational and educational guidance, promotion, placement, teacher evaluation, instruction, and research, to mention just a few — should be based on as much empirical data as possible. Because the standardized and teacher-made achievement tests serve different purposes, school personnel should consider the supplemental value of standardized achievement test scores to teacher-made test scores and teacher observations and judgments, rather than argue that one measurement device is is better than the other.

To compare the pupils in one school with those in another school, a standardized achievement test will be appropriate. To determine whether Johnny has learned his addition skills in Miss Jones' third grade may be better accomplished by using a teacher-made test. Thus, the functions or uses of the two kinds of achievement tests vary. We will consider the use of standardized achievement tests further in the concluding section of this chapter.

CLASSIFICATION OF STANDARDIZED ACHIEVEMENT TESTS

Because certain skills or knowledge may be stressed more at one age (or grade) level than another, we find different kinds of standardized achievement tests: diagnostic tests that are designed to isolate specific strengths and weaknesses of the individual in some particular field of knowledge; single subject-matter achievement tests that are concerned with measuring the pupil's educational accomplishments in a single content area; and survey batteries that consist of a group of tests in different content areas standardized on the same population so that the results of the various components may be meaningfully compared.[16]

These three types of standardized achievement tests differ in their purposes, coverage, and construction. They differ primarily because they

---

[16]Publishers of a number of achievement test survey batteries make the individual tests available in separate test booklets for administration as single subject-matter tests.

are designed to measure different aspects or segments of the pupil's knowledge.[17]

PURPOSES AND USE

All standardized achievement tests are designed to assess pupils' knowledge and skills at a particular point in time. This is true for diagnostic tests, single subject-matter tests, or survey batteries. If we are interested in learning what Mary's specific strengths or weaknesses are, in, say, reading or spelling, we would use a diagnostic test.[18] If we are interested in making a somewhat thorough evaluation of Mary's achievement in spelling, we should use a standardized spelling test rather than the spelling subtest of a survey battery, because the survey battery subtest will ordinarily be shorter, thereby limiting its coverage. If we are interested in learning whether Mary is a better speller than she is a reader, we should use a standardized survey battery where the total test has been standardized on the same sample.[19]

For guidance purposes, it may be advisable to use the results of both a survey battery (which will indicate the relative strengths and weaknesses in many different subject-matter fields) and a single subject matter test that gives more thorough information in a particular area. For example, pupils can initially be given a survey battery as a preliminary screening device. Then, certain pupils can be identified for more thorough investigation. These atypical pupils might then be given a single subject-matter and/or diagnostic test in the area of suspected weakness. The use of such a sequential testing (that is, using the survey battery for an initial screening and a single survey test and/or a diagnostic test for only a few individuals) is an economical approach. Sequential testing can aid the classroom teacher or counselor immeasurably in obtaining relevant data to assist school personnel in providing optimal learning conditions. In the end everyone can benefit — pupils, teachers, and counselors.

COVERAGE AND CONSTRUCTION

Standardized achievement test batteries attempt to measure pupils' knowledge in many diverse areas; single subject-matter tests are restricted to only a single area of knowledge such as grade 11 physics or grade 4 spelling or

[17]Standardized achievement tests can also be classified in terms of their grade or age level.

[18]The teacher must interpret the results of a diagnostic test cautiously. The test does not provide an absolute and irrevocable explanation for the problem (deficiency or weakness) but only offers some suggestions. The psychometric quality of the data provided in these tests is typically inadequate.

[19]If different subject-matter tests have norms based upon different samples, direct comparisons cannot be made because the samples might not be equivalent.

grade 6 language arts. Both types of tests measure the important skills, knowledge, and course objectives. Normally, single subject-matter tests are a little more thorough in terms of their coverage. For example, if a spelling test requires one hour and the spelling subtest of a battery requires 40 minutes, there is more opportunity for the single test to have more items and to thereby increase the content sampling.

Although the survey battery is more convenient to administer than an equal number of single tests and although, for the most part, it is fairly valid for the average classroom teacher, it does suffer from the possibility that some of the subtests might lack the degree of validity desired (because the subtests contain a more limited sampling of tasks). The general consensus, however, is that, despite the more limited sampling of tasks, survey batteries are preferred over a combination of many single subject-matter tests. This is so because the survey battery (1) gives a fairly reliable index of a pupil's relative strengths and weaknesses once it has been standardized on the same population, whereas this is seldom the case for single subject-matter tests (even those prepared by the same publisher); (2) is more efficient time-wise; and (3) is usually more economical. Diagnostic tests may differ markedly from the survey battery or single subject-matter test, depending upon the purposes they are to serve. If we recall that diagnostic tests are designed primarily to assist the teacher in locating or attempting to isolate the genesis of some deficiency, it is not unexpected that we find the diagnostic test to have a thorough coverage of a limited area. For example, both a standardized achievement test of arithmetic skills and/or the arithmetic subtest of a survey battery are concerned with measuring general goals and objectives of the arithmetic curriculum. Hence, both arithmetic tests contain a variety of items on many different arithmetic topics. A diagnostic test, however, may be restrictive in the sense that it is only concerned with one or two aspects of arithmetic such as addition and subtraction. In addition, the diagnostic test will be more concerned with measuring the components that are felt to be of importance in developing knowledge in a complex skill.

There is no appreciable difference among the various types of achievement tests in the technical and mechanical factors involved in their preparation. As mentioned earlier, the major difference among survey batteries, single subject-matter tests, and diagnostic tests is in their purpose. Because they differ in purpose, it follows that they will also differ in the range of material covered. In many instances, it is not possible to identify the type of test an item comes from on the basis of the item format. That is, a test item such as "What percent of 36 is 9?" could conceivably be found in either a survey, single subject-matter, or diagnostic test. About the only way in which one can attempt to distinguish among the various types of achievement tests is to make a study of the breadth or intensity of their coverage.

The development of a good diagnostic test is predicated upon two major assumptions: (1) the ability to analyze skills or knowledge into component subskills, and (2) the ability to develop test items that will validly measure these subskills. It goes without saying that the major problem in constructing a valid diagnostic test rests upon satisfying the former assumption.

SUMMARY

The major distinctions between the various types of standardized achievement tests are in their purpose and ultimate use (and for that reason, they differ slightly in the range of material covered). If an overall assessment in many different areas is desired, and if comparisons are to be made for an individual's relative strengths and weaknesses in various subject-matter areas, a survey battery is desired. If only an assessment in a single area is desired, either a single subject-matter test or a subtest of the battery will suffice. If the teacher is interested in obtaining a clearer picture of particular strengths and/or weaknesses, he should use a diagnostic test. It should be emphasized at this time that the final decision regarding the selection of one test over another should be made by the person(s) using the test. It is essential that the test be valid for his purposes — he is in the best position to know what use will be made of the test results.

EXAMPLES OF ACHIEVEMENT TESTS

In the preceding section, we were concerned with comparing and contrasting the different kinds of standardized achievement tests. At this time, we will present some examples of diagnostic tests, single subject-matter achievement tests, and standardized achievement test batteries that are commonly used in the public schools. In addition, we will also consider some of the factors that are relevant in determining the choice of one achievement test or battery over another.

DIAGNOSTIC TESTS

Diagnostic tests are primarily concerned with the skills or abilities (for example, reading, arithmetic, spelling) that the subject matter experts believe are essential in learning a particular subject. That is, an arithmetic diagnostic test will be concerned with factors that experts in teaching arithmetic think enter into the arithmetic process. Diagnostic achievement tests provide a variety of exercises and problems that maximize the possibility of making errors. In other words, rather than asking only one or two items on addition with carrying or counting off decimals in division, a variety of such problems are presented in a diagnostic test. Also, in addition to the greater number of items, diagnostic tests often have their items graded in difficulty.

Because reading is an integral component of the learning process, the majority of diagnostic tests are for reading. Diagnostic reading tests range from the conventional paper-and-pencil test, where the student reads a sentence and records the error in the sentence, to the oral procedure, where the examiner carefully notes, for example, mispronunciations, omissions, repetitions, substitutions, and reversals of letters. In this latter method — the "thinking aloud approach" — the examiner is in a better position to observe and record errors as they happen and thus to see whether there is any pattern to the error. Understanding not only the kinds of errors made but also obtaining some insight into how the pupil responds and reacts can prove invaluable for future remedial work. For example, in the oral approach, the examiner may note that the pupil is nervous, wary, concerned, and so forth. It is conceivable that in some instances, learning difficulties may be psychomotor or psychological in nature rather than of an intellectual etiology.

A diagnostic test will not only inform the teacher that a pupil is weak or deficient in reading or arithmetic, but will also point out what areas are weak, such as word comprehension or addition with carrying. However, it will not establish causal relationships. In other words, the teacher might learn what the difficulty is but not why the problem is there. For example, let us say that Salvador is weak in algebra. This may be due to his intellectual ability, poor reading skills, psychomotor difficulties, poor study skills, emotional problems, inability to deal with polynomials, and so forth. The teacher must consider such factors to arrive at a reasonable solution to the problem. If not, he may only remedy the immediate algebra problem, but the etiological factors (having not been considered) may manifest themselves in other learning situations.[20]

The manuals of some achievement test batteries suggest that some of their subtests may be used for diagnostic purposes. We strongly caution the user not to consider these subtests as diagnostic because, in most instances, the items were not constructed to measure the components involved in a particular skill such as reading or arithmetic. Before a diagnostic test can be considered valid (1) the component skills subtests should emphasize just a single type of error (such as word reversal in a reading diagnostic test), and (2) the subtest differences must be reliable. This can only be achieved by having subtests that have high reliabilities in themselves and low intertest

[20]The diagnosis of learning problems requires trained specialists — school psychologists and often social workers, physicians, and psychiatrists. The remedial program to be initiated will require special education teachers. Because of this, classroom teachers should leave this area to the specialists, especially for moderate or severe cases.

correlations. Achievement test batteries or single subject-matter tests seldom display these characteristics.

Some of the more common questions asked about diagnostic tests by classroom teachers, counselors, and administrators are as follows:

Q. How does diagnostic testing differ from survey testing?

A. When one administers a standardized achievement test, he is normally concerned only with the total score or possibly the subtest scores. Then appropriate decisions such as grouping, or evaluation of the curriculum are made on the basis of the scores. In diagnostic testing, there is no single score. Rather, there is a detailed analysis (depending upon the test used) of the pupil's work habits. Then, instead of using the test results for, say, grouping, the teacher uses the analysis of test performance plus other information to outline a remedial teaching program.

Q. Do diagnostic tests have norms?

A. Yes and no. Yes, in the sense that a distribution of scores may be presented to designate how students in general have performed. No, in the sense that we think of the norms that accompany other standardized subject-matter (cognitive) or interest tests. The norms accompanying diagnostic tests are not based upon the performance only of those students who are in need of remedial instruction. Because national norms imply a cross-section of pupils throughout the country, it would indeed be difficult to obtain a representative cross-section of failing pupils. On the other hand, a type of norm may be provided by the publisher of a diagnostic test. Such a norm usually contains the classification of types of errors made. The important thing is that when norms accompany a diagnostic test, the sample upon which the normative data are based must be clearly defined.

Q. Are diagnostic tests standardized?

A. Diagnostic tests are standardized in the sense that the instruments are administered under uniform conditions and objectively scored. The fact that subjectivity enters into the interpretation or diagnosis does not detract from the diagnostic test being considered standardized.

Q. What about diagnostic tests that have percentile or grade equivalent norms?

A. Be wary of such tests.

Q. Should diagnostic tests be given to all students?

A. No! Only to those students who are having difficulty. They are too time-consuming to administer, score, and interpret.

Q. How difficult is it to correctly administer a diagnostic test?

A. Very difficult in comparison to other types of achievement tests. Not only must the examiner record the answer given (for young children) but also he must note the kind of error made (for example, leaving out a word when reading a sentence or reversing the letters in a word); he must record the student's thought processes if the student is asked to think aloud; he must note the attitude of the student throughout the test, to mention just a few. Considerable practice is necessary.

It is not possible here to consider in very much detail the variety of diagnostic tests available to the classroom teacher. We have described some of the different methods used to construct diagnostic tests; we have attempted to caution the user to be wary in his interpretation of diagnostic test results (because they are not elegant psychometric instruments with high validity and complete normative data); and we have taken the view that the teacher must be certain every avenue has been explored in his attempt to remedy an evident defect. This section will conclude with a very brief description of some of the more popular diagnostic tests available in the elementary grades.[21] Possibly because of the technical difficulties involved, there is a paucity of valid diagnostic tests.

Reading Diagnostic Tests

Reading diagnostic tests generally measure such factors as reading rate, comprehension, vocabulary, visual and auditory discrimination, and motor skills. As will be evident when reading readiness tests are discussed, the skills measured by reading, reading readiness, and reading diagnostic tests are very similar, as we would expect. The major difference is in the range of material covered and the intensity of coverage.

Q. Do all reading diagnostic tests measure the same thing?

A. No! Although there are more similarities than differences among most standardized reading diagnostic tests, there are nevertheless some basic differences. For example, the Durrell Analysis of Reading Difficulty and the Gates-McKillop Reading Diagnostic Tests are both individually administered. Both measure various factors involved in the reading process but do so in markedly different ways. In the Gates-McKillop, the subtests are analogous to power tests in that the exercises vary in their degree of difficulty. In the Durrell, this is not so. On the other hand, the Gates-McKillop has tests of the child's work-attack skills but the Durrell does not. The strength of the Durrell is in two sets of paragraphs; the Gates-McKillop has eight separate subtests.

Q. How valid are the interpretations that can be made with a reading diagnostic test?

A. This depends upon the test — how the items were selected (or prepared), the test's psychometric qualities, and the adequacy of the norming

---

[21]See Buros' *Mental measurements yearbooks* for a complete description of these and other diagnostic tests.

group. For some tests like the Gates-McKillop, the training and experience of the examiner plays a vital role. The older Gates Reading Diagnostic Tests can be interpreted easily by classroom teachers. The types of interpretations that can be made are governed, to a large extent, by the range of material the test covers. The practical clinical value of the interpretation depends, to a large extent, on the check list of errors (and their validity) the publisher provides.

Gates-McKillop Reading Diagnostic Tests   Bureau of Publications, Teachers College, Columbia University, 1962. Revision of the Gates Reading Diagnostic Tests. Grades 2–6. Two alternate forms (1 and 2). Provides 28 scores. Individually administered. Untimed except for the two flash presentation tests.

The complete test would take several hours to administer and should be given in several sessions. It was designed to identify specific strengths and weaknesses in the child's reading skills by providing a variety of exercises in eight different subtests. Reading is broken up into its many components such as word meaning, sentence meaning, speed, and spelling. These components are not only tested as separate entities, but each of the separate components is measured by exercises varying in degree of difficulty. Hence, if the pupil is unable to recognize words, it is possible, with this test, to determine whether this problem first manifests itself with simple words studied in the first grade, those studied in the second grade, and so forth. No reliability data are presented. The validity evidence must be inferred from the constructs the test authors used to define reading ability. The usual empirical validity data are not presented in the manual. The normative data are unclear. The test is accompanied by an excellent, well-organized manual with many valuable suggestions for profile analysis (modal errors for the various tests are given). The test requires a sophisticated and well-trained examiner for valid interpretation. In fact, this test is most demanding of examiner proficiency insofar as reading diagnostic tests are concerned.

This test has some particularly valuable features:

1. The word recognition subtest is both timed and untimed. Using such a procedure, the teacher can help identify deficiencies in rapid perception. This would be difficult to do if only the untimed test were used.

2. The oral reading test is more than the reading of four paragraphs. Although comprehension is not measured, many other things are — seven types of mispronunciation errors (for example, reversals), and errors of omission, repetition, and addition. These different errors are analyzed in relation to the total number of errors made. Norms are provided for expected errors, and clues and suggestions are provided to help make a specific diagnosis.

3. The manual is full of valuable clues and suggestions for profile analysis and clinical diagnosis. Where appropriate, subtest cross-references are made to assist in diagnosis.

Some of the weaknesses in this test are as follows:

1. Reading comprehension is not measured. And yet, this is an important skill in the reading process. To be able to read is good. To be able to read with understanding is much better.

2. The norm groups for the various subtests are not clearly defined.

3. The interpretation of many of the subtest scores is made relative to the pupil's oral reading level. This can result in misinterpretation — if the oral reading score is incorrect or if a naive teacher thinks errors made by a fifth grader reading at the beginning second-grade level mean the same thing as a third or second grader reading at the same level.

Durrell Analysis of Reading Difficulty New edition. Harcourt, Brace & World, Inc., 1955. Grades 1 through 6. One form. Individually administered. Utilizes a series of paragraphs graded in difficulty, a simple tachistoscope, and a set of cards. The subtests are silent and oral reading, listening comprehension, word analysis, phonetics, faulty pronunciation, writing, and spelling.

The test for nonreaders contains measures of visual memory for word forms, auditory analysis of word elements, letter recognition, rate of learning words, and listening comprehension. A novel but praiseworthy feature of the test is the inclusion of a set of graded paragraphs to measure listening comprehension. Unfortunately, comprehension in both the oral and silent reading tests is measured by sheer, simple recall — a questionable approach, to say the least. Oral reading is measured at each level by means of a single paragraph. If, as the test author suggests, three paragraphs be used to establish the child's reading level, how can this test be used with pupils whose reading level is below third grade? Speed of word recognition (visual) and letter recognition (auditory) are assessed but not the child's word attack skills (syllabication). Validity and reliability data are nonexistent. For each grade, separate norms (based on the high, average, and low subtest scores) are provided. Unfortunately, the description of the sample is unknown. Probably the best feature of this test is the detailed check list of difficulties provided. This check list of reading errors (based on a survey of 4000 children) should be beneficial to inexperienced reading teachers and clinicians. The manual contains suggestions for remedial teaching. An experienced examiner is needed for valid interpretation.

Diagnostic Reading Tests Committee on Diagnostic Reading Tests, Inc., 1963. Three separate batteries: K through grade 4; lower level, grades 4–8; and upper level, grades 7–13. Various forms for the different areas measured at the various grade levels. Each of the three batteries contains an appropriate survey test designed to assess the pupil's general reading proficiency as well as subtests intended to appraise specific reading skills.[22] Individually administered. The user may employ all the subtests in a battery or select only those that are needed for his purpose. Median reliability coefficients are reported for the primary battery (grades K–4) subtests. Reliability coefficients for the other batteries are spotty. Some of the reliabilities that are reported are so low that intrapupil differences would be difficult to justify. The Committee exercised much diligence and effort in developing tests that would be useful to teachers. Not only do teachers have a series of tests with a common design, they also have, with these tests, an instrument that can be used for the cumulative measurement of reading. Many specific suggestions are offered for using the test scores to adapt reading instruction to the needs and abilities of students. The norms are continuously revised. Notwithstanding the virtues of this test, there are certain basic faults incumbent with its use. Specifically, (1) certain selections and items are in need of revision, (2) the format is in dire need of improvement in some of the tests, (3) the test booklets are printed on poor quality paper, (4) the normative data provided are inadequate because of the variation in sample size for the various parts of the test, (5) the literature accompanying the tests is so voluminous that it becomes unwieldy to handle, (6) quartiles and medians are reported for the reading readiness test while percentiles are reported for the other subtests, and (7) validity must be inferred subjectively. It is unfortunate that the potential value of a well-developed, articulated set of tests is marred by inefficiency that could be easily remedied.

Stanford Diagnostic Reading Test (SDRT)   Harcourt, Brace & World, Inc., 1966. Two forms. Two levels: Level I (grades 2.5 to 4.5) and Level II (grades 4.5 to 8.5). Group administered. Seven scores for Level I, eight scores for Level II. Three strictly timed tests and four untimed tests in the Level I battery. Level II battery untimed.

The Level I battery requires about 2½ hours testing time and the test authors recommend that it be administered in four sessions. The Level II battery requires about 90 minutes testing time and the test authors recommend that this level be administered in three sessions. Both the Level I and II batteries are concerned with measuring reading comprehension, vocabulary, and word recognition skills. The Level II battery also measures reading rate. The specific subtests of the Level I battery are reading comprehension, vocabulary, auditory discrimination, syllabication, beginning and ending sounds, blending, and sound discrimination. The subtests of the

[22]There are actually six survey tests: one each for K–1, and grades 1, 2, 3–4, 4–8, and 7–13.

Level II battery are reading comprehension (three scores are obtained: a literal, inferential, and total reading comprehension score), vocabulary, syllabication, sound discrimination, blending, and rate of reading. Content, construct, and concurrent validity were emphasized in the construction of the test. The authors were also guided by an item analysis conducted on about 15,000 students in the try-out program. In addition, teachers who participated in the pilot study were asked for their comments, and these were used in developing the final form. Split-half and alternate-form reliabilities (for the rate of reading test) and standard errors of measurement are reported. The reliability coefficients range from .72 to .97 (majority above .80), and the standard errors of measurement vary from 1.4 to 4.6 raw score units (majority 2.0 or less) for Levels I and II, respectively. The median subtest intercorrelations are moderate, ranging from .48 to .61 for grades 3–8. On the whole, this test demonstrates adequate validity and reliability. As the test authors hasten to add, predictive validity is needed and will be undertaken. Approximately 12,000 pupils were used in the standardization program. Elaborate procedures were employed to make the SDRT norm group duplicate as close as possible the Stanford Achievement Test norm group (with respect to the mean and variance) on the paragraph meaning test. Unfortunately, descriptive information concerning the norm group is conspicuously lacking. Raw scores can be converted to grade scores (reading comprehension subtest only), percentiles, or stanines. The front cover of the test booklet provides space to record the raw scores as well as provides a profile format. A class record and class analysis chart permits summarization of the data for a whole class or group of pupils. The manual is concisely written and contains helpful suggestions to assist the user in test interpretation. Although the classroom teacher can administer, score, and interpret the test, we strongly recommend that, when feasible, an experienced specialist do the actual interpretation and make the suggestions for corrective action.

Diagnostic Arithmetic Tests

With the exception of reading, probably no subject has been more intensively studied than the teaching of arithmetic. And yet, there have been very few new arithmetic tests in the past decade and even fewer new diagnostic tests. Unfortunately, because of the rapidly changing curriculum in the teaching of arithmetic (modern math), the old standbys such as the Diagnostic Tests and Self-Helps in Arithmetic, the Los Angeles Diagnostic Tests, and the Lee-Clark Arithmetic Fundamentals Survey Test may not be too valid today, especially if one is teaching modern math. Certain fundamental skills in arithmetic are taught at the primary level, and regardless of the method of instruction employed, most diagnostic arithmetic tests employ similar kinds of items. Thus, only one such test will be reviewed.

Diagnostic Tests and Self-Helps in Arithmetic   California Test Bureau, 1955. Grades 3–12. One form. Untimed. Four screening tests and 23 diagnostic tests. No scores. No norms.

Each of the 23 diagnostic tests is accompanied by a self-help unit that is on the back of the diagnostic test. Six major areas are surveyed by the series: basic facts (five tests); fundamental operations with whole numbers (five tests); operations with percentages (one test); fundamental operations with decimal fractions (four tests); operations with measures (one test); and fundamental operations with common fractions (seven tests). The four screening tests are designed to measure pupil achievement in whole numbers, fractions, decimals, and general arithmetic skills and knowledge. On the basis of the pupil's performance on one (or more) of the first three screening tests, the appropriate diagnostic test(s) is administered. For example, if the pupil does poorly on Screening Test II, Screening Test in Fractions (the test author suggests that one or more errors is indicative of further testing), he would be given one or more of the Diagnostic Tests in Common Fractions. That is, if he had difficulty in the addition of like fractions, he would be given Test 12, Addition of Like Fractions. The screening test, because it contains only a few examples of the skills needed, would have to be supplemented by a separate test that contains many examples.

The diagnostic tests are essentially power tests that begin with very simple items and then progress in difficulty. Because there are many items dealing with the same concept or skill, the probability of committing an error is maximized, something that is desired in a diagnostic test. The separate diagnostic tests are cross-referenced to assist the teacher in locating the nature of the difficulty. For example, when a pupil multiplies 640 by 23, he may arrive at an incorrect answer for a variety of reasons: (1) he may place the products incorrectly, (2) he may not add the columns correctly, or (3) he may not know how to add with carrying. Therefore, if his performance on the screening test suggested that the pupil had difficulty with multiplication, the teacher would have to see where this error manifested itself. Because of the cross-referencing of the diagnostic tests, the pupil who multiplied 640 by 23 and arrived at an incorrect answer because he didn't add properly could be given Test 1, Addition Facts, and/or Test 6, Addition of Whole Numbers.

The diagnostic self-helps are keyed to the diagnostic test items. The self-helps are, in a sense, remedial exercises that have been worked out in detail. They indicate to the pupil the correct procedure to be used in answering that kind of item. For example, in Test 12, Addition of Like Fractions, the self-help exercises on the addition of fractions with no carrying would be as follows:

1/8   Add the numerators, 1 and 1
1/8
$\overline{2/8}$ = 1/4   Write the sum over the denominator 8

Then, $\dfrac{1+1}{8} = \dfrac{2}{8}$

Reduce 2/8: $\dfrac{2 \div 2}{8 \div 2} = \dfrac{1}{4}$

After working through the self-help exercises, the pupil is encouraged to rework the items that he answered incorrectly.

No reliability and validity data are reported. The test author implies that reliability was increased by having numerous items of the same kind. This may or may not be the case. Content validity was stressed in constructing the test. The test author attempted to analyze the skills needed to perform a particular task. It would have been desirable to present more information as to how these skills were analyzed, who did the analysis, and upon what basis the analysis was done. Do the self-help exercises contribute to learning? Do the diagnostic tests really assist the teacher in locating the nature of the pupils' difficulty, or could essentially similar information be obtained from the arithmetic subtest of a standardized achievement test? Evidence pertaining to these questions is absent in the manual.

The test manual contains numerous suggestions for the effective use of the test results. It also provides the user with a list of the more common errors in operations with whole numbers, common fractions, and decimals.

The Diagnostic Tests and Self-Helps in Arithmetic appears to do an adequate job in surveying specific weaknesses in fundamental arithmetic skills. The first four diagnostic tests contain 100 arithmetic operations involving digits 0 to 9. The basic facts, then, are covered thoroughly. However, there is inadequate provision for the measurement of arithmetic meaning or problem-solving ability. The value of these tests could possibly be increased by having some of the items responded to orally. In this way, the teacher, listening to the pupil "work the problem out loud" could obtain additional information regarding the pupil's work habits. Also, provision of a more complete error list could prove to be beneficial insofar as the teacher's instructional program is concerned.

ACHIEVEMENT TESTS IN SPECIFIC SUBJECTS

Standardized achievement tests are available for nearly every subject (agriculture to zoology) and for every grade level (kindergarten to professional and graduate school). There are, for example, reading readiness tests; reading tests; arithmetic, spelling, and science tests; product scales; and vocational achievement tests. For the most part, reading and arithmetic tests (as well as readiness tests in these respective subjects) are restricted to the primary grades because (1) these skills are primarily developed there and the major emphasis in the first few years of formal schooling is on reading and arithmetic, and (2) the relatively uniform curriculum of the elementary school makes it possible for the survey battery to adequately cover the measurement of the important objectives of instruction. In the secondary grades, because of the nonuniform nature of the curriculum, specialized tests covering a particular course such as Latin, Greek, or psychology are the predominant type.

Readiness Tests[23]

The concept of readiness has changed a great deal from Thorndike's Law of Readiness, which was primarily concerned with an individual's emotional readiness to undertake a new task. Readiness is now concerned with or conceived of, in terms of physical maturation, educational readiness, and general mental ability. In other words, readiness involves a variety of factors that are continually interacting. Hildreth cites seven factors that are to be considered in assessing a first grader's readiness: (1) mental maturity, (2) perceptual maturity, (3) experiential background, (4) linguistic maturity, (5) sensory acuity, (6) social adjustment, and (7) emotional adjustment.[24] These factors are agreed upon by most educational and developmental psychologists. As will be seen in later sections, many of our standardized tests, in reading and arithmetic particularly, are concerned with the measurement of many of these factors.

READING READINESS TESTS   Normally, the first type of standardized achievement test that a pupil receives is a reading readiness test. It is administered either at or near the end of the kindergarten year or very early in the first grade. This test is often considered one of the most important achievement tests that the child takes during his school years. It goes without saying that efficient and adequate reading skills play a vital role in subsequent learning. Hence, anything that can be done (sectioning, placement, and remedial instruction) to provide optimal reading instruction should reap benefits insofar as future learning is concerned.

The major purposes of a reading readiness test are (1) to identify the children who are not yet ready to begin reading,[25] and (2) to identify, for grouping purposes, the children who are at essentially the same level of reading readiness. This grouping will then assist the teacher in providing

[23]Readiness or prognostic tests are sometimes considered aptitude tests because they are used to predict how well the individual will profit from instruction or training.

[24]Gertrude B. Hildreth, *Readiness for school beginners.* Yonkers, N.Y.: World Book Co., 1950.

[25]Whether or not one is ready to begin reading depends upon a variety of factors such as aptitude, psychomotor skills, and mental attitude. For a discussion of these factors, see Albert J. Harris, *How to improve reading ability: A guide to developmental and remedial methods.* (4th ed.) New York: McKay, 1961; and Arthur I. Gates, *The improvement of reading: A program of diagnostic and remedial methods* (3rd ed.) New York: Macmillan, 1947.

appropriate instruction. Reading readiness tests are not designed to predict reading achievement in, say, the sixth or seventh grade. They do provide valuable information insofar as reading ability in the first and second grades is concerned. In addition, reading readiness tests should not be confused with reading diagnostic tests. Although they may indicate weaknesses in certain general broad areas such as word recognition or vocabulary, they are not designed to isolate specific reading defects.

There is a general consensus among reading specialists that a child's readiness to participate in reading, and the extent to which he will learn how to read, are dependent upon a variety of factors: (1) his intellectual ability, (2) eye-hand coordination, (3) motivation to learn how to read, (4) perceptual and visual skills, and (5) knowledge of colors, names of common things, and concepts of time and space. Although there are variations among the many reading readiness tests commercially published, all of them have several of the following types of items:

1. *Motor skills.* The child is required to draw lines, complete a circle, underline words, go through a finger maze.

2. *Auditory discrimination.* The child is either asked to pronounce words after they have been read to him or he is required to select which of several similar-sounding words identify a picture.

3. *Visual discrimination.* The child is required to choose similarities or differences in words, letters, numbers, or pictures.

4. *Vocabulary.* The child's knowledge of the meaning of words is assessed by asking him to either define the meaning of a word, name various objects of the same or different class, or select the correct word to describe a picture.

5. *Memory.* The child may be asked to reproduce a geometrical figure to which he has been exposed for a certain length of time, he may be asked to repeat a story that has been read to him, or he may be required to carry out in sequence a series of instructions that have been presented to him.

The results from only a reading readiness test will not be sufficient to answer all the questions about a child's readiness to learn to read, but they will provide valuable supplementary information to that gathered by observing the child. As we have constantly reiterated throughout this text, the results of any test are best considered as supplementary and complementary information for decision making. Some questions that may be raised regarding reading readiness tests are as follows:

Q. If there is a high correlation between reading readiness test scores and intelligence test scores, why administer a reading readiness test?

A. Yes, there is a high correlation between performance on a reading readiness test and an intelligence test. However, intelligence tests do not survey all the skills and traits the child must have in order to learn to read.

Intelligence tests, by their very nature, are not designed to provide specific information on the child's ability to handle words, whether or not the child can use and manipulate words, whether or not the child has adequate muscular coordination. Reading readiness tests are specifically designed to assess those skills deemed important in the reading process. For this reason, it is recommended that a reading readiness test be administered to kindergarten children, and the intelligence test can be postponed to the first or second grade.

Q. Do all reading readiness tests measure the same thing?

A. No! Although many of them look as if they are doing so because they have vocabulary items, or paragraph reading, or reproduction of objects, there is usually something unique or different about each of the reading-readiness tests available. For example, the Harrison-Stroud Reading Readiness Profiles and the American School Reading Readiness Test both have subtests that assess the child's ability to follow directions. In the former, this is in the "Making Auditory Discriminations" subtest, while in the latter, these skills are measured in the "Following Directions" subtest. However, in the Harrison-Stroud, there is a test of auditory discrimination, but there is no such test in the latter. The American test authors felt that variations in performance could result from variations in administration and, therefore, deleted the measurement of this skill. This is true but is an insufficient reason for omitting such an important task. Steps could be taken to make the administration uniform either by having explicit instructions or by having a recording of the instructions played to the pupils.

Q. How are items selected for reading readiness tests?

A. Once again, there are differences among the various tests. Some test authors, like Harrison and Stroud, attempted to make a job analysis. That is, they specified those skills felt to be important in the reading process and then prepared a test on the basis of this analysis. A somewhat different procedure was employed by the constructors of the Gates and American School tests. On the basis of previously used items and those suggested by experts in the field, they assembled a preliminary pool of items, administered the items, and then selected the items that were statistically sound. Both methods are valid, and no one can say that one is better than the other.

Q. How do I know whether an existing test is valid for my purposes?

A. You don't until you study it carefully! You must study the test manual thoroughly and determine whether the test's objectives are in agreement with your goals. All the test maker can do is indicate what he thinks is important. It is up to the user to judge not only whether he agrees with the test's purposes but also whether the manner in which the test was constructed was valid. For example, the authors of the American School

Reading-Readiness Test felt that auditory discrimination was not important. The Metropolitan Readiness Tests requires the pupil to draw a man. The Harrison-Stroud and American School Tests do not contain this type of item. If the user feels that auditory discrimination is important, he should consider a test other than the American. Similarly, if the user feels that the ability to draw-a-man is vital to the reading process, he would be advised to consider a test other than the Harrison-Stroud or American. The user must also make a thorough analysis of the test items. He cannot judge the purpose of a subtest by merely looking at the items. As we mentioned earlier, both the Harrison-Stroud and the American School tests have items designed to measure the child's ability to follow directions. In the former, this type of item is found as a peripheral task whereas in the latter there is a specific subtest designed to measure this skill. Once again, we reiterate do not judge a test by the names of the subtests!

Q. Should I use an old established test or should I select a new one?
A. This is indeed a very difficult question to answer. Naturally, the old test will usually be accompanied by much data to indicate its validity, especially predictive validity. At the same time, the new tests have had the opportunity to benefit from theoretical advances in teaching methods and from technological advances in test writing and reproduction. Their format can be more up-to-date. For example, a vocabulary test might contain a picture of a telegraph boy delivering a telegram. The boy may be riding a bicycle. Now, this type of item might have been valid in the 1930s and 1940s when telegraph boys did deliver telegrams. But today, telegraph boys are a matter of historical interest. An old test might contain such an item but a newer one should not. One cannot make a blanket statement that a newer test is more valid than an older one. The user should examine many different types of tests, study them carefully, and determine whether the newer tests are really an improvement. A poor new test is not as good as a good old test, technological improvements notwithstanding. A good bet is to select the recently revised edition of a good older test.

Reading readiness tests employ a variety of procedures. All directions are given orally, although on one test, the Harrison-Stroud, one section is devoted to pupils doing the test independently. There are numerous examples or practice exercises provided so that the child will understand what he is to do and how he is to do it. All work is done in the test booklet. The examiner should constantly check the students to be sure that they understand the directions. This should not be difficult because most of the tests are untimed and should under normal circumstances be administered in small groups or individually. Some examples of reading readiness tests follow.

Harrison-Stroud Reading Readiness Profiles Houghton Mifflin Company, 1956. This test, designed for children in grades K–1 is intended to serve three purposes: (1) to ascertain the degree of development of the specific readiness skills to see whether the pupil should be given reading instruction, (2) to determine placement in the first grade, and (3) to designate those skills that are in need of further training either before or during the initial reading period. The test has six subtests: using symbols, making visual discrimination (two scores), using content, making auditory discrimination, using context and auditory clues, and giving names of letters. The testing time varies from 8 to 30 minutes for the various subtests. Approximately 80 minutes of testing time is needed, and the test authors suggest that the test be administered in three sessions. Although the test can be administered either individually or in a group setting, the former is recommended, especially for kindergarten children. No reliability data are presented. The validity data contained in the manual are too sparse to be of any value. Normative data are lacking, hence it is difficult to make valid interpretations.

Lee-Clark Reading Readiness Test   Revised edition. California Test Bureau, 1962. The test's intended grade range is K–1. The test has one form and yields four scores: letter symbols, concepts, word symbols, and a total score. Two of the subtests are timed. Although the test is relatively short and only requires about 20 minutes to administer, it has high predictive validity and reliability for so short a test. The subtest reliabilities range from .83 to .94. However, these reliability coefficients must be interpreted cautiously because they are only based on 170 entering first graders. The percentile and grade equivalent norms provided are based on two different populations (normal and above-average intelligence) that result in problems of interpretation. Also, the norms for the entering first graders and end-of-year kindergarten pupils are based on different but unspecified populations. Considerable supplementary materials are provided. This test serves as an excellent screening device and provides a fairly gross measure for initial grouping purposes. It is not a valid diagnostic test even though the test authors recommend using the test for diagnostic purposes.

Murphy-Durrell Reading Readiness Analysis Harcourt, Brace & World, Inc., 1965. Grade 1. One form. Three subtests: phonemes, letter names (capital and lower case), and learning rate. In addition to the three subtest scores, there is a total score. Raw scores can be converted to percentile ranks, stanines, and quartiles. No time limits, but test authors suggest two testing periods.

Metropolitan Readiness Tests Harcourt, Brace & World, Inc., 1965. Grades K–1. Two forms (A and B). Six subtests: word meaning, listening, matching, alphabet (knowledge of lower-case letters), numbers, and copying. Requires three sessions. Percentile ranks and stanines. Total score and individual subtest scores also expressed in terms of five-level readiness status ratings.

It should be readily evident that there is considerable variation among the various reading readiness tests with respect to the time required for administration, the number of scores obtained, the types of norms provided, and so forth. All, however, are designed to measure the skills the test authors deem important in reading and reading instruction.

USES OF READING READINESS TESTS   The primary use of the reading readiness test is to provide the teacher with basic information about the child's reading skills so that optimal learning conditions can be provided. On the basis of a reading readiness test, a classroom teacher can tailor his teaching program to best fit the needs of each pupil.[26] For example, one student may be deficient in his ability to recognize similarities and differences, while another is having difficulty reading numbers. After ascertaining that the deficiencies are not due to any physical factors, the teacher can institute remedial action where needed. In this illustration, the test is used both as a prognostic device and as a criterion upon which the learning materials are organized and presented by the classroom teacher.

The results of reading readiness tests can also be used by the school principal when there are two or three first grade classes so that the pupils who are at about the same level can be grouped together for instructional purposes. It is much easier to teach groups that are of similar abilities. Naturally, for homogeneous grouping one should also consider other factors. But in the first grade, reading readiness may well be the most important.[27]

Reading Tests

The ability to communicate by means of language is a fundamental necessity in today's society. Reading is one form of communication that must be developed in our pupils. If one were to look at the curriculum in the primary grades, it would be readily obvious that the development of communicative skills — reading, writing, and speaking — make up a major portion of the curriculum. If one were to look at a survey battery, he would find at least one or more subtests for the assessment of a person's reading skills. The subtests might be classified in a variety of ways — reading comprehension, language arts, language skills — but regardless of the rubric used, they are essentially a test of one's ability to read.

[26]Because of the instability of test scores for very young children, the results should be interpreted cautiously.

[27]Intellectual ability is also important. However, many research studies have demonstrated the high correlation between reading and IQ. Some psychologists feel that reading tests are really IQ tests, and vice versa.   The IQ tests that are highly verbal in nature are especially highly correlated with reading readiness tests.

Because we know that all survey batteries, regardless of grade level, have subtests to measure the students' reading proficiency, one might well ask why it is necessary to have, and use, a separate reading test. Is it because the reading tests of the survey battery are invalid? Is it because they are unreliable? Really not. The major reasons for using separate tests for reading skills are (1) survey batteries may not be used until the second, third, or fourth grade, and it is vital that we identify students' reading skills proficiency as early as possible, (2) reading tests should be used if the scores from a survey battery indicate that the pupil is weak in the area, and (3) survey batteries are not as thorough in their coverage in any one area as are separate, subject-matter (or skills) tests.

All reading tests use essentially similar procedures for measuring the pupils' reading ability. Students are typically required to read a series of paragraphs and answer questions about them. Pupils are given items to see whether they are facile with words and sentences. Some tests may employ prose selections only while others may use both prose and poetry to measure comprehension. One test, the Sequential Tests of Educational Progress (STEP), requires the individual to write an essay on specified topics. Some of the tests are oral while others are of the silent-reading type and can be administered in a group setting. Once again, regardless of the manner of assessment, reading tests all serve a common purpose — to see how well the individual can read. As we have mentioned earlier, the reading process is an extremely complex task and involves a variety of factors, some of which are continually interacting and cannot be isolated as distinct entities. No single test attempts to measure all these factors. Some of the factors, such as attitudes involved in reading, or how well a pupil integrates reading in his adulthood, are unlikely to be assessed by any test. Because there is some difference of opinion as to the skills deemed important in the reading process, we see different kinds of reading (or, for that matter, arithmetic, spelling, or science) tests. This is not to say that one standardized reading test is more valid than another. The evaluation of any standardized reading (actually, any achievement) test depends upon the similarity of the user's and test constructor's objectives. You, the user alone must decide whether the objectives you deem important are measured by a test and how well your objectives are measured.

There are many standardized reading tests available. Some are good, some are bad. We will consider just a few of the available reading tests to illustrate their format, technical features, and purpose.

Developmental Reading Tests Lyons and Carnahan, 1961. Four levels: primer reading (grade 1.5), lower primary reading (grades 1.5 to 2.5), upper primary reading (grades 2.5 to 3), and intermediate reading (grades 4–6). Group administered. Testing times for the primary and intermediate tests are 40 and 32 minutes, respectively. One form for the primary series; two for the intermediate test.

This test is an example of how not to publish tests. It has no stated purpose, provides no normative data, and is lacking in reliability and validity data. The three primary tests provide three scores: basic vocabulary, general comprehension, and specific comprehension. The intermediate test provides six scores: basic vocabulary, reading to retain information, reading to organize, reading to evaluate-interpret, reading to appreciate, and average comprehension.

The authors are highly qualified in reading and have the genesis of a good reading test. The test content appears good and could probably be used to prepare a set of valid, reliable, and useful tests. However, much will have to be done with these tests before we would be able to recommend them even for consideration.

Lee-Clark Reading Test   California Test Bureau, 1965. Two levels: primer (grade 1), and first reader (grades 1–2). Two forms for each. In addition, there is an Initial Teaching Alphabet (i.t.a.) edition for both tests but only in a single form. Testing time is about 15 and 25 minutes for the primer and first reader, respectively.

The tests are designed to measure first and second graders' reading ability. This is done with a series of subtests. Both the primer and the first reader provide scores in auditory stimuli, visual stimuli, following directions, and a total score. In addition, the first reader has inference and completion scores. Kuder-Richardson reliabilities reported are .83 and .90 for the primer and first reader, respectively. These should be interpreted with caution because the norm group was somewhat small, no description of it was given, the forms used were not specified, and the time limits might be such that the tests are speeded. Content and concurrent validity were emphasized in the test construction. However, the criterion data for the validity studies are open to question. Vocabulary used in the test was compared with the vocabulary used in first and second grade of three widely used basic reading series and with the Gates' reading vocabulary for the primary grades. But the texts used were not specified. Also, the Gates material was published in 1926, and surely some changes have occurred in the vocabulary level of our children since that time, with our mass media of communication. The data pertaining to correlation studies between these and other standardized achievement tests are difficult to interpret because of the varying reliability and validity of the criterion measures. With respect to the test's validity, it should be noted that heavy emphasis is placed upon identifying words in isolation as well as upon auditory stimuli. Both percentile and grade placement norms are provided. The grade placement norms are difficult to interpret because they are based upon two groups of students: (1)

Group A consists of students of "normal" intelligence who are representative of the various types of reading instruction programs throughout the country, and (2) Group 2 consists of above-average students enrolled in schools where reading is introduced early in the first grade. Other than this information, no data are provided concerning the characteristics of students in the two groups, the manner in which they were selected, and other information that would be of inestimable value in test interpretation. In addition to the grade placement norms, "age in months" data are presented but not elaborated upon. The norms, then, are grossly inadequate. The manuals provide helpful discussions regarding the use and interpretation of scores. Nevertheless, the test authors are to be admonished for their allusion to the reliability of subtest score differences. No data are provided to support this assumption.

The tests are easy to administer and score. They appear to survey the skills necessary for first and second graders learning to read. However, there are so many shortcomings that we strongly urge the user to consider other available reading tests.

Gates-MacGinitie Reading Tests   Teachers College Press, 1965. Replaces the familiar Gates Reading Tests. Six separate tests for grades 1–9: Primary A (grade 1), Primary B (grade 2), Primary C (grade 3), each of which has two forms and provides scores in vocabulary and comprehension; Primary CS (grades 2–3) has three forms and provides scores in speed and accuracy; Survey D (grades 4–6) and Survey E (grades 7–9) each have three forms and provide scores in speed and accuracy, vocabulary, and comprehension. The authors state that Survey F (grades 10–12) is currently in preparation. Testing time varies from 40 to 50 minutes and the test can be administered in either one or two sessions.

The vocabulary test measures the child's ability to analyze or recognize isolated words. In the Primary A and B tests this is done with pictures only, in the Primary C test, a combination of both pictures and words is used, and in the survey tests, words only are used. A picture (or word) is presented and followed by four words (primary) or five words (survey). The pupil is required to recognize the correct word among the foils. This is a power test in the sense that the tasks become increasingly difficult.

The comprehension test measures the child's ability to read whole sentences and paragraphs with understanding. Not only is he required to be able to read but also he must understand what he has read and follow written directions. The Primary A and B tests measure comprehension with 34 passages each; the Primary C test does this with 24 paragraphs. The passages are of increasing length and difficulty — easy to begin with and increasingly difficult as the test progresses. The survey tests measure the pupils' ability to read complete prose passages with understanding. In each of the 21 passages used, from two to three words are missing. The pupil is required to select one word from five that is most appropriate for completing the statement so that the total passage is meaningful.

The speed and accuracy test of the Primary C and survey tests are designed to measure how rapidly the student can read with understanding. The Primary CS test uses 32 short paragraphs while the survey tests each use 36 short paragraphs. Time limits are 7, 5, and 4 minutes for the Primary CS, Survey D, and Survey E tests, respectively. In the allotted time, the pupil is to read the short paragraphs and answer the questions or complete the statements that follow by choosing the most correct word. This test is a speeded test because the authors contend that few students will be able to complete all of the paragraphs.

As is true in any test that attempts to span two or three grades, it is extremely difficult to control the difficulty of the items so that they are not too easy for the upper level students or too difficult for the lower level students. The Gates-MacGinitie tests are no exception, but marked improvement has taken place in comparison to the older Gates Reading Tests.

Validity evidence as such is not presented. The authors do describe the population that was employed in the "try-out" of the test items and say that item analysis was used to determine which items were to be retained. However, neither descriptive data concerning the try-out sample nor information concerning the sources studied to develop items are described. Correlations are reported for each of grades 4 to 9 between the subtest scores and the Lorge-Thorndike Verbal IQ, and range from .18 to .86.

Reliability estimates were by the alternate forms method as well as the split halves procedure and range from .67 to .94. Once again, information concerning the nature of the group studied is lacking. In the main, the reliabilities of most of the subtests are above .80. Because some of the subtests have low reliability, notably the "speed number attempted," extreme caution must be used in interpreting subtest score differences.

The data pertaining to the equivalency of forms was based upon (1) mean item discrimination indices and (2) comparisons of the raw score means and standard deviations for the various forms. Although there is no definite pattern emerging, it would appear that Form 1 is the more difficult.

Tables are provided to convert scores on the 1958 Gates Tests to the 1965 Gates-MacGinitie Reading Tests. Tables are also given to interpret gain scores for either individual pupils or for the whole class. Such gain scores, especially subtest differences, should be interpreted in the light of the subtest's reliability. The explanatory material accompanying these tables has been written in an understandable, uncomplicated fashion. Raw scores can be converted to grade scores, standard scores, or percentiles. Standard score and percentile norms are provided for all the tests. There are separate norms corresponding to the different testing periods used in the standardization. These periods correspond to October and May in the Primary A test and to October, February, and May for the other levels.

The Gates-MacGinitie Reading Tests are more than a revision of the familiar Gates Reading Tests. They are new, attractively printed, easy to administer and score, and now have norms that are more representative of American school children. The norms and various tables provided suffer from the absence of descriptive information concerning the population studied. The content appears to reflect current trends in the teaching of reading as well as in recognizing that the experiential domain of today's student is much broader than it was a decade or two ago. Despite the criticisms noted earlier, the tests should prove to be popular with teachers.

Other Single Subject-Matter Tests

As mentioned earlier, there are a variety of single subject-matter tests available. We could ask (as we did when discussing reading tests), "Why give a separate mathematics test when the battery we use contains a subtest in mathematics?" A survey test for a special subject matter area does not differ in principle from a battery subtest covering the same subject. They are both concerned with assessing the individual's state of present knowledge and contain much the same material. They do differ, however, in their degree or intensity of coverage. For example, an achievement test for arithmetic would contain more items and cover more aspects of arithmetic than would be possible in the battery's arithmetic subtest. Another advantage of the single subject-matter test is that a particular school's objectives might be more in harmony with the objectives of a specific content test than with the subtest of a battery. There are other reasons why we should use single subject-matter tests. One is to obtain more information about a pupil who has done poorly on the subtest of a battery. Another use is for guidance and counseling purposes. Finally, because high schools have less of a uniform curriculum than do elementary schools, conventional test batteries will not have subtests for unique subjects such as Latin, Spanish, or psychology.

We should mention, however, that in the physical and natural sciences, recent curricular changes have not been reflected in most of the standardized tests currently available. This is particularly true for comprehensive survey batteries. Single subject-matter tests (because of production and cost factors) are more apt to be revised with greater frequency than are comprehensive survey batteries. Hence, single subject-matter tests normally reflect curricular changes sooner than batteries. No doubt the next few years will bring forth more tests reflecting curricular changes. Space limitations prevent a more thorough consideration of standardized single subject-matter tests.

ACHIEVEMENT TEST SURVEY BATTERIES

Because survey batteries lend themselves best to a level where there is a common core of subjects and objectives, we find the largest number of them at the primary and elementary levels, although there are survey batteries at all other levels.

When we examine the numerous survey batteries that have been published for the primary and elementary grades, we find more similarities than differences among them. These survey batteries contain tests (actually subtests) in spelling, language usage, reading knowledge, vocabulary, arithmetic reasoning, and arithmetic fundamentals. Survey batteries often provide a total score as well as separate subtest scores. They often provide separate norms (rural-urban, grade, age) to enable the user to make various comparisons. They provide for the conversion of raw scores to standard scores to assist in test interpretation. The most common method of expressing test scores is in terms of grade equivalents,[28] although percentiles are frequently given. In the newer tests, stanines are usually reported.

We will now consider some of the survey batteries used in the elementary and secondary grades. Although there are some standardized tests available for college, and graduate and professional school, these will not be considered.

Metropolitan Achievement Tests Revised edition. Harcourt, Brace & World, Inc., 1962. Consists of six batteries, ranging from grades 1 through 12. The two primary levels have three forms; the elementary, intermediate, and advanced levels each have four forms; and the high school battery has two forms. Although the various tests have timed subtests, the Metropolitan can be considered a nonspeeded test. The working times for the tests vary from 85 minutes at the Primary I level to 282 minutes for the high school battery. The manual recommends that the primary batteries be administered in four sessions; all other batteries need five sessions. All the tests within a particular level are found in a single booklet, although at the upper levels there are separate subtests available in reading (grades 2–9), arithmetic (grades 3–9), science and social studies (grades 5–12), and mathematics and language (grades 9–12). The intermediate and advanced levels have either a partial or complete battery. The optional tests for both levels are the social studies information and science tests. The only two tests that are found at all six levels are a vocabulary test (which even at the Primary I level requires that the subject be able to read) and a reading test. The number of separate subtests varies from four to 13. Content validity was obtained by a systematic analysis of texts, syllabi, and published statements of

[28]See Chapter I for a discussion of the limitations of grade equivalent scores.

educational objectives. The authors also claim validity on the basis of an increase in the proportion of students answering an item correctly in succeeding grade levels. Using such a criterion is both good and bad. It is good because one would expect a seventh grader to know something a fifth or sixth grader does not know. It is bad because it fails to consider that forgetting will occur from, say, fifth to seventh grade, especially of little-used knowledge.

The test items are such that they require knowledge of specific factual information, although understanding and application of knowledge are measured to a slight degree. In the three primary batteries, emphasis is on reading and arithmetic — what we would expect to be stressed in the first four grades — although science knowledge could also have been tested. In the other three batteries (grades 5–12), the major content area emphasis appears to be appropriate — language arts, reading, science, and social studies — but there is still too much emphasis on factual recall and not enough on problem solving or reasoning-type exercises. It would appear that insofar as the mathematics subtest is concerned, the test authors have not been guided by the recommendations and modern curriculum advanced by such groups as the School Mathematics Study Group or the Illinois Commission on School Mathematics.

The data presented regarding the tests' validity are rather meaningless. For example, in the five pre–high school batteries, no summary statistics are presented for the item discrimination indexes. In the high school battery, "mean item validities" are given but the sample upon which they were computed and the method used to calculate the statistic were not explained. With the exception of the high school battery, and the separate parts of the language tests at all levels, the reliabilities within the single grade group range in the .80's and .90's. In the high school battery the reliabilities are somewhat lower, especially for the mathematics and language study skills tests. In the high school battery, the subtest scores are expressed as percentiles and stanines for each grade (9–12). For the batteries below the high school level, the subtest scores are also expressed as grade equivalents. The interpretative manual for the five pre–high school batteries is a model to be emulated by other test publishers and contains many valuable suggestions for the classroom teacher. The high school battery manual, although adequate, unfortunately presents much less information for test interpretation. The test publishers are to be commended for their stand on the development of local norms. At the same time, however, they are open to criticism for their discussion regarding the interpretation of stanines, percentile ranks, and grade equivalents.

Although the Metropolitan has used the traditional type of item, it did introduce a novel feature in the spelling tests at the upper three levels. In the spelling tests of the Primary II and elementary batteries, the pupil writes the words dictated by the examiner. In the spelling tests in the other levels, the word to be tested is presented in the context of a sentence, and the pupil is required to indicate whether the word is spelled correctly (R) or incorrectly (W) or to indicate that he does not know (DK). Further, for those marked W, the pupil is asked to write in the correct spelling. Although the corrected word is not considered in the scoring, and although it is uncertain whether this procedure adds to the validity of the spelling test, it does provide the teacher with some added information that might be valuable for analyzing spelling problems. It is hoped that further research will be conducted to ascertain the efficacy of this approach for the lower-level batteries.

In summary, the Metropolitan Achievement Tests tend to reflect the traditional curriculum. Without a doubt, this battery makes the greatest demand for knowledge of specific facts. The Metropolitan was carefully constructed and standardized. The five pre–high school batteries compare favorably with other standardized achievement survey batteries. This is not so for the high school battery. To provide direction to high school teachers for the improvement of instruction or for curricular changes, the writers would recommend either the Iowa Tests of Educational Development, the Sequential Tests of Educational Progress, or the Stanford Achievement Test.

Iowa Tests of Basic Skills Multilevel edition. Houghton Mifflin Company, 1956. The multilevel edition is intended for use in grades 3–9. It consists of five separate tests — vocabulary, reading comprehension, language skills, work-study skills, and arithmetic skills — and yields 15 scores, the majority of them being in reading and language arts. There are two forms available. The test requires a working time of 279 minutes and should be administered in four sessions. It is a very thorough battery of tests designed to measure functional skills in the core curriculum. The specific content areas such as science or social studies are not covered. An asset of multilevel tests is that, for most students, they circumvent base or ceiling effects. A liability is that stopping and beginning at different places in the test can be very troublesome and confusing for young children. The test reliabilities are quite high — ranging from .70 to .93 for the subtests and from .84 to .96 for the five major tests. The composite reliabilities for the total test range from .97 to .98. The magnitude and pattern of the subtest intercorrelations suggest that the primary skills being measured are reading and vocabulary. Content validity was emphasized in the construction of the test, and the very thoroughness with which it was done is a major strength of the battery. The detail with which the objectives of the various skills were developed attests to the skills and dedication of the test constructors. Teachers will find this material very beneficial for planning remedial instruction. Three types of norms are provided: grade equivalent, grade percentile for individual pupils, and grade percentile for school averages. The two types of percentile norms are provided for the beginning, middle, and end of school year. This latter provision permits flexibility in the testing program. Special percentile norm tables are also provided for regional areas, Catholic schools, and large city schools. The previous editions of this battery were criticized because of their biased sampling — using Iowa children only. This criticism is no longer valid with the latest edition.

Although all the items were carefully constructed, there are some major criticisms that the test user should be made aware of in evaluating this battery. Specifically, these deficiencies are (1) the vocabulary test, although purported to test basic skills has its major focus on the meaning or definition of words, (2) the test of reading comprehension, particularly at the lower grade levels (3–5) appears to be unbalanced with respect to comprehension-type items, (3) the work-study skills test may be biased against children from schools that do not provide this type of educational program, (4) the language skills tests place an inordinate amount of emphasis on capitalization and spelling, and (5) the arithmetic skills test leans quite heavily on content, and is highly verbal.

The test is accompanied by a manual that is both thorough and informative. The manual contains many features that will assist the teacher in using test results to improve instruction. In summary, this test is highly recommended if one wishes to test primarily basic skills. It is a model of test construction and deserves emulation by other test constructors.

California Achievement Tests   Revised edition (1963 Norms). California Test Bureau, 1957. Consists of five levels: grades 1–2 (lower primary), 2.5 to 4.5 (upper primary), 4–6 (elementary), 7–9 (junior high), and 9–14 (advanced). Both primary level batteries have two forms, the elementary and junior high batteries have four forms each, and the advanced level battery has three forms. The batteries at each level attempt to assess the pupil's knowledge and skill in reading vocabulary, reading comprehension, arithmetic reasoning, arithmetic fundamentals, mechanics of English, and spelling. Working time varies from 89 minutes for the lower primary battery to 178 minutes for the junior high and advanced batteries. Content validity was stressed in the construction of all the subtests. Construct validity was studied by obtaining correlations between the subtests of the California Achievement Tests with the nearly comparable Stanford Achievement subtests. The correlations obtained were substantial. Numerous reliability coefficients are reported for the various subtests in the different levels. Estimated reliabilities (K-R 21) for the total scores for all five levels are consistently high, ranging from .95 to .98. K-R 21 reliabilities for total reading, total arithmetic, and total language scores range from .86 to .96. Some reliabilities fall below .80, namely, reading comprehension, arithmetic reasoning, and spelling in the lower primary; spelling in the upper primary; and arithmetic reasoning in the elementary level. Raw scores may be converted to grade placement scores, percentile ranks, standard scores, and stanines. A good feature of this battery is the provision of a table showing the predicted relationship of the California Achievement Test scores with academic aptitude scores obtained from the California Short Form Test of Mental Maturity. Another feature is a section on the cover where the pupil can record his errors so that they are readily evident. Other commendable features are diagnostic suggestions in the test manual, economical and efficient scoring, and provision for appraising handwriting in the spelling test (even though it does not enter into the total score). The test authors attempted to develop a battery of diagnostic tests. However, using these tests or their subscores for such purposes is not recommended until more data on the reliability of test score differences is forthcoming. This survey battery is useful for schools seeking an achievement battery to test only three general skills areas: reading, arithmetic, and language.

Sequential Tests of Educational Progress (STEP) Educational Testing Service, 1963. Consists of four levels (grades 4–6, 7–9, 10–12, and 13–14) with two forms for each level.[29] The batteries at each level have seven tests:[30] reading, writing, mathematics, social studies, science, listening, and essay.[31] With the exception of the essay test, all items are multiple-choice. Administration times vary for the different subtests, but overall testing time is 450 to 500 minutes. The battery is group-administered with the exception of the listening test, which is individually administered. The manual presents evidence for both content and predictive validity. However, the limited empirical data presented in the technical manual indicate that more evidence on predictive validity is necessary. The STEP is designed to assess the overall aims of education rather than the mastery of particular topics, and stress is placed upon the application of knowledge and skills. The Kuder-Richardson reliabilities are generally in the .80's. The somewhat high correlations between the STEP and the SCAT strongly suggest that they are measuring essentially similar constructs. Hence, although both tests are frequently administered, the writers feel that (for most purposes) too little additional information is gathered to warrant the administration of both tests to the same students. Raw scores are converted to percentile bands, which will

[29]The essay test has four forms for each level.
[30]A major portion of the STEP batteries is devoted to the testing of communication skills.
[31]The classroom teacher scores the essay by a product scale technique.

assist in test score interpretation.[32] There are many more additional positive features of the STEP: careful standardization, detailed reporting of norms, a student profile for the six objective tests, a student report form to help the student interpret his own scores, a separate teacher's guide, a comprehensive technical manual with supplements, good format, and a clear and concise manual of directions. Possibly the most important feature of the STEP is its emphasis on application and understanding rather than on factual recall.

As in any product, there are both virtues and limitations. The STEP is no exception. The description of the normative sample is not specified. The norms, even if they are representative, are based upon too few cases at the various grade levels and in a few instances are extrapolated or interpolated values. Statistical manipulations are not bad necessarily, but there is no reason to resort to these when actual data can be provided. The publishers suggest that one use of the STEP is to make school comparisons. And yet, normative data on school means are lacking. Another suggested use made by the STEP's authors is that it can be used to measure pupil growth. This may be a valid claim, but, until normative data from longitudinal studies are forthcoming, we caution the user trying to make meaningful comparisons in student growth. Another deficiency pertains to the conversion from raw scores to converted scores. Because of certain statistical artifacts, such conversions are highly suspect. This therefore results in problems of interpreting pupil growth and of comparing scores from one level to another or within any one level. The majority of the defects mentioned are easily remedied, granted that it would take considerable time, effort, and money. However, the publisher is a reputable firm and should not let such factors detract from this needed research.

The STEP is a good test. There are some who claim that it is not valid for the majority of schools because it stresses the application of knowledge rather than factual recall. The STEP has broken tradition in this respect. Anyone wishing to use the STEP should realize that unless the objectives of his school are in harmony with those of the test, it would be ridiculous to use this test for either evaluating the pupils, the curriculum, or the growth of individual pupils. If one's school subscribes to the traditional curriculum, the STEP is not for him. If one's school is part traditional and part modern, the STEP would serve as an excellent supplementary test.

Some survey batteries span the total elementary and secondary grades with articulated tests. Others cover the upper elementary and secondary grades. Still others are restricted to the high school grades. Although these

---

[32]The percentile bands cover a distance of one standard error of measurement above and below the obtained percentile. This means that the odds are about 2 to 1 that the student's true score falls within the given percentile band. Percentile bands do not reduce the error of measurement.

high school batteries may differ as to the fundamental educational goals emphasized, they all share common purposes — to help the student recognize the deficiencies in his preparation for college and to help predict the student's success in college. We will now briefly consider one of the more popular high school standardized achievement test batteries.

Iowa Tests of Educational Development (ITED)   Revised edition. Science Research Associates, Inc., 1963. There are nine subtests for grades 9–12 designed to measure understanding and application rather than recall of specific facts.[33] The four broad curricular areas of social studies, natural sciences, general mathematics and English are measured by nine separate subtests:[34] understanding of basic social concepts, general background in the natural sciences, correctness and appropriateness of expression, ability to do quantitative thinking, interpretation of reading materials in the social studies, interpretation of reading materials in the natural sciences, interpretation of literary materials, general vocabulary, and use of sources of information. There are two forms. There is a full-length and a modified version for all the subtests except use of sources of information. Each full-length subtest requires from 50 to 65 minutes' working time and each modified subtest (part of the full-length subtest) requires 40 minutes' working time. It is recommended that if the full-length form is used, four half-day sessions of about 2½ hours should be set aside for test administration. The manual contains evidence for both content and predictive validity. With respect to validity, the most essential quality in any test, the test authors discuss content, predictive, construct, and concurrent validity. Unfortunately, they do little more than discuss these. Yes, they do present some empirical data, but these data are a conglomeration of many little studies. Some of these studies report the number of subjects used while others do not.

The test authors' claim for content validity is for the user to take the tests, see what skills and proficiencies are measured, and then decide whether or not these abilities are desirable of a program of general instruction. Suggesting that the user take the test to familiarize himself with it, the items, and the method of administration is commendable — we strongly urge users to do this — but it is no substitute for the test authors describing the rationale used to select the items.

As mentioned earlier, the empirical evidence to demonstrate predictive validity is a compilation of many individual studies. Construct validity was studied by presenting correlations between the ITED and other tests

---

[33]Similar to STEP in this respect. The two differ, however, in other respects. For example, the ITED places greater emphasis on social science and science and less emphasis on communication skills.

[34]There are ten scores for these nine subtests. The first eight subtests are totaled to obtain a subtotal score.

as well as a subtest intercorrelation matrix. It would have been of much more value to present the latter data not only as average within-grade correlations but also separately by grade and sex.

Initially, the ITED was constructed so that each test would yield a reliability coefficient of .91 for students in a single grade. This aim has been fairly well-achieved in the later editions. The split-halves reliability of the full-length version range from .82 to .95 and from .83 to .96 for the class-period (modified) version. Composite score reliabilities range as high as .99. The probable error of any single standard score is approximately 1.2 standard score points. Because of the method used to compute the various reliability coefficients (separately by grade), the variability of scores is restricted, and hence the magnitudes of the coefficients are conservative.

The norms are based on the scores of over fifty thousand pupils tested in the fall of 1962. These students were enrolled in 136 school systems in 39 states. The population of schools was stratified according to geographical location and school size. Reference is made in the manual that the United States Office of Education census data were used but no comparison between these data and the norm data are provided.

Subtest raw scores can be converted to standard scores, which the authors claim can be compared from grade to grade if the tests are administered at the same time each year.[35] The standard scores can be converted to percentile ranks to make subtest comparisons. Percentile rank norms are provided for each subtest in each of the four grade levels. Profile charts are provided for both individual and school averages.[36] A valuable feature for counselors is the inclusion of ITED profiles for high school students who have already been graduated from college. These profiles are broken down by major field. Within each major field, separate profiles are provided for students with A, B, and C averages. Expectancy tables have been developed so that one can predict probable scores on the College Entrance Examination Board tests as well as probable success in college.

Because the authors imply that the major purpose of the test is to tell the teacher what his pupils already know in order that he may tailor the instructional program, one may conceive of the ITED as a quasi-diagnostic test. If so, it should be administered at the beginning of the school year.

---

[35]See Jack Bernard, Achievement test norms and time of year of testing. *Psychol. in Sch.*, 1966, *3* (3), 273–275. He contends that test publishers' norms are relevant only to achievement testing programs that are timed to coincide with the time of year in which the normative data were gathered. See also, Edwin G. Joselyn, Educational growth and the Iowa Tests of Educational Development. *Personnel guidance J.*, 1965, *44* (1), 35–39. Using data from the ITED, his research suggests that the interpretation of growth scores from grade to grade are hazardous even in this case.

[36]We feel that there are insufficient data presented to justify too much faith being placed in the interpretation of an individual's profile. As of now, chance factors play too important a role.

There are some very significant points to raise regarding the validity and utility of the ITED. There is no denying the fact that the ITED measures what it measures quite well. But, what does it measure? And how well does it measure these things in comparison to other tests? The test authors claim that the strength of the battery is in Subtests 5, 6, and 7 — subtests that pertain to the interpretation of literary materials in the social studies and natural sciences. Approximately three hours are spent to measure what should be, or could be measured in a one-hour reading test. The ITED battery takes about eight hours to administer. Is the time spent worth it? The writers feel that because the strength of the test is of a reading nature, the answer is negative. The test authors suggest that the series should be repeated over a four-year period, and yet they present no evidence in terms of longitudinal studies to support their assumption that pupil abilities change that much from one year to another to warrant such a suggestion. Numerous claims are made regarding the predictive validity of the ITED, but nowhere in the manuals are such claims substantiated. There is a paucity of data relevant to test-retest data, intertest correlations, and so forth. The research conducted with the full-length and modified versions shows that the modified version is as valuable as the full-length.

One of the bulletins, *Using the ITED for College Planning*, reports correlations between College Board scores and (1) ITED twelfth-grade composite scores and (2) the quantitative thinking scores. The correlations range from .80 to .87, which are quite substantial. However, it is noted in the bulletin that the ITED provides limited discrimination for SAT scores above 550. This, therefore, severely curtails using the ITED for counseling high school seniors intending to enroll in our more selective colleges.

There is still another perplexing and frustrating aspect of the ITED — the manuals. There is one for the examiner, another for the school administrator, another for the teacher and counselor; there is a college planning manual and various sundry interpretative accessories. Information contained in one manual may be absent in another. This necessitates much searching. It indeed would be valuable to combine all the separate manuals into one.

From a technical standpoint, the ITED appears to have been well constructed. The norms provided are adequate, but the statistical information regarding validity and reliability are very meager. We do not feel that sufficient evidence has been submitted to demonstrate the test's validity.

We will now consider in greater detail one of the most popular and useful standardized achievement test batteries used in our schools: the Stanford Achievement Test. This is not the only good survey battery (others are available), and it is not perfect, as will be evident in the ensuing discussion. The Stanford is selected for detailed discussion becasue it represents one of the better test batteries for surveying school achievement.

CRITICAL EVALUATION OF THE STANFORD ACHIEVEMENT TEST[37]

Grade Level and Content

Primary 1 (Grades 1.2 to 2.5). Included in a single booklet of 12 pages are six subtests: word reading, paragraph meaning, vocabulary, spelling, work-study skills, and arithmetic. Requires 127 to 160 minutes working time and is administered in five sessions.

Primary 2 (Grades 2.5 to 3.9). Eight scores: word meaning, paragraph meaning, science and social studies concepts, spelling, work-study skills, language, arithmetic computation, and arithmetic concepts. The eight tests are presented in a 16-page booklet. Administration time is 185 to 235 minutes. Suggested that the battery be given in seven sessions.

Intermediate 1 (Grades 4 to 5.5). Eight (partial battery) or ten (complete battery) scores: word meaning, paragraph meaning, spelling, work-study skills, language, arithmetic computation, arithmetic concepts, and arithmetic applications are considered in the partial battery. The complete battery includes the social studies and science tests. All tests are contained in a 23 to 31 page booklet. Administration times are 201 minutes (five sessions) for the partial battery and 261 minutes (six sessions) for the complete battery.

Intermediate 2 (Grades 5.5 to 6.9). The partial battery consists of seven tests, and the complete battery contains nine tests. The partial battery consists of the following tests: word meaning, paragraph meaning, spelling, language, arithmetic computation, arithmetic concepts, and arithmetic applications. The complete battery has, in addition, social studies and science tests. The partial battery is contained in a 22-page booklet; the complete battery in a 31-page booklet. The administration times are 192 minutes (five sessions) for the partial battery and 267 minutes (seven sessions) for the complete battery.

Advanced (Grades 7–9). The partial battery — paragraph meaning, spelling, language, arithmetic computation, arithmetic concepts, and arithmetic applications — is administered in four sessions and takes approximately 178 minutes to administer. The complete battery has, in addition, social studies and science tests. It is administered in six sessions and requires 255 minutes testing time. The test booklets for the partial and complete batteries are 20 and 32 pages, respectively.

---

[37]Revised edition published by Harcourt, 1964. Authors of the primary to advanced batteries are: Truman L. Kelley, Richard Madden, Eric F. Gardner, and Herbert C. Rudman. Authors of the high school battery are Eric F. Gardner, Jack C. Merwin, Robert Callis, and Richard Madden.

High School (Grades 9–12).[38] The partial battery consists of seven tests: English, numerical competence, mathematics, reading, science, social studies, and spelling. The working time is 320 minutes. The complete battery also contains an arts and humanities test, a business and economics test, and a technical comprehension test. The complete battery requires a working time of 440 minutes. Although the manual does not suggest the number of testing sessions needed, the writers recommend that a minimum of 4 sessions be contemplated for the full battery and three sessions for the partial battery.

The Stanford Achievement Test at all grade levels is concerned with measuring the outcomes of a core curriculum — spelling, language, reading, and arithmetic skills. At the Intermediate and Advanced levels, the science and social studies tests are optional, but they are required for both the partial and complete high school batteries. The test items were prepared after consultation with subject matter specialists, and careful and considerable analysis of textbooks, word counts, and syllabi.

The paragraph meaning test, which is essentially a reading test, is found at all levels except the high school battery. The word meaning test,[39] in essence, a vocabulary test, is found in the batteries designed for use in grades 2 through 6. The pupils select the word that makes a sentence or statement correct.

The spelling tests in the primary and elementary levels consist of words read by the examiner and recorded by the pupil. In the intermediate, advanced, and high school batteries, the pupil's knowledge of spelling is measured by presenting four words in a group. In each group, the student selects the word spelled incorrectly.

The arithmetic test in the Primary 1 battery attempts to assess the pupil's knowledge of number concepts and measures and his problem-solving ability. All questions are read aloud by the examiner, and the pupil indicates his answer by either (1) drawing a line from one object to another, (2) placing an "X" across the correct answer or (3) recording the numerical answer in the test booklet.

The arithmetic concepts test found at all levels except the Primary 1 (the high school level contains this in the numerical competence test) is concerned with measuring meaning and understanding rather than with just

---

[38]The high school battery has three forms, whereas all other batteries have four forms for each level. English is equivalent to the language subtest in the other levels, reading is similar to paragraph meaning, and numerical competence and mathematics are similar to arithmetic computation and arithmetic concepts, respectively.

[39]Word meaning was included in the Primary 1 battery until the 1964 revision, when it was replaced by a word reading test that measures the pupil's ability to analyze a word without the aid of context clues.

carrying out mechanical operations. The advanced and high school batteries do the best job of reflecting the modern curriculum.

The arithmetic computation tests in the Primary 2, intermediate, and advanced batteries consist of problems in the fundamental arithmetic processes of addition, subtraction, multiplication, and division.

The arithmetic application tests in the intermediate and advanced levels are similar to the problem-solving test in the Primary 2 level in that verbal problems are used to test the pupil's knowledge of the fundamental arithmetic processes.

The arithmetic application tests that are found in the intermediate and advanced levels have more items that involve the reading and interpretation of graphs.

In the high school battery, there is a numerical competence test that includes items designed to measure knowledge of fundamental arithmetic processes such as $\frac{1}{8} + \frac{1}{6} =$　; items testing the pupil's ability to read graphs; and items that require the pupil to translate symbolic terminology before carrying out the required operation.

The high school battery mathematics test consists of two parts — Part A, which emphasizes elementary algebra and geometry, and Part B, which measures knowledge of advanced algebra, trigonometry, and such mathematical concepts as probability and set theory. Part A may be used independently of Part B. Part B should not be used alone because it does not have separate norms.

With the exception of the Primary 1 battery, language is tested at all levels. The language tests in all the batteries include usage (grammar), punctuation, capitalization, and sentence sense. The only difference among the various batteries is the manner in which these skills and knowledge are tested. For example, in the intermediate and advanced batteries, there are separate subtests for usage, capitalization, and punctuation. In the high school battery, however, all these same skills are tested by five paragraphs that may contain a variety of errors. The pupil must decide whether there is an error in (1) capitalization, (2) grammar, (3) punctuation, (4) spelling, or (5) no error. This testing approach differs from the conventional one that presents a set of items that are either correct or incorrect for a specific part of language, such as punctuation or grammar. For example, in the high school battery, the pupil is given a paragraph that contains the sentence *Mary's mother is a good cook*, and he must determine (1) whether or not there is an error and (2) if there is an error, what kind of error is present.

Two additional tests that are common to all the batteries are the science and social studies tests. At the primary level, the science and social studies tests resemble vocabulary tests of science and social studies concepts — which are purported to be independent of the pupil's reading skill. At all other levels, the science tests are designed to assess the pupil's ability to make generalizations and applications.[40] In the intermediate and advanced batteries, the science tests contain items on life science, chemistry, physics, conservation, and the scientific method. In the high school battery, there are items on physical science, life science, and earth science. Part A is concerned primarily with general content, while Part B is designed for students who have taken advanced science courses.

The social studies tests in the intermediate and advanced batteries include items on history, geography, and civics. In the high school battery, the major emphasis is on American and world history, although there are a few items on government, economics, geography, and the reading of maps, graphs, and charts. As in the science test, the four-response, multiple-choice, best-answer type item is used. The social studies tests in the intermediate and advanced battery also contain a subtest of study skills. Included in this section are items dealing with the reading of graphs and tables, map reading, interpretation of a globe, and using library references.[41]

A separate reading test is found in the high school battery. A series of paragraphs of from six to about 40 lines in length are used to measure whether the student is able to make inferences, to comprehend the content, and to ascertain what should be inferred from the material. In the primary and intermediate batteries these same skills are measured by separate subtests.

Figure 3–1 illustrates some of the types of items used in the Intermediate 2 subtests. Although the subtests of the other levels have not been illustrated, the reader should now have a general knowledge of the types of items used. Only after examining and taking the test will the user be able to determine how valid the test will be for his purposes.

Administration

The Stanford Achievement Test can be administered by the classroom teacher without any formal training. The manuals accompanying each battery are well written, complete, and concise for both examiner and examinees. For the pupils, there are examples that are worked out as well as practice items that are attempted before the actual test is begun. If necessary, the examiner can and should give assistance on these practice items.

---

[40]These skills are measured by using a four-response, multiple choice, best-answer type of item. Although the facts needed to make the generalization may not be directly tested, we must assume that the pupil knows these facts before he is able to apply them. Thus, if a pupil missed an item, we do not know whether it was because he could not generalize or whether he in fact did not know the material.

[41]With the exception of how to use a dictionary or library reference, the other skills are incorporated in the kinds of items used in the high school battery.

Figure 3-1

TEST 1: Word Meaning

DIRECTIONS: Read the beginning part of each sentence and the words under it. Decide which of the answers given is *best*. Look at the answer spaces at the right or on your answer sheet (if you have one). Fill in the space which has the same number as the word you have chosen.

SAMPLES

A The name of a color is —

   1 farm   3 red
   2 milk   4 pet   A   1 2 3 4   ○ ○ ● ○

B The day that comes after Monday is —

   5 Sunday   7 Wednesday
   6 Tuesday   8 Saturday   B   5 6 7 8   ○ ○ ○ ○

TEST 2: Paragraph Meaning

DIRECTIONS: Read each paragraph below. Decide which of the numbered words or phrases below the paragraph is *best* for each blank. Look at the answer spaces at the right or on your answer sheet (if you have one). Fill in the space which has the same number as the word(s) you have chosen.

SAMPLES

We went up in an airplane. At first we flew near the A where we could see people and animals. Later we could not see them. Our plane was too B .

A 1 house   3 town
   2 ground   4 hills   A   1 2 3 4   ○ ● ○ ○

B 5 high   7 far
   6 low   8 fast   B   5 6 7 8   ○ ○ ○ ○

TEST 3: Spelling

DIRECTIONS: Read each of the groups of words below. One of the words in each group is misspelled. Find the word that has been misspelled. Look at the answer spaces at the right or on your answer sheet (if you have one). Fill in the space which has the same number as the word you have chosen.

SAMPLES

A 1 dog   3 walk
   2 boy   4 yse   A   1 2 3 4   ○ ○ ○ ●

B 5 this   7 cold
   6 kap   8 tell   B   5 6 7 8   ○ ○ ○ ○

TEST 4: Language   *Part A: Usage*

DIRECTIONS: Read each sentence below. Decide which, if *either*, of the two choices in each sentence is correct in *standard written English*. Look at the answer spaces at the right or on your answer sheet (if you have one). If the choice numbered 1 is correct, fill in the space under the 1. If the choice numbered 2 is correct, fill in the space under the 2. If neither choice 1 nor choice 2 is correct, fill in the space under the N. ("N" stands for "neither.")

SAMPLES

A Joe ^{1} set in the chair. . . . . A   1 2 N   ○ ● ○
     ^{2} sat

B Sally ^{1} ain't here. . . . . B   1 2 N   ○ ○ ○
     ^{2} aren't

Figure 3-1 continued

TEST 4: **Language (Continued)**   *Part B: Punctuation*

DIRECTIONS: In this part, all punctuation marks and capital letters have been left out. Decide which mark of punctuation, if any, is needed after each *underlined* word. If a punctuation mark is needed, find the punctuation mark in the row at the right that has the same number as the underlined word. Then look at the answer spaces at the right or on your answer sheet (if you have one). Fill in the space which has the same letter as the letter beside the punctuation mark you have chosen. If no punctuation mark is needed, fill in the space under the NP. ("NP" stands for "no punctuation needed.")

SAMPLES

C
yesterday we had a holiday

D
mother served cake and ice cream

C a (.)   b (,)

D c (.)   d (,)

a   b   NP
○   ○   ●
c   d   NP
○   ○   ○

TEST 4: **Language (Continued)**   *Part C: Capitalization*

DIRECTIONS: In this part, all capital letters and most of the punctuation marks have been left out. You are to decide whether certain words should be capitalized. These words are *underlined* and have a number above them. You are not to do anything with words that are not underlined. Look at the answer spaces at the right or on your answer sheet (if you have one). Be sure that the number beside the answer space agrees with the number of the word. If the word or phrase should be capitalized, fill in the space under the letter C. ("C" stands for "capital letter.") If a small letter is correct, fill in the space under the letter s. ("s" stands for "small letter.")

SAMPLE

E
mary and tom are going

C   s
E   ●   ○

TEST 4:   **Language (Continued)**   *Part D: Dictionary Skills*

DIRECTIONS: This is a test of your ability to use a dictionary. There are two sections. In this section four words (in boxes) are shown as they might appear in a dictionary, with four definitions given for each word. Below the box for each word are four questions. In the first two questions, the given word is used in a sentence. Read each sentence, then decide which dictionary definition *best* defines the word as it is being used in the sentence. Look at the answer spaces at the right or on your answer sheet (if you have one). Fill in the space which has the same *number* as the definition you have chosen. Two other questions are asked about each word. For each of these, decide which answer is *best* and mark the space which has the same *letter* as the answer you have chosen.

SAMPLES

> **check** (chek) 1. *n.* A pattern in squares of different colors. 2. *v.* To prove true or right. 3. *n.* A mark showing that something has been examined or compared. 4. *v.* To hold back or control.

G Miss Jones made a **check** beside each example.

H The word **check** in the sentence above is —

   a a noun   b a verb   c an adjective   d an adverb

     1   2   3   4
G ◯ ◯ ● ◯

     a   b   c   d
H ◯ ◯ ◯ ◯

TEST 4:   **Language (Continued)**   *Part E: Sentence Sense*

DIRECTIONS: Read each group of words below. Decide if the words make *one complete sentence*, *more than one complete sentence*, or *no complete sentence*. Look at the answer spaces at the right or on your answer sheet (if you have one). If the group of words *can* be correctly punctuated as one sentence by merely putting a period or question mark at the end, fill in the space under the 1. If the group of words *could* be punctuated as two sentences (without changing or omitting any words), fill in the space under the 2. If the group of words is just part of a sentence, fill in the space under the N. ("N" stands for "not a complete sentence.")

SAMPLES

K In 1818 the flag had twenty stars ....
     1   2   N
K ● ◯ ◯

L In the right-hand corner of the flag ...
     1   2   N
L ◯ ◯ ◯

Figure 3-1 continued

TEST 5: **Arithmetic Computation**

DIRECTIONS: Work the example in each box. Then look at the possible answers at the right side of the box and see if your answer is given. If it is, fill in the space at the right or on your answer sheet (if you have one) which has the same letter as the answer you have chosen. If your answer is *not* given, fill in the space which has the same letter as the letter beside the NG (which means "not given"). Use a separate sheet of paper for figuring.

SAMPLE A

$$\begin{array}{r} 6\,4 \\ -2\,3 \\ \hline 4\,/ \end{array}$$

a 31
b 40
c 41
d 42
e NG

a b c d e
A ○ ○ ● ○ ○

TEST 6: **Arithmetic Concepts**

DIRECTIONS: Read each question. Decide which of the answers given below is correct. Look at the answer spaces at the right or on your answer sheet (if you have one). Fill in the space which has the same letter as the answer you have chosen.

SAMPLE

A A dime is worth how many cents?

a 2   c 10
b 5   d 25

a b c d
A ○ ○ ● ○

TEST 7: **Arithmetic Applications**

DIRECTIONS: Work each problem. Then look at the possible answers under the problem and see if your answer is given. If it is, fill in the answer space at the right or on your answer sheet (if you have one) which has the same letter as the answer you have chosen. If your answer is not given, fill in the space which has the same letter as the letter beside NG (which means "not given"). If NG is not listed for an example, one of the given answers is the correct answer. There is no sales tax in any problem on the test unless you are told otherwise. Use a separate sheet of paper for all figuring.

TEST 8: **Social Studies**   *Part A: Content*

DIRECTIONS: Read each question. Decide which of the answers given below is *best*. Look at the answer spaces at the right or on your answer sheet (if you have one). Fill in the space which has the same number as the answer you have chosen.

SAMPLE

A The main business of a restaurant is to sell —

   1 candy   3 groceries   1   2   3   4
   2 clothes   4 meals   A ○ ○ ○ ●

TEST 9: **Science**

DIRECTIONS: Read each question. Decide which of the answers given below is *best*. Look at the answer spaces at the right or on your answer sheet (if you have one). Fill in the space which has the same number as the answer you have chosen.

SAMPLE

A As water boils, it changes to —

   1 ice   3 steam   1   2   3   4
   2 dew   4 snow   A ○ ○ ● ○

Figure 3-1   Sample items reproduced from the Intermediate 2 battery of the Stanford Achievement Test. (Copyright 1964 by Harcourt, Brace & World, Inc. Reproduced by special permission of the publisher.)

Scoring

In both primary batteries, hand scoring is necessary because the answers are recorded in the test booklets. For the other levels, either hand or machine scoring is possible. The directions for scoring are clear and can be easily followed.

On the title page of each battery, there are boxes to record the scores for the separate subtests.[42] In addition, the pupil's profile can be plotted and, comparisons can be made with his grade norm.

Types of Scores

Four types of scores (norms) are used: grade, age, percentile, and stanine. The grade scores can be readily converted to grade equivalents simply by placing a decimal before the last digit. For example, if Johnny's grade score is 76, this means that he is performing at the grade level of 7.6. The manual cautions the user to be wary of grade scores greater than 96, because the grade norms are based on the performance of pupils in grades 1 through 9 tested in the standardization program.[43]

Norming

The standardization of the test was excellent. All Stanford Achievement Test norms are based on the total enrollment in regular classes at each grade level, except for a small group markedly atypical as to age. For all levels, the authors stratified the elementary and secondary school populations on (1) type of school (public, private, segregated, and integrated), (2) geographical location, (3) median family income, and (4) the median level of education of adults over 25 years of age. For the standardization of the primary, intermediate, and advanced level batteries, over 850,000 pupils in 264 stratified school systems from the 50 states and the District of Columbia were tested. Different weighting procedures, however, were used to ascertain the composition of the grades 1–3 and 4–9 samples. For the standardization of the high school battery, over 22,000 students from 58 schools in 39 school systems were used to establish the norms for converting raw scores to standard scores. Smaller numbers of the total group were used to establish the norms for the college preparatory, special semester, and different curricular groups. Each of the norms is further subdivided to correspond to testing periods commonly used in our schools — September to December, January

---

[42]With the exception of the language subtests (where the score is right — wrong), the score for each test is the number correct.
[43]See Chapter I for problems due to extrapolation.

to April, and May to June — the beginning, middle, and end of the school year, respectively.

All subjects in the standardization sample were also given the appropriate level of the Otis Quick-Scoring Mental Ability Test. This provides the user with the means whereby the achievement test score can be compared with intelligence. The caution and thoroughness used to standardize the Stanford Achievement Test makes this test a model for other test publishers to follow.

Reliability

All reliability data are in the form of split-half reliability coefficients, Kuder-Richardson estimates, and standard errors of measurement. The 134 split-half coefficients range from .66 to .95, with all but 13 being above .85. The 122 Kuder-Richardson coefficients range from .71 to .96, with all but 15 being above .85. The majority of the lower coefficients are found for the arithmetic tests in the Intermediate 2 and advanced batteries. For all but the high school battery, each of these values is computed from a random sample of 1000 cases[44] drawn from each of the appropriate grades.

Where more than one grade was used in the standardization, separate reliability coefficients are presented for each subtest for every battery by grades.[45] For example, the reliability data for the language test in the advanced battery are shown:[46]

	r_{11}	$K\text{-}R_{20}$	Standard Error of Measurement
Grade 7	.94	.91	5.0
Grade 8	.94	.92	9.5
Grade 9	.94	.93	8.0

With the exception of the advanced and high school batteries, the majority of standard errors of measurement are in the neighborhood of two to four grade score points. If the grade score standard error of measurement is 4 (that is, 0.4 grade equivalents), and if a pupil obtained a grade equivalent of 6.2, the odds are about 2 to 1 that his true grade equivalent is

[44]The number of cases used to compute the reliability of the high school battery is not indicated in the manual. In the primary batteries, only first and second graders, respectively, were used. The Intermediate 1 battery used only fourth graders; the Intermediate 2 used fifth and sixth graders. The advanced and high school batteries used students in the grade levels for which the test was designed.

[45]The high school battery also presents reliability data for grades 9 to 12 combined, as well as for the separate grades.

[46]The reliabilities reported are corrected split-half reliabilities. The standard error of measurement is expressed in terms of grade scores, and you will recall, is 10 times as large as if reported in terms of grade equivalents.

somewhere between 5.8 and 6.6. In the advanced battery, the standard errors of measurement are primarily in the range of 9 to 11 grade score points (this is to be expected since the population is more homogeneous at the upper levels). In the high school battery, the standard errors of measurement are in the range of 2 to 3 *standard score* points (Note: With the exception of the high school battery, all S_e's are reported in terms of grade score points).

On the whole, the test reliabilities are quite high, considering that they were computed for single grade levels. The publishers are to be commended for their inclusion of grade score standard errors of measurement. However, the interpretation of a test score would have been made easier had the publishers, in the test manual, included some examples of how to use the standard error of measurement.[47] Specifying it is one thing; using it is another.

Validity

Content validity was stressed during the construction of the Stanford Achievement Test. The authors state that a major goal was to make sure that the test content would be in harmony with present-day school objectives and would measure what is actually being taught in today's schools. To achieve this, they made an extensive curricular study by (1) a thorough review of widely used elementary textbooks, (2) a review of research in developmental and educational psychology concerning children's concepts, experiences, and vocabulary at successive age levels, and (3) consultation with subject matter specialists. In addition, item analysis data from the experimental editions guided the test constructors in their attempt to obtain higher validity.

The manual states that the test authors wanted to construct a battery that would measure the knowledges, skills, and understandings commonly considered important in our public schools. The test authors felt that recent, extensive curriculum research and the results of item analyses demonstrated the test's reflection of current instructional goals, materials, and methods. They also indicated that appropriate weight is given both to traditional objectives and to recent curriculum trends. On the whole, the test authors have been successful in their attempts to make the 1964 revision a better test, but have not gone far enough in reflecting curricular change. For example, the arithmetic tests still favor the traditional program.

Some other criticisms pertain to the social studies and science tests. Although one might expect to find items that are assessing the higher mental processes (such as critical thinking ability) we find items measuring study

---

[47]The *Teachers guide for interpretation and use of test results* presents some case studies regarding the interpretation of a pupil's profile. Nowhere, however, is the standard error of measurement illustrated.

skills or factual knowledge.[48] Test interpretation could have been made easier and more valid by providing a table of subtest intercorrelations. In summary, the claim for validity is made on the basis of the description of content sampling. The authors place too much emphasis upon the user's judgment, which, although commendable, is not entirely defensible. Also, if the test is to be used for more than assessment, it must demonstrate predictive validity.

Format

The tests and the administrator's manual for each of the six levels are presented in 8½ by 11 inch booklets. The booklet covers at each level are of a different color. All printing is in black ink on white paper, except the answer portion, which is in the distinctive booklet color. The quality of paper, reproduction, and illustrations is excellent. With the exception of the high school battery, the front page of each test booklet provides space for personal information as well as a place for recording the grade score, percentile rank, and stanines for each test in the battery. Included with each test packet is a class record (and at the lower levels, a class analysis chart) that provides the user with a cumulative picture of the pupils' test performance.

Interpretation and Use

In this section, our attention will be focused on some of the strengths and deficiencies of the Stanford Achievement Test and how they relate to the ultimate value and use of the test scores in the making of valid and reliable educational decisions.

INSTRUCTIONAL USE   A major advantage of this battery is that it provides for a continuous measurement of skills, knowledge, and understanding in the fundamental or core curriculum subjects from grades 1 through 12. This continuous articulation of content permits the teacher or counselor (1) to readily identify persistent strengths or weaknesses and (2) to obtain a global concept of the pupil's growth in the various content areas. The user, after plotting the pupil's performance, will have a chart that "will permit ready identification of areas of strength and weakness, and the magnitude of the departure from typical performance in the various subjects."[49]

The test manual states that the Stanford Achievement Test measures what is being taught in our schools today and that appropriate attention is given

---

[48]This may be more the fault of our elementary and junior high school curricula than poor content validity of the test items.

[49]Stanford Achievement Test, *Manual of directions*, Intermediate 1 battery, p. 18.

to both the traditional and modern curriculum. Teachers can use this test to ascertain whether their goals of instruction are compatible with those measured by the Stanford. However, the teacher must be cautious in his use of the Stanford as the sole criterion of what should be taught in his class. It is a content test rather than a skills test. Hence, the teacher who stresses the development of skills will find the Stanford to lack the degree of validity he desires for his purposes.

There is no denying the fact that the Stanford is one of the most (if not the most) carefully constructed tests with respect to reflecting the curriculum in our public schools. This fact, however, does not negate the possibility that there are marked deficiencies in the test. Some of the specific criticisms of the Stanford are as follows:

1. The language section at the Intermediate 1 level appears to be a speeded test even though the test authors felt that the majority of pupils have sufficient time to complete it. The writers feel that to read about 1500 words in 29 paragraphs and then to be required to answer 60 items (which are not mere factual recall) in 30 minutes will be impossible for the average fourth or fifth grader.

2. The intermediate level batteries, in contrast to the primary level batteries, do not appear to reflect the changes in our mathematics curriculum. The social studies and the science tests, especially the latter, do not reflect curriculum trends.

3. Occasionally, in the social studies tests, we find attitudinal items. For example, one item asks what you should do if pupils are cheating on a test. Although we feel that noncognitive elements should be stressed in our schools, we do not feel that this should be done in the content section of an achievement test.

4. There are certain measurement problems associated with the science and social studies tests, especially at the advanced and primary levels, that make their value questionable. For example, in the advanced battery a score of 31 corresponds to a grade equivalent of 7.2. A score of 33 corresponds to a grade quivalent of 8.0. What is more serious, however, is that the science test consists of 60 items, and the intended range of the test is for grades 7 to 9.

5. Although the norms provided are adequate and are based upon sound sampling techniques, it would have been very valuable insofar as making interschool comparisons is concerned, to have access to at least geographical and even district or city norms. Although this need not be part of the material reported in either the manual or technical supplement, such data should be made available to interested users.

6. Many claims are made regarding the use of the Stanford results for instructional or curricular purposes. Yet, any evidence regarding the predic-

tive validity of the Stanford is lacking. Possibly, this is because the test is so new. We hope that such studies will be forthcoming.

7. Although some evidence is presented regarding the degree of overlap among the tests, no interbattery correlation matrix is presented. Also, regarding the equivalence of the various forms, there are no actual studies reported. These are alluded to in the Technical Supplement,[50] and two studies are reported regarding the comparability of the 1953 and 1964 editions. Other than this, there is no information presented.

These deficiencies, in some instances, are only deficiencies and not errors. Many of them can be readily corrected and, if so, would make the Stanford Achievement Test more useful. They have been discussed primarily to caution the user in his application and interpretation of the Stanford scores. In order to validly appraise his curriculum, his method of teaching, and his pupils' strengths and weaknesses, the teacher should be cognizant of these and other deficiencies.

The Stanford is quite valid for evaluating pupil status and progress. For teachers who frequently like to obtain a cumulative index of their pupils' progress, the Stanford provides a cumulative assessment of pupil knowledge with an articulated series of tests from grades 1 to 12.

Many instances arise when a teacher is interested in knowing whether a pupil is working at the level of his capacity. The Stanford, because it was standardized with the Otis Quick-Scoring Mental Ability Test provides for such information.

The Stanford, as well as other survey batteries, can be used to evaluate the relative strengths and weaknesses of pupils because of its extensive set of subscores. However, provision of many subtests invariably results in short tests (because of time factors), and these short tests have relatively low reliability. Therefore, although we may get an individual profile, it is difficult to interpret, and it may result in gross remedial errors. Although other test publishers sometimes allude to their test as a valid diagnostic tool, the authors of the Stanford *wisely caution against the use of part scores within a given subject area for individual diagnostic purposes.*

In summary, there are many situations where the Stanford can be used for instructional purposes. At the same time, there are certain limitations that preclude absolute faith being placed in the test scores, the thoroughness of construction notwithstanding. The Stanford Achievement Test should not (1) be used for individual diagnosis, and (2) be a major criterion in course planning.

GUIDANCE AND COUNSELING USE   The Stanford Achievement Test is valuable to the counselor because it (1) provides for a cumulative measurement, (2) provides for a ready identification of strengths and weak-

---

[50]*Stanford Achievement Test technical supplement*, 1966.

nesses because of the profile feature, and (3) permits a comparison of the pupil's achievement with his capacity. With test scores from the Stanford, the counselor can assist the student in making a more sound educational or vocational decision than if this data were not available. However, very cautious predictions should be made because the Stanford's predictive validity has not been demonstrated.

The interpretation of the test profile is also fraught with problems. Because stanines are used to construct the profile, this may result in over-interpretation because of the size of the intercorrelations. We recommend percentile ranks.

It is common knowledge that a pupil's obtained score is not his true score. Although the publishers have provided tables indicating the standard error of measurement for the various tests, they have neglected to discuss how this statistic is to be interpreted. This can lead to errors in interpretation by the unsophisticated user.

A table provided for the high school battery that would be of value for the other levels is the standard error of difference table. By using this table, the counselor can ascertain with a fair degree of confidence whether a difference between a score of 46 on the English test and one of 49 on the reading test is a true difference or whether this difference could be solely due to chance. The major value of such tables is that they assist the counselor in determining how much significance, if any, should be attached to the different scores in the test battery. These tables should prevent one from assuming that Johnny with scores of 86 in mathematics and 82 in science, is more proficient in one than the other. They will also assist the counselor in explaining the meaning of, and value to be attached to, test score differences.

The grade equivalents provided are probably often misinterpreted. Because the test's grade norms are based on the performance of pupils in grades 1 to 9 in the standardization program, any grade score beyond 96 must be interpreted cautiously. The test authors are to be commended for their statement that extrapolated scores are very misleading.

The writers feel that although the median battery score is contained in the manual, users should ignore it. It may be very misleading, especially when there is a low intercorrelation among the battery subtests. When this is the case, the median battery score will be more damaging than helpful in making educational decisions.

ADMINISTRATIVE USES   Although results from the Stanford Achievement Test can be used for a multitude of administrative decisions, the more common ones are (1) student selection, classification, and placement and (2) curriculum planning and evaluation.

Selection, Classification, and Placement   Although the Stanford Achievement Test results may be used to select, classify, or place students for particular programs or instructional purposes, the reader should be cognizant of the fact that scores at either extreme (high or low) may be very misleading and could conceivably result in misclassification. In actual practice, the writers recommend when either a very high or very low test score is obtained for a pupil, he should be given either the next higher or lower level battery in a retest situation so that a more valid estimate of his performance might be obtained. For example, let us assume that when Johnny was given the Primary 2 tests, he scored very high. If the teacher wishes to ascertain whether the first score is a relatively accurate picture of his performance, Johnny should be given the next higher level, the Intermediate 1 battery.

Any decisions pertaining to the classification, selection, or placement of students must be made with caution and with as much supporting data as possible. The results of any standardized survey battery should be used as supplementary and not absolute information.

Curriculum Planning and Evaluation   Quite frequently public schools are criticized for not keeping up with changing social conditions. They are claimed to be behind the times. Although we do not feel that the Stanford Achievement Test (nor any other standardized achievement test) should be the sole criterion for evaluating the school curriculum, standardized test results may be invaluable in helping make such decisions. Remember! A good standardized achievement test reflects the important objectives stressed throughout the country. Therefore, if teachers and administrators subscribe to the test's objectives, they should be willing to evaluate their curriculum in the light of test scores obtained from that test. There is little doubt that the Stanford Achievement Test was meticulously constructed and standardized and reflects the opinions of curriculum experts and teachers and syllabi throughout the country. However, the Stanford does not stress the application of knowledge as much as some standardized tests. It is primarily composed of items requiring factual recall; it has not kept pace with the changing curriculum, especially in modern mathematics programs; and it has been constructed by humans, who are not infallible. Recognizing these deficiencies, the administrator using Stanford test scores should be guided in his decisions regarding curriculum revision.

Summary of the Stanford Achievement Test

Despite minor criticisms of the Stanford test — paucity of predictive validity data, conservativeness (which makes it reflect the traditional curriculum), and lack of examples to assist teachers in evaluating the profiles — we recommend it highly. The Stanford series were meticulously constructed and standardized. They provide for continuous measurement with a series of articulated tests from grades 1 to 12. The final decision, however, regarding the tests' validity must rest on the user's instructional objectives.

SUMMARY OF ACHIEVEMENT TESTS

Achievement tests run the gamut from readiness and diagnostic tests to prognostic content-oriented tests (be they single subject matter tests, single survey tests, or survey batteries) and from pre-school to graduate and professional school. All, however, regardless of their format, or types of knowledge and skills surveyed, or types of items used, are designed to give us an index of what the student knows at a particular point in time.

Readiness tests are normally restricted to reading whereas diagnostic tests are confined primarily to reading and arithmetic. These tests are used most frequently in the primary grades and hence the largest number of readiness and diagnostic tests are to be found in grades K–3. Readiness and diagnostic tests differ from the conventional standardized achievement (subject-matter content) tests in that they are in, or attempt to confine themselves to, a very limited area — ascertaining whether the pupil possesses those skills and knowledge to begin a reading program *or* learning the nature of the pupil's difficulties in say reading or arithmetic. The majority of these tests are similar in format and it is nearly impossible to recognize a test only from an inspection of just a few items. There are some differences, however, in the reading readiness tests that are published — these differences reflecting the importance attached to certain facets deemed to be important in beginning to learn to read. For example, one test author might feel that it is essential for the beginning reader to be able to recognize similarities and differences in geometric shapes. Another test author might feel that this skill is unimportant. Hence, if these two authors constructed a reading readiness test, there would be a difference in the kinds of items employed. Diagnostic tests appear to have more similarity than even readiness tests. Their major purpose is to help the teacher recognize the pupil's difficulties and therefore diagnostic tests are constructed so that they permit the pupil to maximize the number of errors he can make. There may be a difference of opinion as to whether a pupil is ready to learn to read, but there is very little difference as to whether he exhibits tendencies of reversals, or omissions when he is reading. It is also important to remember that no single readiness or diagnostic test can assess all the skills and knowledge needed by the pupil to learn effectively.

In addition, we have considered some of the more popular survey batteries that are used at the elementary and secondary levels. If the teacher desires to obtain a better picture of the pupil's knowledge, he is advised to select a standardized achievement test in that particular subject. Single or specific achievement tests are also valuable to the counselor. For example, if a student plans to become a doctor, it would be helpful to know how well he performs on specific biology and chemistry tests because these two areas are of vital importance in medicine (or at least in medical education).

Some of the batteries, such as the Stanford Achievement Test and the California Achievement Tests, provide for continuous measurement from grades 1 through 12. Others are intended for grades 4 to 12 (STEP), or for only high school students (ITED). It should be readily obvious that a survey battery cannot adequately measure all or even most of the outcomes of every (or any) instructional program. However, all batteries attempt to provide measures of achievement in the core subjects by having tests of vocabulary, arithmetic, spelling, reading, and language. The various batteries provide separate subtest scores as well as a total score. Using normative data, the raw scores are transformed to some form of standard score to permit meaningful comparisons among the various subtests.

There are other differences among the various survey batteries. At the primary level (grades 1–3) the content is similar, although the format may differ, from one battery to another. After the fourth of fifth grade, the content of the various batteries differs markedly. Some batteries measure work-study skills, others do not. Some batteries may devote 15 percent of the test to measuring reading comprehension while others will devote about 30 percent. The various batteries also differ in the number of subtests. For example, at the elementary level, the Stanford yields six scores whereas the California Achievement Tests (CAT) gives 18 separate scores.[51] The CAT, STEP, and Stanford Achievement Test measure the fundamental skills of reading, mathematics, and language. The STEP is the only achievement test battery that provides a test of listening ability and that has an essay section where students write themes on selected topics.

The CAT and, to a lesser degree, the Stanford place much emphasis on memory of factual material. The STEP places major emphasis on higher cognitive abilities, such as analysis, synthesis, and interpretation.

The types of norms provided by the Stanford, CAT, and STEP are another point of difference. The CAT provides grade norms, percentile ranks, standard scores, stanines, and grade placement scores. The STEP presents only percentile norms, and the Stanford provides grade equivalent scores, percentiles, and stanines.

Because of the nature of their construction, survey batteries should not be used to obtain a thorough estimate of a pupil's knowledge or skills in a specific area. Although a science or language art subscore can be obtained, this score will normally be influenced by the sample of tasks measured by that particular subtest.

USING ACHIEVEMENT TEST RESULTS

Quite frequently, achievement tests are considered as either single subject-matter tests or survey batteries. This is indeed unfortunate since readiness

[51]Many critics question the validity of so many subscores in a three-hour battery.

and diagnostic tests are also achievement tests in that they provide us with an index of the pupil's knowledge and/or skills.

The authors of many of the better standardized achievement tests and batteries suggest specific uses and supplement this with valuable interpretive examples. At the same time, the ingenious classroom teacher may discover a use that is applicable only in her classroom. It should not be construed that the presentation here is exhaustive. Because of the brevity of our consideration of the use of standardized achievement test results, the remarks to follow should be thought of as only some suggested uses of standardized achievement tests.

The purpose of any standardized achievement test is to provide the user with information concerning the individual's knowledge or skills. However, gathering this information just for the sake of compiling data would be an exercise in futility. The major purpose of gathering achievement test data, or for that matter any kind of data, is to enable the user to make decisions — of selection and classification, for academic and vocational counseling, about the relative effectiveness of two or more methods of instruction — that would be more valid than if such data had not been employed to make the decision. Achievement test results can be used to measure the outcomes of learning, to identify those pupils who are in need of remedial instruction, to identify those pupils who may lack certain fundamental skills (whether they be cognitive, affective, or psychomotor) needed before they can begin reading, to aid in the assignment of course grades, to facilitate learning by the pupils, and as a criterion in evaluating various instructional techniques.[52]

Although we will consider the use of standardized achievement tests under such headings as instructional uses, guidance uses, and administrative uses, the reader should be aware that this classification imposes rigidity in treatment and may result in the fallacious assumption that there is little, if any overlap. Seldom is there a situation where standardized achievement test results serve only a single purpose. Because there will be strengths and weaknesses in *all* standardized achievement tests — for example, the content validity is good but predictive validity is poor; or the normative data are excellent but the test is too time consuming; or the test is valid but the scoring is too complex and requires an experienced examiner to administer and interpret — their limitations must be carefully considered and weighed against their virtues in test selection. In the final analysis, the good is taken with the bad, but we want to be certain that we choose a test with minimum limitations and maximum advantages.

INSTRUCTIONAL USES

Achievement test results can aid the classroom teacher immeasurably. For example, reading readiness test scores can assist the teacher in learning

[52] See Ralph W. Tyler, The education of teachers: a major responsibility of colleges and universities, *The Educational Record* 1958, *39*, 253–261.

which of his pupils possess the skills and knowledge needed to begin the reading program. These test scores can help the teacher group his pupils (tentatively at least) for maximum instructional benefits. Students, who, on the basis of other evidence, demonstrate that they should be successful in reading or arithmetic but who are experiencing difficulty or score poorly on a subject-matter test, may benefit from the administration of a diagnostic test. The diagnostic test can aid the teacher in locating the nature of the difficulty. Diagnostic tests can also be used to identify those students who might benefit from additional remedial work. Diagnostic and readiness tests can be used as an initial screening device to be followed by a more thorough investigation if needed.

Single subject-matter tests and survey batteries can help the teacher ascertain the strengths and weaknesses of his class and thereby suggest modification of his instructional method or the reteaching of certain materials. Or, the teacher can re-evaluate his goals if the data suggest this. He can evaluate the effectiveness of a specific teaching method by using achievement test results.

Standardized achievement tests (excluding readiness and diagnostic tests) can also play an important role with respect to standardizing grading. Quite frequently we hear that Miss Smith is an "easy grader" and that Mr. Jones is a "hard grader." Although standardized achievement tests should not be used to assign course grades, they can be used by both teachers to evaluate their grading practices. For example, when Miss Smith, the easy grader, compares the achievement of her pupils to national and/or local norms and learns that her class is below average, she can then see that the grades she assigned may be misleading. This does not imply, however, that standardized achievement test results be used as the only reference point in assigning course grades. They should be used to give the individual teacher some perspective. Many other factors must be considered before Miss Smith concludes that she is too easy in her grading. The standardized achievement test should be used as supplementary data upon which to obtain a valid estimate of the pupil's achievement, and hence, his final grade.

Achievement test results can be used to help the teacher provide optimal learning conditions for every pupil. In order to do this, the teacher must know as much as possible about every student. Standardized achievement tests will provide some of this needed information. Test results will assist in the grouping of pupils for instructional purposes. They will also be extremely valuable in assisting the teacher to fit the curriculum to each child in a class. Some children should get enrichening experiences, others may require remedial work. For this reason, it is of more value to test students early in the fall rather than the preceding winter or spring.

Occasionally, teachers will use the results of a standardized achievement test as the major criterion in determining the status of their pupils and will then plan their instructional program accordingly. This should never occur. Other factors need to be strongly considered. For example, how well do the test's objectives meet those of the particular teacher? How reliable is a part score in a battery or, for that matter, how reliable are, say, the four or five items used to test the pupil's knowledge of simultaneous equations or atomic structure? Is the course structure centered on skills or on content or on both? Because of these and other considerations, standardized achievement tests should not (1) be a major criterion in course planning and (2) be the focus of the course content to be taught by the teacher. The common single subject matter test, readiness test, survey test, or survey battery should not be used for diagnostic purposes.

GUIDANCE AND COUNSELING USES

Achievement tests can be important in assisting the classroom teacher, principal, school counselor, or clinical psychologist in vocational and educational guidance. In combination with other data, achievement test results can be used to help the student plan his future educational or vocational program. It should be remembered that achievement test data by themselves have limited meaning. They need to be augmented by other information — data about interests, aptitudes, and attitudes — to arrive at the best decision possible. An illustration may help clarify the situation.

Girder, a senior in high school, is interested in studying engineering. The school counselor has a variety of information about Girder. On the basis of a survey battery, Girder's strengths are in verbal skills, and he is deficient in science and mathematics. His interest test scores suggest that he possesses interests shared by journalists. His IQ score indicates that he is of average ability. The counselor should use all this data in helping Girder arrive at a decision concerning the appropriateness of an engineering major in college. The counselor should point out that marked improvement would be needed in science and mathematics in order to succeed in the engineering curriculum. Actually, what the counselor is doing here is making a prediction of probable success based upon test data.[53]

Achievement test results are being used more frequently today in helping high school seniors select a college.[54] With national testing programs becoming more prominent, it is possible for high school counselors to relate achievement test scores to college grades with fairly high validity.

---

[53]Achievement test results are most valid in making educational decisions. They are not as good for vocational guidance because they were not specifically designed with this in mind.

[54]The ACT discussed in Chapter II is really classified as an achievement test but typically is used to make predictions.

Used in this way, the student can be guided to an institution where, because of less competition, he will be more successful and more likely to be graduated.

In conclusion, it must be remembered that achievement test results are not absolute measures and that success in vocational training, graduate, or professional school is dependent upon a multitude of factors, only one of which is prior achievement. Failure to consider these other vitally important factors will result in poor guidance and counseling.

ADMINISTRATIVE USES

Selection, Classification, and Placement

There are many instances where achievement test results are used to select individuals for a particular training program or for a specific vocation. When this is the case, the achievement test must demonstrate high predictive validity.

Selection is more common in industry and higher education than it is in our elementary and secondary schools. For example, a life insurance company may select agents on the basis of an achievement test if it has been found that the test is a good predictor of sales volume. Likewise, a college may select its entering freshmen on the basis of a standardized achievement test if the test has been found to be a valid predictor.

More often today than before (because of man's greater mobility) administrators are confronted with determining where the transfer student should be placed. A fourth grader from Los Angeles should not necessarily be placed in the fourth grade in Syracuse because the schools may not require equal levels of achievement. The results of a standardized achievement test can be used effectively to help the administrator evaluate the transfer student's past performance. This is especially true if the same test is used in both schools. If different tests were used, and no comparisons are possible, the principal should administer the test used in his school.

The data presented in Table 3–2 are for a hypothetical ten-year-old transferring from an ungraded school in Los Angeles to a New York City school in January. The pupil's test scores were obtained in the fall, when he entered the fourth grade. The norms in both schools are based on national norms.

What do we know about this pupil? We know that (1) he is below the average fourth grader except in spelling, (2) he is more like Syracuse third graders than fourth graders, (3) he is more proficient in verbal skills than in arithmetic skills, and (4) if he is placed in the fourth grade, then he may experience a great deal of competition, even to the extent that he might become frustrated and develop a negative attitude toward school.

Table 3–2

Hypothetical Grade Score Equivalents on the Stanford Achievement Test, Primary 1 Battery

Subtest	Transfer Student's Grade Score Equivalent	Mean Grade Score Equivalent for Syracuse 3rd Graders	Mean Grade Score[a] Equivalent for Syracuse 4th Graders
Word reading	3.2	3.5	4.2
Paragraph meaning	3.4	3.4	4.4
Vocabulary	3.4	3.7	4.8
Spelling	4.8	3.8	4.6
Word study skills	3.6	3.6	4.9
Arithmetic	2.5	3.5	4.4

[a]Norms in both schools based on fall testing.

What help can the data in Table 3–2 be to a principal? Would he be likely to make a more valid educational decision with these data than without them? With data such as these, the principal would exercise extreme caution before automatically placing the pupil in the fourth grade because of his age. Now, the principal can either place the pupil in the fourth grade and recognize that the teacher will have to spend extra time with the pupil; or the principal can place the pupil in the third grade and know that he may be out of place physiologically and psychologically. If the pupil is placed in the fourth grade, his teacher will have to understand that he may have difficulty at first, that remedial teaching will be in order, and that additional work will be needed before the pupil will absorb the material as readily as the average fourth grader.

As was discussed earlier, test results can be of help in decision making. In this example, two kinds of decisions must be made: (1) where to place the pupil, and (2) how to best assist the individual after the first decision has been made.

Another example where standardized achievement tests can aid the user is in the classification or placement of students in special courses or programs. The kind of classification possible will depend upon the type of test used and the physical facilities available in the school. For example, if a survey battery is used, a variety of information is provided. The results may suggest that a student take algebra in an average class, reading in a superior class, and social studies in a remedial class. With education moving more and more toward individualized instruction, achievement test results can aid appreciably in fitting the curriculum to the pupil rather than fitting the pupil to the curriculum.

Evaluation of Instruction and Teachers

Some of the misuses of standardized achievement tests are in making educational decisions (regarding the effectiveness of a teacher, of an instructional technique such as a film, of the school curriculum, or of a class or school) solely on the basis of standardized achievement tests results. Teacher effectiveness should not be determined solely on the basis of test results. It would be extremely difficult to compare Miss Smith and Miss Jones, both third-grade teachers in the same school, when we know that one classroom contains an overabundance of bright pupils and that the other contains many slower pupils. Even assuming that the average ability of the two classes are comparable, how can we rate the teachers when Miss Smith, for example, feels certain skills are more easily learned at the end of the term, while Miss Jones prefers to teach these skills at the beginning of the term, but we administer our tests in the middle of the term?

Achievement test results, regardless of their nature, are measures that depend upon past learning. In other words, if Miss Smith's sixth graders are weak in certain arithmetic skills, it may be due to the fact that the essential components of this skill were not developed in an earlier grade. Hence, blaming Miss Smith because her pupils score below national norms would be utterly ridiculous. There is no doubt that teachers play an instrumental role in determining how well their pupils score on achievement tests. However, this is not analogous to the claim that because of this, achievement test results should also be used to rate teachers.

When achievement test results are used to rate teachers, they frequently instill fear into the teachers. This fear conceivably can result in a reduction of teacher effectiveness and in a tendency for "test teaching." Teaching for a test will also encourage undue emphasis on cognitive development, the end result being a lack of concern for the social and emotional development of pupils.

The writers feel that standardized achievement test results can and should (where deemed appropriate) be used to improve the instructional program. Further, we feel that test results should be used to help the teacher rather than to evaluate him. Such self-help can be of marked benefit to the teacher. He can see the strengths and weaknesses of his class (either as a whole or for the individual pupils) if he uses a survey battery. He can, by means of an item analysis, see what skills or facts have and have not been learned. He can, using national norms, make comparisons between his students and students in the same grade nationally. He can, with local norms, compare the status of his students with other students in the same school or in the same school system. He can compare the content of his course with the content deemed appropriate by experts. In conclusion, standardized achievement test results should not be used to evaluate teachers or teaching; they must only be used for constructive self-help.

In summary, although standardized achievement tests are sometimes used to evaluate teachers, the writers strongly oppose this practice — too many factors other than teaching competency can, and do, influence the test score a pupil receives.

Curriculum Evaluation

Achievement test results can also be used as one of the criteria upon which to evaluate the curriculum. For example, 20 years ago it was common practice to delay the teaching of a foreign language until the student reached the seventh or eighth grade. However, it has been found that elementary school children are able to master a foreign language. It has also been demonstrated that with the same amount of training, elementary school pupils do as well on the foreign language achievement test as junior high school pupils. Findings such as these suggest that our curriculum must be flexible. Frequently, achievement test results provide evidence needed to instigate curriculum revision.

The preceding example on the use of achievement test results to study the efficacy of introducing a foreign language in the primary grades is a somewhat simple one. There are instances, however, where the data upon which to base curriculum revision are not so clear-cut.

The profile depicted in Figure 3–2 is for the performance of third graders in a particular school in contrast to the performance of third graders in other schools in the same city. The profile is based upon data collected on the Iowa Test of Basic Skills, which was administered during the first week of classes. Following are some questions and suggested answers:

Q. What does the profile show?

A. Students in the third grade in "Walnut Street" School have an average scaled score performance of about 35 in contrast with the mean scaled score performance of all other third graders of about 60. Also, the "Walnut Street" pupils appear to be more proficient in arithmetic skills than they are in either language or work-study skills.

Q. Are the "Walnut Street" pupils markedly better on one subtest than another? For example, are they better in arithmetic concepts than in reading graphs and tables?

A. It is true that these pupils received the highest and lowest scores on the arithmetic concepts and reading graphs and tables subtests, respectively. This does not mean, however, that they are necessarily better in one than in the other. Much is dependent upon the variability of the pupils and the subtest intercorrelations.

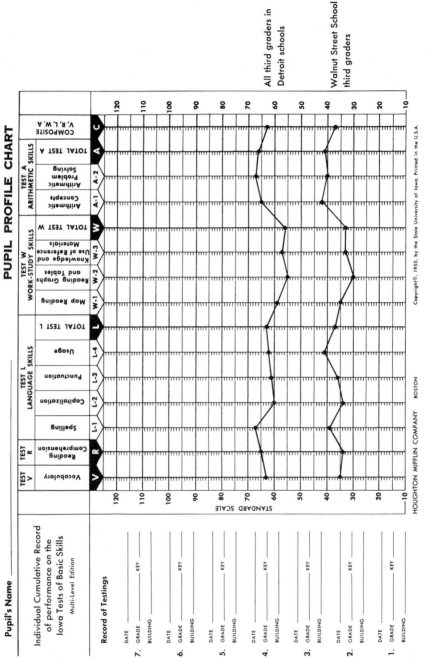

Figure 3-2 Hypothetical profile for third graders in Walnut Street School and third graders in all Detroit schools.

Q. Should the principal change the instructional program at "Walnut Street" School?

A. For this, there is no definite answer. If the "Walnut Street" pupils come, in the main, from an impoverished environment, the decision made could be markedly different than if these pupils were to come from an average or above-average socioeconomic area. In the former, we would have an instance of a poor environment that may not permit pupils to experience verbal and language-type activities, at least the kind that is measured by this or any other standardized achievement test. If the pupils were above-average in intelligence, the principal would have to consider the adequacy of the teachers, the motivation of the pupils, the validity of the test, and other factors before making a decision.

There is no doubt that some modification of the curriculum might be in order for the "Walnut Street" School. The kind of modification (namely, having more free reading, introducing pupils to the public library, or motivating the pupils to achieve at their maximum), however, would be dependent upon the many factors that influence learning. It is conceivable that the curriculum may not have to be modified. Rather, the manner in which the curriculum is introduced may have to be altered. For example, if the test results at the end of the third grade showed that this discrepancy no longer existed, this would suggest that (1) the preparation of the "Walnut Street" pupils in the second grade was markedly different than that of the other third graders when they were in the second grade, or (2) the "Walnut Street" third-grade teachers either taught for the test or were able to make up any deficiencies that existed.

An interesting feature of this hypothetical profile is the strange isomorphism between the "Walnut Street" School third graders and all third graders in the city. The peaks and valleys are nearly identical. Might this indicate something about the curriculum in all the schools? In other words, is it reasonable to expect that more attention might have to be paid certain work-study skills? Not necessarily! From the profile, one is unable to determine the significance of the differences.

In conclusion, we must reemphasize that achievement test scores, whether they be from standardized or teacher-made tests, must be interpreted with caution. Test scores can and do serve as a valuable supplementary criterion upon which to make more valid educational decisions. But, they are supplementary and not absolute, and they are influenced by a myriad of factors.

Grading

In general, standardized achievement test results should not be used to assign course grades. They may be used to assist the teacher in assigning the final course grade provided the test reflects local objectives. As was pointed out earlier, standardized achievement tests are constructed so that they measure broad rather than specific outcomes of instruction. Also, the objectives of instruction may vary, not only from school to school but also from teacher to teacher. For these and other reasons, grades should typically be assigned on the basis of teacher-made tests. These tests, properly constructed, reflect the goals of the individual teacher to a much greater extent than do even the best standardized achievement tests.

In the preceding pages we have attempted to discuss some of the more common uses of achievement test results. As was mentioned earlier, we have not treated all the possible uses. We have neglected to consider using standardized achievement test results for such purposes as (1) motivating pupils, (2) demonstrating to the student what is expected of him, and (3) providing the student with high standards of performance and means whereby he can evaluate his performance. Hopefully, it will be evident that the use of standardized achievement tests is limited only by the resourcefulness and ingenuity of the classroom teacher and that achievement test results should be used as a supplement to other evidence to make sound educational decisions.

CHAPTER SUMMARY

Standardized and teacher-made achievement tests both assess present knowledge so that we may make valid educational decisions. There are differences, however, in the kinds of decisions that can be made with each. Teacher-made tests are usually better for (1) assigning course grades, (2) measuring specific instructional goals, (3) determining how well students are able to perform a particular component of a complex skill, and (4) testing thoroughly a particular unit of instruction. Standardized achievement tests lend themselves more readily to (1) compare performance in different classes, schools, and school districts, (2) assess the relative effectiveness of one method of instruction over another, (3) provide for a cumulative index of pupil growth, and (4) select, classify, and place students.

Standardized achievement tests and teacher-made tests are both concerned with assessing the outcomes of a course of instruction or training. Both are concerned with measuring what the pupils know now, and both employ content validity in their construction. Standardized achievement tests differ from most teacher-made tests in that (1) they are concerned with the broad instructional goals and deal with large segments of knowledge, (2) they are based on general content and learning that is common to schools throughout the country, (3) they are more carefully constructed than is possible for most teacher-made tests, (4) they provide valuable normative data, (5) many of them provide for continuous measurement of the same skills and knowledge, and (6) some of them provide tables for comparing achievement with ability.

The trend today in standardized achievement tests is a movement from testing factual knowledge to testing the pupil's ability to apply and interpret this knowledge.

Finally, it should be recognized that standardized and teacher-made tests are neither absolute nor infallible measures. Before any educational decision is made, a variety of other factors must be considered. Teacher-made and standardized achievement tests complement each other and should be used in this way so as to provide for the optimal development of the individual pupil.

Standardized achievement tests may be classified as diagnostic tests, single subject-matter tests, and survey batteries. Single subject-matter tests can be further subdivided into readiness and prognostic tests. There are few differences among the different kinds of standardized achievement tests with respect to their construction and technical features. They can, and do, differ markedly in their purpose. If a teacher is interested in learning whether a kindergarten pupil is ready for the first grade, he would use a reading readiness test. If he is interested in obtaining a somewhat complete picture of a pupil's strengths and weaknesses in reading, arithmetic, or spelling, he would use a diagnostic test. If he were interested in assessing the pupil's knowledge in 12th-grade Spanish, he would use a single subject-matter test. If he were interested in plotting the strengths and weaknesses of his pupils in the various core subjects, he would use a survey battery. Standardized achievement tests not only lend themselves to assessing the pupils' knowledge now but also are valuable to help the teacher make predictions about future educational progress.

A number of examples were used to illustrate the different kinds of standardized achievement tests available today to the teacher, counselor, specialists, and administrator. There was a brief description of some of these tests and a detailed discussion of a survey battery — the Stanford Achievement Test.

In the final section, the uses of standardized achievement tests were discussed. It was emphasized that they can help the user make more valid educational decisions (be they instructional, guidance, counseling) concerning the pupil.

Standardized achievement tests have come a long way since the Boston Survey in 1845. We anticipate that they will continue to progress in their development.

POINTS TO PONDER

1. Compare and contrast standardized and teacher-made achievement tests. List three specific situations where each would be preferable.

2. Of what value would it be to know the intercorrelations of the subtests in an achievement battery?

3. Which type of validity is most important in an achievement test? Why?

4. You are an elementary school guidance counselor. Your principal assigns you the task of choosing an achievement battery. How do you proceed in your task?

5. First-grade pupils are frequently grouped for instructional purposes on the basis of reading readiness tests. This grouping is not always effective. Does this suggest the elimination of reading readiness tests? Support your answer.

6. There appears to be general consensus, but not universal agreement, on the elementary curriculum. What role should standardized achievement tests play in reducing or increasing the diversity of this curriculum?

7. Mary Poppins scored at the 89th percentile (national norms) on the language subtest of the Stanford Achievement Test. She, however, only received a grade of C on her report card in language arts. How can this be accounted for?

8. Discuss this statement: The California Achievement Tests subscores can be used for diagnostic purposes.

9. What are the problems associated with using standardized achievement test results to evaluate teacher effectivenesss?

10. Given both aptitude and achievement test results for a sixth-grade class, how would you select individuals for an enriched program? What other types of information would be desirable? What potential dangers exist in using test results for this selection procedure?

chapter

IV

interest, personality, and attitude inventories

INTRODUCTION

Should Girder be encouraged to study engineering in college? What are Allan's interests? How can we explain why Beth, who scored at the 95th percentile on the WISC only scores at the 25th percentile on the Stanford Achievement Test? Is Ilene really an aggressive and hostile child? Is Pearl unstrung? Are Ruth's concerns about peer acceptance atypical for an average thirteen-year-old? What are problem check lists? Should teachers interpret noncognitive tests? Are there some noncognitive tests that should be barred from the classroom? Does the information derived from interest, personality, and attitude tests help educators make more valid decisions than could be made if such data were not used? These are some of the questions that will be discussed in this chapter.

It is generally agreed that everyone concerned with the education of children must understand them in their totality in order that optimal learning conditions may be provided. This totality goes beyond academic skills and knowledge. A student's mental health has direct relevance to his ability to learn, his interest in learning, and his attitudes toward the value of an education. Quite frequently, learning difficulties are related to a student's personality, and any attempt to correct the difficulty will be doomed to failure if one does not consider the student's total strengths and weaknesses in both the cognitive and noncognitive areas. Whether an educator realizes it or not, he is influenced by the students' attitudes, values, interests, and general makeup. If a teacher knows that his students dislike history, he could (and hopefully would) employ a variety of techniques to motivate them — films, play acting, and humorous skits — to try to instill a positive attitude toward the value of studying history. If he knows that some students who are poor readers are interested in mechanics, he might use stories with a mechanical flavor in the reading program. All in all, there is no denying the fact that teachers can and do capitalize upon the interests and attitudes of their pupils. However, before one is able to apply knowledge, he must obtain it. Before teachers can use data about their pupils' interests, attitudes, values, and general personality makeup, they must obtain these data.

As the reader studies this chapter it will become increasingly evident that he will not have as much success in measuring noncognitive characteristics as he had in measuring achievement or aptitude. Not only are the techniques less well developed, but even the tests that appear to demonstrate some degree of validity and reliability are fraught with a multitude of methodological problems. Even the best of the measures of typical performance must be interpreted cautiously. The classroom teacher and counselor should be able to interpret problem check lists with minimal training (although the ensuing action will require extensive training and experience). The counselor should be able to interpret the results of interest inventories without too much difficulty. No one, however, unless he has had considerable training and experience, should attempt to interpret measures that are designed to depict abnormality or maladjustment.

There are a variety of procedures by which an individual's behavior can be ascertained: rating scales, anecdotal records, other observational techniques, and pencil-and-paper inventories. Observational techniques such as rating scales, and anecdotal records are among the best methods, especially for adults. They can provide much valuable data, but, for reasons to be discussed later, they may not provide data as valid as that obtained from standardized tests. Standardized, noncognitive tests are uniformly administered and, in general, objectively scored. Many of them also have valuable normative data that enable one to make valid comparisons between a pupil in one community and pupils throughout the country. With standardized, noncognitive tests, one can help ascertain whether Ilene is abnormally aggressive or whether Ruth's concerns about peer acceptance are natural. At this point, one may counter that these questions could be answered by natural observation that would have an additional feature over a testing situation. People are more apt to display their true behavior in natural settings that are informal, unstructured, and nonthreatening. Teachers are able to observe their students in real-life situations. But, are their observations valid? Are teachers objective? Do they know what behavior is significant and what can be overlooked? Can teachers draw correct inferences from observed behavior? As imprecise as noncognitive tests may appear to some, they do provide us with valuable information about the pupil, information that the teacher cannot acquire through observation but that may be necessary to understand the pupil's behavior. There are some who argue that test scores should be used only to supplement teachers' observations. There are others who argue the converse. The important thing to remember is that both teachers' observations and test data provide information about the pupils' behavior, and both should be used.

The classroom teacher, as a member of a professional team vitally concerned with both cognitive and noncognitive behavior, must, in order to be an effective team member, speak the language. Otherwise he will not be able to communicate effectively with other team members — school psychologist, clinician, and counselor. In order to do so, he must know something about noncognitive tests — what they are, what they can and cannot do, the different kinds of noncognitive tests, and so forth — and about the behavior that they measure.

By helping establish optimal positive test-taking attitudes, teachers through their knowledge of noncognitive assessment can indirectly help the counselor to work with the students. Rapport is essential in any testing situation. But it may be more vital in noncognitive assessment, especially when the test is envisaged by the testee as threatening. Also, in noncognitive tests one can fake either good or bad, and the teacher can aid immeasurably in diminishing faking by establishing rapport. The pupil is more apt to trust his teacher with whom he is in daily contact than he is to trust the counselor or clinician whom he sees infrequently. The classroom teacher, especially the one that is trusted and accepted by his pupils, can aid the clinician by breaking the ice and helping the child accept the clinician as someone who is trying to help him.

In summary, knowledge about pupils' interests, personality, and attitudes is important to educators to help them understand pupils better. Knowledge about noncognitive tests (especially interest inventories) is important because they are (1) being used in our schools, especially in the secondary grades, despite the feeling of some that they are of little value, (2) valid in providing us with some information about a student's vocational or avocational interests, (3) more objective than the informal observational approach, and (4) frequently used for research on learning. These kinds of knowledge help teachers communicate effectively with other professionals. We must reiterate that, despite their limitations, standardized noncognitive tests can play an important role in education.

Before discussing the various procedures and tests available to measure noncognitive traits, their advantages and limitations, and their uses and misuses, we must consider some of the methodological problems associated with noncognitive tests: problems of definition, response set, faking, low validity and reliability, and interpretation.

PROBLEMS OF MEASURING NONCOGNITIVE CHARACTERISTICS

There are many unresolved problems in the assessment of noncognitive traits.[1] Because noncognitive assessment (or for that matter, any assessment) involves the differences among individuals as well as changes in behavior over time, validity and reliability are of vital importance. Holtzman[2] has discussed the problems involved in personality measurement (applicable to most noncognitive tests) and raises the following questions: (1) What do we mean by *personality?* (2) How much must we know about an individual before we are truly able to understand his personality? (3) How can one separate personality variance from method variance? (4) Can we ever hope to develop a theory of personality that is comprehensive, systematic, and closely linked with empirical data? It should be evident that, until problems connected with definitions, response sets, validity and reliability, and faking are resolved, noncognitive assessment will be subject to much criticism.

PROBLEMS OF DEFINITION

Noncognitive tests, even more than aptitude or achievement tests, are confronted with the problem of definition. Allport considered at least 50 definitions of personality before he advanced his own. If 100 psychologists were asked to define *personality*, one might get 100 different definitions. This helps account for the inconclusive and often contradictory findings in noncognitive research. Frequently, different researchers arrived at different conclusions because they were studying different variables, even though the variables studied were all labeled the same, for example, *honesty* and *truthfulness.* To some, the terms *attitudes, beliefs, values,* and *interests* are used synonymously and interchangeably. To others, there are definite demarcations. To still others, attitudes and values are considered one category, beliefs and opinions another, and interests still another. The concept of personality has multiple and complex meanings, the various definitions are at best crude, and the techniques for evaluation are sometimes lacking in scientific rigor. Yet, we cannot give up our research or interest in the area of

---

[1]Donald W. Fiske, Problems in measuring personality. In J. M. Wepman and R. W. Heine (Eds.), *Concepts of personality*. London: Aldine, 1963, pp. 449–473. An excellent treatment of measurement problems.

[2]Wayne H. Holtzman, Recurring dilemmas in personality assessment. *J. proj. Tech.*, 1964, *28*, 144–150.

affective development. Grandiose and ethereal constructs such as honesty, beauty, truth, and virtue can be translated to behavioral terms. Once this is done, an attempt can be made to measure these behavioral traits.

Just as we must talk about a specific kind of validity (such as content or predictive) or reliability (stability or equivalence), so, when we discuss a personality trait such as authoritarianism, we must be specific and refer to it as, for example, the "F-Scale's authoritarianism" or "Rokeach's authoritarianism." Until we are able to develop definitions for noncognitive constructs, we will be looking for a needle in a haystack without knowing what a needle looks like.

RESPONSE SET

All noncognitive tests are susceptible to response set, that is, the tendency of an individual to reply in a particular direction, almost independent of content.[3] An individual exhibiting response set answers identical questions (but presented in different formats) differently. For example, he may be predisposed to select the neutral category if a disagree-agree continuum is used, or the "true" statement in true-false items, or he may guess on all items that he is unsure of. There are many types of response set: acquiescence, social desirability, guessing, and sacrificing accuracy for speed (or vice versa).

The response set that has been of most concern in noncognitive measurement is social desirability.[4] This is the tendency for an individual to respond favorably to the items that he feels are socially accepted, such as, "People should be concerned with how their behavior affects others," or "There should be open-housing legislation enacted by Congress." Here, the subject may answer not on the basis of how he truly feels but on the basis of what he thinks is a socially acceptable or desirable answer.

The original goal in the study of response sets such as social desirability was to devise a means whereby their effects could be eliminated (as much as possible) as scaling artifacts. At present, it appears that a controversy exists as to whether we can automatically assume the existence of response sets, and, if they do exist, whether response sets should be measured or eliminated from noncognitive tests.[5] For example, the California F-Scale

[3]Response sets can also be present in cognitive measures. However, in cognitive tests, the response sets can be controlled more easily. For example, guessing can be controlled for in an achievement test through clear directions and correction formulas.

[4]Allen L. Edwards, *The social desirability variable in personality assessment and research.* New York: Holt, Rinehart and Winston, 1957.

[5]Lee J. Cronbach, Response sets and test validity. *Educ. psychol. Measmt.*, 1946, 6, 475–494. Also see Lee J. Cronbach, Further evidence on response sets and test design. *Educ. and psychol. Measmt*, 1950, 10, 3–31, and Leonard G. Rorer, The great response-style myth. *Psychol. Bull.*, 1965, 63, 129–156. Also see Douglas N. Jackson and Samuel Messick, Response styles and the assessment of psychopathology. In Samuel Messick and John Ross (Eds.), *Measurement and personality and cognition.* New York: Wiley, 1962. Also see Douglas P. Crowne and David Marlowe, A new scale of social desirability independent of psychopathology. *J. consult. Psychol.*, 1960, 24, 349–354.

consists of strongly worded opinions most of which express a critical attitude toward human nature. Hence, any tendency to accept these statements may in itself be an indication of authoritarianism, and any attempt to eliminate acquiescence may eliminate or prevent measurement of this important behavioral trait.[6]

If, however, one decides it valuable, steps can be taken to try to control for response set. Cronbach[7] found that response set is particularly prevalent on tests that (1) contain ambiguous items, (2) require the individual to respond on a disagree-agree continuum, and (3) lend themselves to responses in either a favorable or unfavorable direction. Various techniques (such as the forced-choice format) have been used in an attempt to control response set. These techniques have not eliminated the problem completely.

People using personality, attitude, value, and interest tests must pay particular attention to the presence of response sets and must govern their conclusions and recommendations accordingly. More research is needed on response sets: What kinds of people are susceptible? What kinds of items lend themselves to this? Why are some tests affected while others are not? Can (or should) their influence be neutralized?

FAKING

Faking can and does occur on cognitive as well as noncognitive tests, but it is more common on the latter. One psychologist aptly said, "As long as a subject has sufficient education to enable him to answer a personality inventory, however, he probably has the ability to alter his score appreciably in the desired direction."[8] Although an individual can fake either good or bad on a noncognitive test, he can only fake bad (one can fake ignorance, not knowledge) on a cognitive test. The tendency to fake is a characteristic inherent in the individual rather than a test artifact.

Although the examiner expects the subject to give valid information, the examiner does not always receive it. The subject comes to the test and will either be truthful or will lie, depending upon the purpose of the test and his perception of how the test results will be used.[9] Often, responses may be rationalizations or unconscious modifications rather than deliberate lies. A candidate for a vacant position might try to fake good if he has been unemployed for some time or if the new position pays much more than his present job. Quite frequently, an individual is motivated to lie when he knows that his selection or consideration for a particular job depends upon

[6]N. L. Gage and others. The psychological meaning of acquiescence set for authoritarianism. *J. abnorm. soc. Psychol.*, 1957, 55, 98–103.

[7]Cronbach, Further evidence on response sets and test design.

[8]Anne Anastasi, *Psychological testing.* (3rd ed.) New York: Macmillan, 1968, p. 456.

[9]Because of faking, it is very difficult, in clinical psychotherapy, to evaluate the effect of the treatment from test-taking behavior changes.

the types of answers he gives on an interest or personality test. Hence, in his attempt to obtain the job, the subject will do everything possible to create the desired impression.[10] A high school senior, because of his stereotypic impression of a surgeon's life (glamor and prestige), may try to convince his guidance counselor that he likes medicine, or may fake some interest tests to indicate that he has a liking for medicine.

Although the subject will most often try to present himself in a favorable light, there are instances where subjects fake their scores so that they will appear maladjusted or abnormal. A murderer may go out of his way to exhibit tendencies of maladjustment so that he will be judged insane and unfit to stand trial. The tendency to fake bad, that is, to obtain a bad or poor score is most prevalent in testing military personnel, convicts, and mental institution inmates. Most of them may feel they have nothing to lose and everything to gain by demonstrating maladjustment.

Various procedures have been studied and are used to combat faking. One such procedure (perhaps the best) is to establish rapport with the subject and to convince him that in the long run he will be better off if he gives truthful responses. Another method is to attempt to disguise the purpose of the test. This has limited application because the test items may be difficult to disguise from an intelligent subject. However, there are some instances where it is possible to disguise the test's purpose. For example, a researcher interested in studying honesty may prepare a list of book titles, some of which are fictitious. The student is asked to check those book titles he has read. On the surface, the test looks like it is measuring reading interests, but it really is not. It is actually measuring honesty. If a student indicates that he has read a fictitious book, he is obviously lying. Disguising the purpose of a test can also result in some ethical and practical problems, affect the image of psychologists and counselors, and destroy future attempts at establishing rapport.

Another approach to combat faking is to use the forced-choice technique. Here, two or more equally desirable or undesirable statements are presented together, such as

A. I like to read good novels.
B. I like to watch good movies.

The subject is required to choose one answer from the set. One of the answers, however, has been empirically shown to be a more valid predictor of the criterion being studied than are the other(s). The forced-choice method, unfortunately, also has its defects. It requires more time to obtain an equal

---

[10]Russel F. Green, Does a selection situation induce testees to bias their answers on interest and temperament tests? *Educ. psychol. Measmt*, 1951, *11*, 503–515. Also see Alexander G. Wesman, Faking personality test scores in a simulated employment situation. *J. appl. Psychol.*, 1952, *36*, 112–113.

number of responses; it is sometimes resisted by examinees (and may result in negative attitudes toward future testing and/or the counseling interviews); and it may lower the reliability because the choice is more difficult to make.

Still another approach is the construction of scales to *detect* rather than *prevent* faking. Tests such as the Minnesota Multiphasic Personality Inventory (MMPI), the Edwards Personal Preference Schedule (EPPS), and the Kuder Occupational Interest Survey, have special subtests to detect the faker. Of the three, only the verification score (one of its four validity scales) of the MMPI is used to adjust the obtained score. For example, the MMPI has two scale scores (*L* and *F*) to detect faking. Examples of these scale score items are:[11]

> *L*(ie) score — "At times I feel like swearing." An individual who responds False to items such as this is usually not honest in his self-appraisal. A high *L* score suggests that the test responses are invalid.

> *F* score — "I have nightmares every few nights." An individual responding True to this type of item indicates that there may be something wrong with their responses. A high *F* score suggests carelessness or misunderstanding. *F* scores also tend to be high for subjects trying to fake bad.

In conclusion, whatever elaborate procedures are employed by the test to minimize distortion — whether it be by response set, faking, or cheating — we must realize that the subject will only provide the information that he is able[12] and willing to report. People interpreting both cognitive and affective tests (more so the latter) must consider this.

RELIABILITY AND VALIDITY

The reliability of noncognitive tests tends to be considerably lower than for cognitive tests of the same length. In addition, some of the more common procedures for studying reliability may be somewhat inappropriate when it comes to noncognitive tests. Because human behavior is vacillating rather than constant, reliability coefficients derived from test-retest methods (coefficient of stability) will tend to be spuriously low and misleading in

[11]From the Minnesota Multiphasic Personality Inventory. Reproduced by permission. Copyright 1943 by the University of Minnesota. Published by The Psychological Corporation, New York, N.Y. All rights reserved.

[12]There are some instances where incomplete or invalid information is obtained because of the inability of the individual to recall certain events. For example, if a psychiatrist were to ask one to recall significant childhood events, the subject may provide incomplete data, not because he wishes to, but because he is unable to recall it. Recall is also important in dealing with the maladjusted who may repress certain information.

judging the test's precision. Inconsistency in test responses may be either an important aspect of an individual's personality or a test artifact. The split-half and Kuder Richardson methods (measures of internal consistency) are most frequently used to study the reliability of noncognitive tests. Because of low reliabilities, careful attention must be paid to the interpretation of difference scores in a test profile because only marked test-score differences may suggest true intra-individual differences.

It is indeed difficult to ascertain the predictive validity of a noncognitive measure for two reasons: (1) We infer the existence of a behavioral trait on the basis of overt test responses. In other words, we assume that an individual who says he is prejudiced toward Negroes on an attitude test will exhibit this behavior in a real situation. In some instances, making inferences of overt behavior from personality questionnaires is valid, but, because of faking and response set, sometimes they are not. (2) Adequate external criterion data are often lacking.

Some methods used to study the validity of noncognitive tests are contrasted groups, matching, point-by-point comparison, experimentally induced states, and factor analysis.[13]

The research conducted with noncognitive inventories has led to many attempts to improve their validity. Some of the approaches used are (1) using correction scores rather than discarding inventories that appear to be suspect, (2) disguising the purpose of the test,[14] (3) randomly assigning items throughout the test rather than presenting them in blocks, so that the traits being measured do not appear obvious to the examinee, (4) using verification scores to reveal test-taking attitudes,[15] and (5) selecting test items on the basis of empirical rather than a priori grounds. Although these and other approaches are used to improve the validity of personality tests, the evidence today indicates that noncognitive tests still do not approach the criterion-related validity of intellectual measures mainly because of the problem of valid external criterion data.

By this time, it should be readily evident that in noncognitive tests (1) validity and reliability are not as high as in ability tests, and (2) we are most concerned with construct validity and reliability expressed in terms of internal consistency or homogeneity of items. Rather than conclude that noncognitive tests lack the desired degree of validity and reliability needed for making valid educational decisions, we should ask how much informa-

[13]Because these topics are beyond the scope of this text, they are not discussed here.
[14]Daniel N. Wiener, Subtle and obvious keys for the Minnesota Multiphasic Personality Inventory. *J. consult. Psychol.*, 1948, *12*, 164–170, suggests that this be used for subjects who are normal and exhibit social desirability. Obvious items work well for the maladjusted who are honest and seek help.
[15]Such a scale is especially needed when the items are very obvious. Both the Edwards Personal Preference Schedule and the California Psychological Inventory contain a group of items that measure social desirability.

tion can we get from the test and how will it help us. Another way to look at it would be in terms of cost analysis. In the long run, are we able by using noncognitive tests to make less expensive decisions?

PROBLEMS OF INTERPRETATION

Noncognitive tests are really not tests in the sense that aptitude and achievement tests are, because there are not necessarily any right answers. Noncognitive tests are generally interpreted in relation to the traits held by "normal" ("average") people. Hence, although some modal behavior may, to one in a given subculture, seem abnormal, if the subject behaved like the average person in his own subculture, he would not seem abnormal to members of that subculture.

Another problem in the interpretation of noncognitive tests, especially attitude scales, reflects the kinds of responses permitted. Most attitude scale responses provide for a neutral response. But what does a neutral response mean? Does it mean that the individual is really neutral, or does it mean that he is unwilling to commit himself? How does one interpret a neutral response? One way to circumvent the problem of neutral responses is to eliminate this type of response. But, if we do so, might we be eliminating the measurement of a true behavioral trait?

Perhaps the more serious problem in interpreting noncognitive tests is that associated with ipsative forced-choice tests.

Assume one is given a forced-choice item such as

A. I like to build model airplanes.
B. I like to play bridge.
C. I like to collect stamps.

where he is required to select the one statement in the triad that he likes most. Each of the three possible choices is keyed under a different subscale. Thus, if he picks "A," he may receive a point on the scientific scale. If he selects "B," he may receive a point on the sociability scale. If he chooses "C," he may receive a point (but, negative) on the mechanical scale. The essential characteristic of such items is that when a person makes a choice in favor of one subscale (by choosing a particular item) he is at the same time rejecting the other subscales. A test composed of such items (where one is forced to make a choice) gives one an ipsative scale and the scores are ipsative scores. Although multiple-choice cognitive tests also require the individual to make a choice, there is only one correct answer for everyone. Hence, problems associated with ipsative forced-choice tests are unique only to some noncognitive tests.

The essential characteristic of an ipsative scale is that the mean score on all the scales is the same for all persons. Ipsative scores do not reflect the intensity of the subject's feeling, and yet this is something that would be of extreme value in interpreting an individual's responses. For example, three boys purchase vanilla ice cream cones. Does this imply that they all like vanilla ice cream to the same degree? Not necessarily so. Or, if each of the three boys purchased a different flavor, does this signify that the boy who wanted vanilla likes vanilla more than chocolate or strawberry? How much more, if any, does he like vanilla over chocolate? Does he like vanilla more than the boy who chose chocolate?

Ipsative scales only permit intra-individual comparisons. In an ipsative scale, every individual will probably have some high scores and some low scores (he could have all scores at the mean). He can not have all his scores either high or low. Some psychometrists contend that the ipsative forced-choice technique parallels real life in that one is always forced to choose between activity A and activity B. For example, a child, when offered some ice cream, must choose, normally, between chocolate and vanilla. Others argue that this forced choice can sometimes induce frustration in the subject, especially when all the statements (choices) are equally desirable or undesirable.

Even if we were to accept the fact that ipsative forced-choice scales are psychometrically sounder than their free-response counterparts, interpreting a forced-choice profile is very difficult. How does one interpret to a student the profile of an ipsative interest test with ten subscales? One cannot say that his interest in outdoor activities is higher than his interest in musical activities (even though he may have had a higher score on the outdoor scale) because the scores are not absolute. One cannot say that two persons who rank at the 90th percentile in terms of the national norm group have equal outdoor interests because the scores are ipsative. All one can do is give the student some gobbledygook that may confuse and frustrate him.

CONSTRUCTION AND KEYING

Although the construction and keying of noncognitive tests is not a problem of the same proportion as the problems discussed earlier, the fact that problems can arise in trying to key an item leads us to consider it in this section. Because it is extremely difficult at times to distinguish between a particular technique used to construct a test and this same procedure when used to key (score) the test, they will be considered together. Cognitive tests have only a single, accepted, correct answer. Noncognitive tests, on the other hand, need not always be amenable to a "correct" answer. In a noncognitive test, especially one that has been empirically keyed, an item may be keyed one way as the correct answer for plumbers but it may be incorrect for some other group. Three procedures are commonly used to construct and key noncognitive tests: empirical, homogeneous, and logical.

Empirical Construction

In the empirical or criterion method one makes no assumption about the traits or characteristics of people in different occupations but attempts to develop items that will discriminate men (or women) in one group from those in another group. Each item is evaluated in terms of its relationship to the criterion. The criterion for, say, a test of paranoia might be patients in a mental institution who have been diagnosed as paranoiacs. The control group (or normals) could be their visitors. In criterion keying, a person's interests are compared with the interests held by people successful in various occupations.

Items used in the Strong Vocational Interest Blank, the Kuder Occupational Interest Survey, and the Minnesota Multiphasic Personality Inventory were empirically selected and keyed. Although the scoring is usually in terms of unitary weights, differential weights can be assigned in proportion to the difference in responses between the criterion groups.

One virtue of empirical construction (and keying) is that it is very difficult for the examinee to fake his responses. This is true because the examinee does not know how the criterion group responded to the various items (only those items that empirically differentiated among different groups were selected — the items were not selected on sheer faith as in logical keying).

Homogeneous Construction

The test constructor employing the homogeneous method first begins with a large number of items. Then, through factor analysis, clusters are identified, and the items are organized to fit the identified clusters. A psychometric characteristic of a homogeneous-keyed test is that the items of any one scale have high intracorrelations, that is, a common factor runs throughout that scale; the scale intercorrelations are relatively low (or they should be if more than one trait or cluster has been identified).

Logical Construction

In the logical method, the items are selected and keyed on a logical or rational basis rather than on empirical grounds. The test constructor specifies the traits or skills or knowledge needed for the task and then prepares appropriate items. He then scores the items in accordance with his perception of the underlying psychological theory. For example, let us assume that one prepares an interest scale and has as one of his questions, "I like to read blueprints." Logically, one would expect that engineers would like to read blueprints, and if logical keying were used, one would assign a +1 on the engineering scale to those who responded affirmatively. It is conceivable, however, that engineers do not like to read blueprints. If empirical keying had been used to key the test and if it was found that engineers do not like this activity, then one would not assign an individual a $+1$ on the engineering scale to those who responded affirmatively to this item.

MEASUREMENT OF INTERESTS

As was previously mentioned, teachers must be concerned not only with *what* pupils learn, but also with *how* and *why* they learn. People have a tendency to excel or at least to devote more effort and energy to the activities they like. In order for the classroom teacher to best capitalize on the likes and dislikes of his students, it is necessary that he know something of their interests. Interest inventories can assist him in gaining this knowledge. In order for the counselor to aid the student in arriving at a decision in regard to his vocational and educational plans, he also must be cognizant of interest measurement.

Teachers should certainly strive to make their objectives (whether they be cognitive skills, factual knowledge, or wholesome attitudes and values) palatable and interesting to their students. The teacher of ninth-grade social studies might explore students' interests (or at least have the students think about their interests) as they are related to various occupations when he discusses the world of work. The high school teacher who knows that Bill is a poor reader may attempt to provide meaningful learning experiences by capitalizing upon Bill's interests and may assign Bill books that are related to his interests. The fifth-grade teacher working upon addition or subtraction skills may exploit students' interests insofar as the types of story problems used. The important thing to remember is that because pupil interests can influence how well they learn, teachers must be concerned with interest measurement.

ATTITUDES VERSUS INTERESTS

Attitudes and interests are both concerned with likes and dislikes. Both can be related to preferences for activities, social institutions, or groups. Both involve personal feelings about something. It is this "something" that distinguishes attitudes from interests. An attitude is typically conceptualized as being a feeling toward an *object*, a *social institution*, or a *group*. An interest, on the other hand, is conceptualized as being a feeling toward an *activity*.

Attitude and interest inventories share many things in common. They are both highly susceptible to faking, require frank responses from the subject, and, therefore, are able to assess only the characteristics that the individual is able to, or wishes to, reveal.

WHY INTEREST TESTS?

Are not interests unstable, especially for younger children? Does this instability not reflect itself in interest tests being unreliable? Would not the simplest way of ascertaining an individual's interests be to ask him what he likes and dislikes? Are not the interest inventories available today so complex and difficult to intepret that they preclude their use by an untrained classroom teacher?

It has been charged that interest tests are unstable, especially for younger children, but, from adolescence on, interests are not as unstable as many people think. If a teacher or counselor uses an interest inventory for lower elementary school pupils and finds that the results are invalid, this is as much the fault of the teacher as the test. Why condemn interest inventories in general? Yes, the simplest way to ascertain whether an individual would like to be a doctor would be to ask him, but, we know that direct questioning (especially for children between the ages of twelve and fifteen) often results in invalid responses. Yes, interest inventories are difficult for the untrained classroom teacher to interpret, but this does (or should) not imply that the classroom teacher should remain untrained; that he should not know something about interests (how they are measured, how they are related to scholastic achievement, and how they are limited in their value); and that he should not use them or their results. Unless the classroom teacher knows something about interests and interest inventories (actually, most noncognitive measures), he will not be able to communicate effectively with the counselor or clinician,[16] nor will he be able to provide for optimal learning.

Knowledge of an individual's interests provides a sound basis for educational and vocational guidance. Interest inventory results may help the classroom teacher understand why a bright pupil is performing poorly. They can be of assistance to the student, if only to make him think more about his future.

HISTORICAL DEVELOPMENT OF INTEREST INVENTORIES

The study of interests has received its greatest impetus from educational and vocational counseling. School and industrial psychologists share the common concern that the application of test results may permit better decisions to be made by (1) the individual selecting an occupation, and (2) the firm selecting job applicants.

---

[16]See John G. Darley and Theda Hagenah, *Vocational interest measurement*. Minneapolis, Minn.: University of Minnesota Press, 1955, Chapters 2, 4, and 6.

Interest inventories have progressed a great deal from the initial attempts of G. Stanley Hall in 1907 to develop a questionnaire to measure children's recreational interests. Although the measurement of interests was of concern prior to the 1920s, the first, formal, scientific, and orderly approach to the study and measurement of interests began in 1919. In a graduate seminar on interests conducted at the Carnegie Institute of Technology, students and professors developed items to distinguish between members of different occupations. Many inventories evolved from this seminar, the most notable being the Strong Vocational Interest Blank (SVIB). In constructing the original SVIB, two innovations to the measurement of interests were introduced: (1) the items dealt with a subject's likes and dislikes, and (2) the responses were empirically keyed for the different occupational groups. The SVIB was the beginning of "criterion-keying." It was not until 1939 that another standardized interest inventory appeared. In that year, the Kuder Preference Record was published. It differed markedly from the SVIB in construction in that it employed homogeneous keying. Kuder and Strong employed markedly different techniques to develop their initial interest inventories. In both the revised editions of the SVIB and the Kuder, criterion keying was employed. Both authors conceptualized interests, or at least the measurement of interests, differently. Strong employed the very specific description whereas Kuder used the broad category, such as mechanical or scientific rather than engineer or architect. Now, however, both inventories have separate occupational scales as well as general or broad interest clusters. In 1943, the Lee-Thorpe Occupational Interest Inventory (OII) was published. Whereas the SVIB and Kuder both employed empirical and statistical grounds for keying their tests, the OII employed a logical approach. In other words, the OII consists of items that demonstrate logical rather than empirical validity. Still another approach to the construction of interest inventories was used by Guilford and his colleagues. In 1948, Guilford's Interest Survey was published. Two unique features of this inventory were the use of factor analysis in the refinement of the various scales and separate scores for vocational and avocational interests. In 1959, the Geist Picture Inventory was published. It was designed to substitute for the highly verbal inventories. Little evidence has been presented to support the claim that a nonverbal interest inventory is as valid as a verbal interest inventory. Prior to the advent of Guilford's Interest Survey, interest inventories were concerned only with vocational interests. Now, some attention is being paid to avocational interests. Initial standardized interest inventories were designed primarily for college-bound students. There are now inventories designed for use with students who will terminate their education after high school. The Minnesota Vocational Interest Inventory (MVII) published in 1965 is useful for high school students who are occupation-bound rather than college-bound.

Although interest inventories and the study of interest development has progressed in the past decade, much still remains to be done. We still need better theoretical foundations regarding the development of interests; need more knowledge about the relationship of interests to other aspects of human behavior such as ability, intelligence, and personality;[17] and need more evidence regarding the construct of interests. Fortunately, much research is being conducted in the area of interests, and some answers should be forthcoming in the near future.

TYPES OF STANDARDIZED INTEREST INVENTORIES

An individual's interests (his likes and dislikes, his preferences and aversions) can be ascertained in a variety of ways. Super and Crites suggest four approaches that can be used to ascertain an individual's interests: (1) direct questioning, (2) direct observation, (3) tested interests, and (4) interest inventories.[18] Measuring an individual's interests by means of interest inventories has proven to be the most fruitful, encouraging, and valid approach. This method is the only one discussed here. The interest inventory contains statements about various occupations and activities. These statements may be presented singly, in pairs, or in triads. The subject responds to each of the statements in terms of his preference for or aversion to the activity or occupation.

There are at least two dozen standardized interest inventories that are commercially published, some of them designed for vocational guidance only, others for educational guidance only, and others that can be used for both educational and vocational guidance. Some are designed for use with high school seniors, college students, and adults; others with junior high school children. Some are applicable only to students who intend to pursue a college education, whereas others are designed for non–college-bound adolescents. Some are verbal, others pictorial.

Some authors, like Strong, developed interest inventories on the assumption that interests are not a unitary trait but a complex interaction of many traits. Other authors, like Kuder, conceptualized interests as an assortment of unitary traits, and this is reflected in the homogeneity of each of his interest scales. Still other authors constructed their interest inventories on the basis of logical validity. In spite of the different construction approaches (criterion keying, homogeneous keying, and logical keying), all interest

[17]Guilford and his co-workers feel that, in time, interest inventories may be used as personality tests. They suggest — and there is no reason to doubt this — that interests must be related to motives, aspirations, and needs, that interests just do not develop in a vacuum.

[18]Donald E. Super, and John O. Crites, *Appraising vocational fitness by means of psychological tests.* (rev. ed.) New York: Harper & Row, 1962, pp. 377–379.

inventories share the common purpose of assessing an individual's preferences for various activities. Most interest inventories are based on some common assumptions regarding interests: (1) interests are learned rather than innate, (2) interests are often acquired or developed as a result of the individual being engaged in an activity, (3) interests tend to be relatively unstable for young children, but after about age twenty, they tend to become stabilized with little change occurring after age twenty-five, (4) people in different occupations share similar likes and dislikes regarding activities, (5) interests vary in intensity from one person to another, and (6) interests motivate the individual to action.

Because of space limitations, we must restrict our discussion of interest inventories only to those that are most frequently used in our schools. The examples have been selected to illustrate certain principles of test construction.

Empirically Keyed Interest Inventories

Strong Vocational Interest Blank   Revised edition.[19] Stanford University Press, 1966. Seventeen-year-olds and over. 54 occupational scales for men, 34 scales for women. Untimed but takes from 30 to 60 minutes to complete. Two forms for men; three for women.

The SVIB is suitable for older adolescents and adults considering higher-level occupations. It consists of 339 items and provides separate forms for men and women.[20] The items are listed under such topics as (1) occupations, (2) school subjects, (3) amusements, (4) activities, (5) types of people and everyday activities, and (6) a quasi-personality inventory requiring the respondent to rate his abilities and characteristics. The items are both vocational and avocational, and the subject responds to most of the items by means of a three-element choice: like, dislike, or indifferent. Strong attempted to select items that were not influenced or dependent upon previous work experience but that the average adolescent could be expected to know or at least to imagine.

Strong conceived an interest inventory as a group of items that discriminate people in specific occupations from a general group of similar-age subjects (but not in that occupation). To be included in Strong's criterion group (as a member of a specific occupation), the individual had to be between the ages of 25 and 55, employed in that occupation for at least 3 years, and have indicated a liking for his work. For each of the items, the percentage of men (or women) responding "like, dislike, indifferent" were compared with the percentage of "men-in-general" responding in a similar

[19]Men's revision completed; women's revision underway.
[20]The categories are the same for both forms, but the list of occupations and activities differ.

manner. The responses were then assigned weights ranging from $+1$ to -1.[21] A student who receives a high score on the engineer scale, say, displays interests similar to engineers in the norming sample. This is not analogous to saying that the individual would like to be an engineer, that he should study engineering at college, or that he will be successful as a professional engineer. The test score only indicates the similarity of interests shared by the subject and engineers selected for the norming sample.

The various scoring keys are not based on any psychological theory concerning a particular occupation. For example, the physician key is not based on what Strong feels physicians are like. The test data, rather than the test constructor, define the interests of a particular occupation.

In addition to the occupational scales there are two nonoccupational scales that are contained in both the men's and women's forms: academic achievement (AACH) and masculinity-femininity (MF). The SVIB for men also has a specialization level scale (SL) and an occupational level scale (OL). The AACH scale (which replaces the interest-maturity scale of the earlier editions) is intended to provide the user with an indication of the examinee's probable success in college. The MF scale is intended to separate men from women in terms of their preferences. For example, male interests tend to be more technical and impersonal while female interests tend to be related to culture and esthetics. The SL scale is designed primarily for use in counseling students who contemplate attending graduate school or who intend to specialize in a particular profession, such as Pediatrics. The OL scale gives an indication of the respondent's level of aspiration, that is, how aggressive he is, whether he aspires to a managerial level or whether he is content to "plug away" but not advance himself.

The AACH scale is the only nonoccupational scale that appears to possess validity. The other scales, although of possible value, must be interpreted very cautiously. In fact, the writers feel that until further data are forthcoming, they should be ignored.

The evidence for the validity of the SVIB was obtained primarily from longitudinal studies. Strong[22] and others[23] have reported that men originally selecting occupation X and remaining in occupation X obtain higher scores on the occupation X scale than men-in-general. They also tend to have their highest score on that occupational scale rather than on any other. In addition, men who continue in occupation X tend to have higher scores on that scale than men who change from occupation X to occupation Y. Finally, it was found that, in general, men who change from occupation X to occupation Y score higher on Y than in any other occupation.

---

[21]In the older editions the weights ranged from $+4$ to -4.

[22]Edward K. Strong, *Vocational interest blank for men*. Stanford, Calif.: Stanford University Press, 1966.

[23]Darley and Hagenah.

Median-scale test-retest correlations range from .56 (bankers tested over 30 years) to .91 (college sophomores tested after two weeks and young adults tested after 30 days). These retest correlations are quite high considering the time interval. Unfortunately, no odd-even reliabilities are reported for the revised form. Inasmuch as many of the items have been either reworded or replaced in the 1966 revision, it is not completely appropriate to use the data from the earlier editions. It would have been valuable for the authors to provide such data rather than to rely upon the excellent record of the earlier edition to make their point regarding the test's reliability.

Because of the large number of occupational keys, hand scoring is almost out of the question, especially if there are a large number of examinees.[24] To assist the teacher or counselor in interpreting the test scores, the obtained scores on each of the occupational scales (there are 54 occupational scales and four nonoccupational scales for men; 32 occupational and two nonoccupational scales for women) are converted to T scores, and the T scores can be converted to letter grades ranging from A to C. (Actually, the letter grades are A, B+, B, B−, C+, and C). The top 69 percent of, say, successful chemists, would receive A on the chemist scale, and the lowest 2 percent would receive C. Strong says that a score of A signifies that the individual has interests (likes and dislikes) similar to the men classified as successful in their occupation. Individuals with scores of B are less like the norm group, while scores of C signify very little similarity between the individual and the norm group. In addition, the 1966 SVIB for Men profile has a shaded area for each of the occupations to represent the middle third of the men-in-general distribution, as shown in Figure 4–1.[25] These men-in-general bands assist the counselor in making a decision regarding the significance of an interest score.

Without going into a lengthy review of literature about the research conducted with the SVIB, it suffices to say that this inventory has been thoroughly and carefully constructed and standardized, that it displays substantial reliability and predictive validity of occupational choice, and that it can serve a useful purpose in the testing program of our senior high schools.

Minnesota Vocational Interest Inventory The Psychological Corporation, 1965. One form. Untimed, but takes about 45 minutes to administer. Twenty-one occupational scales. Designed for high school students who do not aspire to professional vocations. Reading level of inventory is at about ninth grade.

[24]The manual contains the names and addresses of four commercial firms that provide scoring services for a nominal fee.

[25]In the earlier editions, the "chance bands" were based on test responses arrived at by throwing dice, the boundaries being $\pm 1S_z$ about each mean chance score.

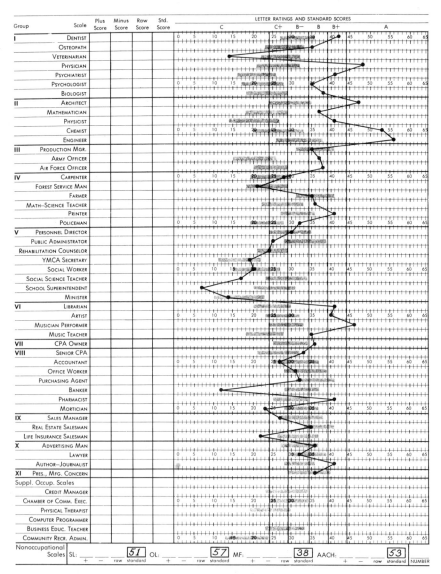

Figure 4-1 Strong Vocational Interest Blank for Men. Reprinted with permission from the MANUAL FOR STRONG VOCATIONAL INTEREST BLANKS FOR MEN AND WOMEN by Edward K. Strong, Jr., revised by David P. Campbell (Stanford: Stanford University Press, 1966), p. 14.

The MVII consists of 474 items that are arranged in 158 triads. In each triad the examinee is required to indicate the activity he likes most as well as the one he likes least. The MVII differs from many other interest inventories in that it is concerned with measuring the interests of non–college-bound youth who might be considering occupations at the semiskilled and skilled levels. Scoring keys have been developed for occupations ranging from baker to warehouseman. In addition, keys are available for nine area or interest scales, the area scales being comparable to the interest clusters of the SVIB. The validity of the occupational scales has been ascertained in a variety of ways. One type of validity reported is the percent of overlap between the criterion group and the tradesmen-in-general. The median percent overlap is 40 percent (a respectable value). The overlap statistic represents the percentage of classification errors. With a 40 percent overlap, a scale would misclassify about 20 percent of the total group. Validity is also expressed in terms of the difference in scores obtained between people in various occupations. In this respect the MVII scales do not do as well as they do in separating criterion groups from tradesmen-in-general. For example, food service managers score as high on the stock clerk scale as do stock clerks. This suggests that the two have similar interests, and yet we know that the nature of the work is quite different for the two occupations. A similar situation exists with regard to the discrimination between food service managers and bakers. The MVII does not seem to make as good a separation between different cccupational groups as does the SVIB, but this may be due to the nature of the interests in skilled trades being less well defined. Test-retest reliabilities over a 30-day period ranged from .64 to .88 with a median reliability of .82 for the occupational scales, and from .62 to .87 with a median reliability of .84 for the area scales. The reliability coefficients may be misleading, considering the size and homogeneity of the sample and the time interval (98 students in a Minneapolis high school and a time interval of 30 days). Data collected over a longer time interval as well as a more representative sample would be more desirable. Performance is reported on the profile in terms of standard scores. There is a shaded area accompanying each of the 21 occupational scales, this area representing the range of scores for the middle third of a group of skilled tradesmen drawn from the tradesmen-in-general population. The test authors recommend using this shaded area as a reference point in deciding upon the significance of an individual's scores.

The MVII is a promising instrument and should find a useful purpose in counseling students who intend to go into skilled, nonprofessional occupations. At present, it suffers from an inadequate standardization and has too few empirical studies to support any real claim for validity and reliability. What has been reported in the manual is respectable — we only ask that more respectability (in terms of "hard" data) be offered. The MVII does not appear to be as fakable as some of the other interest inventories. Even so, faking can occur, and, as is suggested in the manual, the MVII should not be used in employment selection programs. It is easy to administer and score; the quality and format are good; many counselors' suggestions are contained in the manual; and it can be used with ninth graders, although one must recognize that the interests of young teenagers may still not be crystallized. All in all, teachers and counselors in systems where the majority of students enter into skilled or semiskilled nonprofessional occupations should find the MVII an asset to their existing testing program.

Kuder Occupational Interest Survey, Form DD   Science Research Associates, Inc., 1964. Replaces Kuder Preference Record, Form D. High school students and adults. One form. Untimed but takes about 30 minutes to complete. Thirty core scales.

The OIS consists of 300 items arranged into 100 triads. It, like the Minnesota Vocational Interest Inventory, is a forced-choice[26] test where the subject chooses the one statement he likes most and the one he likes least. The OIS can be used for 11th and 12th graders, college students, and adults. There are 79 occupational scores and 20 college-major scores reported for men. For women, there are 56 occupational scores and 20 college-major scores. In addition, there are nine experimental scales. The various occupational scales can also be combined into one of 17 different interest areas or clusters. These clusters range from an enjoyment of outdoor activities to a preference for acting spontaneously. The validity of the OIS rests primarily upon concurrent validity studies. Tables are presented to show how well the inventory separates men (or women) in one occupation from people in other well-defined criterion groups. The inventory does this quite satisfactorily and holds up in cross-validation studies. Validity was also studied by (1) errors of misclassification, that is, where, say, a banker received a higher score on a scale other than the banker scale, and (2) job-satisfaction studies. The data reported demonstrates that the OIS has respectable concurrent validity. Unfortunately, no data are presented on the predictive validity of the OIS because of its newness. Also, very little data are furnished regarding other psychometric characteristics of the scales[27] and/or items that would help answer whether the inventory has construct validity. Although internal

---

[26]Research has aptly demonstrated that fixed-response category formats are quite susceptible to severe response bias. An attempt was made in the OIS and MVII to correct for this by employing a forced-choice format that, although it does not control completely for response set, does tend to minimize it.

[27]A table in the manual's appendix does contain the intercorrelations of 23 core scales. Another table presents the intercorrelations of scores for the 17 interest areas, but there are no scale intercorrelations presented.

consistency measures are not too important when the purpose of a test is to separate different occupational groups, test-retest reliability is of vital importance. When one considers that these scores may be used to advise and counsel a student regarding his future occupation or profession, the user must demand proof that the interests being measured are stable over time. Kuder presents a few reliability studies that span over a two-week period but this cannot compare with some of the SVIB data spanning as much as a 30-year period. The OIS still must prove itself insofar as stability is concerned.

The OIS has a verification key (something the SVIB does not) that can assist the counselor in ascertaining how honest and careful a subject was in responding to the inventory. Although such a score is of value and, from the data presented, this scale appears to be valid, approximately the same amount of space is devoted in the manual to this scale as is devoted to reliability or validity.

The OIS has been carefully constructed and has some features not found in other interest tests.[28] It contains an interpretative leaflet for the examinee that is well written. The manual is also well written and contains some useful suggestions for the counselor. The discussion on the development of the test and the description of the criterion groups is clear and should prove of value to the counselor considering the use of the OIS. A major disadvantage of the test is that it can only be scored by the publisher. As mentioned earlier, more data on validity and reliability are needed.

Homogeneous-Keyed Interest Inventories

Kuder General Interest Survey (GIS), Form E   Science Research Associates, Inc., 1964. Grades 6–12. One form. Untimed but takes about one hour to administer. Provides 11 scores.

The GIS is a revision and downward extension of the Kuder Form C. It is more suitable for junior high school students than was Form C, and its reading level is sufficiently low to permit its use with high school students who have a limited vocabulary. The GIS consists of 552 statements that are grouped into 184 triads. The subject selects the statement or activity liked "most" and the one liked "least" in each of the triads. Kuder contends that the scoring is such that the GIS is not a purely ipsative scale, even though it is of a forced-choice format. Kuder offers some rational arguments concerning the nonipsative nature of the GIS, but the writers feel he has stretched the point in his argument. The GIS has been constructed with

---

[28]For females, the scores for certain occupations and college majors are reported using data based on the male groups. This is done where opportunities are present for either sex in an occupation, for example, medicine.

younger people in mind: (1) it has a vocabulary that is at the sixth-grade level, and (2) it attempts to avoid using occupational titles (the meanings associated with them are relatively unstable, especially for younger people). The GIS is suitable for students in grades 6 to 12, and research is now underway to see whether it is valid for adults.[29] The GIS differs from the Kuder Occupational Interest Survey and the SVIB in that it expresses vocational preferences only as cluster areas rather than specific occupational choices. There are ten occupational scales: outdoor, mechanical, computational, scientific, persuasive, artistic, literary, musical, social service, and clerical. In addition, there is a verification scale. The number of items assigned to each scale varies from 16 in the musical scale to 70 in the persuasive scale. Because the scales do not contain an equal number of items, the raw scores not only can vary from individual to individual but also do vary from one scale to another. Although this may not confuse the trained counselor, it probably will confuse the student because the GIS can supposedly be self-administered, -scored, and -interpreted.

The relative newness of the GIS precludes furnishing predictive data. It is hoped, however, that, when such data are forthcoming, they will be published in a supplementary manual. It is also hoped that the validity data for the GIS will be more inclusive than that for its predecessor (Kuder Form C), which is woefully inadequate with respect to specific occupational criterion data. Another form of validity is content or face validity. When one glances through the inventory, he is apt to notice that the activities referred to are biased in favor of middle-class American values. There are only a few items that relate to activities that the underprivileged could be expected to experience. This strongly suggests that the GIS not be used in poverty areas or in schools that have a major proportion of their pupils coming from a racial or economic ghetto. A third aspect of validity presented in the manual pertains to the intercorrelations among the eleven scales. Although homogeneous keying attempts to produce scales that have highly intracorrelated items but low intercorrelations (among the scales), we are unable to explain some of the obtained correlations. For example, should there be a substantial correlation between the musical and artistic interest scales? One would expect so, but the correlations are .02 and .03 for boys and girls, respectively. Inasmuch as the profile leaflet encourages self-interpretation, this dependence upon the relatedness (or unrelatedness) of the constructs measured can result in misuse and should be clarified.

---

[29]Attempting to construct an inventory that is useful for both young people and adults can lead to many difficulties. For example, in an attempt to make the items palatable to younger people (for example, "have a teacher find fault with a paper of yours in front of the class"), one risks the loss of rapport of adults. On the other hand, trying to please adults may result in items dealing with activities unfamiliar to younger people, (for example, "decide whether to publish stories writers send to a magazine").

The reliability estimates provided are in terms of stability data, and Kuder-Richardson measures of internal consistency. The test-retest data are based upon a small group of boys and girls retested after a 6-week interval and also on 311 boys and 328 girls tested first in the sixth or seventh grade and then four years later. It is the latter data that are of most interest. The average correlations for boys and girls are .50 and .43, respectively. This would therefore severely limit the use of the GIS for making individual and possibly even group predictions for sixth and seventh graders. It would be of value to have data demonstrating whether the highest scores tend to remain high and the lowest scores tend to remain low. Such data are especially of significance in vocational and educational counseling.

The normative data are adequately presented in the manual. The descriptions of the sampling procedures used and the nature of the standardization sample are clear. It would appear that the publishers exercised care in attempting to obtain a fairly representative sample. In the main, they achieved this with a fair degree of success, even though some of the geographical regions are slightly under- or overrepresented.

Raw scores are converted to percentiles, and these percentile scores are then used to prepare the test profile. This procedure does not eliminate the possibility that the reported score may be an inaccurate representation of the subject's interest. For example, an individual can obtain a high percentile score and still have little interest in the area, and vice versa. Because the percentiles of ipsative scores can result in interpretative problems for college students who have taken tests-and-measurements courses, what then can we expect from a seventh grader interpreting his own profile?

A somewhat disturbing feature of the profile leaflet is the description of the various interest areas. Specific references are made to occupations or vocations, and these occupations are then grouped within a larger interest cluster. For example, in defining a persuasive interest, the publishers say that most salesmen, personnel managers, and buyers have high persuasive interest. Yet, no empirical evidence is presented in the manual to support such a claim. For this reason, we feel that the user should exercise extreme caution in interpreting the test profile. We further suggest that, because of possible misinterpretation of the profile leaflet (especially by younger pupils), the counselor or teacher does the actual interpretation.

In conclusion, we are pleased that an attempt has been made to try to measure the interests of younger people in the Kuder General Interest Survey. Our knowledge of the development and stability of interests is not complete, but this should not dissuade us from trying to measure them. Our interest, however, in the development of such an inventory should not make us sacrifice quality. From the data presented in the manual regarding the test's validity and reliability, it would appear that the the test was published before sufficient and adequate predictive validity data were obtained.

Logically Keyed Interest Inventories

Lee-Thorpe Occupational Interest Inventory   Revised edition. California Test Bureau, 1956. One form. Two levels: intermediate (grades 7–12) and advanced (grades 9 to adulthood). Ten scores. Untimed, but takes about 45 minutes to administer.

The OII consists of 120 pairs of statements and has a forced-choice format. The authors began with definitions of occupations listed in the *Dictionary of Occupational Titles*[30] and established six broad categories or fields of interest: personal-social, natural, mechanical, business, arts, and sciences. The ten scores that are obtained can be grouped into one of three categories: (1) fields of interest, (2) types of interests (verbal, manipulative, and computational), and (3) levels of interests. Within each of the six fields of interest, tasks were selected to represent the three levels of interest or responsibility (high, low, and medium). Validity and reliability data are lacking. The relationships found between field and type scores are misleading and are, to a large extent, an artifact of the inventory. The normative data provided are not only inadequate but also misleading. In general, the OII should be used only for research purposes until the authors can present empirical data to demonstrate the inventory's validity and reliability.

COMPARISONS AMONG SELECTED INTEREST INVENTORIES

There is very little difference, if any, among the various interest inventories with respect to their general purpose. All are concerned with an assessment of one's likes and dislikes for various occupations so that the examinee, with the help of a trained counselor, can make more valid decisions regarding future educational or vocational plans than if interest inventory data were not available. There are, however, some marked differences between the various standardized interest inventories with respect to their method of construction, scoring, ease of administration, and ease of interpretation. Also, they differ in the grade level at which they can be used.

Method of Construction

The Strong Vocational Interest Blank (SVIB), Minnesota Vocational Interest Inventory (MVII), and Kuder Occupational Interest Survey (OIS) employed criterion keying (contrasted groups). The SVIB and MVII used as their criterion groups, men-in-general, whereas the OIS compared men in one occupation with those in many other occupations. The OII employed logical keying, and the GIS used homogeneous keying. All but the SVIB employed a forced-choice format to try to control for response sets.

---

[30]Published by the United States Employment Service (USES) and contains descriptions of virtually all occupations.

Grade Level and Content

Neither the SVIB nor the OIS should be used for students who are not at least juniors in high school. The OII can be used for seventh graders, but the results should be interpreted cautiously. The Kuder GIS can be used for bright sixth graders. The MVII can be used for pupils in the ninth grade (about fifteen or sixteen years old).

With respect to content, there is very little difference, if any, between the Kuder and Strong inventories. They stress activities and interests related to professional occupations and vocations. These inventories, however, differ from the OII and the MVII, which are concerned more with nonprofessional occupations, especially the MVII. The OII items are more heterogeneous than the SVIB or Kuder items, and hence the OII may be more difficult to interpret. Because the OII is based on the *Dictionary of Occupational Titles*, it may sample many activities with which the student has little knowledge or experience. All interest inventories, regardless of their content, are concerned with ascertaining an individual's likes and dislikes for various activities and occupations. The Kuder scales are the only ones that contain a verification key.

Administration and Scoring

All interest inventories are untimed but take about 30 to 60 minutes to administer. None require any formal training for either administration or scoring. They are all group administered but can be individually administered if the situation warrants it. Preparation for testing conditions is minimal because no equipment is needed. One can say that interest inventories are, in a sense, self-administering.

The five inventories discussed here differ markedly in their ease of scoring. The OII and the GIS are relatively easy to score and can be either hand or machine scored. The SVIB and the OIS are complex to score, and hand scoring is out of the question. In fact, the OIS can only be scored by the publisher. The MVII is between the two extremes.

Validity and Reliability

The amount of evidence supporting claims for validity and reliability differs among the interest inventories. If one were to conceptualize a continuum

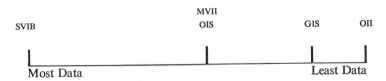

Figure 4-2 Empirical evidence for validity and reliability.

running from most to least empirical evidence in support of reliability and validity data, the results would be as depicted in Figure 4–2.

Although the GIS does not have too much data to substantiate its predictive validity, it does have a little more than the OII. Remember that the GIS is a relatively new instrument but that the OII has been around for some length of time and the authors have failed to heed the criticisms regarding their paucity of validity and reliability data.

Interpretation

One may think that the less complex an inventory, the easier is its interpretation. This does not hold true, at least for interest inventories. All interest inventories are difficult to interpret properly. If they are to be used for more than exploratory devices, they should be interpreted only by a trained counselor or psychologist. Of the five inventories discussed earlier, the OII and the GIS convey more general (rather than specific) information and hence may be frustrating to some students. It is one thing to tell a student that he exhibits the interests shared by chemists or lawyers, but it is something else when you tell him that he has scientific interests. What are scientific interests? In using either the SVIB, the OIS, or the MVII, the counselor can be both specific (using the separate occupational scores) and general (using the cluster or area interest scores), but with the OII or the GIS, the counselor can only be general in his evaluation of the examinee's interests.

The SVIB, OIS, and MVII are better for job orientation because the scores tell one what men in a specific vocation or profession (as well as people in broad areas such as scientific, mechanical, and business) like and dislike. Unlike the OII and the GIS, we do not have to infer an individual's interests from a general scale such as personal-social or computational.

The degree of confidence that a counselor can place in his interpretation is directly related to both the validity and the stability of the instrument(s) used. There is no denying that the SVIB has had more research performed with it, that there have been many longitudinal studies conducted with it, and that it has, in essence, stood the empirical test. To a somewhat similar degree, the same can be said about the OIS. However, little, if anything, can be said about the MVII or the GIS because they are so new. Unfortunately, the OII is an old test that never provided data on its psychometric quality.

Regarding interpretation, one must keep in mind that the Kuder tests and the MVII, because they are forced-choice inventories, are ipsative rather than normative scales. This means that the choice of one response automatically results in the rejection of the other(s). In other words, an ipsative scale results in a high score in one scale to be accompanied by a low score in another scale. Therefore, any attempt to interpret the absolute difference in scores or the degree of difference between a score of 40 on Scale A and a score of 46 on Scale B is most difficult.

The OII (because it is more descriptive of vocations than either the SVIB, Kuder GIS, MVII, or OIS) may be more susceptible to responses being made in terms of stereotypes that the examinee holds rather than in terms of interests per se. In addition, the OII and MVII are not as applicable to higher level professional occupations as is either the Kuder Occupational or the SVIB.

Although similar labels, such as *scientific*, may be attached to scales in the various interest inventories, the counselor must be cautious in inferring that scales having the same designation are measuring exactly the same trait or characteristic. Just as one should not judge a book by its cover, the counselor should not interpret a scale by its name. The counselor must be thoroughly familiar with the test, the operational definitions of the terms used to describe the scale, and the theoretical orientation of the test constructor. All of these reinforce our position that, for other than exploratory information, the user be trained in terms of both formal course work and practical experience.

The OIS and the SVIB are relatively unsatisfactory for people entering occupations that are below the professional-managerial level, even though there are many scales that are occupational in nature. Of the two tests, the OIS is more suitable for persons contemplating lower-level occupations. This is not to imply that these authors felt the measurement of interests for skilled workers was futile. Indeed, this was not the case. Strong goes so far as to recommend some inventories to be used with individuals contemplating skilled, nonprofessional occupations. The nature of the research conducted in the development of the Strong and the OIS was such that the inventories are biased in favor of professional and managerial people. Use of either the SVIB or the OIS for high school seniors who intend to enter the apprenticeship program of skilled craftsmen is strongly discouraged. In fact, using these inventories for these persons is a misuse (the MVII would be appropriate here).

In conclusion, there are some similarities as well as marked differences among the various interest inventories. Although Strong and Kuder originally approached the measurement of interests differently, their tests are now very similar. Strong adopted the interest clusters advocated by Kuder, and Kuder adopted the specific interest areas used by Strong. Although criticisms can be leveled at any of the interest inventories, the deficiencies of the Strong and Kuder inventories are mild in comparison to the deficiencies of the OII. One reviewer of the OII went so far as to say that this is a good example of how efficient packaging and advertising can make a worthless test appear to be valid.[31]

[31]See Edward S. Bordin's review of the OII in Oscar K. Buros (Ed.), *The third mental measurements yearbook*. New Brunswick, N.J.: Rutgers University Press, 1949, pp. 666–667.

USING INTEREST INVENTORY RESULTS

As might be expected, the greatest utility of interest inventory results is for guidance and counseling — vocational, educational, and personal. Used appropriately, these tests scores may help an individual crystallize his interests by having him think about his future plans or may clarify some misconceptions that he has about future occupational or vocational goals. It should be stressed here that it is not the test scores per se that help achieve this self-discovery. It is the professional interpretation made of the test scores. Those who interpret interest test scores must be thoroughly trained and familiar with interest inventories: their uses and misuses, their fallibility, their stability, and their general value in helping make sound educational and vocational decisions.

Before considering the various uses of interest inventory results by educators, we feel that it would be appropriate to summarize what we have learned about the nature of interests and interest inventories.

1. Interests tend to become progressively more stable with age (particularly after adolescence), but they are never permanently fixed. Although a broad area of interest, such as medicine, may not change, there can be a shift in one's interests regarding general practice versus specialization or regarding different specialties. Using interest inventory results to counsel students who are not yet juniors in high school into making specific vocational decisions is to be discouraged because at this age, interests are changeable. Interest test scores can and should be used in discussions about various occupations and professions. Interest inventories that claim they are valid for junior high school children or for elementary school children should display predictive validity over a long time interval before much faith is placed in their results. Only the Strong has demonstrated empirically that its results are quite reliable (in terms of long-term stability) for individuals around 25 years of age.

2. Interest inventories are susceptible to response set and faking; some more so than others. The user should therefore interpret the results of interest inventories accordingly.

3. Interest inventory scores can be influenced by the ambiguity of the questions asked. For example, two people can respond to the item "Like to play bridge" in the same way but for different reasons. One individual may answer "Like" because it affords him an opportunity to meet people and establish future contacts even though he may dislike bridge. Another person might answer "Like" for different reasons. He may like bridge because of the challenge it offers; yet, this person might not like people and may avoid them whenever possible. This example indicates that the responses to interest inventory items are relative rather than absolute indicators of likes

and dislikes. It is of vital importance that interest inventories be carefully constructed so as to remove the influence of ambiguity as much as possible.

4. Interest inventories are verbal in nature. The examinee must be able to comprehend what is being asked of him. Although the reading levels of the interest inventories vary, nearly all presume that the examinee can read at least at the sixth-grade level.[32] This therefore precludes the use of such inventories as the SVIB, OIS, GIS, and OII for illiterates and students who have a reading deficiency. The verbal nature of these interest inventories also leaves open the possibility of misunderstanding or misinterpreting, even though there may be little ambiguity in the items.

5. Interest inventories do not do very well in predicting job success, academic success, job satisfaction, or personality adjustment. There is no interest test on the market that will permit one to say that Johnny should become a doctor, lawyer, or carpenter. There is no interest inventory that will indicate whether or not Johnny will be happy or successful in vocations or occupations in which he has obtained high scores. This does not mean that interest inventories have no predictive validity. They do, but they are not as valid as our cognitive measures. There is a slight relationship between interest inventory scores and academic success (correlations normally are about .30). And, there is a slight relationship between interest scores and such things as job success and personality. This, however, should not necessarily be interpreted as evidence of a relationship that is of practical significance (even though it may be of statistical significance), nor should it be construed as a cause-and-effect relationship. In predicting job satisfaction, it should be remembered that many factors must be considered, of which interests are but one factor. The relationship between interest scores and job success is vague because of the problem of obtaining a valid measure of job success. Interest inventory scores may be related to various measures of job and/or academic success and satisfaction. However, the nature of the relationship is such that interest scores alone should never be used to predict future success or satisfaction. It is because the untrained user may make exaggerated statements regarding the probability or degree of success (or satisfaction) in a profession or vocation that we find interest inventories being severely and unduly criticized. Once again, we reiterate that in many instances the instrument is made the scapegoat.

[32]G. Frederic Kuder, *Occupational Interest Survey general manual*. Chicago: Science Research Associates, 1966, p. 2. No data are furnished to support this contention. In a study by Fritz W. Forbes and William C. Cottle, A new method of determining the readability of standardized tests. *J. appl. Psychol.*, 1953, *37*, 185–190, they demonstrated that the reading grade levels were 8.7 for the old Kuder and 11.4 for the old SVIB. Because the revised editions are not that different, the writers suggest that the user ascertain the reading level needed for the test he intends to use.

Although persons may have a natural tendency to accent the negative and eliminate or forget the positive, we hope that this tendency is not exercised when interest inventories are concerned. When used properly, interest inventory results can provide valuable information for the teacher and counselor — information that is more valid than that obtained by non-standardized approaches — so that he will better understand the pupils' cognitive and noncognitive behavior.

Guidance Purposes

After cognitive measures, interest inventory results play the greatest role in vocational and educational counseling. Interest inventory results are beneficial to both the counselor and the counselee. The counselor can use the results as an introduction to the interview. The interest test may be used as a gambit in situations where it is difficult to establish rapport. The counselor can use the test results to help open the way to discussing other problems such as academic difficulty, personal-social relationships, and the like. The counselee, on the other hand, has an opportunity to view himself as he described himself. He can look at his present plans and see, with the assistance of the counselor, whether his aspirations are realistic. The counselee can use the test results as leads for further consideration. The counselee and counselor can use the test results to see whether the expressed interests are related or unrelated (whether they all fit into a pattern such as humanitarian or technical or whether they are distinct), whether the program that the counselee is intending to follow is compatible with his profile of interests and abilities, and whether the counselee's vocational or avocational goal will be realized by the program he is now following.

Interest test results, if used cautiously, can help an individual find himself in terms of the activities he feels are important and interesting. Interest test results should not be used for classroom selection purposes (though they may be useful for classification). They should not be used to tell Johnny that he should enter the field of engineering. They should not be used as a major criterion in vocational and educational counseling. High scores on an interest inventory are not analogous to saying that the individual has either the aptitude or potential for success in a particular vocation. The test scores only provide a relative index of the individual's likes and dislikes, and for some inventories, it is possible to compare the student's interests with those of individuals who are successful in a vocation or profession. In actual practice, interest inventory results should only be used for their valuable ancillary information. Other factors such as ability, aptitude, motivation, and the like must be considered. Finally, the total profile rather than just part of it must be considered so that as complete a picture as possible of the individual's interests can be obtained.

Instructional Purposes

Although interest inventory results can be used for grouping students, they normally are not used for this purpose. In a somewhat indirect fashion, interest inventory results can be used by the classroom teacher to provide optimal learning conditions. Take for example, the junior high school student who is a poor reader. Recognizing the limitations of interest inventory scores for junior high school students, the teacher who knows that Billy likes mechanics, may attempt to motivate him to read more by suggesting books, magazines, or articles that are of mechanical content. Hence, although the test score is not used as an instructional device per se, it is used to provide a learning experience that may be quite beneficial insofar as Billy's reading is concerned.

Interest inventories can be used as a learning device. For example, in the unit on "Work" in Social Studies, the teacher can have the students take an interest test. He can use this technique to get the students to think somewhat systematically about the relationships between personal interests and occupational choice. Any interest inventory used in a group fashion should be used for discussion purposes only. Hopefully, divergent thinking rather than convergent thinking will ensue.

SUMMARY

Knowledge about an individual's interests can be of much value to the classroom teacher, or counselor (as a gambit for a discussion between the student and counselor regarding the student's vocational plans), and the individual (they can help him give some considerations to professions and vocations that he might never have thought about).

Interests can be assessed in a variety of ways: expressed, manifest, tested, and interest inventories. Research has indicated that interest inventories are the most valid.

The three techniques most frequently used to construct interest inventories are: logical-keying, homogeneous-keying, and criterion-keying. Although the two men most renowned for their work in the area of interest measurement, Strong and Kuder, employed different approaches in the initial development of their inventories, the revised editions of the Strong and Kuder are more similar than different. The interest patterns or clusters identified or at least designated by Kuder and Strong have, in the main, been confirmed by empirical research.

Despite the fact that interest inventories have certain limitations (fakable, susceptible to response set, may be answered on the basis of stereotypes, and may be difficult to interpret especially if they are ipsative forced-choice tests) they do have much value in vocational and educational counseling *if* and *when* used properly.

Some inventories, like the Kuder and Strong are designed for individuals who plan to attend college and aspire to managerial or professional roles. Other inventories, such as the MVII, are designed for students who plan to enter into apprenticeship programs after leaving high school.

More research is needed about the relationship between the scores of the various inventories. There have been many instances reported in the literature regarding such discrepancies. Needless to say, research directed to resolving such discrepancies (which can play a significant role in vocational guidance) will permit the counselor to make a more valid interpretation of the test profile.

Interest inventories have come a long way from Strong's initial attempts in the 1920s. They are not only becoming more refined but they are beginning to emphasize or at least recognize the need for a theoretical position on the development of interests. They can assist the counselor in establishing rapport. They can help the student by giving him something to consider or reflect upon; by providing him with some ideas that he can develop more fully by reading and discussion. They can help the teacher organize meaningful learning experiences. All in all, they can help school personnel obtain a more complete picture of the individual by providing valuable data about his likes and dislikes. Such data are best obtained from standardized interest inventories.

PERSONALITY ASSESSMENT

There is no denying that personality characteristics are or should be of concern to classroom teachers. It is generally agreed that education must be as concerned with attitudes, values, and interests to the same degree as it is concerned with the development of cognitive skills and knowledge. What value will society accrue from individuals who can solve a quadratic equation or are able to detect the components of LSD but who are hostile or aggressive? Education should be concerned with developing a well-rounded individual.

Technological changes during the past decade have created new demands from our students as well as our schools. In order to provide optimal learning conditions, educators must know as much as possible about the *process* as well as the *product* of learning. They must recognize that *what* a person thinks may be just as important as *how* he thinks. Quite often, what and how an individual learns can be markedly influenced by his personality makeup.

WHAT PERSONALITY IS

Judging from the variety of definitions posited in psychology texts, it would appear that everyone knows (or thinks he knows) what personality is, but no one is able to define it precisely. *Personality*, as *intelligence*, differs in meaning depending upon who gives the definition. To the layman, *personality* is frequently defined in terms of (actually confused with) one's reputation, such as "he's easy-going, she's sweet and understanding." In other words, the layman tends to define one's personality in terms of what other people think of one. To the clinician, personality is a complex interaction of many factors that are difficult to isolate and analyze. Although there are a variety of definitions posited by psychologists, we subscribe to the one given by Allport because he has attempted to synthesize the various definitions into a meaningful whole: "Personality is the dynamic organization within the individual of those psychophysical systems that determine his characteristic behavior and thought."[33] Regardless of the definition one subscribes to, it should be readily evident that personality is a complex interaction of many factors.

> Personality does not depend upon a few characteristics alone but upon the interaction of practically all the traits of an individual ... all contribute to the personality, and not as separate entities but as an organized system.[34]

The marked discrepancies in the definition of *personality* have arisen primarily because of idiosyncratic feelings regarding the existence of these traits and their operational definitions. Hence, two tests may measure the trait of authoritarianism, but the construct may be viewed differently by the two psychologists who contructed the tests.

Returning to our question "What is personality?" it should be evident that it is the total individual — his cognitive and noncognitive traits. In this text, however, we will restrict our discussion of personality assessment to problem check lists, general adjustment inventories, and projective tests. We recognize that an individual's interests, his attitudes, and his opinions are an integral component of his general makeup (as are his cognitive traits).

We must emphasize that personality tests, with possibly the exception of some problem check lists, should not be administered and interpreted by the classroom teacher. The assessment of an individual's behavior is

---

[33]Gordon W. Allport, *Pattern and growth in personality*. New York: Holt, Rinehart and Winston, 1963, p. 28.

[34]Laurence F. Shaffer, *The psychology of adjustment*. New York: Houghton Mifflin, 1936, p. 282.

dependent upon the synthesis of many particles of information. Valid synthesis should and can be undertaken only by persons trained in this area.

HISTORICAL DEVELOPMENT OF PERSONALITY MEASURES

Man has always been aware of individual differences, and sometimes he has had the tendency to attach arbitrary labels (such as *hostile, mean,* or *cooperative*) to people and has failed to realize that these labels can be damaging. In the fourth and third centuries B.C., Theophrastus and Hippocrates divided men into different types. (It is interesting to note that over 2000 years later, Sheldon[35] attempted to classify personality on the basis of physical characteristics.) However, early attempts to classify personality into types or categories on the basis of physiognomy, by glandular secretions, and body build have been largely abandoned today.

In the 1880s, Galton devised the first personality questionnaire when he wanted a standardized procedure for studying mental imagery. In the ninteenth century, G. Stanley Hall used a personality questionnaire in his study of adolescent development, and Kraeplin and Sommer worked with free association tests. Both Galton and Hall were moved to devise personality questionnaires so that they could gather data that could not be obtained by the observational method. In 1905, Jung published a free-association test to measure emotional complexes. In 1910, Kent and Rosanoff, in the United States, used free-association techniques to expose some of the subconscious personality traits and to ascertain whether they could be used to discriminate among various mental disorders. The first inventory primarily concerned with individual assessment was the Woodsworth Personal Data Sheet (WPDS). This inventory was used during World War I as a screening device to detect soldiers who might break down mentally in battle. Although it was not intended to replace the thorough psychiatric interview, it did (like the Army Alpha and Beta for intelligence) offer a speedy method of testing large numbers of individuals at induction centers and isolating those deserving of more thorough attention. The WPDS was the model used to develop many of our personality inventories.

In 1921, in Bern, Switzerland, Rorschach published what is now known as the Rorschach Ink Blot Test. This was, and still is, one of the most well-known personality measures. In 1921, Pressey published his Group Scale for Investigating the Emotions, and Voelker's Test of Trustworthiness appeared. In 1923, Downey's Will Temperament Test was published, which introduced a novel approach in assessing personality. In the Downey test, the subject's personality is measured under different conditions, such as

---

[35]William H. Sheldon and others, *The varieties of human physique.* New York: Harper & Row, 1940.

writing with one's eyes open and then with them closed. In 1935, another unstructured projective test, the Thematic Apperception Test, by Murray and Morgan, was published.

During World War II, personality testing was aided immeasurably by psychometric advances, notably factor analysis and the forced-choice technique. Before this time, personality inventories frequently consisted of a hodgepodge of items, the items being based on behavioral characteristics that were arbitrarily chosen. Cattell, Thurstone, Eysenck, and Guilford have all used the factor-analytic approach in their attempts to develop empirical rather than rational personality tests.

During the past decade or so, research on personality assessment has tended to focus less upon techniques and more upon the development of a theory of personality. It is one thing to use factor analysis, but no technique will ever replace the need for formulating constructs on the basis of personality theory. An example of a personality test based upon theory is the Edwards Personal Preference Schedule (EPPS), which is based on Murray's needs theory. Today, emphasis in personality testing is directed toward the assessment of normal behavior.

TYPES OF PERSONALITY TESTS[36]

Personality can be measured in a variety of ways. Three commonly used approaches to study personality are: (1) see what the individual says about himself (self-report inventories), (2) see what others say about the individual (sociometric inventories), and (3) see what the individual does in a particular kind of situation (observational techniques).

Another way in which personality tests can be classified is in terms of the method in which one's behavior is studied or in the manner in which the stimuli are presented. Stimuli can be presented as either *structured* or *unstructured*. The structured test consists of items or questions that can be interpreted in relatively the same way by all examinees (for example, "Do you daydream?"). The unstructured test (sometimes referred to as the projective test, although projective devices can be either completely unstructured or semistructured) consists of ambiguous pictures or ink blots to which the examinee responds according to his interpretation of the stimulus. In the structured test, the subject projects his feelings when describing the ambiguous stimulus or completing the incomplete statement or word. Unstructured tests differ from structured tests in that they are usually not quantitatively scored, although they could be. Structured personality tests are objectively scored with predetermined keys, and the individual's scores are then compared with the responses of the standardization sample.

[36]Tests are used here in their broadest context; that is, we are considering rating scales and check lists as tests.

Personality tests can further be classified in terms of their method of construction. As discussed earlier in the chapter, three common approaches used to construct personality tests are (1) criterion keying (used in the MMPI and the California Psychological Inventory), (2) factor analysis (used in the many Cattell personality tests), and (3) the logical approach (used in the Bernreuter Personality Inventory). In essence then, personality tests can be differentiated in terms of *how* they do what they do rather than in terms of *what* they do. However, it is essential that the reader be cognizant of *what* they do. That is, does the test attempt to isolate problems, or does it attempt to give an indication of possible adjustment?

In this chapter, we will consider only the self-report inventories — be they structured or unstructured — recognizing that, although other techniques provide valuable information, they are typically locally constructed rather than commercially standardized tests.

STRUCTURED SELF-REPORT INVENTORIES

Structured self-report inventories are the most common type of personality tests used in schools (and industry) today. They are a basic tool in the diagnosis of illness, whether it be physical or mental. Just as the physician will ask what hurts you, where it hurts, and when it started, the psychiatrist and clinician will ask whether one has nightmares and whether one has a tendency to daydream. The answers to these kinds of questions, over the years, have been found to be more indicative of maladjustment than those to other questions that could be asked. When such questions are selected and put together in a list to be checked off by the examinee, it is a test or inventory. Self-report inventories can be classified into either problem check lists or general adjustment inventories. They can also be classified in terms of their method of construction: criterion groups, factor analysis, or the logical approach. All, however, are structured.

Problem Check Lists

Problem check lists are the most applicable personality measure in our public schools because of their limited demand upon formal training and experience for the examiner. In fact, one can go so far as to say that no formal training is required to administer and score a problem check list. Interpretation, on the other hand, demands training, sophistication, and experience. It is one thing to administer a check list and still another to interpret it. For example, let us assume that Peter indicates he has difficulty with his brothers and sisters. What can, should, or does one do? Naturally, the untrained teacher should obtain professional assistance in whatever action he undertakes. In fact, we strongly recommend that assistance in the interpretation of, and subsequent action to, a problem check list be obtained from a qualified counselor or clinician. Sibling rivalry, in Peter's case may appear, on the surface, easy to deal with. However, it is usually more complex than that and therefore requires professional training.

Problem check lists can be used by the classroom teacher to confirm some of his subjective impressions that he obtained by observation. For example, in Peter's case, the teacher may have noticed that Peter is depressed or moody, whereas a few months earlier he was a happy child. Problem check lists can be used by the teacher (or counselor) to obtain a better understanding of the pupil — his problems, his behavior. It is quite conceivable that a pupil like Peter will suddenly begin doing poor, sloppy work. Possibly, from the results of a problem check list, the teacher will be able to learn that Peter's performance is because of something that is bothering him rather than because of laziness. Problem check lists, especially when administered to the whole class, will make pupils less self-conscious and willing to reveal their problems. This is especially true if the teacher discusses the general findings. The pupil is then able to see that he is not atypical, that other pupils are also bothered or concerned about a variety of things. Problem check lists also serve as excellent screening devices for the counselor. On the basis of their results and an interview, the counselor may suggest more thorough treatment if needed.

It should be remembered that problem check lists are just that — they do not make any claims to measuring personality traits. In problem check lists, the individual checks only the statements that are applicable to him (and that he wishes to check) and that he is consciously aware of. Problem check lists have their greatest value in acting as a communication vehicle between the pupil and the counselor. The test results can help save the counselor much valuable time by indicating what the problem appears to be and can help establish rapport between the pupil and counselor.

Problem check lists are essentially concerned with such areas as family, peer relationships, finances, study skills, health, and relations with adults. Even so, they differ slightly in their format. In some, the pupil only checks the statements that he perceives as problems. In others, the pupil can indicate the degree of severity: minor, moderate, severe. In still others, the pupil can write a statement about the problem, thereby allowing him to explicate.

Mooney Problem Check-List Revised edition. The Psychological Corporation, 1950. Untimed, but takes about 30 minutes. Has four levels: (1) Junior high school for grades 7 to 9, which yields seven scores (health and physical development; school; home and family; money, work, the future; boy-and-girl relations; relations to people in general; and self-centered concerns). (2) High school for grades 9 to 12, which yields 11 scores (health and physical development; finances, living conditions, employment; social and recreational activities; social-psychological relations; personal-psychological relations; courtship, sex, marriage; home and family; morals and religion; adjustment to school work; the future — vocational and educational curriculum; and teaching procedures). (3) College for grades 13 to 16, which yields the same scores as the high school. (4) Adult, which measures problems in nine areas (health, economic security, self-improvement, personality, home and family, courtship, sex, religion, and occupation).

The items used were selected after a thorough analysis of written statements of problems by over 4000 students and through adults' statements of problems, a survey of the literature, and the authors' counseling experience. Some examples of the items used are:

Have trouble with my teeth.

Not living with my parents.

I want to learn how to read better.[37]

For each of the levels, provision is made for the student to indicate whether he would like to discuss his problems with someone. In the high school and college forms, the student can specify the person with whom he would like to discuss his problems.

In the Mooney, the subject responds to each of the items only if he is worried or concerned. Because this is not a test in the usual sense, we find validity and reliability data lacking, although the manual does report a few studies. It would indeed be helpful if more data were provided. There is no normative data — the authors claim that local norms are more appropriate in a check list.

The Mooney, as other problem check lists, is designed to provide ancillary and supplementary information about the student. There are no right or wrong answers as such but only indicated problems or areas of concern. The authors make frequent cautions to the user regarding the instrument's interpretation and applicability. They are conservative when they say:

At all times the counselor must keep in mind that the *Problem Check-List* is not a test. It does not yield scores on traits or permit any direct statements about the adjustment status of the person who made the responses. Rather, the *Problem Check-List* is a form of simple communication between the counselee and the counselor designed to accelerate the process of understanding the student and his real problems.[38]

---

[38]*Mooney Problem Check-List manual*, p. 5.

The writers, recognizing that most personality tests are beyond the training and qualifications of the classroom teacher (and even the school psychologist unless he has taken specialized advanced training), feel that a critical evaluation of a personality test should be on an inventory that has particular relevance to, and can be administered and interpreted (tentatively at least) by the classroom teacher. With this in mind, we have selected an example of a problem check list, the Billett-Starr Youth Problems Inventory, because no formal training is required for its administration and scoring.

A CRITICAL EVALUATION OF THE BILLETT-STARR YOUTH PROBLEMS INVENTORY (BSYPI)

Grade Level and Content

Two levels: grades 7–9 and 10–12. The purpose of this inventory is to help school personnel quickly identify the self-acknowledged problems of students in grades 7 to 12. The junior high school form contains 432 problems. The senior high school form contains 441 problems. The problem areas assessed are physical health and safety, getting along with others, boy-girl relationships, home and family life, personal finance, interests and activities, school life, personal potentialities, planning for the future, mental-emotional health, and morality and religion. A twelfth score is the total score. The number of problems in each of the 11 areas varies from nine to over 80.

Some examples of the problems and areas are:

Getting Along with Others: I argue too much.
I don't know how to act with jealous people.

School Life: I don't like school.
I wonder if I'll pass.

Morality and Religion: I can't believe in any religion.
I often tell lies.[39]

No attempt was made to assign problems randomly, but all problems of a similar nature (no indication is given in the manual as to *how* and/or *why* a problem was assigned to a particular area) were grouped together. Such a procedure might encourage faking, but if rapport is established between pupil and teacher, this should be minimized.

[39]Irving S. Starr and Roy O. Billett, Billett-Starr Youth Problems Inventory. New York: Harcourt, Brace & World, 1961. Items reproduced by permission of the copyright owners, the authors.

Administration

The BSYPI is untimed. However, the test authors recommend that 80 minutes and 70 minutes be designated for administering the junior and senior high school forms, respectively. The test authors suggest that if time is at a premium, the various areas may be administered separately (one or two at a time). We question this. How reliable would the results be? Would there be any differences occurring over a period of time? Are scores obtained in a single session comparable to those obtained in multiple sessions? How can the norms be used if multiple sessions are employed? The absence of answers to questions such as these preclude multiple testing sessions unless the results are to be used for class discussion purposes only.

No formal training is needed to administer this inventory. The manual contains abundant information on the mechanics of administration and scoring. The classroom teacher or a teacher's aide should have no difficulty administering this inventory.

Scoring

Pupils respond to each of the items by means of a three-element key: **NP** means no problem, **S** means that the statement is somewhat of a problem to him, and **M** means that the item is much of a problem to him. The pupil crosses out the appropriate symbol.

Because this is a problem check list rather than a test with right and wrong answers, scoring is done by hand. Only items marked **M** or **S** are counted.[40]

Types of Scores

Total scores may be evaluated by reference to percentile norms for each sex reported separately for the two levels. In addition, quartile norms are presented for each of the area scores. A difficulty in interpreting the quartile norms is encountered for the areas where there are only a few items. For example, in the area of personal finance, there are 9 items. However, checking as little as two problems in this area will move the student from the bottom quarter to the top quarter of the distribution. Such lack of differentiation between the extremes suggests that interpretations would be subject to much error. We recommend that either more problems be added to such areas or that comparable areas be combined for test interpretation.

---

[40]It is recommended in the manual (p. 7) that no distinction be made between an **S** or **M** response in scoring. The contention that this method of responding improves "the student's general attitude and the validity of his responses" is not supported by empirical evidence.

Norming

The test was administered to 8675 students in 30 junior and senior high schools. No stratification was used, and it would appear that the sample is biased in favor of the eastern and southern regions. Only one midwestern state was used, and no schools from the western states were included in the standardization program. Although the authors contend that both rural and urban pupils were used, they present no information concerning the composition of the sample except for grade and sex distributions. The test authors recommend local norms. But they also make the point (possibly with tongue in cheek) that the sample should *not* be considered as representative. Yet, they confuse the issue when they state that "there is no known reason to suspect that the distribution of number of problems marked or the percent of students marking each problem would differ substantially if a more representative group had taken the Inventory."[41]

Reliability

As is true with nearly all problem check lists, reliability data are not reported. The authors of such inventories contend that the typical methods employed to ascertain reliability, namely, test-retest reliability, are not applicable. This may be true for test-retest reliability over a prolonged period of time because human behavior is vacillating rather than static. Also test-retest within a few days can be misleading because the subject's perception of his problems may be changed simply by going through the check list. We agree that some reliability estimates may be in error because we are dealing with human behavior. We contend, however, that the test authors should present reliability data, and then the user should evaluate these data in their proper perspective. As the inventory is now, we are unable to make even an intelligent estimate of its reliability.

Validity

The instrument's principal claim to validity rests upon the manner in which it was constructed. The items are based upon the acknowledged problems written by a large number of students. The validity data presented in the manual support the contention of the test authors that these statements are problems students admit. Although these statements may be considered to constitute a universe of student problems, no data are presented to indicate how thoroughly or adequately this domain of behavior was sampled. Techniques used in other personality inventories such as correlations with

[41]*BSYPI manual*, p. 15.

other standardized tests, comparison of test performance with case histories, and matching could and should have been used. Once again it should be mentioned that these comments are applicable to most check lists and not just to the BSYPI. Although the authors imply that there is agreement between the results of counselor interviews and test scores, they do not offer any evidence regarding the extent of agreement or the method employed.

Format

The items are contained in a 12-page booklet measuring eight and one half inches by eleven inches. All printing is in black ink on white paper with bold type used for the **NP** and **M** responses. Italics are used whenever references are made to brother/sister, mother/father, or boys/girls. Because of the large number of items, it would have been desirable had the publisher spread out the problems. In this way, reading would have been easier. The front page of the test booklet has spaces to record the number of problems checked "Some" or "Much" for each of the 11 areas measured.

The examiner's manual is well written and easily understood. In addition to discussing what is commonly found in such manuals — validity, reliability, norms — a few suggestions are interspersed here and there regarding test interpretation. Unfortunately, neither the technical data presented nor the cursory interpretative comments do much to assist the test user.

Interpretation and Use

The BSYPI is most suited for guidance and counseling. A novel (although not original) feature of the BSYPI is the labeling of certain items as indicators of "urgent" or "very serious" problems so as to demand immediate attention. The test authors had a committee of 20 experts (school counselors, school psychologists, professors of psychology, and the like) rate each statement of the inventory on a three-point scale: minor, in-between, and very serious problem. This is an admirable undertaking, but unfortunately, too many questions remain unanswered: Because as many as 15 percent of the standardization group checked these labeled items, is it not conceivable that there will be a spuriously high rate of false positive identifications (that is, identifying an individual as a problem case when, in reality, he is not)? Because the ratings were made "blind," that is, not applied to any specific situations or cases of maladjustment, the user should interpret these "urgent" problems accordingly. As of now, no evidence has been presented regarding their validity or utility in identifying students with behavioral problems. The BSYPI should only be used for preliminary screening and then should be followed up with more thorough interviews where the scores deem it advisable. Although it lacks the voluminous data associated with the Mooney, it appears to be a promising inventory. Time will tell how valid it is.

SUMMARY OF PROBLEM CHECK LISTS   Problem check lists must be accepted at face value. They are composed of items that are intended to be representative of problems that people face in different areas such as home, family, school, and occupation. No claim is made that they measure personality characteristics, and, in fact, the authors caution the user in the manual to avoid adopting this view. The responses only reflect the areas that the student is willing (or consciously aware of) to discuss. The responses to problem check lists should not be considered as a test or subtest score. The teacher and counselor should use the responses as a guide for further exploration. If used in this way, problem check lists are quite valid and helpful.

The Mooney and the BSYPI differ very little in purpose, format, and scoring. As of now, the Mooney Problem Check-List is accompanied by more substantial research data (no doubt because it has been around for so long). The BSYPI is still too new to have proven its validity.

Problem check lists are primarily used to identify individuals who are concerned with social and personal relationships. Another type of structured self-report inventory is the adjustment inventory. This type is concerned primarily with the identification of neuroticism and pathological deviation. In addition, there have been developed structured self-report inventories that are most concerned with the assessment of narrowly defined behavior characteristics such as sociability, masculinity-femininity, and introversion-extraversion. These latter inventories place major emphasis on the measurement of individual differences within the normal range of deviation. They will not be discussed here because of their limited educational value.

General Adjustment Inventories: Criterion Groups

The Adjustment Inventory   Consulting Psychologists Press, Inc., 1963. One form. Two levels: Student form for grades 9–16 (research edition published in 1962), and adult form (published in 1938). The revised student form has six scores: home, health, submissiveness, emotionality, hostility, and masculinity. The adult form also provides six scores: home, occupational, health, social, emotional, and a total score. Untimed, but requires about 30 minutes to administer.

The Adjustment Inventory consists of 200 items that are answered Yes, No, or ?. In the revised form, three criteria were used to select items: (1) correlating the scale against external criteria such as similar scales and ratings of experts, (2) eliminating items that have little intrascale correlations, and (3) writing items on rational or a priori grounds. Hence, we may say that the revised scale contains some items that have predictive validity evidence and other items that have logical validity evidence. Concurrent validity was studied by correlating the subscores with those of similar tests, and the resulting correlations are quite high, being about .72 (with the exception of the Bell masculinity-femininity scale and those of the MF scales of the MMPI where the r's were .38 for women and .13 for men). The split-half reliabilities are all in the .80's.

The test is accompanied by an excellent manual with many interpretative guidelines. The normative data are still scanty. Percentile norms are given for 295 boys and 372 girls in grades 10 to 12; college norms are based on 316 men and 347 women in their freshmen to junior year. Unfortunately, both standardization samples are biased because of geographical limitations. The adult form contains the same number of questions, is answered in the same way, and was constructed with the same general principles as the revised student form. Odd-even reliability coefficients range from .80 to .89.

It should be emphasized that the validity of The Adjustment Inventory is as good as, and better than, most pencil-and-paper adjustment inventories. The student form is used more extensively than the adult form. The items were carefully selected and were randomly placed throughout the test to prevent or minimize acquiescence. Its principal functions are as an indicator of subjects requiring counseling, as a guide to help the trained clinician conduct the interview, and as an aid to a better understanding of the individual.

California Psychological Inventory (CPI) Consulting Psychologists Press, Inc., 1960. One form. Untimed, but requires about one hour to complete. Appropriate for ages 13 and over. Provides 18 scores: dominance, capacity for status, sociability, social presence, self-acceptance, sense of well-being, responsibility, socialization, self-control, tolerance, good impression, communality, achievement via conformance, achievement via independence, intellectual efficiency, psychological mindedness, flexibility, and femininity.

The author attempted to construct an instrument that would provide for a comprehensive, multidimensional assessment of normal persons in various settings. It consists of 480 statements that are responded to on a true-false dichotomy. The number of items in each scale varies from 22 to 56, the median being 37. Eleven of the scales were constructed on the basis of criterion group performance. Pupils were initially labeled as dominant or sociable by their high school principals, and the test scores were studied to see if they differentiated between these two groups. Cross-validation samples were then used to see whether the scales were valid. On this basis, the other ten scales were constructed, and it would appear that they are quite valid when judged against actual behavior criteria of contrasted groups. Three scales were empirically derived to provide the verification scales. Four of the scales were based on rational grounds. The author claims that personality traits can be classified into four categories: (1) measures of poise, ascendancy, and self-assurance, (2) measures of socialization, maturity, and responsibility, (3) measures of achievement potential and intellectual efficiency, and (4) measures of intellectual and interest modes. Later factor analytic studies, however, demonstrated that five scores would be needed to glean the information from the 18 scales. Possibly more important was that these studies suggest that some of the scales are improperly classified.

The test-retest reliabilities for high school students (one-year interval) are .65 for males and .68 for females. No doubt, if the reliability coefficients were internal consistency or split-half method estimates, they would tend to be higher. The norms are based upon 6000 males and 7000 females from a wide geographical area, differing in age and socioeconomic status. In addition, separate mean profiles for high school and college students of each sex are presented. Total scores are also presented for 30 special groups for each of the 18 scores.

Although the author might have indicated more confidence in his test's reliability than is justified by the evidence, one cannot deny that it is one of the best personality tests available. It was carefully constructed, is supported by much empirical evidence, has an excellent manual, and reports intercorrelations between the CPI and other widely used personality tests such as the MMPI and the Bernreuter.

General Adjustment Inventories: Logical Approach

Some authors employ criterion groups to select their items. Others employ factor analysis to assist them in selecting their items. Still others use no empirical evidence per se but construct their test on the basis of a logical or armchair philosophy. In other words, they conceive of a construct as manifesting itself in a particular type of behavior and then prepare items to measure that behavior.

The Personality Inventory Consulting Psychologists Press, Inc., 1938. One level, grades 9 to 16 and adults. Untimed. Requires less than 30 minutes to complete. Provides six scores:[42] self-sufficiency, neurotic tendency, introversion-extroversion, dominance-submission, confidence, and sociability.

The test consists of 125 items to which the examinee responds by means of a three-element key: Yes, No, ?. The items were selected from four existing inventories. The correlations between the Personality Inventory and these four scales varied from .67 to .94. Validity for such a test must necessarily be based on its predictive power. The manual contains very little validity evidence (actually, only a correlation table between the original four tests and the marker scales that were used to derive the weighting scheme).

---

[42]An early factor analysis by Flanagan and subsequent research has demonstrated only two independent factors (self-confidence and solitariness). Therefore, instead of these six scores, there should be but two, those based on the factor analytic studies.

The voluminous research gathered with this inventory have produced negative findings. Reliability coefficients reported in the manual (split-halves) range from .85 to .92 for college samples and from .78 to .86 for high school samples. Test-retest coefficients reported in the literature are somewhat lower. The 1938 norms are percentile equivalents and are provided for high school boys and girls, college men and women, and adult men and women. Excellent features of this test are that it takes relatively little time to administer and that there has been a great deal of data collected with it.[43] There are, however, many defects that warrant serious consideration before using it. Specifically, some of the more pronounced deficiencies are (1) it is not recommended for selection programs because it is too susceptible to faking, (2) it really only measures two traits, even though six scores are provided, (3) the scoring is cumbersome, and (4) the normative data is dated (the manual still reports data gathered in 1935). About the only commendable feature of this test is that it has information based on over 30 years of experience with it, and all information points out the same thing: Look for another personality test.

General Adjustment Inventories: Factorial Scales

If one subscribes to the definition of personality as a multitude of traits continually acting and interacting, it is necessary that some method be devised to isolate and measure these traits. And, in order to measure these traits, it is necessary to select appropriate items. One procedure used to identify the existence of traits is termed *factor analysis*. Factor analysis attempts to account for the interrelationships among a number of items in terms of some underlying factors. The test-maker normally begins with a construct, prepares a number of items, and administers these items to a group of subjects. Then he uses factor analysis to ascertain whether the items selected do in fact measure the underlying traits that he specified. This approach has been used by Eysenck, Guilford, Thurstone, and Cattell to construct their personality tests. Factor analysis has done much to increase our understanding of the components of aptitude, achievement, and personality and has resulted in purer measures of these components.

Thurstone Temperament Schedule   Science Research Associates, Inc., 1953. Suitable for students in grades 9 to 16 and adults. One form. Untimed, but takes about 15 minutes to complete. Because it is based upon the responses of normal individuals, it does not claim to classify personality disorders.

---

[43]William H. Whyte, Jr., *The organization man*. New York: Doubleday, 1956, p. 209. Whyte writes that, in 1953, over 1,000,000 copies of this test were sold. He then goes on to **give** psychological testing in industrial use and the Bernreuter in particular a scathing **attack.** The Bernreuter is deserving of this attack, but psychological testing is not. One bad **apple** does not ruin the barrel of apples if the apple is removed early enough.

Prior to developing this test, Thurstone factor-analyzed some of Guilford's scales and found that only seven of his 13 factors accounted for the test's variance. He then proceeded to construct his schedule to measure these seven factors, which he labeled as active, vigorous, impulsive, dominant, stable, sociable, and reflective. The test contains 140 items — 20 for each trait. Responses are made in terms of Yes, No, ?. The schedule is self-administering, and, because it is based upon the responses of normal individuals, it does not lay any claim to abnormal personality classification. The reliabilities of the seven scales vary from .45 to .86 with a median reliability of .64. This low reliability is to be expected when only 20 items are used in each scale. The manual contains norms for various occupational groups and would no doubt be of value to personnel directors. If some validity data could be gathered for educational decision making, the schedule may prove to be a valuable instrument in a high school counseling situation.

Evaluation of General Adjustment Inventories

Throughout the preceding discussion we have stressed that the user be very cautious in the interpretation of noncognitive test results. Problems of validity, reliability, language (ambiguity and/or interpretation made of such words as *usually* or *good*), faking, response set, scoring, and interpretation are such that they preclude the use of most personality inventories by the classroom teacher. Nevertheless, as discussed earlier in this chapter, the teacher must know something about the area of personality and personality assessment in order that he provide for optimal learning conditions. We feel that it is just as (if not more) valuable for the teacher and counselor to know what is bad about tests as it is for them to know what is good about tests. In addition, as we mentioned earlier, teachers and counselors must realize that they are still able to obtain more reliable and valid information about the noncognitive characteristics of their pupils with tests than they can by other means. It is for this reason that we have spent some time discussing general adjustment inventories.

General adjustment inventories are of value because they (1) help establish rapport between counselor and counselee by having some basis upon which to begin an interview, (2) permit the examinee to express problems that are of relevance (or those which he thinks are of relevance or importance) to him, and (3) provide the counselor or clinician with more information about the individual so that a global picture of the individual is obtained.

UNSTRUCTURED INVENTORIES

Structured self-report inventories are not the only manner in which an individual's behavior can be measured. Another standardized approach to the assessment of personality is the one frequently used by the clinician: the unstructured or projective test. Whereas self-report structured inventories require the subject to describe himself, projective tests call upon the individual to interpret objects other than himself. These objects may be pictures, incomplete sentences, drawings, and the like. Anastasi classifies projective techniques into five types: associative techniques (Rorschach Ink Blot Test), construction procedures (Thematic Apperception Test), completion tasks (Rotter Incomplete Sentence Test), ordering devices (Szondi Test), and expressive methods (Machover Draw-A-Person Test).[44] In the latter, both product and process are evaluated. Projective tests may also be differentiated from self-report inventories in many other ways: (1) Projective tests normally present unstructured stimuli while self-report inventories are predominantly structured.[45] The unstructured task permits the individual to project his feelings, these feelings reflecting his needs, motives, and concerns. (2) Projective tests (because they are innocuous) are more resistant to faking and the influence of response set than are self-report inventories.[46] (3) Projective tests are interesting and novel and hence can easily be used with young children or with individuals who are afraid of a formal, pencil-and-paper test. (4) Projective tests can be either verbal or nonverbal, but self-report inventories are verbal and hence are not applicable to illiterates and very young children. (5) Self-report inventories, at least most of them, can be objectively scored, but projective tests are very susceptible to the subjective feelings of the scorer, even when certain guidelines are used in the scoring. (6) Projective tests usually are based upon or reflect psychoanalytic theory such as that of Jung or Freud. (7) Projective

(a)   (b)

Figure 4-3   Structured and unstructured stimuli.

[44]Anne Anastasi, *Psychological testing.* (2nd ed.) New York: Macmillan, 1961, p. 566.

[45]The difference between structured and unstructured stimuli depends upon the degree of agreement regarding the stimuli. If there is consensus that the object in Figure 4–3(a) is a cup or at least a receptacle to hold something, it would be termed a structured stimulus. If there is lack of agreement because of the ambiguity of the stimulus in Figure 4–3(b), it would be termed unstructured.

[46]Even though a maladjusted person may attempt to fake his responses, it is quite conceivable that his faked reponses will indicate that he is maladjusted.

tests normally utilize a global approach in the assessment of personality[47] and often go beyond personality syndromes per se and concern themselves with creativity and critical-thinking ability.

Both projective tests and self-report inventories share many things in common: (1) they have low validity and reliability, (2) they only provide some of the information needed to obtain a better understanding of the individual, and (3) they can be administered either individually or in groups. With the exception of problem check lists, both structured and unstructured personality tests should only be interpreted by qualified persons. Because the administration, scoring, and interpretation of projective tests is complex and because of the formal training and experience needed to work with them, we will dispense with an evaluation of some of those commercially available. Instead, we will evaluate projective tests in a general fashion. Too often, the critics of projective techniques are too severe in their criticism while the proponents of this method are too glib and make sweeping and often unwarranted assumptions regarding the test or technique used. Because of the conflicting research evidence that has been presented and because of the possible confusion that might exist in the readers' minds, we feel it is well worth a few minutes to try to summarize some of the major findings about projective tests. Because we have already discussed some of the psychometric problems associated with noncognitive tests in general, we will discuss here only the factors that are most pertinent to projective tests.

Reliability

The common methods used to estimate a test's reliability are usually inappropriate when it comes to projective tests. It is difficult to use the split-half method for many of the projective tests because few component scores are obtained. When separate component scores are obtained, such as on the Rorschach, the final score is based upon the interpretation of the final test result and not the initial response. Therefore, if one uses the split-half method, he is testing the reliability of the interpretations rather than the reliability of the test. This is not to say that the reliability of interpretation is not important — it is very important. However, if we are concerned with the test's reliability, it is that aspect that we should study, and the split-half method will not suffice.

Because projective tests do not really have a standardized method of scoring (and even of administration because the probing artifact is an integral part of the test's administration) we expect to find scorer unreliability. Because the final interpretation of a projective test's responses is a synthesis of numerous factors and because this synthesis can be markedly influ-

---

[47]Color, movement, size, and so forth are frequently considered in interpreting a test protocol.

enced by the examiner, the matter of scorer reliability is very important. Many research studies with the Rorschach have demonstrated that the scorer reliabilities are not as low as we might expect. They are lower than what is obtained when studying scorer reliability of cognitive tests, but this is to be expected. Studies on the scorer reliability of the Thematic Apperception Test have reported coefficients ranging from .54 to .91. Most people recognize that the reliability of projective tests will be lower than that for other structured self-report inventories. We are more concerned with the sweeping statements that advocates of projective tests make about the reliability of these tests than we are with the magnitude of the reliability coefficients obtained.

Validity

Although valid external criterion data are difficult to obtain for all non-cognitive tests, it would appear that the data are most difficult to obtain for projective tests. For this reason, projective tests must rest their claim for validity upon logical rather than empirical grounds. Research has shown that projective instruments such as the Rorschach and TAT are of moderate value in discriminating between normal persons and those who are mentally ill. These tests do a better job for markedly deviant personalities than for those who are only slightly askew from normality. Unfortunately, however, many people use projective techniques for making fine discriminations. In terms of their supplemental role in aiding the clinician in making a diagnosis, projective tests may be useful. Only the user can conclude whether logical validity should be considered a replacement for empirical validity. Until the examiner's influence can be removed or at least controlled, projective tests will tend to be of questionable validity. Until some consensus of agreement can be reached between the theoretician and the practitioner, the concept of the validity of projective techniques will remain questionable.

Administration and Scoring

Projective tests, in contrast to other personality tests and cognitive measures, are woefully inadequate insofar as objective scoring and administration is concerned. In addition, they lack the precise normative data accompanying aptitude, achievement, and interest tests.

Projective tests, because of their examiner influence, must by necessity be administered, scored, and interpreted only by skilled clinicians who have had considerable training not only in terms of academic preparation but in the use of the instrument. There are many schools of thought regarding the manner in which a protocol of the Rorschach or TAT is to be interpreted. Regardless of the method used to interpret the test protocol, the examiner must be thoroughly familiar with the test and the underlying theory. This is another reason why projective tests should not be part of the regular school testing program and why they should not be administered by the ordinary classroom teacher.

Value and Use

Projective tests do have certain advantages in comparison to self-report, general adjustment inventories. As mentioned previously, these are (1) response set is minimized, (2) they are not subject to ambiguous statements and semantics such as "Do you have frequent nightmares?" (What is *frequent?* What is a nightmare?), and (3) they are open-ended and thus permit the individual to discuss whatever he wishes. In addition, projective tests can be used with illiterates and are particularly useful for working with young children who treat the instrument as a game.

SUMMARY

Personality inventories (adjustment inventories) are not yet ready for general use in our schools and should not be part of the test battery that is normally and routinely administered in school testing programs. Even the best of them must be used with caution and only by trained and experienced clinicians. With the exception of the problem check lists one may go so far as to say that personality assessment should be barred from the classroom teacher. This does not imply, however, that personality assessment should be barred from the public school. In order to gather empirical data (data that has been lacking for personality tests in general and projective techniques in particular), it is necessary to administer tests to pupils. The test results, however, should be used primarily for counseling and research rather than for making instructional decisions. Until personality tests achieve the stature of our cognitive measures and of some of the interest scales, they should be handled with great caution.

ATTITUDE AND VALUE ASSESSMENT

How many times have you heard:

Johnny is a bright enough boy, but he just isn't interested in school.

I wonder what is wrong with Mary? She is above average in ability but performs poorly in science and mathematics.

I think that Peter is prejudiced.

How do attitudes, values, beliefs, and opinions differ?

Should the classroom teacher be concerned with attitudes?

In this section, an attempt will be made to demonstrate the need for the classroom teacher to know something about the attitudes of his pupils, how attitudes are related to learning, and some of the techniques currently used to measure attitudes.

Attitudes are the end product of the socialization process. They influence an individual's responses to objects, situations, other persons, and groups of persons. If we know a person's attitude toward an object, we are better able to predict his reaction to that class of objects. Attitudes are not fixed but are quite malleable, especially in young children. Because education can be considered one of the vehicles that may be used to change attitudes, it is desirable that teachers be aware of attitudes: what they are, how they are measured, and how they may be changed. Research has demonstrated that there is a positive correlation between attitudes and learning. This is another reason for teachers to know something about attitudes. Unless a pupil has a favorable attitude toward education, he will just occupy a seat in the classroom, and teaching him can be quite difficult. Research has demonstrated that, at best, only about 50 percent of the variation in grades is accounted for by cognitive or intellectual factors. A large part of the unaccounted variance is, no doubt, due to affective factors, some of which are attitudes. In the final analysis, education must be concerned not only with *how* people learn but also with *why* they learn — how people feel and behave, their likes and dislikes.

Attitude assessment really has no history of its own, possibly because it is an integral part of social psychology. Nevertheless, there have been some definite approaches used to study attitudes and values. In the 1920s, Thurstone's adaptation of psychophysical methods to quantifying judgment data represents an important milestone in attitude scale construction.[48] A few years later, Likert proposed an entirely different approach to the construction of attitude scales.[49] After World War II, a major effort in attitude scale construction was in developing techniques that would ensure unidimensionality or homogeneity of items.[50] As yet, these techniques are not refined, although they do show great promise. The most recent trend is toward multidimensional scaling.

WHAT AN ATTITUDE IS

Attitudes are a predisposition to respond overtly to social objects. This statement is alluded to, in part at least, by the numerous definitions posited

[48]Louis L. Thurstone and Ernest J. Chave, *The measurement of attitude.* Chicago: University of Chicago Press, 1929.

[49]Rensis A. Likert, A technique for the measurement of attitudes. *Arch. Psychol., N. Y.,* 1932, No. 140. The Thurstone method requires that items be classified by judges into 11 piles, and scale values are then assigned to each item. In the Likert method, items are selected on an item discrimination basis.

[50]An excellent treatment of Guttman's scalogram analysis and Lazarsfeld's latent structure analysis is found in Leon Festinger, The treatment of qualitative data by scale analysis. *Psychol. Bull.,* 1947, *44,* 149–161.

by social psychologists. There are, however, some differences as is seen by the following definitions. Krech defines an attitude as "an enduring system of positive or negative evaluations, emotional feelings, and pro or con action tendencies with respect to a social object."[51] Campbell defines an attitude as "a syndrome of response consistency with regard to social objects."[52]

Attitudes are not directly observable but are inferred from one's overt behavior, both verbal and nonverbal. You cannot see prejudice but you can observe the behavior of one who is prejudiced. Thus, on the basis of observations of a person's consistent behavior pattern to a stimulus, we would conclude that he displays this or that attitude.

Attitudes are learned. Because they are learned, they can be changed, if it is deemed necessary. However, one cannot alter, modify, or reinforce something until he knows the status of that something. And, one of the more valid ways to measure this something is to use a standardized test. For this reason, it is important that teachers know something about attitudes and the methods by which they can be measured.

EVALUATION OF ATTITUDE SCALES

Whereas cognitive measures are classified in terms of their purpose, attitude tests are classified in terms of their method of construction. There are three major types of attitude scales: (1) summated rating scales such as the Minnesota Scale for the Survey of Opinion (Likert-type), (2) equal-appearing interval scales such as the Thurstone and Remmers scales (Thurstone-type), and (3) cumulative scales (Guttman-type).[53]

The usefulness of any test or scale depends upon its reliability, validity, norms, and ease of administration, scoring, and interpretation. We will now briefly summarize how these factors relate to attitude scales.

Reliability. Attitude scales, by and large, have reliabilities around .75. This is much less than obtained for cognitive measures and hence the results obtained from attitude scales should be used primarily for group guidance and discussion.

Validity. In general, attitude measures have less validity data available than do other noncognitive measures. This is in part because of the problems inherent in measuring attitudes and in part because many of them were constructed primarily for research purposes.

[51]David Krech and others, *Individual in society.* New York: McGraw-Hill, 1962, p. 177.
[52]Donald T. Campbell, The indirect assessment of social attitudes. *Psychol. Bull.*, 1950, 47, p. 31.
[53]Allen L. Edwards, *Techniques of attitude scale construction.* New York: Appleton, 1957. See also Hermann H. Remmers, *Introduction to opinion and attitude measurement.* New York: Harper & Row, 1954.

The correlations obtained between the scale scores and observed behavior are typically low. Nevertheless, knowledge of the disparities between expressed attitudes and actual behavior is useful in understanding and working with the individual.

Norms. In the majority of instances, there are no norms accompanying standardized attitude scales. The user must be careful in his evaluation of a published test, especially one that has employed the Likert method. The interpretation of Likert scores is based upon the distribution of sample scores and, therefore, has meaning only by making comparisons to the norm group. Naturally, one can prepare local norms. Even if appropriate sampling techniques have been employed to select the standardization sample and even if the normative data are adequate, the fact that conditions affecting attitudes are so viable leads us to suggest that very recent norms be used. For example, American attitudes toward Japan were markedly different on December 6 and 8, 1941.

Administration, Scoring, and Interpretation. In contrast to the projective tests considered in the previous section, attitude scales are easy to administer and score. They require no formal training and can be handled easily by the classroom teacher. The interpretation of attitude test scores, on the other hand, is an entirely different matter. Because of psychometric problems, the user should be cautious in the interpretations he makes.

Despite some of the limitations just noted, the results obtained from attitude scales can be useful in educational planning and evaluation. Acquisition of desirable attitudes is one of the major goals in our schools. Without knowledge of the prevailing attitudes of the pupil, class, or school, it would be difficult to plan accordingly.

In summary, attitudes are predispositions to respond overtly to social objects. A variety of definitions has been posited, but all agree that attitudes guide and direct an individual's behavior. For this reason, it is imperative that teachers know something about attitudes, how they are formed, how they are changed, and how they relate to the learning process.

Attitude scales can be constructed in a variety of ways. Attitude scales are highly susceptible to faking, and, therefore, care must be taken to establish rapport between pupil and teacher. In addition, one's interpretation should be guided by the knowledge that attitude scales can be faked. Attitude scales are beset with a multitude of methodological problems that make their interpretation precarious. Nevertheless, attitude scales can often be used by the classroom teacher to obtain a better understanding of his pupils.

ASSESSMENT OF PUPIL STUDY HABITS AND ATTITUDES TOWARD SCHOOL

As has been mentioned at various points in this text, the matter of how well a student does on an aptitude or achievement test is dependent upon factors other than basic ability or intelligence. Some of the factors that must be considered in assessing or appraising an individual's academic performance are (1) mental maturity, (2) motivation, (3) study habits, (4) study skills, and (5) attitude toward the value of an education, teachers, school, and courses. The brightest student (speaking in terms of IQ) may be performing at a somewhat mediocre level. He may be getting C's and D's whereas we would predict from a valid measure of his IQ that he should be receiving A's and B's. On the other hand, the intellectually poorer student might be getting B's although we would predict that he would obtain C's. Why the discrepancy between predicted achievement and realized achievement? No doubt, how the pupil studies and his attitudes regarding education play a significant role in an explanation of such discrepancies.

We will now briefly consider two standardized study habits and skills inventories.

Survey of Study Habits and Attitudes (SSHA) The Psychological Corporation, 1965. Two forms: H (for grades 7–12) and C (for college students and high school seniors). Untimed, but majority of students complete the SSHA within 20–35 minutes. Seven scores (based upon for basic scales): delay avoidance (DA), work methods (WM), study habits (SH = DA + WM), teacher approval (TA), education acceptance (EA), study attitudes (SA = TA + EA), and study orientation (SO = SH + SA or the total of the four basic scales).

The SSHA was designed (1) to identify the students whose study habits and attitudes are different from the students who do well in their academic work, (2) to assist students who might benefit from improved study habits (this improvement may come about as a result of counseling and/or instruction on how to study), and (3) to predict academic success for high school and college students. The SSHA consists of 100 items such as

Daydreaming distracts my attention from my lessons while I am studying (DA).

My teachers criticize my written work for being poorly planned or hurriedly written (WM).

My teachers make their subjects interesting and meaningful to me (TA).

I feel that I would study harder if I were given more freedom to choose subjects that I like (EA).[54]

which attempt to assess the "motivation for study and attitudes towards academic work" syndromes rather than just the mechanics of study. This perhaps is the most differentiating factor of the SSHA from other study habits inventories. Subjects respond to each item by means of a five-element key ranging from Rarely (0–15 percent of the time) to Almost Always (86–100 percent of the time). In an attempt to control for response set, the "acceptable" (keyed) responses are randomly distributed at both ends of the continuum. The extreme positions are weighted twice that of the near-extreme positions. That is, if an item is keyed Rarely or Sometimes, a Rarely response is given a weight of 2 and a Sometimes response is given a weight of 1.

Both logical and empirical validity were stressed in the test's development. Items were chosen on the basis of interviews with students, and each item was empirically validated (correlations of the SSHA with grades, teacher's ratings, and aptitude scores) as to its applicability to the problem. For Form H (grades 7–12), student advice was obtained so that the language would be clear and meaningful to junior and senior high school students. The validity data presented in the test manual show that the SSHA is independent of scholastic achievement and that there is an increase in the predictive efficiency of grades when the SSHA is used in combination with aptitude test scores. Internal consistency (.87 to .89) and test-retest (.83 to .88) reliability estimates are reported for Form C. Test-retest reliabilities for Form H vary from .93 to .95. It is unfortunate that these data are based on only Texas students, especially because the correlation data reported for Form C show differences between college students in Texas and those in other parts of the country. Percentile norms are reported separately for each of the seven scores. For Form H, norms are provided for grades 7 to 9 combined and grades 10 to 12 combined. The Form H norming sample appears to be heavily weighted in favor of Texas students and students from the south-western region of the country.

To aid in test interpretation, the percentile scores can be plotted on the diagnostic profile sheet, that is on the reverse side of the answer sheet. (See figure 4–4) The pupil's scores can then be compared to the performance of the norm group and his strengths and weaknesses identified. In addition, a separate counseling key is provided. This key enables the teacher or counselor to identify critical responses — those items that differentiate between high and low scholastic achievers. Still, the test authors recommend that the counselor and student make a detailed item-by-item analysis of the responses. It would have been desirable had the test authors presented more descriptive information on the development of this key.

In summary, the SSHA was well conceived in its development. It is easy for the pupil to understand and complete the inventory. It is easy to administer and score. It stresses the motivational and attitudinal aspects of study more than any other study habits inventory.

California Study Methods Survey (CSMS)   California Test Bureau, 1958. Grades 7–13. Three subtests: attitudes toward school, mechanics of study,

DIAGNOSTIC PROFILE FOR SURVEY OF STUDY HABITS AND ATTITUDES

W. F. Brown and W. H. Holtzman

Name **Lehmann** (Last) **Allison** (First)   Date **12-21-68**

School **Grant Park**

Age **13**   Sex **F**   Form of SSHA **H**

Circle Grade or Year in School:

High School: 7 ⑧ 9 10 11 12   College: Fr. Soph. Jr. Sr.

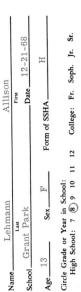

Profiling Your SSHA Scores

To find out how you did on each scale of this survey, look at the numbers in the row marked "Percentile." Your percentile on each scale shows your relative standing in the group of people described on the "Norms Used" line at the bottom of the chart. For example, if your norms group is college freshmen and your percentile on the TA scale is 45, it means that 45 per cent of the freshmen received lower scores than yours on the TA scale, while 55 per cent of them received higher scores. Thus, your percentile tells where you rank in comparison with others in your norms group.

You can complete your profile by making a heavy line across each column at the level which corresponds to your percentile rank on that scale. For example, if your percentile rank on the DA scale is 65, make a heavy line across the DA column halfway between 60 and 70. Draw a line corresponding to your percentile rank for all seven scales.

Then start at the horizontal line you have drawn and black in each column up to or down to the 50th percentile line. Since the 50th percentile line represents the score made by the middle student of your group, the vertical bars above that line on your profile show those scales on which you have scored higher than the middle student and the bars below that line show the scales on which you scored lower.

What Your SSHA Scores Mean

High scores on *SSHA* are characteristic of students who get good grades; low scores tend to be characteristic of those who get low grades or find school work difficult. Therefore, your scores on the *SSHA* scales can indicate your strengths and weaknesses in the areas measured by the survey, and also help to predict future academic achievement.

What the SSHA Measures

(DA) DELAY AVOIDANCE—your promptness in completing academic assignments, lack of procrastination, and freedom from wasteful delay and distraction.

(WM) WORK METHODS—your use of effective study procedures, efficiency in doing academic assignments, and how-to-study skills.

(TA) TEACHER APPROVAL—your opinions of teachers and their classroom behavior and methods.

(EA) EDUCATION ACCEPTANCE—your approval of educational objectives, practices, and requirements.

(SH) STUDY HABITS combines the scores on the DA and WM scales to provide a measure of academic behavior.

(SA) STUDY ATTITUDES combines the scores on the TA and EA scales to provide a measure of scholastic beliefs.

(SO) STUDY ORIENTATION combines the scores on the SH and SA scales to provide an overall measure of study habits and attitudes.

Grades 7,8,9 Combined

Figure 4-4 Diagnostic profile for survey of study habits and attitudes. Reproduced from SSHA Manual. Copyright © 1966 by The Psychological Corporation, New York, N.Y. 10017. All rights reserved as stated in the Manual and Catalog.

and planning and system. Separate score for each subtest plus a verification score and a total score. Untimed, but requires about one class period.

The CSMS was designed to assess the habits, attitudes, and knowledge needed for maximum scholastic achievement. The survey consists of 150 questions to which the student responds Yes or No. The major emphasis of the CSMS is on the mechanics of study, but this survey resembles the Survey of Study Habits and Attitudes in that it also stresses attitudinal factors such as motivation. The items used in the CSMS resemble those illustrated in the previous inventories. Content, construct, and concurrent validity were stressed in the development of the survey. The writers are a little disturbed at the validity evidence reported. The test author examined the psychology of learning reported in four textbooks, which were published as early as 1935 and as late as 1942. Surely, the theory of learning has undergone some change since then! Construct validity was studied by comparing the responses of 100 high and 100 low achievers. In addition, in the preparation of the mechanics of study subtest the responses of 200 high achievers and 200 low achievers were compared. The criteria upon which high and low achievement were based are not described. Nor are the samples used defined as to type of school, sex, and age. Concurrent validity was studied by correlating each of the scores with grade-point averages. The correlations between the CSMS subtest scores and GPA varied from .32 to .58; the correlations between the subtest scores and achievement test scores ranged from .11 to .48. Test-retest and internal consistency reliability estimates are reported in the manual. For the total score, they appear to be adequate. They are too low, however, for the separate subtest scores. Because the subtest intercorrelations are very close to the subtest reliabilities, the difference scores obtained are questionable as to their significance. The test author does not feel this way when he says, in the manual, that "the usefulness of the separate scales are not reduced to any appreciable extent." We feel that they are, and we caution the user accordingly. This is especially true for the scores of eighth graders. The data suggest that the CSMS increases the predictive efficiency of a student's GPA (from .66 to .75).

Raw scores are converted to percentiles and normalized T scores. Norms are reported for each of the three subtests and the total score separately. Inasmuch as research has indicated a sex bias in grades, one wonders why the test author did not report the data for males and females separately.

Because of the manner in which the verification score was developed, it is quite possible that a student wishing to fake good (exemplify proper and desirable study habits and attitudes) could go undetected. The manual states that a verification score of 17 is the critical cutoff point. Yet, simple random guessing would give one a score of 15, which is close enough to be suspected by the examiner. Also, an individual responding Yes to every item would obtain a verification score of more than 20, and he would go undetected. All in all, the verification score is not very good for careless students or for those who might well have a negative attitude toward school.

The CSMS appears to have been carefully constructed, although more information is needed. The directions are simple and clear. The uses of the test results are briefly discussed in the manual. The subtest reliabilities are too low to place much confidence in interpreting subtest score differences. The verification score is highly suspect. The CSMS may be of value in calling the student's attention to study habits that he might profitably undertake.

In conclusion, study habit inventories have a place in the classroom and can be administered, scored, and interpreted by the classroom teacher. Although the majority of them stress the process of locating information, the Survey of Study Habits and Attitudes and the California Study Methods Survey stress attitudes and motivational aspects. Study habits inventories, as with all self-report techniques, are dependent upon the respondent's honesty — they are only surveys of self-report. The essential question, "Do the results of a study habit inventory in combination with previous GPA yield a higher cross-validated multiple R than do only previous GPA?" remains unanswered for most study habit inventories.

CHAPTER SUMMARY

In this chapter we have considered a broad spectrum of noncognitive tests: (1) interest inventories, (2) problem check lists, (3) general adjustment inventories, (4) projective tests, and (5) attitude and value measures.

There are many problems associated with the assessment of affective characteristics (faking, malingering, response set, validity and reliability) that are usually not encountered to as great an extent in cognitive measures. For this reason, affective measures must be interpreted with a great deal of caution.

Although the interpretation of most noncognitive tests, with the exception of the problem check lists, is beyond the training and experience of the classroom teacher, this is not tantamount to concluding that they should not be used in the school. They do serve a valuable purpose. They provide the user with some added information that might permit him to arrive at a better understanding of the individual. And teachers are, or should be, interested in learning as much about their pupils as is humanly possible.

A variety of methods can be used to study noncognitive traits. One can employ observation, questionnaires, or tests. The tests may be self-report inventories or they may be projective techniques. There are advantages and disadvantages associated with each approach. In this chapter we have concerned ourselves solely with the discussion of standardized approaches in the study of personality. This emphasis on standardized assessment techniques should not be construed as evidence that they are always more valid than, say, the observational approach or the use of sociometric devices.

Just as adjustment inventories and projective tests give no clue as to the intensity of feeling, interest inventories do not provide us with an absolute measure of one's interests. Personality tests can only assist us in identifying subjects who are in need of assistance and possibly in ascertaining where or what are the problems. However, if used judiciously and if proper rapport is established and maintained, they do permit the user to obtain a more complete understanding of the subject, and they provide the subject with an opportunity to express and then discuss his feelings.

For a number of reasons, attitudes and values have been considered as one rather than as separate traits. Attitude tests have been evaluated in terms of their (1) reliability, (2) validity, (3) normative data, and (4) administration, interpretation, and use. Because there are very few standardized attitude tests available for use in the elementary and secondary grades, the writers recommend that in many, if not most, instances, the classroom teacher would be well advised to construct his own scales. A brief discussion of tests of study habits and attitudes was presented.

Although psychologists have not approached the degree of sophistication in the assessment of affective measures as they have in the measurement of cognitive abilities, much research is presently underway to improve personality measures. With time, personality measures should become more reliable (if they do not, this will be because of the fact that human behavior is not stable rather than because of poor tests), they might become more valid for predictive purposes, and they might become less complex to score. Judging from the cornucopia of research studies, should these not be attained, it will not be a reflection of the lack of devotion and concern of researchers in the field of noncognitive assessment.

POINTS TO PONDER

1. Approximately 50 percent of the variance in grades among individuals can be accounted for by aptitude and achievement tests. Using noncognitive tests in addition does not increase this percentage very much. How do you account for this?

2. Write definitions for the following terms: *truthfulness, aggressiveness, rigidity, succorance,* and *deference.* Compare your definitions with those of your classmates. Do your definitions differ? If so, does this mean you would interpret personality inventories measuring these traits differently?

3. Should response sets be controlled in personality inventories? (You may wish to do a thorough review of the literature before discussing this.)

4. How would you employ empirical keying for the Strong Vocational Interest Blank so that it might be used to differentiate the interests of "good credit risks" from "poor credit risks"?

5. What would be the problems of developing a predictive interest inventory for fifth graders?

6. Rank the following types of standardized tests in terms of the necessity for frequent revision: achievement, aptitude, attitude, interest, problem check lists, projective, and self-adjustment inventories. Give reasons for your ranking.

7. What instructional use would you make of the results of a problem check list?

8. As a new counselor, you find that your predecessor had been routinely administering a self-adjustment inventory as part of the school testing program. You are called to a school board meeting to explain the various tests used. Would you defend the use of the self-adjustment inventory? Why?

9. Recognizing the limitations of noncognitive tests, what arguments can you advance to support their use in the public schools?

10. Develop a 20-item scale to measure teachers' attitudes towards culturally deprived children. What type of reliability estimate should you gather? How would you validate such a scale?

chapter

V

educational testing:
a broader viewpoint

By now the reader should have some insights about various testing principles as well as some knowledge about the various types of tests appropriate for school use. The selection, administration, scoring, and interpretation of different kinds of tests have been discussed in some detail. However, educational testing involves more than principles and techniques. We must consider how people feel about tests. How does the public think tests can and cannot help in educational decision making? What will educational testing be like in the future? What makes a good school testing program, and how should one be established? This last chapter is designed to present a broader view of educational testing through a discussion of these issues. It is organized into three major headings: (1) "Planning and Administering a School Testing Program," (2) "Public Concern about Testing," and (3) "Future Trends in Testing."

PLANNING AND ADMINISTERING
A SCHOOL TESTING PROGRAM

An important aspect of any good school testing program is that the program be a cooperative venture from the planning stage through the recording and interpretation of the results. Teachers, administrators, counselors, and, to some extent, both parents and students all need to understand the program and to realize that it is designed for their benefit. Without such a realization, the program cannot achieve its full potential. Needless to say, if the original program planning is conducted by only a single individual or special interest group, the rest of the professional staff, the parents, and the students cannot necessarily be expected to endorse and adopt the program with enthusiasm.

Cooperative planning not only leads to more enthusiastic test use, it also leads to a better and more complete program. Teachers, counselors, administrators, parents, and students have overlapping yet somewhat unique needs to be met from testing programs. The unique needs of each group may not be well known to others. For example, the instructional decisions of teachers require somewhat different data from that needed for curricular decisions made by administrators. If a member of each group does not have an opportunity to assist in the planning of a program, that program will more than likely be incomplete. Thus, a committee representing all interest groups should actively participate in the planning of a testing program.

Though it is extremely important that many subgroups be represented in the planning so that a variety of viewpoints is obtained, the final decisions should be the responsibility of the professional staff. By having parents and students involved, they will have a better understanding of the what and why of testing programs. The specific decisions (for example, which achievement battery should be used) should be left to the school staff. The actual administration of the program should be made the responsibility of only a single professional person. This individual should be one who (1) is well trained in tests and measurements and is dedicated to the philosophy of measurement (that is, that test results do aid in decision-making processes); (2) can communicate and cooperate with the various interest groups in the school; and (3) has at least a little tolerance for, and expertise in, administrative duties because the total program from planning to ordering tests, administering tests, seeing to the scoring, analysis, recording, and appropriate distribution and interpretation of results does require administrative "know-how." This role is typically filled by a counselor who has special interest and training in testing.

STEPS IN PLANNING A TESTING PROGRAM

There are several steps necessary to plan a good testing program. The first, and probably the most important, step is that the planning committee specify as clearly as possible the purposes of the testing program for their school. They must translate general objectives into specific behavioral objectives. As has been repeatedly emphasized, different tests serve different purposes, and without some purposes in mind the committee would be hard put to even designate areas the program should cover let alone to select the best instruments. Although schools will surely have some different purposes, there are many commonalities. Most schools will expect their testing program to serve some instructional, guidance, and administrative purposes. Hopefully, all schools will also use their testing program for research purposes, although it may be that no test would be selected solely for its research uses. (Except, of course, when the research is funded by an external agency!)

Second, after thorough consideration has been given to what a testing program should accomplish, the committee must determine the practical aspects of the testing program. There are always unfortunate limitations such as lack of money and too few or inadequately trained personnel. Once priorities have been set, the committee is ready to make some decisions about what specific tests should be given; the when, how, and who of administration, scoring, and analysis; the system of record keeping; and the methods of distributing and interpreting results. Table 5–1 provides a sample check list for the committee and/or administrator of the testing program to follow.

We have no desire to irritate our readers by condescendingly spelling out the detailed specifics in administering a testing program. We do want to emphasize though that details are important. Many a testing session has been less than ideal because someone overlooked a detail. Sufficient tests, answer sheets, and pencils should be available. An administrator's test manual is necessary. There does need to be sufficient time for the test. Adequate seating space must be provided. It often is necessary to have proctors. And secretaries do need to be given directions about what to do with those little gummed labels with numbers on them that are returned from the scoring service!

A TYPICAL SCHOOL TESTING PROGRAM

As mentioned, testing programs can and should vary, depending upon such characteristics as the size of the school, the characteristics of the student body, and the number and quality of the pupil personnel workers. Nevertheless, there are some commonalities among school testing programs. Surveys of school testing programs, indeed, show a great many similarities. For example, a 1963 survey[1] indicates that almost all (96 percent) of the Michigan public schools that have a testing program use tests of general intelligence. The average child takes four such tests while in school. Eighty percent of the Michigan school systems use aptitude batteries. Achievement batteries are used by 93 percent of the schools, five being the average number of times a child would take such a battery. Reading readiness tests

[1]Frank B. Womer, *Testing programs in Michigan schools*. Ann Arbor, Mich.: University of Michigan Press, 1963, 64 pp.

Table 5–1

A Check List of Factors Affecting the Success of a Testing Program[a]

	Check
1. *Purposes of the program*	
Clearly defined	_____
Understood by parties involved	_____
2. *Choice of tests*	
Valid	_____
Reliable	_____
Appropriate difficulty level	_____
Adequate norms	_____
Easy to administer and score	_____
Economical	_____
Best available for purpose	_____
3. *Administration and scoring*	
Administrators well trained	_____
All necessary information provided	_____
Scorers adequately instructed	_____
Scoring carefully checked	_____
4. *Physical conditions*	
Sufficient space	_____
Sufficient time	_____
Conveniently scheduled	_____
5. *Utilization of test results*	
Definite plans for use of results	_____
Provision for giving teachers all necessary help in using scores	_____
Provision for systematic follow-up on use of results	_____
6. *System of records*	
Necessary for purpose	_____
Sufficient for purpose	_____
Convenient form for use	_____
7. *Personnel*	
Adequately trained for the purpose	_____
8. *Affiliated research*	
Full advantage taken of results	_____
Provision for special studies, analyses, etc.	_____

[a]Reproduced from Roger T. Lennon, *Planning a testing program*, Test Service Bulletin No. 55, issued by Harcourt, Brace & World, Inc., New York. Reproduced by special permission of the publisher.

are used by about 50 percent of the schools. Interest inventories are used in about 65 percent of the schools. Few schools use personality inventories as part of the regular testing program.

It should be stressed that these figures depict the percentage of schools that used these various tests in their regular testing program administered to all pupils. It does not include the tests that schools would use with individual pupils. The percentages would have all been higher had that been the case, particularly the percentages of interest and personality inventories used.

On the basis of the Michigan and other surveys, one might conceptualize a typical testing program (to be routinely administered to all students) as illustrated in Table 5–2. This typical program is not necessarily the best pattern for all schools. Other tests such as individual intelligence tests, special aptitude and achievement tests, and various types of interest, value, attitude, and personality inventories should be available for use with individual students.

The specific tests chosen depend upon the characteristics and needs of each school district, but we strongly recommend that the same achievement battery be used at the designated grade levels to provide some continuity. Naturally, if the content validity of a specific test used at the lower grades is inappropriate in a higher grade, the switching of achievement batteries is warranted. Also, it is helpful if schools use general intelligence tests that have been normed on the same population as the achievement battery.

Because various states have different testing requirements, programs may differ from the one given so as to follow those regulations. We have mixed feelings regarding these external state regulations. They do serve a useful

Table 5–2

A Typical School Testing Program

Grade	Kind of Test
K	Reading readiness
1 or 2	General intelligence
4	Achievement battery
5	Achievement battery
5	General intelligence
6	Achievement battery
7	Achievement battery
8	Multifactor aptitude test
10	Achievement battery
11	General intelligence
9, 10, 11 or 12	Interest test

purpose by forcing schools to maintain minimum testing programs. On the other hand, external regulations always mean a certain amount of rigidity, and there is the danger of being forced to administer tests that the schools will not use either because they have no objectives relevant to those tests or because they are inadequately staffed to correctly use the results. It may also lead to duplication of testing. Some schools overtest. Perhaps this is due to external funds being made available to the schools who follow certain prescriptions.

If all schools would adopt the position that a test not be given unless the results are to be used, there would be less testing. However, what is needed in most schools is probably not less testing but better use of the tests now being given. That is not to say that there is no overlap in many testing programs that exist. For example, schools will occasionally administer both the DAT and a general intelligence test in the same grade, even though research shows fairly conclusively that the VR + NA score of the DAT correlates very well with scores from most group intelligence tests. Some aptitude and achievement tests are so highly correlated that we may well question whether both need be given. Any unnecessary duplication of testing or administration of tests whose results remain unused should be eliminated. This is a waste of time and materials, and this results in a negative attitude toward testing by all involved — pupils, teachers, and parents.

DISSEMINATING, RECORDING, AND INTERPRETING SCHOOL TEST RESULTS

Factors to be considered in test selection, administration, scoring, and one aspect of interpretation (knowledge about the meaning of the scores) have been covered in Chapter I. More should be said about the distribution and recording of the test results and about the interpreting of test scores to others. If the test results are to be effectively used they must (1) be made available (and interpreted) as quickly as possible to the appropriate personnel and (2) be recorded and filed in a fashion that facilitates their use. How test results are disseminated and recorded will vary from school to school because school facilities differ. However, for each test, the test administrator (with the help of his committee) must decide (1) to whom the test results should be distributed, and (2) a method of disseminating information that will be efficient and yet insure correct and adequate communication.

Dissemination

We do not regard results of aptitude or achievement tests as private information between the test taker and some other single individual such as the school psychologist. We take the position that the results of all achievement and aptitude tests should be disseminated to all professional staff members in the school, the individuals who were tested, and the parents of those individuals. In fact, there is precedent for the opinion that parents have a legal right to the test information contained in the official school record.[2] Other people, such as prospective employees, should only receive this information with the student's permission.

Goslin,[3] upon presenting public school principals with a series of items concerning reasons to use standardized tests, found that the four reasons that received the highest vote of importance all involved dissemination of test result information to the pupils and parents. He also found that over 60 percent of the public secondary school students and parents of elementary school children sampled, felt that intelligence test information should be routinely reported to them. In contrast to this desire, Goslin found that approximately half the teachers in his sample had never given a pupil even a general idea of his intelligence, although nearly all teachers felt they ought to have free access to such information about their students. Goslin uses this type of evidence to conclude that there is a "need for a clear statement of policy regarding the dissemination of test scores and information resulting from test scores, both by teachers and other school personnel."[4] We certainly concur with that statement. This clear statement of policy should come from the local school district and not from textbook writers. The policy should be dependent upon such school characteristics as student-counselor ratio, measurement competencies of the teachers, and whether or not in-service training is available for measurement-naive teachers. The important point is that some qualified professional interpretation of aptitude and achievement test scores should be made to every parent and child.

Interest inventory results should, in general, be made available (that is, recorded where all would have access to it) to the same three groups — professional staff, students, and parents — but active dissemination and discussion of the information need only be done with the students. Naturally, any interested parent should be able to receive professional interpretation of their child's interest test scores. Teachers should know what kind of interest inventory information is available and where it can be obtained. They should be strongly urged to avail themselves of this information and to use it, much as they would other data in the cumulative record, to aid in the full understanding of each individual child.

As a matter of normal routine, personality and attitude inventory results should not be made available to anyone except the student without his explicit permission. One way to minimize faking is to alleviate anxiety about

[2]*Van Allen* v. *McCleary*, 27 Misc. 2d81, 211NYS, 2d 501 (Sup. Ct. Nassau Co.) 1961.

[3]David A. Goslin, *Teachers and testing.* New York: The Russell Sage Foundation, 1967, pp. 19, 77, 92.

[4]Goslin, p. 86.

who will have access to the test results and about how they will be used. If a counselor or school psychologist wishes to obtain an accurate measure from a student, the counselor may well emphasize the confidential nature of the information. If confidentiality is promised or even implied, it should not be broken. Oftentimes, however, the professional who gathered the information will deem it beneficial for the student to share the information with others such as parents or teachers. If so, he should obtain the student's permission to release the data. It should be pointed out that whether or not counselors or school psychologists legally enjoy privileged communication as do physicians or attorneys is debatable. The New York ruling referred to before specified that parents could obtain the "official school records." These could also be subpoenaed. Counselors might argue, however, that their records (including personality test scores) are not a part of the "official school records."

Recording

The recording of the test results not considered private information between student and psychologist is certainly a task that can be accomplished by trained clerks. Even these results, however, are not in the public domain, and the clerks should be cautioned to treat the results as confidential. The test results are generally stored in pupils' cumulative folders. In the future they will no doubt be placed in computer storage. In either case, one must somehow insure that the information is readily available for those who should have access to it and not available to those who should not have access to it. These two goals are hard to reach simultaneously. Test results must be kept under lock and key, but teachers should have easy access to them and be encouraged to use them. Of course, some teachers are not knowledgeable enough to use test results correctly. This places us somewhat in an ethical dilemma when we suggest that aptitude, achievement, and interest test results be made available to all the professional staff. However, it is really the teachers' ethical responsibility. Teachers should know how to use most, if not all, of the scores in the areas mentioned. If not, they should surely realize their limitations in the area and not obtain the information.

Interpreting Test Information to Others

Just as the parent and pupil have a right to certain kinds of test information, the school has the responsibility to communicate this information so that it will be understood correctly and used appropriately. This means that raw test score information would probably not be disseminated. The major aspects to be communicated are (1) what information the test score gives us, (2) the precision of this information, and (3) how the information can be appropriately used.

Many times confusion exists as to what information the test score provides. This may be due to one of two reasons: (1) the type of score (that is, percentile, stanine, and so on) may not be understood and (2) the construct being measured may not be understood. These problems can be overcome, but the educator needs to be sufficiently aware of the possible confusion that can take place in a parent's or pupil's mind. For example, confusion concerning the type of score may result from mistaking percentiles for percentages, while a misunderstanding of a construct may be the result of confusing aptitude with interest. Even administrators, counselors, and teachers do this! If a professional can make such a mistake, it emphasizes the fact that we must be very careful in interpreting to others what the test is measuring.

The precision of the test information is another important aspect of test interpretation. What needs to be interpreted is an accurate impression of a test's accuracy. This, of course, varies from test to test. There has been much concern in the past about laymen not being aware of the imprecision of the tests. The attempt by some to differentiate between IQ's only one point apart illustrates insensitivity to the concept of errors of measurement. This danger of overinterpretation should be guarded against. Although a teacher or counselor cannot teach a parent or student about the theoretical concepts of reliability or standard error of measurement, they certainly can and should communicate the general idea. A good way to do this is through band interpretation. Presenting a range of values encompassing $\pm 1S_e$ from the observed score as indicating where the individual would probably score if he retook the test usually gets across the point of imprecision. The idea of band interpretation is most often accomplished using percentile bands, although raw scores or z or T score bands could be used. Percentile bands are reported for the better constructed tests. If not reported, they can easily be computed for any test that reports percentiles and a standard error of measurement. One simply looks up the percentiles that correspond to $X \pm 1S_e$. One can be about 68 percent confident that a person's true percentile will be within this range. A possible misinterpretation of percentile bands is that a person unsophisticated in this type of score may think that the percentile corresponding to a person's observed score is halfway between the two percentile end points. (Or, as mentioned earlier, it is possible to confuse percentiles and percentages.) Because percentiles are rectangularly distributed and observed scores are typically distributed in a fairly normal fashion, this will not be the case — except when a person's observed score is equal to the mean of the distribution. Thus, if percentile bands are used, the percentile for the observed score should be given along with the two end percentiles.

Although many people overinterpret small differences in scores, it is also true that other people place too little faith in test results and under-interpret score differences. This has probably become even more true because of the recent criticisms of testing that have received so much space in the press. In particular, students who score poorly on tests have a tendency to discount the results. Although a teacher or counselor should not argue with a parent or student over the accuracy of a test score, the precision of a test should not be underplayed. There has been much talk recently about the importance of a good self-concept. This is fine, but there is no evidence to suggest that a person who has an inaccurately high self-concept will make better decisions than a person who perceives himself accurately. In fact, a good decision, by definition, is dependent upon an accurate self-concept, not a good self-concept.

It is possible that people will understand what characteristic has been measured and how accurately it has been measured without understanding how this information is useful to them. For example, for an individual to know that he is at about the 80th percentile on a test measuring creativity may not be particularly useful to him. It is up to the test interpreter to help the individual understand how that information is related to the decision he must make.

Although not ideal, it is certainly adequate to present group interpretations of the achievement and aptitude test results to teachers. Parents and students who are somewhat less sophisticated with regard to test interpretation should receive more individualized interpretations.

The interpretation of the interest inventories is best done individually, although group interpretations of some interest inventories are appropriate. If the purpose of the interest inventory is primarily to start the student thinking about how his interests relate to his educational plans and the world of work, then group interpretation is appropriate. If the interest inventory data are to be used to assist the individual in an immediate educational or vocational decision, then individual interpretation of the data in a counseling situation is necessary.

Any interpretation of personality inventory results should be done in an individual interview by qualified personnel. Because of problems inherent in personality measures, we strongly recommend that they be discussed in general terms only.

Much more could be said concerning specific techniques of test interpretation.[5] Separate courses should be taken in counseling techniques of test interpretation beyond an introductory course. The main point to be made here is that, in any interpretation of test data, the focus should always be on the student, not on the test score.[6]

[5]See James H. Ricks, *On telling parents about test results.* Test Service Bulletin No. 54. New York: The Psychological Corporation, December 1959.
[6]For a further discussion, see Leo Goldman, *Using tests in counseling.* New York: Appleton, 1961.

EXTERNAL TESTING PROGRAMS

By *external testing programs* we mean those tests that are administered under the control of agencies other than the school. These tests often are administered in the school, by school personnel, but the school is not officially in charge. Examples of such tests are the College Entrance Examination Board (CEEB) tests, the Preliminary Scholastic Aptitude Test (PSAT), the American College Testing Program Exam (ACT) and the National Merit Scholarship Qualifying Test (NMSQT). These tests are all used for college admission or scholarship selection purposes. The problem is that different colleges have different requirements, so that, unless a student knows for sure what college he will be attending, he ends up being forced to take several tests. There has been some concern from school personnel[7] about the amount of student time and money these tests consume. These tests do overlap to a considerable degree, and many persons have wondered whether the tests could not be equated statistically so that only one of these tests need be taken and the score on it converted into equivalent scores on the other tests. The problems of equating these tests have been discussed considerably in the literature,[8] and the general concensus of the psychometric experts is that such tests cannot really be equated because they measure, in part, different constructs. However, the scores could be made comparable enough that college admission and scholarship officers could, if they wished, accept the scores from one test as a substitute for other test scores. Because error of measurement exists in all tests anyway and because tests are never used as the sole criterion, it seems some flexibility is justifiable.

PUBLIC CONCERN ABOUT TESTING

With the increased use of testing in schools, industry, and government, it is natural and appropriate that the public show interest in and concern for this enterprise. What started as a spark of concern has been fanned into a burning flame by writers criticizing tests in what has come to be a typical journalistic exposé fashion.[9] The validity of the criticism expressed in the

[7]See, for example, Joint Committee on Testing of the American Association of School Administrators, National Education Association, *Testing, testing, testing.* Washington, D.C.: the Association, 1962.

[8]See, for example, E. F. Lindquist, Equating scores on non-parallel tests. *J. educ. Measmt.*, 1964, *1*, 5–9 and William H. Angoff, Technical problems of obtaining equivalent scores on tests. *J. educ. Measmt.*, 1964, *1*, 11–13.

[9]See, for example, Hillel Black, *They shall not pass.* New York: Morrow, 1963; Martin L. Gross, *The brain watchers.* New York: Random House, 1962; and Banesh Hoffmann, *The tyranny of testing.* New York: Crowell-Collier-Macmillan, 1962.

numerous books and articles is probably inversely proportional to the public acclaim they have received. Yet, all of them have been of value — if for no other reason than for forcing psychometricians to defend themselves against the sometimes unjust criticisms. Psychometricians, of course, share the legitimate concerns of the public and are attempting to improve all aspects of their profession. Although many concerns have been voiced and many issues are involved, the most important ones revolve around the ethics of test use and the possible dire consequences of testing.

The public asks or should ask questions such as the following:

1. Who is qualified to administer and interpret tests?
2. What kinds of tests should be given?
3. How should test results be used?
4. Who should have access to test results?
5. Are tests fair?
6. Are our children being overtested?
7. Are our children being undertested?

The answers to questions like these are not independent of each other. For example, the kinds of tests that should be given depend upon the qualifications of the user and upon the proposed uses of the tests. Because public concern encompasses so many specific yet interrelated aspects of testing, it is difficult to present the topic completely in any tightly organized fashion. We have, therefore, chosen in this part of the chapter to focus on three issues that seem of most concern to the public: (1) the use (or misuse) of test scores for making decisions about individuals, (2) the invasion of privacy issue, and (3) the fairness of tests to minority groups. Needless to say, these issues are neither mutually exclusive nor exhaustive.

THE USE (OR MISUSE) OF TEST SCORES

The consequences of misusing tests can be quite severe. Examples of misusing tests are legion. Some of these have already been discussed. The important point is that misusing tests is prevalent. This does not lead us to the conclusion that testing is bad but, rather, that we must concentrate our energies toward the goal of educating people how to correctly use test results. Most of the problems related to test misuse bear upon the overgeneralizations made by users rather than because the tests per se are invalid. Most test constructors display integrity and professional honesty concerning how these tests can be used. However, when an educator uses a test he is not qualified to use, this is not professional honesty.

Many people criticize the faulty decisions made through misusing test information. Fewer people realize that a far more costly misuse of tests is not to give them at all. Even if only a few more students made better decisions with the help of test information than they would have made without that information, the long-term benefits usually far outweigh the initial costs of testing.

Correct test use involves all aspects of testing, from selection to interpretation. We don't wish at this time to go back into the problems of selection, interpretation, and so forth. However, as pointed out in Chapter I, tests are used to help make decisions. If test information is used correctly, it is impossible to make (in the long run) poorer decisions using this additional information. Thus, if the public desires accurate decision making, their concern should not be whether tests should be used but, rather, whether tests are used properly. Users of tests have an ethical responsibility to be qualified to administer, score, and interpret tests properly. Unfortunately, there are many test users who do not assume this responsibility. A pertinent question is who should stipulate users' qualifications. Is it the responsibility of the test publishers to be sure unqualified users do not obtain copies of tests? Should a professional organization as the American Psychological Association set up standards? Should states have certification requirements? Should a federal agency control this? Any suggested answer to this would probably raise as much controversy as to who should assume responsibility for our safety while we ride in automobiles. The APA does have a set of ethical standards that covers test publication and test interpretation, but they cannot police nonmembers.[10] There are also some test publishers, not guided solely by the profit motive, who distribute only to those users who appear qualified. Whether or not we can ever arrive at a consensus on how to control the qualifications of test users, the problem is a legitimate one. It is an ethical issue we must somehow deal with.

Ethical issues of testing, however, go far beyond the qualifications of the user. Such questions as to whom should test scores be released and what kinds of questions do we have the right to ask are also relevant. These will be discussed under the following section.

THE INVASION OF PRIVACY ISSUE

Assume you are a counselor in a school system working with a disturbed youngster. You feel additional information about the youngster will enable you to deal with him more effectively. Do you have the right to ask him to answer "true" or "false" to such questions as the following?

1. I have never been in trouble because of my sex behavior.
2. I have never indulged in any unusual sex practices.

[10]See *Ethical standards of psychologists*, Washington, D.C.: The American Psychological Association, 1953. Included in this statement is a general description specifying the minimum levels of training for administering various kinds of tests.

3. I believe there is a Devil and a Hell in afterlife.
4. I have had some very unusual religious experiences.
5. There is something wrong with my sex organs.[11]

These are examples of some of the more personal questions taken from the Minnesota Multiphasic Personality Inventory (MMPI). Criticism has arisen from many people concerning whether asking questions such as these is not an invasion of privacy. Why should we tell anyone whether or not we have ever indulged in any unusual sex practices? Some people have even suggested that the very asking of such questions is harmful to the person taking the test. Irate citizens have been known to burn answer sheets from tests containing such questions.[12] Under the spur of a Congressional investigation, the Peace Corps and the United States Civil Service Commission have eliminated many such questions. The Peace Corps also decided to give trainees the right to refuse to take the MMPI and now requires destruction of the answer sheets and of any written evaluation of test scores.

What really is the invasion of privacy issue? What is the fuss all about? It, of course, varies from person to person. Some people actually find it distasteful and degrading to read such personal questions. They certainly wouldn't want their daughters to read such "dirty" questions! The knowledge that some people feel this way tells us something about their psychological makeup. Their objections, however, are probably not valid objections to the asking of such questions. There is no known evidence to suggest that the reading of such questions makes a person more neurotic, more psychotic, or less moral.

Other people object on different grounds. Some are concerned not about having to read or answer such questions but, rather, about how the answers will be used. This gets us into such problems as scorers' qualifications, their ethics, and storage of test information. What if the answer sheets to such tests as the MMPI are kept and filed? Who then will have access to these files? An ethical and knowledgeable qualified user would never reveal to a third party an answer to a specific question. Seldom would he even interpret such an answer to the client himself. He would, instead, look at the patterns of responses as recorded on the profile sheet. But what about others who may have (or at some later date obtain) access to the files? Could not, for example, a lot of political hay be made by reporting a candidate's answers to the questions cited above! The merits of permanently storing data are that (1) we will have more information available to help

---

[11]From the Minnesota Multiphasic Personality Inventory. Reproduced by permission. Copyright 1943 by the University of Minnesota. Published by The Psychological Corporation, New York, N.Y. All rights reserved.
[12]Gwynn Nettler, Test burning in Texas. *Amer. Psychologist*, 1959, *14*, 682–683.

make decisions about individual people and (2) we will be able to improve our tests and learn more about people in general by doing follow-up research. The dangers center around who does (or may in the future) have access to the stored information. Will clerks have access to the data? Can it be subpoenaed? The public concern about what data is kept on file is a very real and important concern, but this should be recognized as at least, in part, a separate issue from whether we have a right to originally ask personal questions.

In making a personnel decision about a person, do I have a right to pry into his personality? Many psychologists would argue yes. As Hathaway[13] points out, once you decide, for example, that a Peace Corps worker should not be maladjusted, then how will you find this out? If, for reasons of privacy, investigation of personal items is prevented, is not this analogous to the prudery that would not permit medical doctors to examine the body? In the authors' opinion, this analogy holds, and the conclusion is that qualified psychologists should have the right to ask personal questions if the questions are pertinent. (We should not have to strip before the receptionist — only before the medical doctor, and we would object to having a medical doctor examine our body if the examination was irrelevant.) The problem is that laymen have a hard time judging the relevancy of what a professional does. How do we know whether or not it is relevant for a medical doctor to check our blood pressure and perform a urinalysis? How do we know whether or not it is relevant for a psychologist to ask us if we love our mother? If tests are not relevant, they are invasions of privacy. If they are relevant, they are not invasions of privacy.

Commentators on the "invasion of privacy" topic should stick to the important issues, that is, the relevancy of the information gathered, qualifications of the gatherer, immediate use to which information is put, and what is done about the storage of such information. They would, thus, find that they share the same concerns as the professional psychologists. Some people carry their worries about invasion of privacy to the extreme. If we really were never allowed to find out anything about another person, then we would not even be allowed to give classroom achievement tests to find out how much the student has learned![14]

FAIRNESS OF TESTS TO MINORITY GROUPS

It would be nice to believe that every logically thinking person in the United States is against unfairness of any sort. The question to be discussed is

[13]Starke R. Hathaway, MMPI: Professional use by professional people. *Amer. Psychologist*, 1964, *19*, 204–210.

[14]See, for example, Supplement. *J. educ. Measmt.*, 1967, *4*, (1), 1–31 for a series of position papers on the Invasion of Privacy issue.

certainly not should we be fair but, rather, what is fairness? What practices are and are not fair? Do tests discriminate against the disadvantaged? What is and is not discrimination? According to Webster to *discriminate* can be defined as either (1) "to make a distinction; to use good judgment" or (2) "to make a difference in treatment or favor on a basis other than individual merit."[15]

Tests can and do help us make distinctions. Tests are used to identify differences within and among individuals and within and among groups or classes of people. That is the whole purpose of testing. If there were no differences in test scores (that is, if tests did not discriminate), they would be worthless.

Is it possible for tests to discriminate in an unfair sense (that is, using the second definition of discrimination)? Suppose that a company uses a selection test on which it can be shown that Negroes typically do less well than whites. Is the test unfair for revealing this difference? Many would say so. The test is certainly discriminating under the first definition, but is it unfair discrimination? To be sure, we could use test results to help us unfairly discriminate. For example, we could require that Negroes receive higher scores in order to be hired (or vice versa, as some advocate). This would be discrimination of the second type. This, however, would be an example of unfair use of test results rather than the use of an unfair test.

But, even if we don't set up this kind of unfair differential standard, is the test still unfair just because Negroes, on the average, do poorer? This depends on the degree to which the test is relevant (or valid) for selecting prospective employees. If, indeed, there is a reasonable correlation between job success and test scores, it would seem that selection on the basis of test scores is a wise one and not unfair, even though members of some subcultures do better than members of other subcultures.

If, however, a test does tend to discriminate (differentiate) between races or other subcultures and if the differential scores are *not* related to what we are predicting (such as on-the-job success), then the test is unfair. This could occur for many reasons. For example, the test may demand knowledge that is dependent upon having been raised in a certain cultural environment, whereas the criterion may not depend upon this knowledge. Or, perhaps some subgroups do not do as well on tests, not because they don't know the material, but because they lack test-taking skills. This lack of test-taking skills may well not affect the performance on the criterion at all. Thus, it can be seen that the question of test fairness is really one of test validity. A test may differentiate Negroes from whites and be fair (valid) for some purposes and not for others. Differentiation alone is not what makes a test unfair.

---

[15]*Webster's seventh new collegiate dictionary*. Springfield, Mass,: Merriam, 1965, p. 238.

As mentioned earlier, in the last decade or two, well-meaning psychologists have sought to devise culture-free intelligence tests. Such tests have attempted to ask only those items that do not differentiate among groups coming from different cultures. The advocates of such procedures argue that this gives them a test that is independent of environmental influences and as close as possible a measure of innate ability. In general, these tests have not been well accepted by most psychologists. It is very doubtful whether we could ever devise a paper-and-pencil test to measure innate ability (whatever that is). Certainly, scores on present tests are influenced by environmental factors. There is no debate with that. But, does that make them unfair? Clifford, a Negro educator, has said,

> To disparage testing programs for revealing the inequities which still exist in the social, the economic, the educational, and the cultural domains of American life is as erroneous as it would be for residents of Bismarck, North Dakota, to condemn the use of thermometers as biased, when, as this is being written, the temperature of Bismarck is −11°F and in Miami, Florida it is 83°.[16]

Ausubel states the case as follows:

> The intelligence test . . . proposes to measure functional capacity rather than to account for it. If the culturally deprived child scores low on an intelligence test because of the inadequacy of his environment, it is not the test which is unfair but the social order which permits him to develop under such conditions.
>
> By the same token we would not say that the tuberculin test is unfair or invalid (a) because the lower-class child really does not have any greater genic susceptibility to tuberculosis but happens to live in an environment that predisposes him to this disease, and (b) because it measures exposure to a particular disease which happens to be related to lower social class status rather than to one which is not so related. In terms of operational functional capacity, an intelligence test is no less fair or valid because a low score is reflective of cultural deprivation than because it is reflective of low genic endowment. Furthermore, to argue that test scores are valid is not to claim that they are necessarily immutable irrespective of future environmental conditions, or to defend those aspects of the social system that give rise to the culturally deprived environment.[17]

[16]Paul I. Clifford and Joshua A. Fishman, The impact of testing programs on college preparation and attendance. *The impact and improvement of school testing programs.* NSSE Yearbook LXII, Part II, p. 87.

[17]David P. Ausubel, *The influence of experience on the development of intelligence.* Paper read at the Conference on Productive Thinking in Education sponsored by the NEA Project on the Academically Talented Student, Washington, D.C., May 24, 1963.

It should be pointed out that both Clifford's and Ausubel's statements are based on the assumption that whoever interprets the intelligence test scores will realize that they are not direct measures of genetic capacity and that they are influenced by environmental conditions. Although the test is not unfair, it would be an unfair use of a test score to intepret it as irrefutable evidence of only genetic capacity.

The moderator approach to studying validity is one that has considerable merit in ameliorating the problems associated with potential test bias. Using this approach, separate validities may be obtained for different subgroups (for example, Negro and white) in the same situation. This is done by using separate correlation cofficients (and regression equations) for the two groups. Thus, each person is compared with others within his own subgroup.

In summary, tests should not be considered unfair just because they discriminate. That is what tests are supposed to do. Tests, however, can be invalid and therefore unfair; people can give unfair interpretations of the results (be they valid or invalid); or one can set up differential standards on tests and thereby use test results unfairly.

In general, although there would be important exceptions that should be investigated, the effect of using objective measures such as test data is to make social class barriers more permeable. Some of the ivy-league schools are good examples of this effect. Prior to selection on the basis of objective test information, some of these schools were homogeneous with respect to social class and somewhat heterogeneous with respect to ability. Now, just the reverse is true. Making decisions on the basis of objective measures is really more fair than making them on affective feelings (positive or negative) we have toward different subcultures.

CONCLUSION ON PUBLIC CONCERN ABOUT TESTING

It is good that people feel free to voice their concerns. There are many legitimate concerns about testing. Many of the concerns about testing, however, have not been relevant. If there are problems associated with test accuracy (there are), and if the misuse of tests has led to unfortunate consequences (it has), the appropriate procedure is to correct the problems, not to stop testing. We maintain that in many instances the issues of concern to the public such as invasion of privacy and unfair tests are problems associated with test use rather than with the psychometric properties of the tests. Psychologists are in part to blame for this misuse. They have an obligation to educate the public as to how tests should be used and as to how they are being used. However, much of the negative affect of the public toward tests is precisely because tests are used as they should be, to help make decisions. In our society, decisions must be made. These decisions are not always pleasant to the people involved. Because tests help make decisions, they have been attacked. Unfortunately, there are some individuals who assume that by doing away with tests we could avoid making decisions. That is not the case. Decisions must be made! Decisions will always be made! Information helps us make decisions. Tests provide information. As professionals, we must insure that valid tests are used for making appropriate decisions. We must not and cannot be intimidated by irresponsible critics of the testing movement. If we let this happen, we may as well relegate the task of education to the unqualified.

FUTURE TRENDS IN TESTING

It is always hard to predict. Even with tests carefully designed to help predict specific future behavior, we often cannot make accurate predictions. Yet the authors of the text — without the aid of specific test results! — are audacious enough to make some tentative predictions concerning educational testing. In 1963, each of nine test specialists made ten-year projections of testing.[18] It may be interesting to read and check the accuracy of those nine seers. We will not comment on all observed trends or predict future trends in all possible areas. We comment only on those areas that are most salient to educators.

CONTENT OF ACHIEVEMENT TESTS

The rapid expansion of knowledge in subject matter areas and improved instructional methods have resulted in considerable curricular revisions. In the past, the content of standardized achievement tests has lagged behind curricular change. Although some published tests have been the impetus for curricular change (this is not necessarily bad because test authors are generally subject matter experts), in general the test publishing industry has followed rather than led in this endeavor. We have already noted in Chapter III that achievement tests are moving away from questions based on factual recall to those designed to measure understanding and application. This trend will continue as tests are revised in accordance with curricular changes. In spite of real efforts to update tests, we feel a realistic prediction is that test content will continue to lag behind curricular content. This is unavoidable if the curriculum is to determine test content rather than vice versa. It takes a considerable length of time to publish a good test, and the curriculum is, and should be, dynamic rather than static.

[18]Robert H. Bauernfeind, *Building a school testing program*. Boston: Houghton Mifflin, 1963, pp. 296–318.

MEASURES OF CURRICULA ASSESSMENT

A closely related area in which we might hope to see improvement is the development of tests to evaluate the new curricula. Stake[19] suggests that although some tests may be appropriate to differentiate among individuals, these same tests are not appropriate to assess the impact of an instructional program. He states:

> Discriminability among students is important for instruction and guidance, but for development and selection of curricula, tests are needed that discriminate among curricula. Different rules for test administration are possible, and different criteria of test development are appropriate, when the tests are to be used to discriminate among curricula. . . .
>
> I am dismayed by my colleagues who believe that these same tests (standardized achievement tests) can be used to satisfy the needs of the curriculum evaluator.[20]

As implied in the last sentence of this quote, not all psychometricians would agree that different criteria of test development, let alone different tests, are necessary for curricular assessment. Most would feel, however, that tests designed for curricular evaluation must be more comprehensive than the typical achievement tests. Surely, in determining which curriculum is best, we are concerned with more than just how much knowledge is gained. Self-concepts, interest in the subject matter, and long-range effects on behavior are all appropriate goals. In this sense the development of measures of curricular assessment will be a more challenging task than many we have faced in the past. On the other hand, because the test results will be used to make decisions about groups rather than individuals, the tests will not need to have the high reliabilities and validities we expect in the instruments we use to help in individual decision making.

In the past, educators have undertaken curriculum studies with the conventional achievement tests. This may be a serious limitation of previous curriculum research. At this point in time there is a paucity of exposition about the appropriate testing domain and the psychometric properties required for these kinds of tests. Even less work has been done in actually developing tests for curricular evaluation. We expect considerable activity in this realm of evaluation in the years ahead.[21]

---

[19]Robert E. Stake (Ed.), Perspectives of curriculum evaluation, AERA Monograph Series on Curriculum Evaluation. Skokie, Ill.: Rand McNally, 1967, pp. 1–12.

[20]Stake, pp. 5–6.

[21]For further information, see Lee J. Cronbach, Course improvement through evaluation. *Teachers coll. Rec.*, 1963, *64*, 672–683 and Robert E. Stake, Countenance of educational evaluation. *Teachers coll. Rec.*, 1967, *68*, 523–540.

NATIONAL ASSESSMENT PROGRAMS

As a larger percent of public expenditures is funneled into education, there has been a growing awareness for the need to assess the outcomes of education. In 1964 the Carnegie Corporation appointed an Exploratory Committee on Assessing the Progress of Education (ECAPE) and named Ralph Tyler as Chairman. In a 1965 White House Conference on Education, John W. Gardner in essence supported this type of exploratory action and predicted "that sooner or later the American people will want to know what they are getting for their money."[22]

Members of ECAPE were plagued somewhat by critics who have been concerned with the dangers of such an assessment program. The primary fear of most of these critics was that somehow such an assessment program "*would result in a centrally controlled* [read "dictated"] *curriculum,*" and would "*stultify the curriculum.*"[23] The authors of this text (as well as the members of ECAPE) are puzzled by these fears, but nonetheless they exist. A good part of the committee's time was originally spent in an attempt to communicate their plans to other educators and laymen and to alleviate the fears of those who have reacted in such a manner. Many speeches were made and articles written in an attempt to spell out how the objectives of national assessment differ from the other educational uses of evaluation. As Tyler pointed out:

> The most frequent use of evaluation is to appraise the achievement of individual students. . . . A second use of evaluation is to diagnose the learning difficulties of an individual student . . . A third use of evaluation is to appraise the educational effectiveness of a curriculum. . . .
>
> There is a fourth use of evaluation which is to assess the educational progress of larger populations in order to provide the public with dependable information to help in the understanding of educational problems and needs and to guide in efforts to develop sound public policy regarding education. This type of assessment is not focused upon individual students, classrooms, schools or school systems, but furnishes over-all information about the educational attainments of large numbers of people.
>
> The distinction may be illuminated somewhat by comparing the situation in education and in the field of health. The public has information about the incidence of heart diseases, cancer, and other diseases for different age and occupational groups, and for different geographic regions. This information is useful in developing public

[22]Reported in *The New York Times*, July 25, 1965.
[23]Harold C. Hand, National assessment viewed as the camel's nose. *Phi Delta Kappan*, 1965, *47*, pp. 9, 10 respectively.

understanding of the progress and problems in the field of health where greatest effort and support may be needed. At the same time, physicians have evaluative procedures to diagnose diseases, to appraise the progress patients are making and to evaluate the effectiveness of treatments. The physician's evaluative techniques are devised to serve his purposes and the public health assessments are designed to provide the public with helpful information. One type does not take the place of the other.[24]

The first two uses Tyler mentions are, of course, those where one would employ an achievement test such as those discussed in Chapter III of this book. For the third use, one would employ a test of the type Stake[25] advocates. The fourth use, that of national assessment, requires, according to Tyler, a still different type of examination.

There are many scholars not threatened by the national assessment program who feel that enough data are already available through our existing extensive school testing programs and from other national projects such as Project TALENT to meet Tyler's stated objectives. They are not convinced a still different type of evaluation is necessary. Ebel,[26] for example, feels that a different kind of examination is not necessary. Making use of Tyler's medical evaluation analogy, he suggests that, indeed, the public could not obtain information concerning the incidence of heart disease other than by making use of the same evaluative procedures the physician uses in making the diagnosis in the first place. Regardless of how we argue the analogy, there remains the possibility that different kinds of assessment devices are needed.

As we have mentioned again and again, a test is not valid or invalid. Validity is a matter of degree, and the degree of validity changes from one situation to another. A test that may be very valid for one kind of assessment may not be valid at all for other assessment purposes. Existing tests are quite valid for many purposes, but they may not be valid in national assessment. ECAPE members feel different kinds of measures will be more appropriate.

To develop an assessment program that would hopefully meet the fourth use Tyler mentioned, the committee first developed some general policies governing such important questions as what kinds of testing instruments would be prepared, who would prepare such instruments, the sample to be tested, and to whom the findings would be released. Space limitations do not permit us to go into detail concerning the decisions and the reasons

[24]Ralph W. Tyler, The objectives and plans for a national assessment of educational progress. *J. educ. Measmt.*, 1966, *3*, 1–2.
[25]*Perspectives of curriculum evaluation.*
[26]Robert L. Ebel, personal communication.

for them. Basically, the plan was to assess a sample from each of 768 sub-populations stratified on the following variables: sex (2); geographic region (4); age group (4), ages 9, 13, 17, and adult; population density (4); socioeconomic level (2); and race (3). Sets of exercises were developed with the help of various agencies and subject-matter specialists. These exercises were based on objectives that curriculum experts, public school teachers, and leading lay citizens felt were important.

The findings, when completed, will be released to the public. It is hoped that the results will provide the type of information necessary to help educators in their continuing efforts to upgrade the education of the nation's youth. There should be continual assessment of our educational product. Otherwise, we may be content to perpetuate the status quo, the end result being a stagnation of our product.

COMPUTER-AIDED TESTING

Anyone who has read the technical manuals accompanying the better standardized tests realizes that computers already play a large role in the educational testing enterprise. Computers are used in the development of tests by aiding in the processes of norming, deriving types of scores, computing item analyses, estimating reliability and validity, and a host of other tasks. Computers are also used in the process of scoring and the reporting of results. For example, the Houghton Mifflin Scoring Service (HMSS) will report information such as the following to each school that has taken the Lorge-Thorndike Intelligence Tests.

1. Nine derived scores for each answer sheet
2. A list report (in triplicate) of pupils' scores
3. Class averages
4. Building averages
5. System averages
6. Local norms data
7. Interpreted and punched IBM cards for each pupil

This last service allows the schools who have access to computers to easily analyze these data in any way they see fit. But, in spite of the already considerable use of computers by testing companies, we can hopefully expect much more.

Perhaps most important is the expected increase in the use of computers within the school itself. An exciting area of research that may well have a significant and lasting impact is in using computers to administer tests.[27]

[27]John F. Vinsonhaler, James E. Molineux, and Bruce G. Rogers, *An experimental study of computer-aided testing.* Computer Institute for Social Science Research Report, Michigan State University, 1965.

This automated approach not only would free professional staff time for other duties but also would eliminate administrator variability as a source of error in test scores, thus improving their reliability.

Use of computer administration will also facilitate test selection and the use of sequential testing. Computers could easily be programed to present items of appropriate difficulty for an individual, as judged by that individual's responses to previous items, thus providing "tailor-made" tests. These tests would be much more efficient than existing tests; that is, more worthwhile information on a student could be gathered per unit of time.

The use of computers in the school should facilitate teaching-testing cooperation. The immediate storage, analysis, and print out of a student's examination results would help the teacher plan instructional processes. The research begun by Flanagan[28] is an excellent example of using evaluation via computers to aid in teaching.

Finally, we would be remiss if we did not mention the research being conducted on grading essays by computer.[29] As depicted by the accompanying cartoon (Figure 5–1), there are still some problems connected with this task, but Page and his associates have indeed come a long, long, way. Judging from the past successes of those who have been interested in discovering (or inventing) educational applications for computers, we do not want to bet too much against the eventual routine use of computers for building, administering, scoring, recording, and interpreting the majority of tests used in the public schools. Although a single school, or even a small school district, may not own a computer, time sharing would permit even the smallest school to avail itself of such facilities.

AFFECTIVE DOMAIN TESTING

Psychometrists vary in their opinions concerning the future of testing in the affective domain. Ebel, writing in 1963, hopefully predicted "less demand for paper and pencil tests of poorly defined personality traits such as motivation, creativity, leadership, adjustment, etc."[30] Siegel, on the other hand, states that we should "look for a relative de-emphasis of IQ testing and measurement in the cognitive area . . . we will see a heavier emphasis on tests designed to assess creativity and noncognitive factors."[31]

There is no doubt that in the past, tests of the noncognitive factors have been of poorer psychometric quality than their counterparts in the cognitive domain.

[28]John C. Flanagan, Functional education for the seventies. *Phi Delta Kappan*, 1967, *49*, 27–32.

[29]Ellis B. Page, The imminence of grading essays by computer. *Phi Delta Kappan*, 1966, *47*, 238–243.

[30]Robert L. Ebel in Robert H. Bauernfeind, *Building a school testing program*. Boston: Houghton Mifflin, 1963, p. 315.

[31]Laurence Siegel in Robert H. Bauernfeind, p. 306.

Great Scot! It's just flunked Hemingway.

Figure 5-1 Cartoon by Margaret McGarr. Reprinted by permission from the
PHI DELTA KAPPAN, January 1966.

Although the authors of this text do predict increased testing in the
affective domain, we are not in favor of this unless increased testing is done
with better tests and/or unless better measures of the criterion behavior
are developed. We are in agreement with Ebel that, hopefully, there will
be less demand for tests of *poorly defined* personality traits. However,
we are optimistic concerning the possibilities of improving the tests in this
area. We think some of the psychometric problems mentioned in the previous chapter can, at least to some extent, be either circumvented or overcome. The important task of improving the constructual definitions is not
solely or even primarily the job of psychometricians. It is the task of all
psychologists. Whether or not tests of noncognitive variables will ever be
really successful as selection instruments is debatable because the problem
of faking will always exist to some degree.

APTITUDE TESTING

There is still considerable controversy among psychologists as to the meaning of terms like *aptitude, capacity, intelligence,* or *creativity*. Although
current trends can be described, it is somewhat more risky to make predictions concerning future trends. Guilford's[32] book summarizes his research and others' but has not been out long enough to allow one to judge
what impact it may have. However, there seems little doubt but that the
multiaptitude model of the structure of intelligence will continue to gain in
popularity.

[32]J. P. Guilford, *The nature of human intelligence*. New York: McGraw-Hill, 1967.

The attempt to measure creativity will consume much research energy. The prediction by Siegel quoted in the previous section mentions an emphasis on creativity testing. He has certainly been correct in his prognosis thus far, and we predict the trend to continue.

QUALITY VERSUS QUANTITY

It is the authors' hope, if not their prediction, that the years ahead will bring a reduction in the number of tests designed to test the same constructs. There are far too many tests of poor quality on the market. The fact that Buros[33] lists 1219 tests, many of them scathingly criticized, is indicative of the extent of this problem. We would much prefer to see fewer tests and those then of higher quality.

Buros obviously feels the same way. In the preface of *The Sixth Mental Measurements Yearbook* he writes:

> When I initiated this test reviewing service in 1938, I was confident that frankly critical reviews by competent specialists representing a wide variety of viewpoints would make it unprofitable to publish tests of unknown or questionable validity. Now, 27 years and five *Mental Measurements Yearbooks* later, I realize that I was too optimistic. . . . Despite unfavorable reviews in the MMY's, the publication and use of inadequately validated tests seem to be keeping pace with the population explosion.[34]

Probably the only way for our hope to materialize is for the consumers to stop purchasing inadequate tests. This, of course, cannot happen unless consumers are capable of making good judgments. This leads to our last prediction.

CONSUMER COMPETENCE

Smith states that "educational measurement is not in the control of test authors or publishers. It is in the hands of test users. . . ."[35] One of Anderson's eight "dreams and expectations" for educational testing is "increased sophistication on the part of test users."[36]

It is the truthfulness of Smith's statement that makes Anderson's dream so enormously important. Tests can be important and useful tools. Used correctly by competent personnel, tests will continue to play an increasingly important role in educational institutions. Tests used incorrectly by incompetent, unprofessional staffs may do more harm than good. There have

---

[33]Oscar K. Buros, *The sixth mental measurements yearbook.*
[34]Buros, pp. xxiii–xxiv.
[35]Arthur E. Smith in Bauernfeind, p. 308.
[36]Scarvia A. Anderson in Bauernfeind, p. 302.

been, in the past, far too many instances of incorrect use of tests by school personnel. Hagen and Lindberg, writing in 1963, made 16 recommendations concerning staff competency in testing. Three recommendations that pertain directly to classroom teacher competency are as follows:

Recommendation 12. In order to discharge their functions in the testing program effectively, the classroom teachers must have a basic understanding of the evaluative process and the place of the testing program in the total evaluation of the students and the educational program.

Recommendation 13. Classroom teachers should know the general types of tests available and be aware of their uses, strengths, and limitations.

Recommendation 14. Classroom teachers should be able to combine available test data with other records and to interpret them as they relate to individual children in their classes.[37]

Unfortunately, neither these recommendations pertaining to classroom teacher competencies nor the recommendations they make concerning other professional staff competencies have been realized in many schools. It is our hopeful prediction that professional educators' competencies in test use will increase to an acceptably high level. If not, tests will continue to be misused in educational institutions. In that case, the public, who is concerned about all aspects of education, will revolt against the use of standardized tests in the schools.

A FINAL WORD

We have covered in this book some of the basic aspects of standardized testing in education. It was not intended that this book cover all that any single teacher may wish to know about standardized tests. It was our purpose to present the minimum information with which every professional worker in the school (teacher, counselor, social worker, or principal) should be familiar. It is sincerely hoped that the readers who expect to be closely involved in school testing programs will continue their education in this important field.

POINTS TO PONDER

1. We have suggested in this chapter that pupils, parents, and teachers all be involved in setting up the school testing program. What part should

[37]Elizabeth Hagen and Lucile Lindberg, Staff competence in testing. *The impact and improvement of school testing programs.* NSSE Yearbook 62, Part II, 1963, p. 249.

each play? What are the dangers of such a heterogeneous committee?

2. In what fashion should standardized test results be reported to parents and teachers and to elementary, secondary, and college students?

3. Assume you are in a financially troubled school district and are only allowed to give one aptitude test and two achievement batteries in grades K to 12. At which grade levels would you administer the tests?

4. Some states have a uniform state-wide testing program. Are you in favor of such programs? Explain your position.

5. It is typical school policy to have a student's cumulative record accompany him as he moves from one grade to the next or from one school to another. What are the advantages and limitations of this policy? Under what conditions could it constitute an invasion of privacy?

6. Under what circumstances would it be appropriate to ask very personal questions in a standardized test?

7. Assume a test has been developed that can differentiate between teachers who are pro and anti union. Does the school superintendent have a right to use this instrument in helping decide who to (a) hire and (b) promote?

8. What would be the benefits to society of developing a test on which all subcultures perform equally well? How have you defined subculture?

9. A college uses test ABC for admission purposes. Research has demonstrated that the test is a reasonably valid predictor ($r = .58$) of college GPA. Research has also shown that some subcultures do less well on this test than others. What further evidence needs to be gathered to answer the question of whether the test discriminates unfairly?

10. If it is possible for a test to be administered by either a teacher or a computer, are two sets of norms necessary? Why?

APPENDIX A

Selective List of Test Publishers

American College Testing Program, P. O. Box 168, Iowa City, Iowa, 52240

American Guidance Service, Inc., 720 Washington Avenue, S.E., Minneapolis, Minnesota, 55414

Australian Council for Educational Research, Frederick St., Hawthorn E.2 Victoria, Australia

The Bobbs-Merrill Company, Inc., 4300 East 62nd Street, Indianapolis, Indiana, 46206

Bureau of Educational Measurements, Kansas State Teachers College, Emporia, Kansas, 66801

Bureau of Educational Research and Service, University of Iowa, Iowa City, Iowa, 52240

California Test Bureau, Del Monte Research Park, Monterey, California, 93940

Center of Psychological Service, 1835 Eye Street, N.W., Washington, D.C., 20006

Committee on Diagnostic Reading Tests, Inc., Mountain Home, North Carolina, 28758

Consulting Psychologists Press, Inc., 577 College Avenue, Palo Alto, California, 94306

Cooperative Test Division, Educational Testing Service, Princeton, New Jersey, 08540

Educational and Industrial Testing Service, P.O. Box 7234, San Diego, California, 92107.

Educational Test Bureau, Division of American Guidance Service, Inc., 720 Washington Avenue, S.E., Minneapolis, Minnesota, 55414

Guidance Centre, Ontario College of Education, University of Toronto, 371 Bloor Street, W., Toronto 5, Ontario, Canada

Harcourt, Brace & World, Inc., 757 Third Avenue, New York, New York, 10017

Hayes Educational Test Laboratory, 7040 North Portsmouth Avenue, Portland, Oregon, 97203

Houghton Mifflin Company, 2 Park Street, Boston, Massachusetts, 02107

Institute for Personality and Ability Testing, 1602 Coronado Drive, Champaign, Illinois, 61822

Lyons and Carnahan, 407 East 25th Street, Chicago, Illinois, 60616

National Foundation for Educational Research in England and Wales, the Mere, Upton Park, Slough, Bucks, England

Ohio Scholarship Tests, State Department of Education, 751 Northwest Boulevard, Columbus, Ohio, 43212

Personnel Press, Inc., 20 Nassau Street, Princeton, New Jersey, 08540

The Psychological Corporation, 304 East 45th Street, New York, New York, 10017

Psychometric Affiliates, 1743 Monterey, Chicago, Illinois, 60643

Public Personnel Association, 1313 East 60th Street, Chicago, Illinois, 60637

Public School Publishing Company, 4300 East 62nd Street, Indianapolis, Indiana, 46206

Scholastic Testing Service, Inc., 480 Meyer Road, Bensenville, Illinois, 60106

Science Research Associates, Inc., 259 East Erie Street, Chicago, Illinois, 60611

Scott, Foresman and Company, 433 East Erie Street, Chicago, Illinois, 60611

Sheridan Supply Co., P.O. Box 837, Beverly Hills, California, 90213

Stanford University Press, Stanford, California, 94305

C. H. Stoelting Co., 424 North Homan Avenue, Chicago, Illinois, 60624

Teachers College Press, Teachers College, Columbia University, New York, New York, 10027

United States Government Printing Office, Washington, D.C., 20402

University of London Press, Ltd., Little Paul's House, Warwick Square, London E.C.4, England

Western Psychological Services, Box 775, Beverly Hills, California, 90213

APPENDIX B

A Glossary of 100 Measurement Terms
Roger T. Lennon[1]

This glossary of technical terms used in educational and psychological measurement is primarily for persons with limited training in measurement, rather than for the specialist. The terms defined are the more common or basic ones such as occur in test manuals and simple research reports. In the definitions, niceties of usage have sometimes been sacrificed for the sake of brevity and, it is hoped, clarity.

The definitions are based on study of the definitions and usages of the various terms in about a dozen widely used textbooks in educational and psychological measurement and statistics, and in both general and specialized dictionaries. There is not complete uniformity among writers in the measurement field with respect to the usage of certain technical terms; in cases of varying usage, either these variations are noted or the definition offered is the one that the writer judges to represent the "best" usage.

academic aptitude. The combination of native and acquired abilities that is needed for school work; likelihood of success in mastering academic work, as estimated from measures of the necessary abilities. (Also called *scholastic aptitude.*)

accomplishment quotient (AQ). The ratio of educational age to mental age; $EA \div MA$. (Also called *achievement quotient.*)

achievement age. The age for which a given achievement test score is the real or estimated average. (Also called *educational age* or *subject age.*) If the achievement age corresponding to a score of 36 on a reading test is 10 years, 7 months (10-7), this means that pupils 10 years, 7 months achieve, on the average, a score of 36 on that test.

achievement test. A test that measures the extent to which a person has "achieved" something—acquired certain information or mastered certain skills, usually as a result of specific instruction.

[1] Published as *Test Service Notebook No. 13* (New York: Harcourt, Brace & World, Inc.). Compiled with the assistance of Claude F. Bridges, John C. Marriott, Frances E. Crook, and Blythe C. Mitchell, Division of Test Research and Service. Reprinted with the permission of Harcourt, Brace & World, Inc.

age equivalent. The age for which a given score is the real or estimated average score.

age norms. Values representing typical or average performance for persons of various age groups.

age-grade table. A table showing the number or per cent of pupils of various ages in each grade; a distribution of the ages of pupils in successive grades.

alternate-form reliability. The closeness of correspondence, or correlation, between results on alternate (*i.e.* equivalent or parallel) forms of a test; thus, a measure of the extent to which the two forms are consistent or reliable in measuring whatever they do measure, assuming that the examinees themselves do not change in the abilities measured between the two testings. (See RELIABILITY, RELIABILITY COEFFICIENT, STANDARD ERROR.)

aptitude. A combination of abilities and other characteristics, whether native or acquired, known or believed to be indicative of an individual's ability to learn in some particular area. Thus, "musical aptitude" would refer broadly to that combination of physical and mental characteristics, motivational factors, and conceivably other characteristics, which is conducive to acquiring proficiency in the musical field. Some exclude motivational factors, including interests, from the concept of "aptitude," but the more comprehensive use seems preferable. The layman may think of "aptitude" as referring only to some inborn capacity; the term is no longer so restricted in its psychological or measurement usage.

arithmetic mean. The sum of a set of scores divided by the number of scores. (Commonly called *average, mean.*)

average. A general term applied to measures of central tendency. The three most widely used averages are the *arithmetic mean*, the *median*, and the *mode*.

battery. A group of several tests standardized on the same population, so that results on the several tests are comparable. Sometimes loosely applied to any group of tests administered together, even though not standardized on the same subjects.

ceiling. The upper limit of ability measured by a test.

class analysis chart. A chart, usually prepared in connection with a battery of achievement tests, that shows the relative performance of members of a class on the several parts of the battery.

coefficient of correlation (r). A measure of the degree of relationship, or "going-togetherness," between two sets of measures for the same group of individuals. The correlation coefficient most frequently used in test development and educational research is that known as the *Pearson (Pearsonian) r*, so named for Karl Pearson, originator of the method, or as the *product-moment r*, to denote the mathematical basis of its calculation. Unless otherwise specified, "correlation" usually means the product-moment correlation coefficient, which ranges from .00, denoting complete absence of relationship, to 1.00, denoting perfect correspondence, and may be either positive or negative.

completion item. A test question calling for the completion (filling in) of a phrase, sentence, etc., from which one or more parts have been omitted.

correction for guessing. A reduction in score for wrong answers, sometimes applied in scoring true-false or multiple-choice questions. Many question the validity or usefulness of this device, which is intended to discourage guessing and to yield more accurate rankings of examinees in terms of their true knowledge. Scores to which such corrections have been applied— e.g., rights minus wrongs, or rights minus some fraction of wrongs—are often spoken of as "corrected for guessing" or "corrected for chance."

correlation. Relationship or "going-togetherness" between two scores or measures; tendency of one score to vary concomitantly with the other, as the tendency of students of high IQ to be above average in reading ability. The existence of a strong relationship—i.e., a high correlation—between two variables does not necessarily indicate that one has any causal influence on the other. (See COEFFICIENT OF CORRELATION.)

criterion. A standard by which a test may be judged or evaluated; a set of scores, ratings, etc., that a test is designed to predict or to correlate with. (See VALIDITY.)

decile. Any one of the nine percentile points (scores) in a distribution that divide the distribution into ten equal parts; every tenth percentile. The first decile is the 10th percentile, the ninth decile the 90th percentile, etc.

deviation. The amount by which a score differs from some reference value, such as the mean, the norm, or the score on some other test.

deviation IQ. See INTELLIGENCE QUOTIENT.

diagnostic test. A test used to "diagnose," that is, to locate specific areas of weakness or strength, and to determine the nature of weaknesses or deficiencies; it yields measures of the components or sub-parts of some larger body of information or skill. Diagnostic achievement tests are most commonly prepared for the skill subjects—reading, arithmetic, spelling.

difficulty value. The per cent of some specified group, such as students of a given age or grade, who answer an item correctly.

discriminating power. The ability of a test item to differentiate between persons possessing much of some trait and those possessing little.

distractor. Any of the incorrect choices in a multiple-choice or matching item.

distribution (frequency distribution). A tabulation of scores from high to low, or low to high, showing the number of individuals that obtain each score or fall in each score interval.

educational age (EA). See ACHIEVEMENT AGE.

equivalent form. Any of two or more forms of a test that are closely parallel with respect to the nature of the content and the difficulty of the items included, and that will yield very similar average scores and measures of variability for a given group.

error of measurement. See STANDARD ERROR.

extrapolation. In general, any process of estimating values of a function beyond the range of available data. As applied to test norms, the process of extending a norm line beyond the limits of actually obtained data, in order to permit interpretation of extreme scores. This extension may be done mathematically by fitting a curve to the obtained data or, as is more common, by less rigorous methods, usually graphic. See Fig. 1. Considerable judgment on the test maker's part enters into any extrapolation process, which means that extrapolated norm values are likely to be to some extent arbitrary.

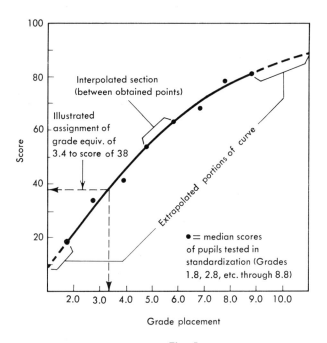

Fig. 1

factor. In mental measurement, a hypothetical trait, ability or component of ability, that underlies and influences performance on two or more tests, and hence causes scores on the tests to be correlated. The term "factor" strictly refers to a theoretical variable, derived by a process of *factor analysis*, from a table of intercorrelations among tests; but it is also commonly used to denote the psychological interpretation given to the variable —i.e., the mental trait assumed to be represented by the variable, as verbal ability, numerical ability, etc.

factor analysis. Any of several methods of analyzing the intercorrelations among a set of variables such as test scores. Factor analysis attempts to account for the interrelationships in terms of some underlying "factors," preferably fewer in number than the original variables; and it reveals how much of the variation in each of the original measures arises from, or is associated with, each of the hypothetical factors. Factor analysis has contributed to our understanding of the organization or components of intelligence, aptitudes, and personality; and it has pointed the way to the development of "purer" tests of the several components.

forced-choice item. Broadly, any multiple-choice item in which the examinee is *required* to select one or more of the given choices. The term is best used to denote a special type of multiple-choice item, in which the options, or choices, are (1) of equal "preference value"—i.e., chosen equally often by a typical group, but (2) of differential discriminating ability—i.e., such that one of the options discriminates between persons high and low on the factor that this option measures, while the other options do not.

frequency distribution. See DISTRIBUTION.

grade equivalent. The grade level for which a given score is the real or estimated average.

grade norm. The average score obtained by pupils of given grade placement. See NORMS, MODAL AGE.

group test. A test that may be administered to a number of individuals at the same time by one examiner.

individual test. A test that can be administered to only one person at a time.

intelligence quotient (IQ). Originally, the ratio of a person's mental age to his chronological age $\left(\dfrac{MA}{CA} \right)$ or, more precisely, especially for older persons, the ratio of mental age to the mental age normal for chronological age (in both cases multiplied by 100 to eliminate the decimal). More generally, IQ is a measure of brightness that takes into account both score on an intelligence test and age. A *deviation IQ* is such a measure of brightness, based on the difference or deviation between a person's obtained score and the score that is normal for the person's age.

The following table shows the classification of IQ's offered by Terman and Merrill for the Stanford-Binet test, indicating the per cent of persons in a normal population who fall in each classification. This table is roughly applicable to tests yielding IQ's having standard deviations of about 16 points (not all do). It is important to bear in mind that any such table is arbitrary, for there are no inflexible lines of demarcation between "feeble-minded" and "borderline," etc.

Classification	IQ	Per cents of all persons
Near genius or genius	140 and above	1
Very superior	130–139	2.5
Superior	120–129	8
Above average	110–119	16
Normal or average	90–109	45
Below average	80–89	16
Dull or borderline	70–79	8
Feeble-minded: moron,	60–69	2.5
imbelicile, idiot	59 and below	1

interpolation. In general, any process of estimating intermediate values between two known points. As applied to test norms, it refers to the procedure used in assigning interpreted values (e.g., grade or age equivalents) to scores between the successive average scores actually obtained in the standardization process. In reading norm tables, it is necessary at times to *interpolate* to obtain a norm value for a score between scores given in the table; e.g., in the table given here, an age value of 12–5 would be assigned, by interpolation, to a score of 118. See Fig. 1. under EXTRAPOLATION.

Score	Age Equiv.
120	12–6
115	12–4
110	12–2

inventory test. As applied to achievement tests, a test that attempts to cover rather thoroughly some relatively small unit of specific instruction or training. The purpose of an inventory test, as the name suggests, is more in the nature of a "stock-taking" of an individual's knowledge or skill than an effort to measure in the usual sense. The term sometimes denotes a type of test used to measure achievement status prior to instruction.

Many personality and interest questionnaires are designated "inventories," since they appraise an individual's status in several personal characteristics, or his level of interest in a variety of types of activities.

item. A single question or exercise in a test.

item analysis. The process of evaluating single test items by any of several methods. It usually involves determining the difficulty value and the discriminating power of the item, and often its correlation with some criterion.

Kuder-Richardson formula(s). Formulas for estimating the reliability of a test from information about the individual items in the test, or from the mean score, standard deviation, and number of items in the test. Because the Kuder-Richardson formulas permit estimation of reliability from a single administration of a test, without the labor involved in dividing the test into halves, their use has become common in test development. The Kuder-Richardson formulas are not appropriate for estimating the reliability of speeded tests.

machine-scorable (machine-scored) test. A test that may be scored by means of a machine. Ordinarily, the term refers to a test adapted for scoring on the International Test Scoring Machine, manufactured by International Business Machines Corporation. In taking tests that are to be scored on this machine, the examinee records his answers on separate answer sheets with a special electrographic pencil. These pencil marks are electrically conductive, and current flowing through them may be read on a suitably calibrated dial as a test score. The machine distinguishes, by means of appropriate keys, between right and wrong answers, and can combine groups of responses in order to yield total or part scores, weighted scores, or corrected scores.

matching item. A test item calling for the correct association of each entry in one list with an entry in a second list.

mean. See ARITHMETIC MEAN.

median. The middle score in a distribution; the 50th percentile; the point that divides the group into two equal parts. Half of the group of scores fall below the median and half above it.

mental age (MA). The age for which a given score on an intelligence test is average or normal. If a score of 55 on an intelligence test corresponds to a mental age of 6 years, 10 months, then 55 is presumably the average score that would be made by an unselected group of children 6 years, 10 months of age.

modal age. That age or age range which is most typical or characteristic of pupils of specified grade placement.

modal-age norms. Norms based on the performance of pupils of modal age for their respective grades, which are thus free of the distorting influence of under-age or over-age pupils.

mode. The score or value that occurs most frequently in a distribution.

multiple-choice item. A test item in which the examinee's task is to choose the correct or best answer from several given answers, or options.

multiple-response item. A special type of multiple-choice item in which two or more of the given choices may be correct.

N. The symbol commonly used to represent the number of cases in a distribution, study, etc.

normal distribution. A distribution of scores or measures that in graphic form has a distinctive bell-shaped appearance. Figure 2 shows such a graph of a normal distribution, known as a *normal curve* or *normal probability curve*. In a normal distribution, scores or measures are distributed symmetrically about the mean, with as many cases at various distances above the mean as at equal distances below it, and with cases concentrated near the average and decreasing in frequency the further one departs from the average, according to a precise mathematical equation. The assumption that mental and psychological characteristics are distributed normally has been very useful in much test development work.

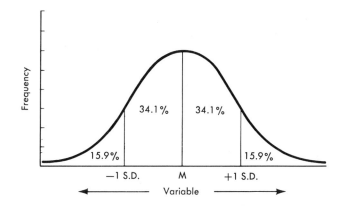

norm line. A smooth curve drawn through the mean or median scores of successive age or grade groups, or through percentile points for a single group. See Fig. 1 under EXTRAPOLATION.

norms. Statistics that describe the test performance of specified groups, such as pupils of various ages or grades in the standardization group for a test. Norms are often assumed to be representative of some larger population, as of pupils in the county as a whole. Norms are descriptive of average, typical, or mediocre performance; they are not to be regarded as standards, or as desirable levels of attainment. Grade, age, and percentile are the most common types of norms.

objective test. A test in the scoring of which there is no possibility of difference of opinion among scorers as to whether responses are to be scored right or wrong. It is contrasted with a "subjective" test—e.g., the usual essay examination to which different scorers may assign different scores, ratings, or grades.

omnibus test. A test (1) in which items measuring a variety of mental operations are all combined into a single sequence rather than being grouped together by type of operation, and (2) from which only a single score is derived, rather than separate scores for each operation or function. Omnibus tests make for simplicity of administration: one set of directions and one over-all time limit usually suffice. *Otis Quick-Scoring Mental Ability Tests: Beta* or *Gamma Tests* are omnibus-type tests, as distinguished from tests such as *Terman-McNemar Test of Mental Ability* or *Pintner General Ability Tests: Verbal,* in which the items measuring various operations are grouped together, each with its own set of directions.

percentile (P). A point (score) in a distribution below which falls the per cent of cases indicated by the given percentile. Thus the 15th percentile denotes the score or point below which 15 per cent of the scores fall. "Percentile" has nothing to do with the per cent of correct answers an examinee has on a test.

percentile rank. The per cent of scores in a distribution equal to or lower than the score corresponding to the given rank.

performance test. As contrasted with *paper-and-pencil test,* a test requiring motor or manual response on the examinee's part, generally but not always involving manipulation of concrete equipment or materials. *Cornell-Coxe Performance Ability Scale, Arthur Point Scale of Performance Tests,* and *Bennett Hand-Tool Dexterity Test* are performance tests, in this sense. "Performance test" is also used in another sense, to denote a test that is actually a work-sample, and in this sense it may include paper-and-pencil tests, as, for example, a test in accountancy, or in taking shorthand, or in proofreading, where no materials other than paper and pencil may be required, but where the test response is identical with the behavior about which information is desired.

personality test. A test intended to measure one or more of the non-intellective aspects of an individual's mental or psychological make-up. Personality tests include the so-called *personality inventories* or *adjustment inventories* (e.g., *Heston Personal Adjustment Inventory, Bernreuter Personality Inventory, Bell Adjustment Inventory*) which seek to measure a person's status on such traits as dominance, sociability, introversion, etc., by means of self-descriptive responses to a series of questions; *rating scales* (e.g., *Haggerty-Olson-Wickman Behavior Rating Schedules*) which call for rating, by one's self or another, of the extent to which a subject possesses certain characteristics; *situation tests* in which the individual's behavior in simulated life-like situations is observed by one or more judges, and evaluated with reference to various personality traits; and *opinion* or *attitude inventories* (e.g., *Allport-Vernon Study of Values*). Some writers also classify interest inventories as personality tests.

power test. A test intended to measure level of performance rather than speed of response; hence one in which there is either no time limit or a very generous one.

practice effect. The influence of previous experience with a test on a later administration of the same test or a similar test; usually, an increase in the score on the second testing, attributed to increased familiarity with the directions, kinds of questions, etc. Practice effect is greatest when the interval between testings is small, when the materials in the two tests are very similar, and when the initial test-taking represents a relatively novel experience for the subjects.

probable error. See STANDARD ERROR.

product-moment coefficient. See COEFFICIENT OF CORRELATION.

profile. A graphic representation of the results on several tests, for either an individual or a group, when the results have been expressed in some uniform or comparable terms. This method of presentation permits easy identification of areas of strength or weakness.

projective technique (projective method). A method of personality study in which the subject responds as he chooses to a series of stimuli such as ink-blots, pictures, unfinished sentences, etc. So called because of the assumption that under this free-response condition the subject "projects" into his responses manifestations of personality characteristics and organization that can, by suitable methods, be scored and interpreted to yield a description of his basic personality structure. The *Rorschach* (ink-blot) *Technique* and the Murray *Thematic Apperception Test* are the most commonly used projective methods.

prognosis (prognostic) test. A test used to predict future success or failure in a specific subject or field.

quartile. One of three points that divide the cases in a distribution into four equal groups. The lower quartile, or 25th percentile, sets off the lowest fourth of the group; the middle quartile is the same as the 50th percentile, or median; and the third quartile, or 75th percentile, marks off the highest fourth.

r. See COEFFICIENT OF CORRELATION.

random sample. A sample of the members of a population drawn in such a way that every member of the population has an equal chance of being included—that is, drawn in a way that precludes the operation of bias or selection. The purpose in using a sample thus free of bias is, of course, that the sample be fairly "representative" of the total population, so that sample findings may be generalized to the population. A great advantage of random samples is that formulas are available for estimating the expected variation of the sample statistics from their true values in the total population; in other words, we know how precise an estimate of the population value is given by a random sample of any given size.

range. The difference between the lowest and highest scores obtained on a test by some group.

raw score. The first quantitative result obtained in scoring a test. Usually the number of right answers, number right minus some fraction of number wrong, time required for performance, number of errors, or similar direct, unconverted, uninterpreted measure.

readiness test. A test that measures the extent to which an individual has achieved a degree of maturity or acquired certain skills or information needed for undertaking successfully some new learning activity. Thus a *reading readiness test* indicates the extent to which a child has reached a developmental stage where he may profitably begin a formal instructional program in reading.

recall item. An item that requires the examinee to supply the correct answer from his own memory or recollection, as contrasted with a *recognition item,* in which he need only identify the correct answer.
e.g., "Columbus discovered America in the year   ?   "
is a recall item, whereas
"Columbus discovered America in *a* 1425 *b* 1492 *c* 1520 *d* 1546"
is a recognition item.

recognition item. An item requiring the examinee to recognize or select the correct answer from among two or more given answers. See RECALL ITEM.

reliability. The extent to which a test is consistent in measuring whatever it does measure; dependability, stability, relative freedom from errors of measurement. Reliability is usually estimated by some form of *reliability coefficient* or by the *standard error of measurement.*

reliability coefficient. The coefficient of correlation between two forms of a test, between scores on repeated administrations of the same test, or between halves of a test, properly corrected. These three coefficients measure somewhat different aspects of reliability but all are properly spoken of as reliability coefficients. See ALTERNATE-FORM RELIABILITY, SPLIT-HALF COEFFICIENT, TEST-RETEST COEFFICIENT, KUDER-RICHARDSON FORMULA(S).

representative sample. A sample that corresponds to or matches the population of which it is a sample with respect to characteristics important for the purposes under investigation—e.g., in an achievement test norm sample, proportion of pupils from each state, from various regions, from segregated and non-segregated schools, etc.

scholastic aptitude. See ACADEMIC APTITUDE.

skewness. The tendency of a distribution to depart from symmetry or balance around the mean.

sociometry. Measurement of the interpersonal relationships prevailing among the members of a group. By means of sociometric devices, e.g., the *sociogram,* an attempt is made to discover the patterns of choice and rejection among the individuals making up the group—which ones are chosen most often as friends or leaders ("stars"), which are rejected by others ("isolates"), how the group subdivides into clusters or cliques, etc.

Spearman-Brown formula. A formula giving the relationship between the reliability of a test and its length. The formula permits estimation of the reliability of a test lengthened or shortened by any amount, from the known reliability of a test of specified length. Its most common application is in the estimation of reliability of an entire test from the correlation between two halves of the test (*split-half reliability*).

split-half coefficient. A coefficient of reliability obtained by correlating scores on one half of a test with scores on the other half. Generally, but not necessarily, the two halves consist of the odd-numbered and the even-numbered items.

standard deviation (S.D.). A measure of the variability or dispersion of a set of scores. The more the scores cluster around the mean, the smaller the standard deviation.

standard error (S.E.). An estimate of the magnitude of the "error of measurement" in a score—that is, the amount by which an obtained score differs from a hypothetical true score. The standard error is an amount such that in about two-thirds of the cases the obtained score would not differ by more than one standard error from the true score. The *probable error* (P.E.) of a score is a similar measure, except that in about half the cases the obtained score differs from the true score by not more than one probable error. The probable error is equal to about two-thirds of the standard error. The larger the probable or the standard error of a score, the less reliable the measure.

standard score. A general term referring to any of a variety of "transformed" scores, in terms of which raw scores may be expressed for reasons of convenience, comparability, ease of interpretation, etc.

The simplest type of standard score is that which expresses the deviation of an individual's raw score from the average score of his group in relation to the standard deviation of the scores of the groups. Thus:

$$\text{Standard score } (z) = \frac{\text{raw score } (X) - \text{mean } (M)}{\text{standard deviation } (S.D.)}$$

By multiplying this ratio by a suitable constant and by adding or subtracting another constant, standard scores having any desired mean and standard deviation may be obtained. Such standard scores do not affect the relative standing of the individuals in the group nor change the shape of the original distribution.

More complicated types of standard scores may yield distributions differing in shape from the original distribution; in fact, they are sometimes used for precisely this purpose. *Normalized standard scores* and *K-scores* (as used in *Stanford Achievement Test*) are examples of this latter group.

standardized test (standard test). A systematic sample of performance obtained under prescribed conditions, scored according to definite rules, and capable of evaluation by reference to normative information. Some writers restrict the term to tests having the above properties, whose items have been experimentally evaluated, and/or for which evidences of validity and reliability are provided.

stanine. One of the steps in a nine-point scale of normalized standard scores. The stanine (short for *standard-nine*) scale has values from 1 to 9, with a mean of 5, and a standard deviation of 2.

stencil key. A scoring key which, when positioned over an examinee's responses either in a test booklet or, more commonly, on an answer sheet, permits rapid identification and counting of all right answers. Stencil keys may be perforated in positions corresponding to positions of right answers, so that only right answers show through when the keys are in place; or they may be transparent, with positions of right answers identified by circles, boxes, etc., printed on the key.

strip key. A scoring key arranged so that the answers for items on any page or in any column of the test appear in a strip or column that may be placed alongside the examinee's responses for easy scoring.

survey test. A test that measures general achievement in a given subject or area, usually with the connotation that the test is intended to measure group status, rather than to yield precise measures of individuals.

test-retest coefficient. A type of reliability coefficient obtained by administering the same test a second time after a short interval and correlating the two sets of scores.

true-false item. A test question or exercise in which the examinee's task is to indicate whether a given statement is true or false.

true score. A score entirely free of errors of measurement. True scores are hypothetical values never obtained by testing, which always involves some measurement error. A true score is sometimes defined as the average score of an infinite series of measurements with the same or exactly equivalent tests, assuming no practice effect or change in the examinee during the testings.

validity. The extent to which a test does the job for which it is used. Validity, thus defined, has different connotations for various kinds of tests and, accordingly, different kinds of validity evidence are appropriate for them. For example:

(1) The validity of an achievement test is the extent to which the content of the test represents a balanced and adequate sampling of the outcomes (knowledge, skills, etc.) of the course or instructional program it is intended to cover (*content, face,* or *curricular validity*). It is best evidenced by a comparison of the test content with courses of study, instructional materials and statements of instructional goals, and by critical analysis of the processes required in responding to the items.

(2) The validity of an aptitude, prognostic, or readiness test is the extent to which it accurately indicates future learning success in the area

for which it is used as a predictor (*predictive validity*). It is evidenced by correlations between test scores and measures of later success.

(3) The validity of a personality test is the extent to which the test yields an accurate description of an individual's personality traits or personality organization (*status validity*). It may be evidenced by agreement between test results and other types of evaluation, such as ratings or clinical classification, but only to the extent that such criteria are themselves valid.

The traditional definition of validity as "the extent to which a test measures what it is supposed to measure," seems less satisfactory than the above, since it fails to emphasize that the validity of a test is always specific to the purposes for which the test is used, and that different kinds of evidence are appropriate for appraising the validity of various types of tests.

Validity of a test *item* refers to the discriminating power of the item—its ability to distinguish between persons having much and those having little of some characteristic.

name index

subject index

Academic Promise Tests, 106
Achievement tests, 127–200
  administrative uses, 192
  classification of, 137
  content, future of, 287
  definition of, 73
  diagnostic tests, 140–149
  differences among types, 137–139
  dissemination of results, 276
  examples of, 140–186
  guidance uses, 191
  history of, 129, 132

  in specific subjects, 149–160
  instructional uses, 189–191
  misuse of results, 194
  standardized versus teacher-made,
    132–136
  survey batteries, 161–186
  uses of, 10, 188–198
  versus aptitude tests, 73–74
Adjustment inventories, general, 247–
  251
  criterion groups, 247–249
  evaluation of, 251